THE BEST TEST PREPARATION FOR THE
SAT II: Subject Test
PHYSICS

David K. Bross
Physics Teacher
Parkway West High School
Ballwin, Missouri

Michael L. Lemley
Physics Teacher
Buckhannon-Upshur High School
Buckhannon, West Virginia

Michael H. Farmer
Physics Teacher
Greenville Technical College
Greenville, South Carolina

Larry Weathers
Physics Teacher
The Bromfield School
Harvard, Massachusetts

Research & Education Association
61 Ethel Road West • Piscataway, New Jersey 08854

The Best Test Preparation for the
SAT II: SUBJECT TEST IN PHYSICS

1999 PRINTING

Printed in the United States of America

Library of Congress Catalog Card Number 96-71059

International Standard Book Number 0-87891-870-1

Research & Education Association
61 Ethel Road West
Piscataway, New Jersey 08854

CONTENTS

PHYSICS COURSE REVIEW

THE PRACTICE TESTS

ABOUT THE TEST

The SAT II: Subject Tests are developed and administered for the College Board by Educational Testing Service (ETS). The test development process involves the assistance of educators throughout the country, and is designed and implemented to ensure that the content and difficulty level of the test are appropriate.

Although some colleges require SAT II: Subject Tests as part of their admissions process, most colleges use the scores from the SAT II: Subject Tests for student placement purposes. Test scores are used as a means of determining a student's aptitude for a particular course of study.

The SAT II: Subject Test in Physics is one hour in length and consists of 75 multiple-choice questions. These questions are designed to measure your knowledge of physics and your ability to apply that knowledge. The general difficulty level of the test is designed for students who have taken a one-year introductory course in high school physics. To assist you in preparing for the exam, the College Board has provided the following list of exam topic percentages: mechanics (34–38%); electricity and magnetism (19–23%); waves (18–22%); heat, kinetic theory, and thermodynamics (8–12%); modern physics (8–12%); miscellaneous (measurement, math skills, laboratory skills, 2–4%). Concept application percentages are also provided: recall (20–33%); single-concept problem (40–53%); multiple-concept problem (20–33%).

Primarily, the test assesses your knowledge and understanding of the most significant concepts in physics and your ability to apply that knowledge. Laboratory experience will contribute to your understanding of some of the questions on the test. Since the mathematical calculations are limited to simple algebraic, trigonometric, and graphical relationships, students are not permitted to use electronic calculators or slide rules during the test. For the majority of the test, the principal system of units is the metric system.

To receive information on upcoming administrations of the exam, consult the publication *Taking the SAT II: Subject Tests,* which can be obtained from your guidance counselor or by contacting:

College Board SAT Program
P.O. Box 6200
Princeton, NJ 08541-6200
Phone: (609) 771-7600
Website: *http://www.collegeboard.org*

ABOUT THE REVIEW

The review in this book is designed to refresh your knowledge and further your understanding of the test material. It includes problem-solving techniques you can use to enhance your scores on the exam. Also included in the review are extensive discussions and examples to sharpen your skills in physics. Topics covered in the review include:

➤ Vectors and Scalars

➤ Mechanics

➤ Electricity and Magnetism

➤ Waves and Optics

➤ Physical Optics

➤ Heat, Kinetic Theory, and Thermodynamics

➤ Modern Physics

SCORING THE TEST

When you take the actual Physics Test, your test will be scored electronically by a scanning machine. For each correct answer, you will receive one point. For each incorrect answer, you will lose one-fourth of a point. This method compensates for random guessing. All unanswered questions will not be counted. In order to score your practice test follow this procedure:

Step 1: Check your answers to the test questions against the answers in the answer key.

Step 2: Determine the number of correct answers. Do not count any unanswered questions. Enter the result here: _____

Step 3: Determine the number of incorrect answers and divide this number by four. Do not count any unanswered questions. Enter the result here: _____

$$\frac{\text{Total incorrect answers}}{4} =$$

Step 4: Subtract the result in Step 3 from the number of correct answers in Step 2. Round this number to the nearest whole number. This is your raw score. Enter the result here: _____

To convert your raw score to a scale score, use the table that follows.

SAT II: Physics Score Conversion Table

Raw Score	College Board Scaled Score	Raw Score	College Board Scaled Score	Raw Score	College Board Scaled Score
75	800	40	670	5	450
74	800	39	660	4	440
73	800	38	650	3	430
72	800	37	650	2	430
71	800	36	640	1	420
70	800	35	640	0	410
69	800	34	630	− 1	410
68	800	33	630	− 2	400
67	800	32	620	− 3	390
66	800	31	610	− 4	390
65	800	30	610	− 5	380
64	800	29	600	− 6	370
63	800	28	600	− 7	370
62	790	27	590	− 8	360
61	790	26	580	− 9	350
60	780	25	580	− 10	350
59	780	24	570	− 11	340
58	770	23	570	− 12	330
57	770	22	560	− 13	330
56	760	21	550	− 14	320
55	760	20	540	− 15	310
54	750	19	540	− 16	310
53	750	18	530	− 17	300
52	740	17	530	− 18	290
51	730	16	520	− 19	290
50	730	15	510		
49	720	14	510		
48	720	13	500		
47	710	12	490		
46	700	11	480		
45	700	10	480		
44	690	9	470		
43	690	8	470		
42	680	7	460		
41	670	6	450		

ABOUT RESEARCH & EDUCATION ASSOCIATION

Research & Education Association (REA) is an organization of educators, scientists, and engineers specializing in various academic fields. Founded in 1959 with the purpose of disseminating the most recently developed scientific information to groups in industry, government, high schools, and universities, REA has since become a successful and highly respected publisher of study aids, test preps, handbooks, and reference works.

REA's Test Preparation series includes study guides for all academic levels in almost all disciplines. Research & Education Association publishes test preps for students who have not yet completed high school, as well as high school students preparing to enter college. Students from countries around the world seeking to attend college in the United States will find the assistance they need in REA's publications. For college students seeking advanced degrees, REA publishes test preps for many major graduate school admission examinations in a wide variety of disciplines, including engineering, law, and medicine. Students at every level, in every field, with every ambition can find what they are looking for among REA's publications.

Unlike most test preparation books—which present only a few practice tests that bear little resemblance to the actual exams—REA's series presents tests that accurately depict the official exams in both degree of difficulty and types of questions. REA's practice tests are always based upon the most recently administered exams, and include every type of question that can be expected on the actual exams.

REA's publications and educational materials are highly regarded and continually receive an unprecedented amount of praise from professionals, instructors, librarians, parents, and students. Our authors are as diverse as the subjects and fields represented in the books we publish. They are well-known in their respective fields and serve on the faculties of prestigious universities throughout the United States.

ACKNOWLEDGMENTS

In addition to our authors, we would like to thank Dr. Max Fogiel, President, for his overall guidance which has brought this publication to its completion; Larry B. Kling, Quality Control Manager of Books in Print, for his supervision of revisions; Robert Gelinas, Editorial Assistant, for coordinating revisions; and Marty Perzan for typesetting the book.

SAT II:
PHYSICS

Course Review

CHAPTER 1

VECTORS AND SCALARS

BASIC DEFINITIONS OF VECTORS AND SCALARS

A vector is a quantity that has both magnitude and direction. Some typical vector quantities are: displacement, velocity, force, acceleration, momentum, electric field strength and magnetic field strength.

A scalar is a quantity that has magnitude but no direction. Some typical scalar quantities are: mass, length, time, density, energy and temperature.

Note: In this book, vectors are indicated by bold type.

ADDITION OF VECTORS (a + b) — GEOMETRIC METHODS

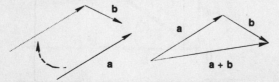

(i) Attach the head of **a** to the tail of **b**.

(ii) By connecting the head of **a** to the tail of **b**, the vector **a + b** is defined.

Figure 1 — Triangle Method of Adding Vectors (Head-to-Tail)

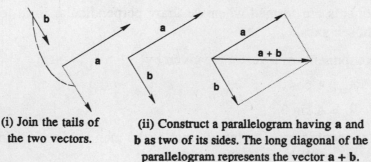

(i) Join the tails of the two vectors.

(ii) Construct a parallelogram having **a** and **b** as two of its sides. The long diagonal of the parallelogram represents the vector **a + b**.

Figure 2 — The Parallelogram Method of Adding Vectors (Tail-to-Tail)

SUBTRACTION OF VECTORS

The subtraction of a vector is defined as the addition of the corresponding negative vector. Therefore, the vector $P - F$ is obtained by adding the vector $(- F)$ to the vector P, i.e., $P + (- F)$. See the following figure.

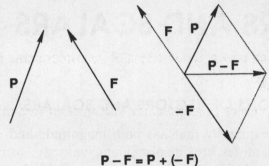

$$P - F = P + (- F)$$

Figure 3 — The Subtraction of a Vector

THE COMPONENTS OF A VECTOR

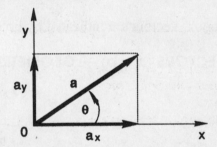

Figure 4 — The Formation of Vector Components on the
Positive X - Y Axis

a_x and a_y are the components of a vector $\mathbf{a}$. The angle θ is measured counterclockwise from the positive x-axis. The components are formed when we draw perpendicular lines to the chosen axes.

The components of a vector are given by

$$A_x = A \cos \theta$$

$$A_y = A \sin \theta$$

A component is equal to the product of the magnitude of vector A and cosine of the angle between the positive axis and the vector.

The magnitude can be expressed in terms of the components.

$$A = \sqrt{A_x^2 + A_y^2}$$

For the angle θ,

$$\tan \theta = \frac{A_y}{A_x}.$$

A vector **F** can be written in terms of its components F_x and F_y

$$\mathbf{F} = \mathbf{i}F_x + \mathbf{j}F_y$$

where **i** and **j** represent perpendicular unit vectors (magnitude = 1) along the x- and y-axis.

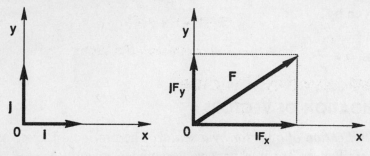

(a) The unit vectors **i** and **j** of the two-dimensional rectangular coordinate system.

(b) The components F_x and F_y.

Figure 5 — Vector Components and the Unit Vector

THE UNIT VECTOR

A Unit Vector in the direction of a vector **a** is given by

$$u = \frac{\mathbf{a}}{|\mathbf{a}|} = \frac{\mathbf{a}}{a} = \left(\frac{a_x}{a}\mathbf{i}\,\frac{a_y}{a}\mathbf{j}\right).$$

ADDING VECTORS ANALYTICALLY

Analytical addition involves adding the components of the individual vectors to produce the sum, expressed in terms of its components.

To find **a** + **b** = **c** analytically:

i)   Resolve **a** in terms of its components:

$$\mathbf{a} = \mathbf{i}a_x + \mathbf{j}a_y$$

ii) Resolve **b** in terms of its components:

$$\mathbf{b} = \mathbf{i}b_x + \mathbf{j}b_y$$

iii) The components of **c** equal the sum of the corresponding components of **a** and **b**:

$$\mathbf{c} = \mathbf{i}(a_x + b_x) + \mathbf{j}(a_y + b_y)$$

and

$$\mathbf{c} = \mathbf{i}c_x + \mathbf{j}c_y$$

and the magnitude

$$|c| = \sqrt{c_x^2 + c_y^2}$$

with θ given by

$$\tan \theta = \frac{c_y}{c_x}.$$

MULTIPLICATION OF VECTORS

Multiplication of a vector by a scalar. The product of a vector **a** and a scalar k, written as $k\mathbf{a}$, is a new vector whose magnitude is k times the magnitude of **a**; if k is positive, the new vector has the same direction as **a**; if k is negative, the new vector has a direction opposite that of **a**.

The Scalar Product (Dot Product). The Dot Product of two vectors yields a scalar:

$$\mathbf{a} \cdot \mathbf{b} = ab \cos \theta.$$

The Vector Product (Cross Product). The Cross Product of two vectors yields a vector:

$$\mathbf{a} \times \mathbf{b} = \mathbf{c} \quad \text{and} \quad |c| = ab \sin \theta.$$

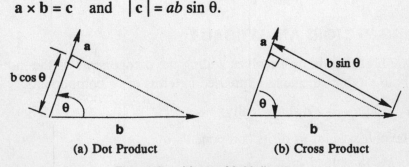

(a) Dot Product   (b) Cross Product

Figure 6 — Vector Multiplication

4

The direction of the Vector Product $a \times b = c$ is given by the "Right-Hand Rule":

i)   With a and b tail-to-tail, draw the angle θ from a to b.

ii) With your right hand, curl your fingers in the direction of the angle drawn. The extended thumb points in the direction of c.

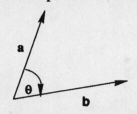

Figure 7 — The Direction of the Vector Product,

$c = a \times b$ ($|c|$ = ab sin θ), is into the page.

CHAPTER 2

MECHANICS

KINEMATICS

Kinematics is a branch of mechanics in which motion along straight lines and curves is studied. The fundamental concepts described here are the basis for mechanical physics.

The concept of motion involves several important ideas, the first of which is speed. Speed is the time rate of motion, or simply, the distance traveled within a given time unit. To calculate a speed, the equation is

$s = d/t$

where s is the speed, d is the distance traveled, and t is the time to travel the distance. If, for example, a member of a track team were to run 100 meters in a time of 11.5 seconds. his speed would be 100 m/11.5s, which is 8.7 m/s.

The understanding of speed leads to a more complex concept known as velocity. Velocity is complex in that it consists of two parts, speed *and* direction. If a mass travels a given direction, its time rate of motion is now considered a velocity. The numeric speed value is called the magnitude and the direction is specified. Examples of velocity values are 250 m/s south, or 50 m/s 10° north of west. When calculating velocity values, the equation is similar to the speed equation:

$$v = d/t=$$

where v is the velocity, d is the distance, and t is the time. The magnitude of velocity can also be represented graphically.

Graph A shows the change in distance versus the travel time. The velocity is represented by the slope of the line. Since the slope of the line is constant, the magnitude of the velocity is constant. However, if the slope of the representative line changes during the time period, then the velocity is variable. Variable velocity is shown on Graph B.

Once again, the equation and graphs only represent the magnitude of the velocity, but the direction of the motion must be specified. This directional aspect makes velocity a vector quantity. Vectors are lines which can be used to graphically examine velocity. Because of their nature, vectors are more mathematically complex than numeric magnitudes. By examining the following velocity vector problem, the nature of vectors may be better understood.

An airplane flies east with a velocity of 150 km/hr. The wind at this time has a velocity of 45 km/hr south. What is the plane's resultant velocity? To solve the problem, a graphic representation is made using vectors. (See Figure 8.) By adding the wind vector to the plane vector, we find a resultant vector, v_r, at some angle south of east. In a scalar drawing, the

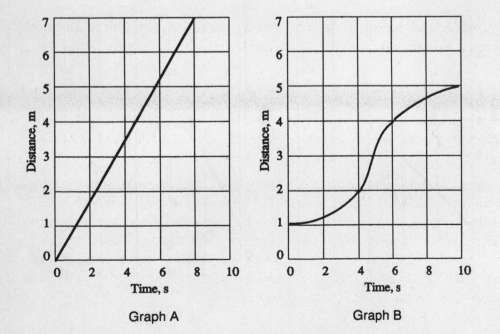

Graph A

Graph B

resultant velocity, v_r, is equal to the length of v_r in centimeters times the 10 km/hr scale. For example, if v_r is 15 cm, then the velocity is 15 × 10 or 150 km/hr. The angle is measured with a protractor, and we find the direction of v_r to be some angle south of east. Directional angles should always be measured from the nearest horizontal or vertical reference, in this case, east.

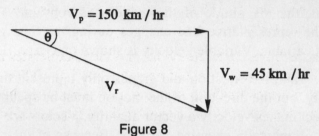

Figure 8

Without a scale drawing we solve the problem trigonometrically, beginning with the tangent function:

$\tan \theta = 45/150 = 0.3$

$\theta = \arctan 0.3 = 16.7° \text{ S of E}$

$\sin \theta = 45/V_r$

$v_r = 45/\sin 16.7° = 156.6 \text{ km/hr}$

When an object changes in velocity, it is accelerating. Acceleration is

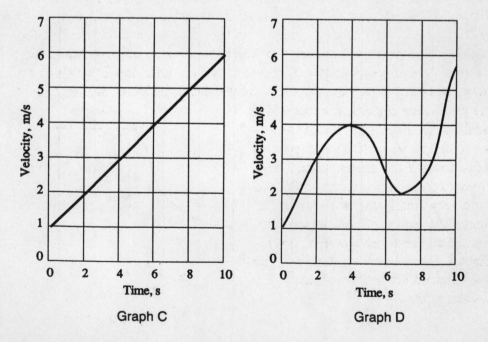

Graph C

Graph D

the rate of change of velocity within a given time period. Acceleration, a, is the change in velocity divided by the time interval for the change. The equation is

$$a = \Delta v / \Delta t.$$

As with a velocity, acceleration can be represented graphically as the slope of a line for a velocity versus time graph. It can also be constant, (Graph C), or variable, (Graph D).

If a car is traveling at 20 km/hr, and then accelerates to 60 km/hr in 5 seconds, the acceleration would be (60 - 20)/5 = 40/5 = 8 km/hr/s. This means that for each of the 5 seconds, the velocity increases by 8 km/hr. The acceleration equation can be solved for a final velocity so that

$$v_f = v_i + a\Delta t.$$

Combining this equation with the velocity equation, $v = d/t$, we can produce an equation with which we may solve for the distance traveled by an accelerating object:

$$\Delta d = v_i\Delta t + \tfrac{1}{2}a\Delta t^2.$$

Since acceleration is defined as a change in velocity, it is possible to accelerate by changing only the direction of the velocity and have the magnitude remain the same. An example of this idea is that if you were walking 3 m/s east, then turned and walked 3 m/s south, you have accelerated. If these directional changes were to occur constantly in equal amounts, then the resulting path of motion would be circular. Circular motion is the result of centripetal acceleration, which means acceleration towards a center point. Figure 9 shows a circular path and 2 positions for the same object. Upon examination, we see the direction of the velocity at any given time is perpendicular to the radius of the path. The velocity direction changes in such a way so as to move toward the center, hence, centripetal acceleration. Assuming θ and d are very small, the path will be circular. The force which causes centripetal acceleration is called the centripetal force because this force is also directed toward the center of the circular path.

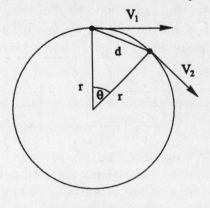

Figure 9

Uniform circular motion has its own unique quantities of velocity and acceleration. Since the displacement along a circle can be measured by angles, velocity about a circular path is known as angular velocity, ω, so that

$$\omega = \Delta\theta \, / \, \Delta t$$

where $\Delta\theta$ is the change in angular displacement and Δt is the time interval for that change. Angular acceleration, α, relates to angular velocity by

$$\alpha = \Delta\omega \, / \, \Delta t$$

where $\Delta\omega$ is the change in angular velocity, and Δt is the time interval for that change.

DYNAMICS

The foundation concept in the study of dynamics is the force. Forces are phenomena which pull or push on masses. Gravity is one such force. Gravity pulls masses toward the Earth. Gravity accelerates all masses at 9.8 m/s². This means that small masses fall at the same rate as larger ones. However, the air around the Earth can cause objects to fall more slowly. If we consider objects falling in a vacuum, then we can make predictions about their motion. Any equation involving acceleration, a, can be adapted for gravitation acceleration by replacing a with g; 9.8 m/s². Figure 10 shows the fall of a mass starting from rest. As the mass falls, it gains velocity at 9.8 m/s². The velocity after any given time of fall is

$$v = g\Delta t.$$

If we examine a 3 second fall, then

$$v = (9.8)\,(3) = 29.4 \text{ m/s.}$$

We also see that as the velocity increases, the distance traveled per second also increases. The distance an object falls in a given time is shown

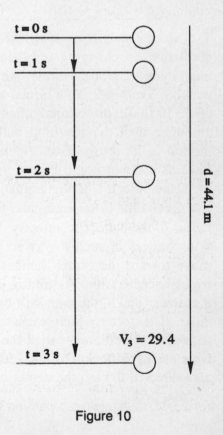

Figure 10

by

$$\Delta d = \frac{1}{2} g \, \Delta t^2.$$

Again looking at a 3 second fall, the distance fallen is

$$\Delta d = \frac{1}{2} (9.8) (3^2) = 44.1 \text{ meters.}$$

An additional application of free falling objects is the parabolic motion of a projectile. Projectiles, such as a bullet, baseball, etc., have motion characteristics in two dimensions simultaneously. However, these horizontal and vertical motions are independent of one another. Figure 11 shows the path of a projectile with a velocity of 100 m/s at 30° above horizontal.

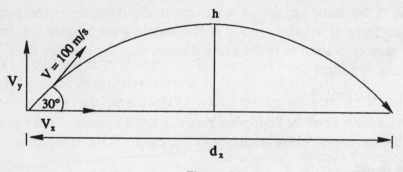

Figure 11

Since v is at an angle, the horizontal motion of the object is a result of the horizontal component of v, $v_x = v \cos 30°$. The vertical motion results from the vertical component $v_y = v \sin 30°$. Accordingly, the X motion is analyzed with a linear equation, and the Y motion is analyzed with falling object equations. The maximum height of a projectile, h, is the point at which $v_y = 0$. The time to reach maximum height is half the time of the total flight, and is given by

$$t = v \sin \theta / g.$$

For our example,

$$t = (100) \sin 30° / 9.8 = 5.1 \text{ s.}$$

By substitution,

$$h = v^2 \sin^2 \theta / 2g.$$

Thus $h = (100)^2 \sin^2 30° / (2) (9.8) = 127.55 \text{ m.}$

Since the total time is twice the time to maximum height or 10.2 s, the horizontal distance can be found by $d_x = v_x t$.

$$d_x = v_x t = v \cos \theta \, t = (100)(\cos 30°)(10.2) = 883.3 \text{ m}$$

Masses tend to resist the effect of forces due to a characteristic known as inertia. Inertia is the platform for Newton's First Law of Motion. The first law states that if a mass is at rest, its inertia will act so as to keep the mass at rest. Also, if a mass is moving, its inertia acts to keep the mass moving with a constant velocity. This idea helps to explain orbiting satellites or planets. Once the motion is established, it will not change unless some external force acts to change the motion. The force is defined by Newton's Second Law of Motion. Mathematically,

$$\mathbf{F} = m\mathbf{a},$$

where $\mathbf{F}$ is the force applied in a particular direction, m is the mass to which the force is applied, and $\mathbf{a}$ is the acceleration resulting from the force. The acceleration is in the same direction as the applied force. The dimensions of a force are

$$\mathbf{F} = (\text{kg})(\text{m/s}^2)$$

which is called a newton. Suppose a race car has a mass of 2000 kg. What force must the engine exert to accelerate the car at 50 m/s²? Since

$$\mathbf{F} = m\mathbf{a},$$

$$\mathbf{F} = (2000)(50) = 100,000$$

newtons of force. Newton's Third Law of Motion involves two forces. This law states that when one mass exerts a force on another, the second mass will exert a reaction force equal in magnitude and opposite in direction to the first. As stated earlier, the force of gravity pulls masses toward the Earth. Newton developed a gravity relationship known as the Universal Law of Gravitation. The idea is that all masses exert a pulling force on all other masses. The attraction between two masses is directly proportional to the product of their masses, and inversely proportional to the square of the distance between their centers. The equation is

$$\mathbf{F} = \frac{Gmm'}{d^2}$$

where G is the universal gravitational constant. The value of G is 6.67×10^{-11} Nm²/kg². The laws of motion and gravitation describe the basic ideas regarding forces. However, the study of forces requires a closer examination.

The motion of planets and satellites can be approximated by considering their orbits as circular. The gravitational force between the masses is the centripetal force which maintains circular motion. From the Law of Gravitation,

$$\mathbf{F} = Gmm'/d^2$$

and the centripetal force is given by,

$$\mathbf{F}_c = m\omega^2 r.$$

Since $\mathbf{F} = \mathbf{F}_c$ and d can be considered the radius of the orbit,

$$Gmm' / r^2 = m\omega^2 r$$

$$\omega^2 = Gm' / r^3$$

This equation is the determination of the angular velocity for planetary or satellite orbits where m' is the larger mass which holds the planet or satellite. This equation also shows that the mass of the orbiting satellite, m, does not affect its velocity. If we wish to place a satellite in orbit 75,000 km above the Earth, the velocity required to maintain this orbit is,

$$\omega^2 = Gm' / r^3$$

where G is 6.67×10^{-11} Nm^2/kg^2, m' is the mass of the Earth, equal to 5.96×10^{24} kg, and r is the radius, 7.5×10^7 m.

$$\omega^2 = (6.67 \times 10^{-11}) (5.96 \times 10^{24}) / (7.5 \times 10^7)^3$$

$$\omega^2 = 3.97532 \times 10^{14} / 4.21875 \times 10^{23}$$

$$\omega^2 = 9.4229807 \times 10^{-10}$$

$$= 3.07 \times 10^{-5} \text{ rad/s}$$

Since one radian is the angle at which the circumference traveled equals the radius, the linear velocity is,

$$v = (3.07 \times 10^{-5} \text{ rad/s}) (7.5 \times 10^7 \text{ m/rad})$$

$$= 2302.5 \text{ m/s} = 2.3 \text{ km/s}$$

Forces are vector quantities, with magnitude and direction. This means they are added in the same manner as velocity vectors. When forces are added in this manner, they produce a Net Force, which is the final effect resulting from a force combination. If all forces counteract each other so that the net force is zero, then a translational equilibrium has been established. Equilibrium is the state of an object which is at rest. If a positive net force is applied to a mass, it will accelerate according to the second law of motion. Forces applied in the same or opposite directions add together arithmetically. For instance, a 20 N force east and a 13 N force east will result in a net force of 33 N east. Conversely, a 400 N force north added to a 150 N force south results in a net force of 250 N north. Once again, forces that combine at angles other than 0° or 180° require a vector diagram and trigonometric functions to calculate. The determination of net forces from force combinations is known as force composition.

PROBLEM

> Two forces act on a point. One is 10 N east and the other is 30 N 30° south of west. What are the magnitude and direction of the resultant net force?

Solution

To solve, a diagram is needed. Figure 12 shows the proper position and proportion of the forces. If we now diagram the addition of the 30 N force to the 10 N force, we create a triangle which shows the resultant force, F_r. Since the F_r is opposite the known angle, the law of cosines is applied to find the magnitude of F_r.

$$F_r = \sqrt{F_1^2 + F_2^2 - 2(F_1)(F_2)(\cos \theta)}$$

$$F_r = \sqrt{10^2 + 30^2 - 2(10)(30)(\cos 30°)}$$

$$F_r = 21.9 \text{ N}$$

To find the direction of F_r, the law of sines is applied:

$$\frac{\sin \theta_1}{F_1} = \frac{\sin \theta_2}{F_2} = \frac{\sin \theta_r}{F_r}$$

solving for θ_2,

$$\sin \theta_2 = (\sin 30°)(30) / 21.9 = 0.685$$

$$\theta_2 = \arcsin 0.685 = 136.8°$$

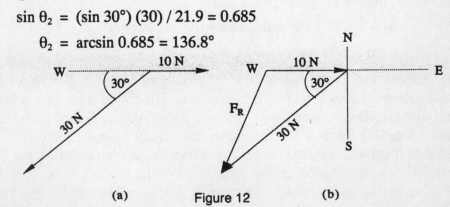

(a) Figure 12 (b)

This is the angle in question but is not considered the proper direction for F_r. F_r is 136.8° from east, but the west reference is closer. In this case,

$$\theta = 180° - \theta_2 = 180° - 136.8° = 43.2° \text{ S of W}$$

$$F_r = 21.9 \text{ N} \quad 43.2° \text{ S of W}$$

Forces are not always combined into a composite force. Many situations involve a process known as force resolution. Resolving forces means to reduce a given force to its perpendicular components. Examine Figure 13 below.

Shown here is a force of 100 N 40° S of W. The question is what amount of the force is south and what amount is west. Adding the forces in triangular form, shown in Figure 13b, shows F_s as the sine of 40° and F_w as the cosine of 40°.

$$\sin 40° = F_s / 100$$

$$F_s = \sin 40° (100) = 64.3 \text{ N south}$$

$$\cos 40° = F_w / 100$$

$$F_w = \cos 40° (100) = 76.6 \text{ N west}$$

Net forces applied to objects cause motion. Sometimes, one object must slide over another to move. When this occurs, a new force must be considered, friction. Frictional forces resist the sliding motion of objects by acting parallel to the sliding surfaces in the direction opposite the motion. The magnitude of friction depends upon certain situations. First, the nature of the surfaces which are in contact. Smoother surfaces have less friction than rough surfaces. Also, friction depends on the magnitude

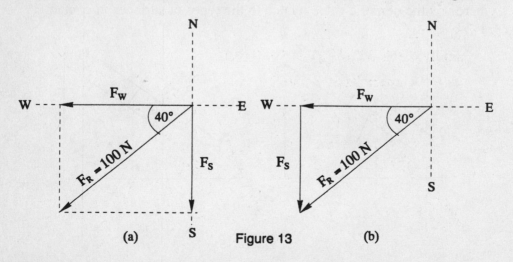

(a)   Figure 13   (b)

of the force pressing the surfaces together. In looking at Figure 14, we
see a block on an incline. The weight
of the block is shown as force F_w. If
F_w is resolved into its components, we
see that the component F_p is parallel
to the surface and could cause motion.
Component F_N is the pressing force
perpendicular to the surface. This
force is known as the *normal* force,
hence, F_N. Figures 15a and 15b show
the friction force, F_f, which is parallel
to the surface. In Figure 15a, F_f is op-

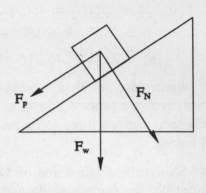

Figure 14

posite F_p. If the block is at rest or sliding down the incline with a constant
velocity, then F_f will equal F_p. If F_p is larger than F_f, then the block must
accelerate down the incline because of the net force in that direction. If a
force, F_a, is applied to the block, parallel to the surface and up the incline,
as shown in Figure 15b, then F_f will be in the direction of F_p. For F_a to
cause upward motion, it must be at least as large as the sum of F_p and F_f:

$$F_a = F_p + F_f.$$

Once again, the amount of friction is determined by F_N and the contact surfaces. The surface factor can be incorporated using the ratio of F_f to
F_N, which is unique to each case. This value is the coefficient of sliding
friction, μ. In this ratio,

$$\mu = F_f / F_N$$

where μ is the numeric value related to the types of surfaces in contact.

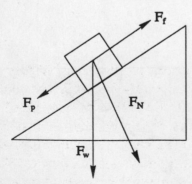
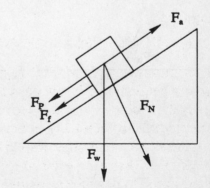

Figure 15

PROBLEM

The coefficient of friction between a metal block and an inclined surface over which it will slide is 0.20. If the surface makes a 20° angle with the horizontal, and the mass of the block is 80 kg, what force is required to slide the block up the incline at a constant velocity?

Solution

To solve, diagram the problem and identify all forces. The weight of the block, F_w, would be 80 kg times the gravitational acceleration for Earth, $g = 9.8$ m/s².

$$F_w = (80) (9.8) = 784 \text{ N}$$

To resolve F_p and F_N,

$$F_p = \sin 20° (F_w)$$
$$= \sin 20° (784) = 268 \text{ N}$$
$$F_N = \cos 20° (F_w)$$
$$= \cos 20° (784) = 737 \text{ N}$$

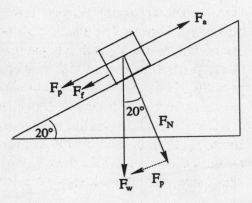

Figure 16

Since the block is moving up the incline, F_f is in the direction of F_p. To produce constant velocity up the incline,

$$F_a = F_p + F_f.$$

Since μ is given as 0.20, $\mu = F_f / F_N$ becomes $F_f = \mu F_N$.

$$F_f = \mu F_N = (0.20) (737) = 147 \text{ N}.$$

Solving for F_a,

$$F_a = F_p + F_f = 268 + 147 = 415 \text{ N}.$$

Until now we have viewed forces acting on objects as if they were acting on a single point. Every object has a center of gravity. The center of gravity is that point within an object where all the mass is considered to be concentrated. If all forces act on the center of gravity, then their behavior is the same as the point objects we have examined. If, however, forces act on points other than the center of gravity, a new situation occurs. Torque is the term used to describe a positive net force which causes rotation of an object about a fixed pivot point. If the torques applied counteract each other, the net torque is zero. This condition is known as rotational equilibrium, and no rotation will occur. If a net torque is present, then the object will rotate. In examining Figure 17, we see a uniform bar, pivoted at the geometric center which is also the location of the center of gravity. The weight of the bar, 20 N, acts downward at the center of gravity. F_a is a force of 10 N up acting 5 cm left of pivot, and F_b is an 8 N force up acting 7 cm right of pivot. The torque, T, provided by each force is found by $T = Fd$, where F is the force and d is the distance from the pivot.

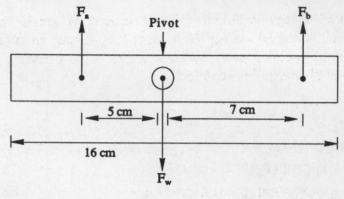

Figure 17

T for F_a is $T = 10(5) = 50$ N(cm)

T for F_w is $T = 20(0) = 0$ N(cm)

T for F_b is $T = 8(7) = 56$ N(cm)

Rotation in the direction of F_a would be clockwise or positive torque. Rotation in the direction of F_b would be counterclockwise or negative torque.

T net = T clockwise + T counterclockwise

T net = 50 + (- 56) = - 6 N (cm)

This means the net torque is 6 N (cm) counterclockwise, and the bar will rotate counterclockwise. It is important to realize that forces applied at the pivot point *do not* create torque.

During rotational motion, the rotational inertia of the mass tends to resist motion changes according to the first law of motion. The amount of net torque is related to the inertial value by

$T = I\alpha$,

where I is the rotational inertia and α is the angular acceleration.

ENERGY AND MOMENTUM

When forces move objects through some distance, it is said that *work* has been done on the object. Work is the product of the force causing the motion and the distance through which the object is moved:

$W = F\Delta d$.

Energy is defined as the ability to do work. Energy can take a variety of forms, and can change forms at any given time.

Potential energy is an energy form caused by gravity or elasticity. Gravitational potential energy is produced by lifting an object to some height through which gravity may accelerate it. To calculate the gravitational potential energy for an object,

$E_p = mgh$,

where m is the mass, g is gravitational acceleration, and h is the height through which the object may be accelerated. Thus, a 100 kg boulder at the top of a 25 meter high cliff would have an

$E_p = (100)(9.8)(25) = 24,500$ joules.

A second type of potential energy is produced by elasticity, such as the stretching or compression of a spring. When a spring is stretched or compressed beyond its equilibrium position, then it applies a force so as to return to equilibrium. The energy which applies the force is the elastic potential energy. To calculate the elastic potential energy,

$E_p = \frac{1}{2}k(d^2)$,

where d is the distance from the equilibrium position and k is the force constant for the spring. The value of k depends upon the nature of the spring.

Elastic potential energy within a spring can provide a special type of repetitive motion known as *Simple Harmonic Motion*. Any object which moves over the same path repeatedly in equal time intervals has periodic motion. When the mass on the spring in Figure 18 is stretched and released, it is accelerated upward with a force proportional to the displacement from equilibrium. When the mass moves back towards equilibrium, it will accelerate past it. This causes compression of the spring which applies a force in the opposite direction with the same result. The motion of the mass will continue in a periodic oscillation. This linear oscillation is simple harmonic motion.

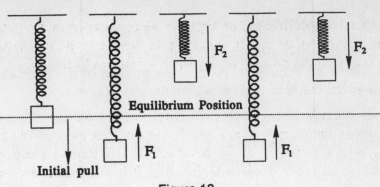

Figure 18

Kinetic energy is a form of energy which is produced by the motion of an object. Kinetic energy depends upon the mass and velocity of an object. To calculate kinetic energy,

$$E_k = \frac{1}{2} mv^2.$$

If a 2000 kg automobile is traveling at 12 m/s, then its kinetic energy is

$$E_k = \frac{1}{2} (2000) (12)^2 = 144,000 \text{ joules.}$$

The study of energy leads to a very important concept known as the Law of Conservation of Energy. This law states that the sum of all energy of all forms is equal to the total amount of energy within a system. Furthermore, the total energy in a system has a *constant* value. Figure 19 shows various amounts of different types of energy. The sum of those energies is also represented. At some point, some of the energy present may change form, as shown in Figure 20. Although the energy may change its form, *the sum of the energies will always equal the same constant total.*

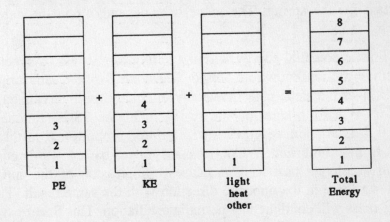

Figure 19

Laws of conservation also apply to other areas of motion study. The quantity of motion an object possesses is known as its momentum. The momentum, **p**, is the product of an object's mass and velocity,

$$\mathbf{p} = mv.$$

Momentum is also a vector quantity. For the motion of an object to change, its momentum must change. For example, a train and a car may be traveling with the same velocity, but the train will require a larger force to stop because its mass is much larger, thus it has a greater momentum to overcome. Momentum is involved in another idea regarding motion called impulse. Impulse is the product of a force and the time interval over which it acts. The impulse

$$F\Delta t = m\Delta v,$$

hence, an impulse is equal to a change in momentum.

The Law of Conservation of Momentum, as with energy, states that the sum of all momentum in a system is always equal to the same constant total amount. If an object in a system loses momentum, then another object somewhere in that system must gain momentum to preserve the total amount of momentum. This idea can be better understood by studying collisions. Objects transfer momentum between one another when they collide. If momentum is conserved, then the total momentum before and after the collision is equal. The equation:

$$(m_1v_1 + m_2v_2) \text{ before} = (m_1v'_1 + m_2v'_2) \text{ after}$$

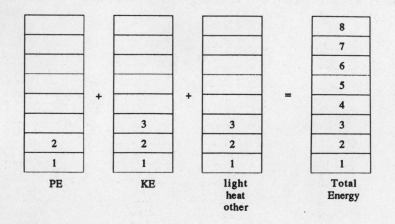

Figure 20

is used to calculate momentum magnitudes for a two object collision in one dimension. The sum of momentum before the collision is equal to the sum of momentum after the collision. Remember that momentum is a vector quantity and if collisions occur in two or three dimensions, then momentum must be calculated in the same manner as force and velocity vectors.

Angular momentum is the quantity of rotational motion. Angular momentum, in rotational terms, is $I\omega$, where I is the rotational inertia and ω is the angular velocity of the object.

CHAPTER 3

ELECTRICITY AND MAGNETISM

ELECTROSTATICS

Electrostatics is the study of stationary electrical charges. The Basic Law of Electrostatics states that charges which are alike repel one another, while charges which are opposite attract each other. Electric charge is measured in a unit known as a Coulomb. One Coulomb of charge is equivalent to 6.25×10^{18} electrons, which means that one electron holds a charge of 1.6×10^{-19} coulombs. The forces of repulsion and attraction acting on point charges are proportional in the same manner as gravitation between two masses. Figure 21 shows two sets of charges which are separated by a distance, d. In Figure 21(a), the opposite charges produce attraction forces, and in Figure 21(b), the similar charges produce repulsion forces.

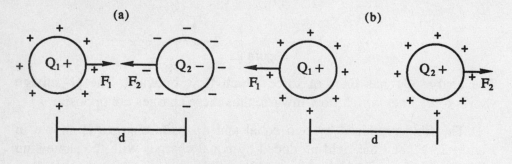

Figure 21

The magnitude of the forces is shown by

$$\mathbf{F} = \frac{kQQ'}{d^2}$$

where $\mathbf{F}$ is the force, k is a constant, Q and Q' are the magnitudes of the charges, and d is the distance between the centers of Q and Q'. For calculating forces between charges in air,

$k = 8.93 \times 10^9 \ \text{Nm}^2/C^2$.

In a vacuum,

$k = 8.987 \times 10^9 \ \text{Nm}^2/C^2$.

To calculate the force between a $3C$ charge and a $7C$ charge which are 0.60 m apart in air, Coulomb's Law shows

$\mathbf{F} = kQQ' \ / \ d^2 = (8.93 \times 10^9) \ (3) \ (7) \ / \ (0.60)^2$

$\mathbf{F} = 5.21 \times 10^{11} \ \text{N}$

Since both charges have the same sign, $\mathbf{F}$ is positive. This means that the force is repelling the charges. Opposite charges result in negative forces, which shows attraction.

Forces between charges occur because each charge generates an electric field. An electric field is that region in space in which a charge could experience an electric force. Electric fields are shown by lines of electric forces as in Figures 22 and 23.

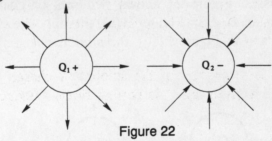

Figure 22

The charge $Q+$ has lines of force which flow outward. The $Q-$ charge shows force lines which flow inward, thus these charges are opposite.

The field produced by two equal and opposite charges is shown in Figure 23(a), and the field produced by equal charges with the same sign is shown in Figure 23(b). In Figure 23(a), the force lines complement each other, flowing out of one charge into the other. In Figure 23(b), the force lines oppose each other, causing the repulsion effect. Any charge particle, such as $q+$, which enters an electric field would experience a force according to Coulomb's Law and the direction of the force would be tangent to a given force line.

Electric Field Intensity, ε, at any point in the field is the force per unit of positive charge at that point. Thus,

$\varepsilon = \mathbf{F} / q,$

where F is the force in newtons on charge q in coulombs. If a charge of $0.75C$ in an electric field experiences a $0.5N$ force, the field intensity would be

$\varepsilon = \mathbf{F} / q = 0.5/0.75$

$= 6.7 \, N/C.$

If an electric field acts on and moves a charge from one point in a field to another, then these points are said to differ in electrical potential. By moving the charge, the field does work on the charge. The potential difference, V, between two points in an electric field is the work done per unit charge as the charge is moved, and is measured in volts. One volt is that potential difference which does one joule of work when moving a one coulomb charge.

ELECTRIC CIRCUITS

The existence of a potential difference is the energy which moves electric charges. When moving many charges through a conductor, the rate at which they flow is referred to as electric current, I. More specifically,

$I = Q/t,$

such that current is a measure of the amount of charge which passes a given point within a given time. As current flows, conductors may resist

(a)   (b)

Figure 23

the movement. This opposition to current flow is called resistance. The resistance within a conductor depends on the nature and material of that conductor.

When conductors offer resistance, they convert some of the current's kinetic energy into heat. The actual amount of heat generated by a resistance can be determined by Joule's Law; the heat produced in a conductor is directly proportional to the resistance, the square of the current, and the time the current is maintained.

$$\Delta H = I^2 Rt/J,$$

where ΔH is the heat in calories, I is the current, R is resistance, t is the time, and J is the mechanical heat equivalent, 4.19 joules/calorie.

PROBLEM

> What amount of heat is produced by a 10 ohm resistor which carries 0.3 amps of current for 3 minutes?

Solution

Since T must be expressed as seconds, $t = 3$ min $= 180$ sec. Therefore

$$H = I^2 Rt / J = (0.3)^2 (10) (180) / 4.19 = 38.7 \text{ calories.}$$

The relationship among potential differences, V, current, I, and resistance, R, is essential in the analysis of direct current electric circuits. This relationship is known as Ohm's Law,

$$V = IR.$$

Let's examine Figure 24.

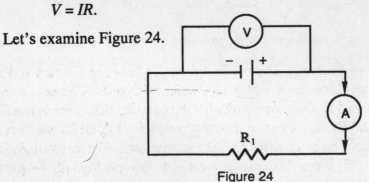

Figure 24

The potential difference in this circuit is provided by a one cell battery,

and would be measured with a voltmeter,

$\left(\text{V}\right)$.

Assuming the resistance of the wire to be insignificant, the circuit resistance is equal to the resistance, R, which is 3 ohms. If our ammeter,

$\left(\text{A}\right)$,

reads a current of 0.5 amps, what is our voltmeter reading? By Ohm's Law,

$$V = IR = (0.5)\,(3) = 1.5 \text{ volts.}$$

Examination of the following circuits will provide more insight into the laws for DC electric circuits.

Electrical circuits can be connected in series of parallel configurations. A series means that the electrical devices are connected such that the current *must* go from one device to the next. Parallel connections provide different paths for current flow.

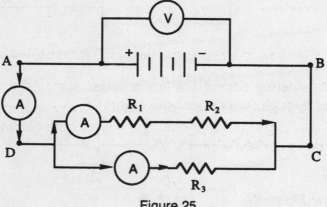

Figure 25

Examination of Figure 25 shows the difference between a series and a parallel connection. Between A and B is a series of 3 cells. The set of resistors between C and D show two paths for the current. Some current will pass through R_1 and R_2, and some will pass through R_3. R_1 and R_2 are in series since the current must go through both in that path. The resistor R_3 is parallel to the R_1 - R_2 series because any current through R_3 will *not* pass through the R_1 - R_2 series and vice versa.

Mathematical analysis of circuits is more complex. When considering a series of voltages, they are added to a sum or total voltage as in Figure 26. Thus, for voltages in series,

$$V_t = V_1 + V_2 + V_3 \ldots + V_n.$$

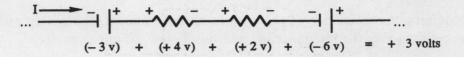

$$(-3v) \quad + \quad (+4v) \quad + \quad (+2v) \quad + \quad (-6v) \quad = \quad + 3 \text{ volts}$$

Figure 26

For parallel voltages, the connections are such that each device is essentially connected to the same two points as in Figure 27. This means that the voltage for each device is equal. Thus, for voltages in parallel,

$$V_t = V_1 = V_2 = V_3 \ldots = V_n.$$

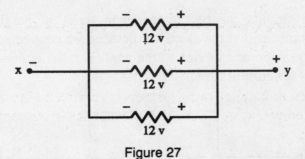

Figure 27

When considering current through a series, we find that the same current passes through each device as in Figure 28.

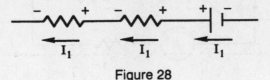

Figure 28

Thus, for currents through a series,

$$I_t = I_1 = I_2 = I_3 \ldots = I_n.$$

This seems logical since the current has no other path. For currents through parallel branches, we find that current which reaches a divided path *must* divide so as to send some current through all branches. The amount of current through a branch depends upon the resistances encountered in that branch. Thus, for parallel circuits,

$$I_t = I_1 + I_2 + I_3 \ldots + I_n$$

as shown in Figure 29.

To examine resistances in series, they are added to a sum just as the voltages. Thus, for resistances in series,

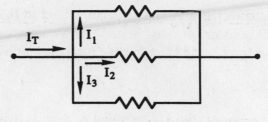

Figure 29

$$R_t = R_1 + R_2 + R_3 \dots + R_n$$

as shown by Figure 30.

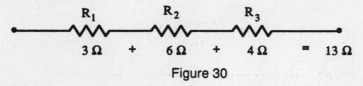

Figure 30

For resistances in parallel, we find a more complex situation. The resistance value equivalent to the parallel resistor set is the reciprocal sum of those resistors.

$$\frac{1}{R_{eq}} = \frac{1}{R_1} + \frac{1}{R_2} + \frac{1}{R_3} \dots + \frac{1}{R_n}$$

as in Figure 31.

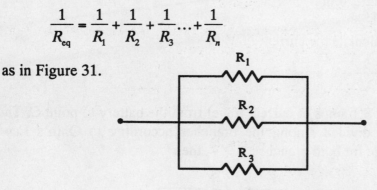

Figure 31

We can now apply these ideas to the circuit in Figure 32 to both analyze the circuit and better understand the relationships.

Given that the voltage for each cell is 3 V and $R_1 = 2\ \Omega$, $R_2 = 3\ \Omega$, and $R_3 = 7\Omega$, find the total current, I_t; the current through R_1 - R_2, I_1; and the current through R_3, I_2.

To begin, we must realize that Ohm's Law can apply to the total circuit, any section of the circuit, or any device within the circuit. First, the reading on the voltmeter will be the total for 3 batteries in series;

$$V_t = V_1 + V_2 + V_3 = 3 + 3 + 3 = 9 \text{ volts.}$$

Since point C is connected to A and D is connected to B, then the voltage across the parallel resistor set must be 9 V. If we now calculate the total resistance of our set, we could calculate the total current by

$$I_t = \frac{V_t}{R_t}.$$

To calculate R_t, we must apply the rules series and parallel resistors. Since R_1 and R_2 are in series, they are added together. But, their series combination is parallel to R_3. Since there are no other resistances to consider, R_t will equal R_{eq} for our set. Thus,

$$\frac{1}{R_t} = \frac{1}{(R_1 + R_2)} + \frac{1}{R_3}$$

$$\frac{1}{R_t} = \frac{1}{5} + \frac{1}{7}$$

$$\frac{1}{R_t} = 0.2 + 0.143 = 0.343$$

$$R_t = \frac{1}{0.343} = 2.9\,\Omega$$

Now we may calculate the current I_t,

$$I_t = \frac{V_t}{R_t} = \frac{9}{2.9} = 3.1 \text{ amps.}$$

This means that 3.1 amps of current travel from the battery to point C. The current is then divided among the branches according to Ohm's Law. Since the voltage for both branches is 9 V, then

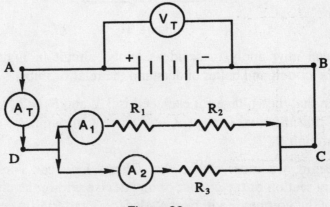

Figure 32

$$I_1 = \frac{V}{(R_1 + R_2)} = \frac{9}{5} = 1.8 \text{ amps}$$

$$I_2 = \frac{V}{R_3} = \frac{9}{7} = 1.3 \text{ amps}$$

Please note that $1.8 + 1.3 = 3.1$ amps. The sum of the divided currents must equal the total current.

Another device which may be used in a circuit is a capacitor. A capacitor is a combination of conducting plates which are separated by some insulating material. They are used to store electric charge within a system. The plates are given a potential difference which causes a charge build up on each plate. The ratio of the charge on either plate to the potential difference is called capacitance. Capacitance is measured in farads. One farad is the capacitance when one coulomb of charge on a capacitor results in a potential difference of one volt between the plates. The charge on a capacitor can be increased by using dielectric materials for insulators rather than air. The magnitude of the charge increase is different for different materials. If an air capacitor has a charge Q_1, and a second dielectric capacitor has a charge Q_2 under the same potential difference, then $Q_2 > Q_1$ by a factor of k, the dielectric constant for the given material. Thus, $Q_2 = kQ_1$.

As with other devices, the capacitance value for combinations of capacitors depends upon the connections within the circuit. Figure 33 shows capacitors in parallel which are added to a sum:

$$C_t = C_1 + C_2 + C_3 \ldots + C_n.$$

Also, capacitors in series add to a reciprocal sum:

$$\frac{1}{C_t} = \frac{1}{C_1} + \frac{1}{C_2} + \frac{1}{C_3} \ldots + \frac{1}{C_n}.$$

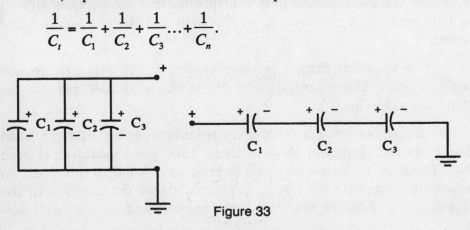

Figure 33

ELECTROMAGNETISM

Magnetism is a concept closely related to electricity, and shows many similarities to electrical phenomena. Magnetism is a property of charge in motion. In most situations, electrons within the structure of materials have two types of motion. First is the revolution of electrons about the nucleus of an atom. This gives the atom magnetic properties (Figure 34). The second is the motion of the electron spinning on its axis, causing magnetic effects. Most electrons are paired with opposite spins so as to neutralize their magnetism.

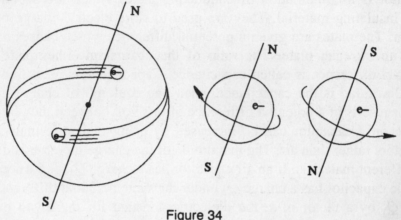

Figure 34

Although it is true that all atoms have these magnetic properties, we know that not all materials act as magnets. Iron is the most common magnetized substance. For the most part, atoms within the iron crystal are grouped in areas determined by their magnetic properties. These areas are called domains. The orientation of these domains is essentially random and crystallize in such a way so as to cancel the effects of each other. If the crystal is subjected to an intense magnetic field, the domains will all align themselves in the direction of the field and become a permanent magnet.

Just as electrical charges produce electric fields, magnets produce magnetic fields. Magnetic fields flow out of the north pole and into the south pole, as in Figure 35.

Once again we see that the opposite poles complement each other and have a force of attraction between them. Like poles would repel each other. The lines shown are magnetic lines of flux. A line of flux is drawn so that the tangent to the line at any point shows the direction of the magnetic field. Keep in mind that both magnetic and electric fields sur-

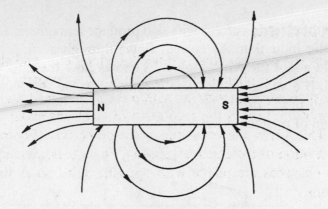

Figure 35

round the source in three dimensions, not in a single plane as they are shown here.

The strength of a magnetic field is related to the flux density. Flux density is a measure of the number of flux lines per unit area perpendicular to the lines. This idea is shown in Figure 36.

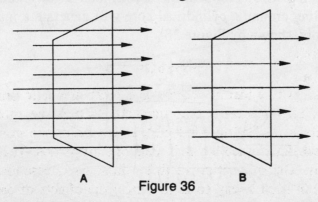

A   Figure 36   B

Given that the areas designated in *A* and *B* are equal, then the magnetic field in *A* is stronger than the field in *B* since more flux lines pass through the equal area. Thus, the field in *A* is more dense than the field in *B*.

Flux density can be calculated by

$B = \phi / A,$

where *B* is the flux density, ϕ is the number of flux lines, and *A* is the area of flux. Since flux lines are measured in webers, *B* is considered to be webers/m^2 which is called a tesla.

The flow of electric current will also produce a magnetic field. This is electromagnetic induction. As current flows through a wire, it induces a magnetic field about the wire. Figure 33 shows how the direction of flux can be found. If a straight conductor is grasped in the right hand with the thumb pointing in the direction of current, then the fingers wrap the wire in the direction of magnetic flux.

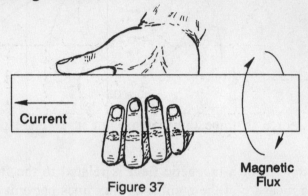

Figure 37

If conducting wire is looped into a coil, then a new situation occurs. Current traveling around a cylindrical core will generate a magnetic field through the core, shown by Figure 38.

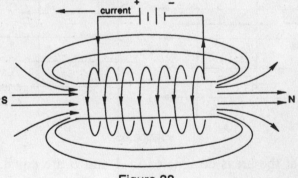

Figure 38

To find the direction of flux, Figure 39 shows that if the coil is grasped with the right hand so that the fingers wrap in the direction of the current, then the thumb will point in the direction of magnetic flux.

It is also possible to induce electricity with magnetism. As seen in Figure 40, a magnet, oriented with the north pole on the right side, moving to the right toward a loop of wire will induce a counterclockwise current in the wire loop. This is an illustration of Lenz's law which states that the induced current will be in a direction to oppose the change in magnetic flux that produced the current. The counterclockwise *induced* current produces a magnetic field (as found from the right hand rule) with the north pole oriented on the left which opposes or repels the magnet moving toward the right. If the magnet were pulled away from the loop, the induced current would be clockwise and the induced magnetic field reversed to attract the magnet and thus oppose its motion moving away from the coil.

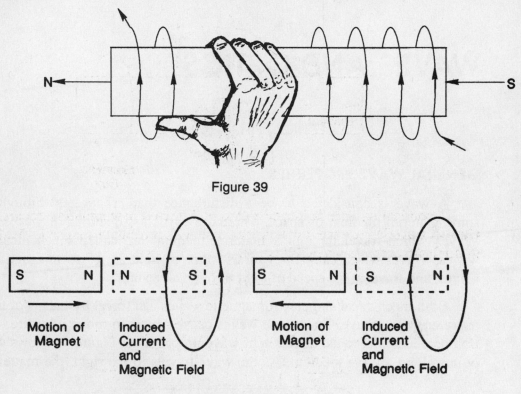

Figure 39

Figure 40

CHAPTER 4

WAVES AND OPTICS

GENERAL WAVE PROPERTIES

A wave is considered to be a disturbance that propagates through some material medium or space. There are two classifications of waves. Waves which travel through a material medium are called mechanical waves. Waves which carry the various forms of light are electromagnetic waves, and travel at the speed of light through a vacuum.

Both mechanical and electromagnetic waves can travel by means of a transverse type wave. Transverse waves cause matter to move in a direction perpendicular to the direction of wave propagation. Figure 41 shows 4 points along a wave medium. As the wave travels to the right, the matter

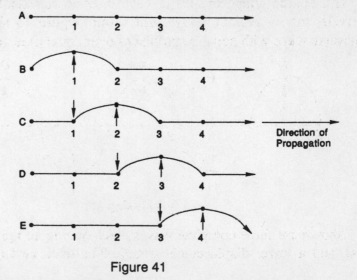

Figure 41

within the medium moves up, then down as the wave passes. Thus, the wave is transverse.

A second type of mechanical wave is the longitudinal or compression wave. Longitudinal waves cause material in the medium to move parallel to wave propagation. Figure 42 shows a compression wave pulse through a coil spring. When released, the compressed area attempts to spread out which will compress the coils to their right. This process continues throughout the length of the spring.

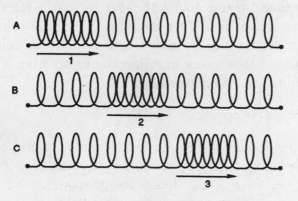

Figure 42

Sound waves are the best example of compression waves. The shock from a sound compresses the air near the source which sends a compression wave through the air in all directions. You hear the sound when the compression shock hits your ear drum.

If a source which creates a wave does so repeatedly at equal time intervals, then a periodic wave will result. Figure 43 shows a periodic transverse wave with equal disturbances over equal time periods.

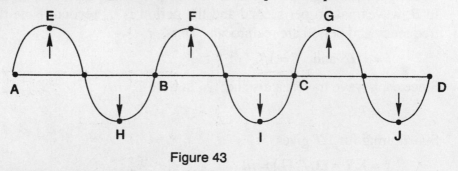

Figure 43

Shown are three complete waves, each having an upper displacement crest, and a lower displacement trough. The distance from a point on a wave to the same point on the next is called one wavelength. For our wave, the wavelength, λ, (lambda), could be measured from A to B, one crest and one trough; from E to F, crest to crest; or from H to I, trough to trough.

A wave which travels through one crest and one trough has completed one cycle. If we measure the number of waves which pass a given point in a specified time interval, then this is known as wave frequency. Frequency, f, is measured in cycles per second which is a hertz. The period, T, for a wave is the time for one complete wave to pass a reference point. Finally, a wave that moves in a given direction must have velocity in that direction. Wavelength, frequency, period, and velocity all relate to each other. Figure 44 shows two waves traveling one meter from X to Y. Each wave can travel from X to Y in one second.

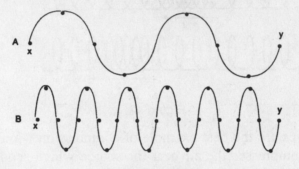

Figure 44

Looking at wave A, we find that in one second, two complete waves will pass point Y which gives a frequency equal to 2 hz. For wave B, six waves pass Y in one second which gives a frequency of 6 hz. Since the waves are traveling 2 per second in A, the period for wave A is $1/2$ second. In B, waves pass 6 per second and the period is $1/6$ second. Note that the frequency and period are reciprocals. Thus,

$$f = 1/T \quad \text{and} \quad T = 1/f.$$

Since each wave travels a distance, λ, in time T,

$$v = \lambda/T.$$

Substituting for $1/T$ gives

$$v = \lambda/T = (1/T)\,(\lambda) = f\lambda$$
$$v = f\,\lambda$$

This final equation is true for all periodic waves, transverse or longitudinal, regardless of medium material.

One interesting idea regarding wave velocity is the Doppler Effect. This effect refers to a wave which originates from a source which is traveling with some velocity. In essence, the source velocity appears to be added to or subtracted from the wave velocity. The Doppler Effect is best explained by examining sound waves.

The frequency of a sound wave determines a characteristic known as pitch. Interpreting pitch is how the human ear distinguishes among frequencies. The higher the frequency, the higher the pitch. If the source of sound is in motion relative to the listener, then the Doppler Effect occurs, and the pitch heard is not the true pitch of the wave. Figure 45 shows the Doppler Effect. Remember that sound travels by compression waves, but for this diagram they are shown as transverse.

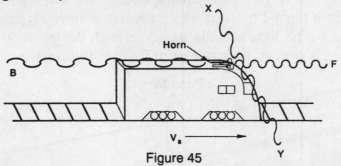

Figure 45

The listeners at positions X and Y hear the wave perpendicular to the motion of the train. These waves are unaffected by the motion of the source, and the true pitch is heard. Listener F hears a wave which is traveling the same direction as the course. As the source approaches, the frequency heard increases and the pitch is higher. Listener B hears the opposite effect. Since the sound is moving opposite the source, the frequency heard decreases and the pitch is lower.

GEOMETRICAL PROPERTIES

Waves have many geometrical and optical properties. For the purposes of explanation, these descriptions will be made using light waves.

Waves can be reflected. This means that waves bounce off a surface, such as a mirror. The reflection of waves follow certain geometric principles. In Figure 46, the line XY is the surface of a plane mirror. Line AB is an incident light ray which strikes the surface at B. The dotted line NB is the normal reference line per-pendicular to the surface. Line *BC* is the reflected light ray. The first law of reflection states that the angle of incidence, measured from the normal to the incident ray, is equal to the angle of reflection, *r*, measured from the normal to the reflected ray. The second law of reflec-tion simply states that the inci-

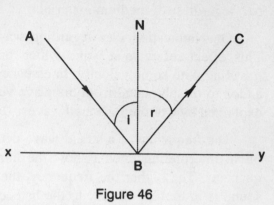

Figure 46

dent ray, the reflected ray, and the normal all lie in the same plane.

Reflection of light can cause the formation of images. Real images are formed by converging light passing through an image point, and vir-tual images are formed by light which appears to have diverged from an image point, but no light actually passes through this point. Two rays of light are needed to locate an image point from an object point.

Plane Mirror

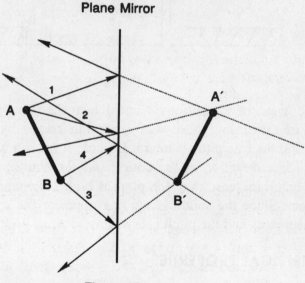

Figure 47

Figure 47 shows the location of the image of object line *AB*. Rays 1 and 2 begin at point *A* and are reflected according to the first law. *The point at which reflected rays intersect is the image point.* Since the re-flected rays for 1 and 2 are diverging, they appear to have intersected behind the mirror. Tracing these reflected rays back, we find the intersec-

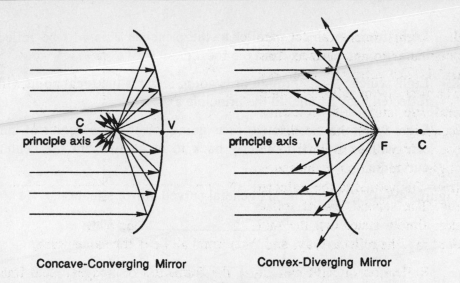

Concave-Converging Mirror   Convex-Diverging Mirror

Figure 48

tion at A'. B' is found by tracing rays 3 and 4 in a similar manner. Line $A'B'$ is the virtual image for line AB since there is no light behind the mirror. Note that for plane mirrors, the images are always virtual, erect, and equal in size to the object and appear to be the same distance behind the mirror as the object is in front.

Curved spherical mirrors present a greater challenge. Spherical mirrors are sections of a sphere used as a reflecting surface. The study of curved mirrors involves specific terminology. Figure 48 shows a concave converging mirror which has the reflecting surface inside the sphere, and a convex diverging mirror which has the reflecting surface ouside the sphere. The exact center of the mirror is called the vertex, V. An imaginary line which passes through the vertex perpendicular to the face of the mirror is the principle axis. Along the axis lies point C, which is the center point of curvature for the mirror and represents the center of the sphere from which the mirror was taken. Any line from C to the mirror is normal to the mirror and is a secondary axis. Point F is the focal point of the mirror. It is located exactly half the distance from V to C. Any light ray that is parallel to the principle axis will converge to or appear to diverge from the focal point. The distance from V to F is called focal length.

These mirrors will also form images whose characteristics can be determined graphically or mathematically.

When graphing images from spherical mirrors, the following rules simplify the process.

1. Light from an object parallel to the principal axis will be reflected back through or away from the focal point.

2. Light which passes through or is going towards the focal point will be reflected back parallel to the principle axis.

3. Light which passes through or is going towards the center of curvature will be reflected directly back to or away from the center of curvature.

Figures 49(a) - (f) show the six general curved mirror situations.

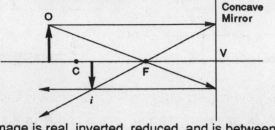

Figure 49(a) — Image is real, inverted, reduced, and is between C and F.

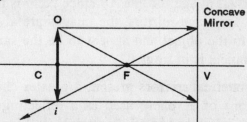

Figure 49(b) — Image is real, inverted, equal in size, and is at C.

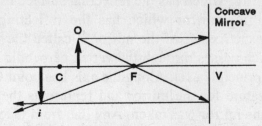

Figure 49(c) — Image is real, inverted, enlarged, and is beyond C.

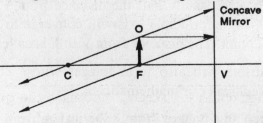

Figure 49(d) — The reflected rays are parallel, no image is formed.

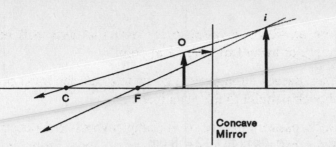

Figure 49(e) — Image is virtual, erect, enlarged, and is behind the mirror.

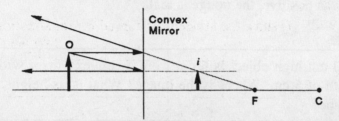

Figure 49(f) — Image is virtual, erect, reduced, and is between V and F.

The mathematical equation for mirrors relates the distance from V to the object, d_o, the distance from V to the image, d_i, and the focal length, f.

$$\frac{1}{f} = \frac{1}{d_o} + \frac{1}{d_i}$$

When solving for the variables we find,

$$f = \frac{d_o d_i}{(d_o + d_i)} : d_o = \frac{d_i f}{(d_i - f)} : d_i = \frac{d_o f}{(d_o - f)}$$

The nature of diverging light is such that d_i is negative for virtual images, and f is negative for convex mirrors. All other quantities are considered positive. The size of an image is related by

$$\frac{h_i}{h_o} = \frac{d_i}{d_o}$$

where h_i is the height of the image and h_o is the height of the object. This shows that the size ratio is equal to the distance ratio for each situation. Since height cannot be negative, h_i is always positive and any negative sign on a d_i value is ignored.

PROBLEM

A 4 cm high object is placed 12 cm from a concave mirror with a focal length of 8 cm. Where is the image? What is the height? What is its type?

Solution

Solve for d_i,

$$d_i = d_o f / (d_o - f) = (12)(8) / (12 - 8) = 96/4 = 24 \text{ cm}$$

and solve for h_i,

$$h_i = d_i h_o / d_o = (24)(4) / 12 = 8 \text{ cm.}$$

Since d_i was positive, the image is real.

PROBLEM

A 10 cm high object is 6 cm from a convex mirror with a focal length of 5 cm. Where is the image? What is its height? What is its type?

Solution

Solve for d_i, remember d_i is negative for convex mirrors.

$$d_i = d_o f / (d_o - f) = (6)(-5) / [6 - (-5)] = -30/11 = -2.7 \text{ cm}$$

Solve for h_i, remember h_i is positive.

$$h_i = d_i h_o / d_o = (2.7)(10) / 6 = 4.5 \text{ cm}$$

Since d_i was negative, the image is virtual.

Another characteristic of waves is that they can be refracted. As light travels from one medium to a second medium with a different optical density, it will bend. Optical density is measured by how fast light will pass through the medium. The higher the optical density, the slower light will pass through. This change in velocity results in the bending of light we call refraction. Figure 50 shows how a ray is refracted.

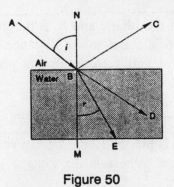

Figure 50

Line *AB* is the incident ray. Line *NM* is the perpendicular normal at the point of refraction. Line *BC* represents a small amount of light reflected by the surface. Line *BD* is the original path of the incident ray, and *BE* is the refracted light ray. The incident ray and refracted ray are related by Snell's law:

$$n = \sin i / \sin r$$

where *n* is a property of an optical medium known as the Index of Refraction. It is the ratio of the sine of the incident angle to the sine of the refraction angle. The index of refraction can also be expressed in terms of the speed of light:

$$n = c / v_m$$

where *c* is the velocity of light in a vacuum and v_m is the velocity of light in any medium.

The refraction of light can be summarized in three laws. First, the incident ray, the refracted ray and the normal are in the same plane. Second, the index of refraction for any medium is constant for any incident angle. And third, light rays which pass from lower to higher optical densities are bent toward the normal. Rays from higher to lower densities are bent away from the normal. The third law is shown by Figure 51.

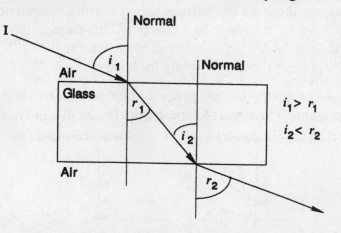

Figure 51

According to law three, it would be possible to reach an angle of refraction equal to 90° when moving from higher to lower densities, shown by Figure 52.

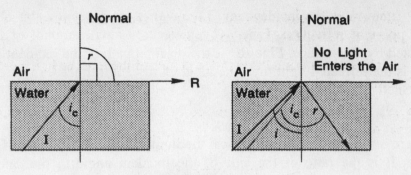

Figure 52

The angle of incidence which produces the 90° refraction is called the critical angle, i_c. If the angle of incidence is larger than i_c, then all light is reflected by the surface. This effect is called Total Internal Reflection. Since i_c is a characteristic of the medium, it is related to the index of refraction by $\sin i_c = 1/n$, thus $i_c = \arcsin 1/n$.

The most useful type of refraction is the bending of light with lenses. Much of the terminology is the same as for curved mirrors, but there are differences to recognize.

First, light passes through lenses. This means that a concave lens will diverge light and convex lenses will cause light to converge. These properties are opposite those for the corresponding mirrors. Another difference is that lenses have no reference to a center of curvature, although there are special situations regarding a distance twice the focal length, $2f$. Finally, the rules for diagrams change slightly for lenses.

1.   Light which enters the lens parallel to the principle axis will exit so as to pass through or appear to come from the focal point.

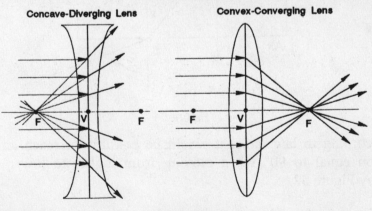

Figure 53

2. Light which passes through the focal point of a *convex lens* will exit the lens parallel to the principle axis.

3. Light which passes through the center of the lens, at *V*, is not bent and exits along the same path.

Figures 53 and 54 show the nature of these lenses and the general image formations.

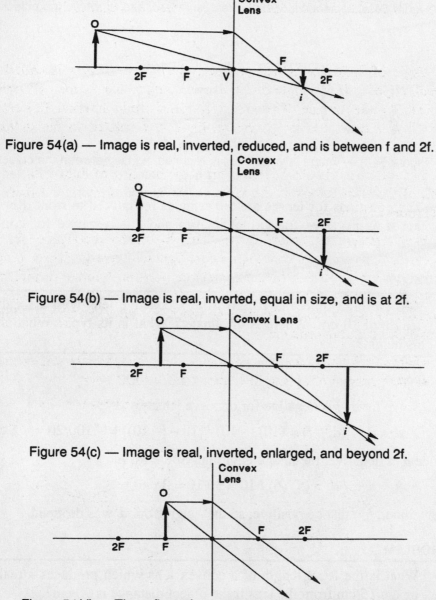

Figure 54(a) — Image is real, inverted, reduced, and is between f and 2f.

Figure 54(b) — Image is real, inverted, equal in size, and is at 2f.

Figure 54(c) — Image is real, inverted, enlarged, and beyond 2f.

Figure 54(d) — The reflected rays are parallel, no image is formed.

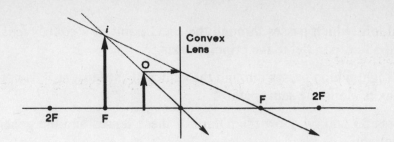

Figure 54(e) — Image is virtual, erect, enlarged, and is behind the object.

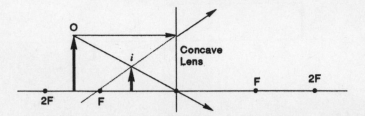

Figure 54(f) — Image is virtual, erect, reduced, and is between the object and the lens.

The equations for lenses are the same as for curved mirrors. Remember that d_i is negative for virtual images and f is negative for concave lenses.

PROBLEM

A 6 cm high object is 10 cm from a concave lens with a focal length of 10 cm. Where is the image? What is its type? What is its height?

Solution

Solve for d_i, f is negative for concave lenses.

$$d_i = d_o f / (d_o - f) = (10)(-10) / [10 - (-10)] = -100/20 = -5 \text{ cm}$$

Since d_i is negative, the image is virtual. Solve for h_i,

$$h_i = d_i h_o / d_o = (5)(6) / 10 = 30/10 = 3 \text{ cm}.$$

Remember, h_i must be positive, so the - sign from d_i was dropped.

PROBLEM

What is the focal length of a convex lens which produces a real image 15 cm from the lens if the object distance is 30 cm?

Solution

Solve for f,

$$f = d_o d_i / (d_o + d_i) = (30)\,(15)\,/\,(30 + 15) = 450\,/\,45 = 10 \text{ cm.}$$

CHAPTER 5

PHYSICAL OPTICS

PHYSICAL OPTICS

The behavior of waves can be affected by other waves or by instruments designed to produce a desired effect. When two or more waves come together, the resulting phenomenon is known as interference. Figure 55 shows two transverse waves. The maximum displacement of a crest or trough from the center is the amplitude of the wave. Here, amplitude a_1 is half that of a_2.

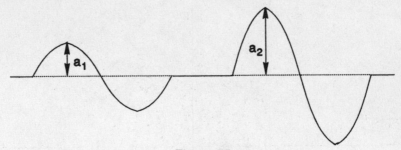

Figure 55

When waves interfere with each other, it is the amplitudes which are affected, which indirectly affects the energy of the wave. Figure 56 shows two identical waves, A and B, traveling from X to Y.

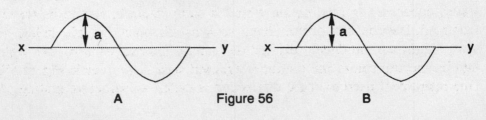

Figure 56

If these waves are added together, we have constructive interference. The crests of *A* and *B* will combine as well as their troughs. This would create a new wave, *C*, found in Figure 57.

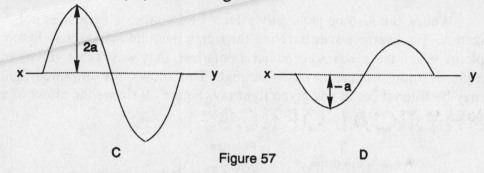

C   Figure 57   D

If wave *A* were to combine with wave *D*, then each crest would combine with a trough, effectively cancelling out both waves. This effect is destructive interference.

The examination of interference creates definite patterns within a wave system. Figure 58 shows a double point source interference pattern. Each solid line is a crest and the dotted lines are troughs. Considering these to be sources of light, dark regions appear at points of destructive interference and bright regions appear where constructive interference occurs.

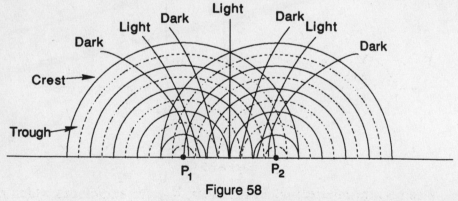

Figure 58

Waves can be bent by a process known as diffraction. Diffraction is the spreading of light into an area behind an obstruction. When light waves encounter an obstruction which is comparable in size to its wavelength, diffraction can occur. Items such as slit openings, pin holes, or sharp edges can produce a diffraction pattern. Diffraction separates light into its spectral colors and produces light and dark regions as in Figure 58. One instrument used to cause diffraction is called a diffraction grating. A grating is a transparent slide with etched lines which cause diffraction. Each grating could have hundreds or thousands of lines per centimeter of surface.

Waves can also be physically effected by a process known as polarization. Transverse waves traveling through a medium may vibrate in any plane. When these waves encounter a polarizer, only waves that vibrate in a predetermined plane may pass through. This shows that unwanted light may be filtered out of any given light ray. Figure 59 shows the effect of a polarizer.

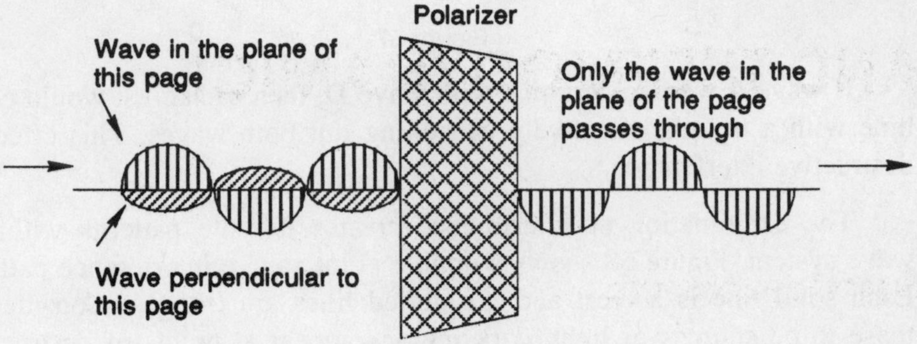

Figure 59

CHAPTER 6

HEAT, KINETIC THEORY, AND THERMODYNAMICS

THERMAL PROPERTIES

Much of the energy we deal with day to day is heat energy. Hot objects cool off over time and some substances burn and release heat. When a substance is hot, it has more thermal energy than when it is cold. The thermal energy of matter is the total potential and kinetic energy associated with the internal motion of the constituent particles. The term *heat* is actually a reference to the amount of thermal energy which is released, absorbed, or transferred from one body to the next.

Although heat and temperature are related, they are different quantities. A temperature is a quantity proportional to the *average* kinetic energy of the internal particles. For scientific purposes, temperature measurements must be made on the Celsius or Kelvin scales. The Kelvin scale is an absolute scale containing no negative temperatures. 0°K is called the absolute zero of temperature. At this point, molecular motion is at a minimum, thus it is the lowest possible temperature. In the lab, temperatures can be made on the Celsius scale and then converted to Kelvin degrees. The magnitude of 1C° is equal to that of 1°K. The difference is that 0° Celsius is assigned to the freezing point of water. 0°K is 273° below this point. Therefore

$$°K = °C + 273°.$$

When a body absorbs heat, its temperature will increase. The amount of heat needed to change the temperature of a body 1° is the heat capacity.

heat capacity = $\Delta H / \Delta T$

where ΔH is the heat needed to cause the temperature change ΔT. Since heat capacity is affected by the mass of material, it is not considered a descriptive property of matter. If, however, we consider different substances with equal mass, we have a property unique to each substance known as specific heat. Specific heat is the heat capacity per unit mass of substance. Specific heat, c, is given by

$c = \Delta H / m\Delta T.$

From this we can see that $\Delta H = mc\Delta T$, which allows the change in heat to be calculated since m and T are measurable, and c can be found on a prepared table of specific heat values. Examine the following problems.

PROBLEM

What is the specific heat of copper if a 150g sample absorbs 6930 calories which increases the temperature from 20°C to 520°C?

Solution

Solve for c,

$c = \Delta H/m\Delta T = 6930/ (150) (500) = 6930 / 75000 = 0.0924 \text{ cal/g}°C.$

PROBLEM

How many calories of heat are required to raise the temperature of 875g of copper 200°C?

Solution

Solve for ΔH,

$\Delta H = mc\Delta T = (875) (0.0924) (200) = 16{,}170 \text{ cal.}$

Another specific property of substances is Thermal Expansion. Except in a few instances, materials expand when heated, and contract when cooled. If we consider the expansion of solids in one dimension, then we are referring to linear expansion. The change in length per unit length of a solid for a 1° change is called the Coefficient of Linear Expansion. From this we conclude that the longer an object is, the greater the expansion will be per degree. This is shown in Figure 60.

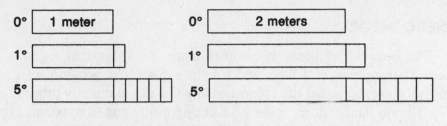

Figure 60

First note that the expansion shown here is greatly exaggerated for the purposes of the diagram. The rods begin at 0°. At 1°, the rods will expand according to their coefficients. Since the 2 meter rod is twice as long, its expansion is twice as much per degree. This is also illustrated at 5°. This means that the change in length, Δl, is equal to the product of the original length, l, its temperature change, ΔT, and the coefficient of linear expansion, α, such that

$$\Delta l = \alpha l \Delta T.$$

The coefficient for aluminum is 2.3×10^{-5} / °C. If a 12 meter aluminum rod is heated from 20° to 100°, what is the length of the rod at 100°?

$$\Delta l = \alpha l \Delta T = (2.3 \times 10^{-5})\,(12)\,(80) = 0.022 \text{ m}$$

The new length of the rod is

$$12 \text{ m} + 0.022 \text{ m} = 12.022 \text{ m}.$$

We must remember that solids expand in three dimensions. If two dimensions are examined, then the coefficient of area expansion is twice the linear coefficient. For three dimensions, the coefficient of volume expansion is 3 times the linear coefficient.

Liquids also expand when heated. Since liquids have no definite shape, we consider the volume expansion, ΔV, such that $\Delta V = \beta V \Delta T$. β is the coefficient of volume expansion.

Water is an exception to the expansion rules. When water is in the solid form of ice, it has an open hexagonal crystal structure which is necessary because of the bond angles of water molecules. This structure requires more space than if the molecules were free to move within the bond angle of another water molecule. Because of this, water has its maximum density at 40°C at which point heating or cooling will cause expansion.

KINETIC THEORY

The behavior of gases is complex since the volume of a gas is not fixed. There are several laws which help explain the behavior of gases. Charles' Law states that the volume of any dry gas is directly proportional to its Kelvin temperature, if the pressure upon the gas is constant. Figure 61 illustrates Charles' Law. Under P_1, the gas has a larger volume at a higher temperature. The Charles' Law equation is

$$V' = VT' / T,$$

where V' is the new volume, T is the original temperature, V is the original volume, and T' is the new temperature. To make a calculation, the temperatures must be in Kelvin degrees. Charles' Law can be applied to the following problem.

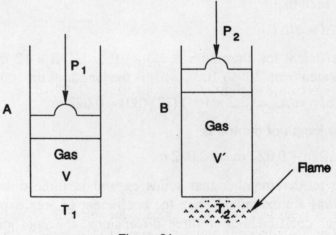

Figure 61

PROBLEM

What is the new volume of 3 liters of oxygen which is heated from 20°C to 50°C under constant pressure?

Solution

Convert °C to °K,

°K = °C + 273°

56

$20 + 273 = 293°$ and $50 + 273 = 323°$.

Solving for V',

$$V' = VT' / T = (3) (323) / 293 = 3.3 \text{ liters.}$$

Boyle's Law states that the volume of any dry gas is inversely proportional to the pressure exerted on it, if the temperature is constant. Figure 62 illustrates Boyle's Law. The increase in the pressure from P_1 to P_2 decreases the volume of the gas.

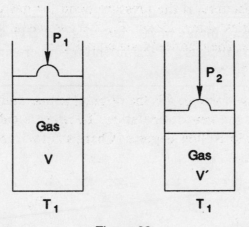

Figure 62

Since the pressure and volume are inversely proportional, their product is a constant. This means that

$$PV = k \text{ and } P'V' = k.$$

The Boyle's Law equation is

$$V' = VP / P'.$$

Pressure is measured in atmospheres, atm. One atmosphere is the pressure of the Earth's atmosphere at sea level, and is called standard pressure. Standard temperature is 0°C or 273K. These values are often referred to as STP (standard temperature and pressure). Boyle's Law can be applied to the following problem.

PROBLEM

What pressure is needed to reduce 10 liters of a gas at STP to a volume of 2 liters?

Solution

Solve for P',

$$P' = VP / V' = (10)(1) / 2 = 5 \text{ atm.}$$

The combination of these two laws gives the Combined Gas Law Equation.

$$PV / T = P'V' / T'$$

PROBLEM

What is the new volume of 20 liters of gas at STP which experience a pressure increase of 2 atm and a temperature increase of 75°?

Solution

A 2 atm increase means

$$P' = 1 + 2 = 3 \text{ atm}$$

$$T = 273° \text{ and } T' = 273 + 75 = 348°K$$

Solving for V',

$$V' = PVT' / P'T = (1)(20)(348) / (3)(273)$$

$$= 6960 / 819 = 8.5 \text{ liters.}$$

Amedeo Avogadro found that at the same temperature and pressure, different gases had densities proportional to the molecular weight. The molecular weight is the sum of all the atomic masses for all atoms that form the molecule. He also found that if you have a mass in grams of a substance equal to the molecular weight of the molecule, then the number of particles present in that mass would be equal for all substances. This is known as the gram equivalent weight. For example, helium has an atomic mass of 2. Avogadro said that 2 grams of helium contains 6.02×10^{23} atoms of helium. Further, if you had 44 grams of carbon dioxide with a molecular weight of 44, then you would have 6.02×10^{23} particles of CO_2. 6.02×10^{23} is called Avogadro's Number.

One gram-molecular weight is commonly called a mole. One mole of a substance is that mass which contains Avogadro's Number of particles. Under these conditions, any PV/T ratio is the same for one mole of any gas, and can be expressed as a constant, R. R is the Universal Gas Constant.

$R = PV/T$

Since this is true for any number of moles present, $nR = PV/T$. This equation is most commonly written as

$PV = nRT$

The Ideal Gas Law

PROBLEM

To apply the ideal gas law, 15g of carbon dioxide, CO_2, occupy a volume of 13 liters under 1.5 atm of pressure. What is the temperature of the CO_2?

Solution

Determine the number of moles of CO_2.

$CO_2 = C + O + O = 12 + 16 + 16 = 44$ g/mol

15 grams × 1 mol/44 g = 0.34 mol CO_2

Solving for T,

$T = PV/nR = (1.5)\,(13) / (0.34)\,(0.082) = 699°K.$

For one mole of a gas at STP, the volume is 22.4 liters. The value of R is

$R = PV/nT = (1\ atm)\ 22.4\ L)/(1\ mol)\ (273°) = 0.082\ L\ atm/mol°K.$

THERMODYNAMICS

Heat energy can be changed into other types of energy. This is the concept of Thermodynamics. The following information deals with converting heat into mechanical energy. The energy which is transferred is the internal energy a substance possesses. Internal Energy is the total potential and kinetic energy of the particles within the substance. These particles include the molecules, atoms, ions, and subatomic particles.

Heat is one form of internal energy. Mechanical energy is considered work and is measured in joules. An equivalent amount is measured in calories. One calorie is equal to 4.19 joules of work. This factor is the mechanical heat equivalent.

The transformation of heat into mechanical energy is governed by the First and Second Laws of Thermodynamics. The first law states that the energy supplied to a system in the form of heat is equal to the work done by the system plus the change in internal energy of the system. Thus, there is no loss of energy. To state the law mathematically, ΔH is the quantity of heat added to a substance with internal energy equal E_i. This addition causes an increase in internal energy to E_f and also does a quantity of work, W. Thus, $\Delta H = (E_f - E_i) + W$.

The second law states that it is impossible to construct an engine whose only effect is to extract heat from a source at a single temperature and convert all the heat into work. The examination of a basic heat engine can help clarify the second law.

In an engine, the working substance goes through a given cycle. The heat taken by the cycle is converted into work. However, any heat which is not converted must be delivered to a low temperature heat reservoir or "heat sink." The heat sink absorbs the exhaust from the cycle. Figure 63 illustrates the basic process for heat engines.

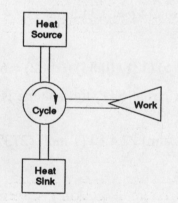

Figure 63

In essence, the second law says that heat flows from objects with high temperatures to objects with low temperatures. In a single temperature system, no heat flows.

The efficiency of a heat engine, e, is equal to the work done during one cycle divided by the heat added during the cycle.

$$e = W / \Delta H$$

From the first law, we find that the work is the difference between the heat taken in and the heat exhaust,

$$W = \Delta H_i - \Delta H_e.$$

Therefore,

$$e = (\Delta H_i - \Delta H_e) / H_i$$

$$e = 1 - \Delta H_e / \Delta H_i$$

Since the ratio of the heats is equal to the ratio of the temperatures,

$$e = 1 - T_e / T_i \times 100\%.$$

From this we conclude that the efficiency can be increased by raising the temperature of the source, lowering the temperature of the sink, or both. Maximum efficiency is achieved by keeping the source temperature as high as possible while keeping the sink temperature as low as possible. Examine the following problems.

PROBLEM

What is the efficiency of a heat engine which has an input temperature of 300°C and a sink temperature of 150°C?

Solution

Solving for e,

$$e = 1 - T_e / T_i = 1 - (150 / 300) = 1 - 0.5 = 0.5$$

$$e = 0.5 \times 100\% = 50\%$$

PROBLEM

What input temperature is necessary to increase the efficiency of the engine in the above problem by 30% if the sink temperature remains the same?

Solution

Solving for T_i, for $e = 80\%$,

$$T_i = T_e / (1 - e) = 150/(1 - 0.8) = 150 / 0.2 = 750°C.$$

CHAPTER 7

MODERN PHYSICS

NUCLEAR STRUCTURE AND TRANSFORMATION

Early atomic scientists believed that atoms were composed of an equal number of positive and negative electrical charges even though the actual internal structure of these charges was undetermined. Ernest Rutherford performed an experiment which led to a new theory of atomic structure.

Rutherford shot a beam of positively charged alpha particles through a thin layer of gold foil. The alpha particle had a velocity of 1.6×10^7 m/s and the thickness of the foil was 1×10^{-7} m. He found that most of the particles passed through the foil as if it had not been there. But unexpectedly, he found that one of 8,000 alphas was deflected backward by the foil. From this and other data, Rutherford concluded that the positive charge in an atom must be concentrated at a single point. This is the only possible structure which could repel an alpha as was observed. Therefore, Rutherford's atom contained a nucleus in which 99.95% of the mass is concentrated, holds all the positive charge within the atom, and is surrounded by the negative charge. The positive nuclear particles are now known as protons. Protons have a mass of 1.007276470 amu which is equivalent to $1.6726485 \times 10^{-27}$ kg. This mass is 1836/1837 of the mass of hydrogen which contains one proton as the nucleus and one electron. Thus, the electron's mass is only 1/1837 of the mass of hydrogen, 9.1×10^{-31} kg or 0.00054858026 amu.

The number of protons in the atom nucleus is called the atomic number. If the nucleus is composed entirely of protons, then the mass of atom would be the sum of all the proton masses. This is not the case, however, since atomic masses are considerably larger than this sum. James Chadwick isolated a neutral particle he called a neutron. From his experiments it was evident that neutrons were regular components of atomic nuclei with a size comparable to a proton and a slightly higher mass of 1.008665012 amu or $1.6749543 \times 10^{-27}$ kg. Thus, the atom nucleus is composed of positive protons and neutral neutrons. Once again, these nucleons provide for 99.95% of the atomic mass.

It may seem strange that many protons may be compacted into the nucleus of an atom without repelling each other electrically. Protons and neutrons in a nucleus are held together by the Nuclear Binding Force. Nuclear binding is a unique attraction force which acts between nucleons which are closer than 2.0×10^{-15} m. The magnitude of the binding energy can be found by considering the nuclear mass defect. Measurements show that the mass of a nucleus is always less than the sum of the masses of its individual particles. This is true because of mass to energy conversion according to

$$E = mc^2.$$

Thus, when particles combine to form a nucleus, a small amount of mass is converted to energy. The energy released is the nuclear binding energy. To find the binding energy of a helium nucleus, examine the following information:

helium nucleus = 2 protons + 2 neutrons

2 protons = 2 × 1.007276 = 2.014552 amu

2 neutrons = 2 × 1.008665 = 2.017330 amu

total of 4 nucleons = 4.031882 amu

mass of helium nucleus = 4.001509 amu

nuclear mass defect = 0.030373 amu

Nuclear energies are measured in electron volts. One electron volt is the energy needed to move an electron through a potential difference of 1 volt. Since electron volts are small, energies are more commonly measured in Megaelectron volts, 1×10^6 electron volts. The conversion of one amu to energy yields 931 MeV. To find the binding energy of helium,

0.030373 amu × 931 MeV/amu = 28.3 MeV or 7.1 MeV/nucleon

One important characteristic of many nuclei is Radioactivity. This is the spontaneous breakdown of unstable nuclei with the emission of particles and/or rays. This process is most commonly referred to as radioactive decay. A heavy nucleus can decay by emitting two kinds of particles, alpha or beta, or by the emission of gamma rays. The alpha particle is a helium nucleus. Alphas travel at one tenth the speed of light, are positively charged, and can be stopped by a sheet of paper. Betas are electrons which travel near the speed of light, have a negative charge, and have more penetrating power than alphas. Gamma rays are waves which carry no mass and no charge, travel at the speed of light, and have high energies.

The emission of these radiation particles cause conversion to a new isotope of the same element, or cause a transformation to a new element. Uranium 238 is radioactive and decays by a series of reactions. We can examine nuclear transformations by looking at some of these uranium decay reactions. Uranium 238 decays by the emission of an alpha particle. The reaction is,

$$^{238}_{92}U \rightarrow \, ^{234}_{90}Th + \, ^{4}_{2}He$$

The letters shown are the element symbols. The number written as the superscript is the atomic mass of the isotope, and the number written as the subscript is the number of protons in the nucleus, which is the atomic number. Uranium 238 emits an alpha which carries away 2 protons and 2 neutrons. Thus the mass is reduced by 4 nucleons, 238 - 4 = 234. Losing 2 protons gives the atomic number of 92 - 2 = 90. This means that the element now present is element 90, Thorium. This thorium isotope has a mass of 234 amu. In nuclear equations, the sum of the masses and the proton numbers must be equal on either side. Reactions which emit gamma rays do not change the atom, since gammas carry no mass and no protons. Thorium 234 is also radioactive and will decay by the emission of a beta particle. By looking at the following equation, we can predict the resulting element and its mass.

$$^{234}_{90}Th \rightarrow \, ^{0}_{-1}e + \, ^{?}_{?}?$$

The symbol for beta shows that it carries no mass and a -1 proton number. These numbers are significant in that betas must come from a transformation which results in the loss of a neutron and the gain of a proton. Thus, the mass is the same but the element will change. Since,

$$234 = 0 + ? \text{ and } 90 = -1 + ?$$

then

$$^{234}_{90}\text{Th} \rightarrow \ ^{0}_{-1}\text{e} + \ ^{234}_{91}\text{Pa}$$

Thus, the element produced is Protactinium 234. After 14 such reactions which produce radioactive products, Uranium 238 will be reduced to a very stable Lead 206 atom.

As a particular number of radioactive atoms decay, it is logical that the amount of decay activity will decrease over time since there are fewer atoms of the original element left. The time period associated with a decay rate is called Half-Life. Simply, the half-life is the time necessary for exactly half of the radioactive atom to decay. The following chart and graph show an example half-life analysis for Iodine 131. Given that the half-life for Iodine 131 is 8 days:

Time in days	Number of I -131 atoms	Number of half lives
0	100%	0
8	50%	1
16	25%	2
24	12.5%	3
32	6.25%	4
40	3.125%	5

Shown graphically, we see how the decay activity decreases over time.

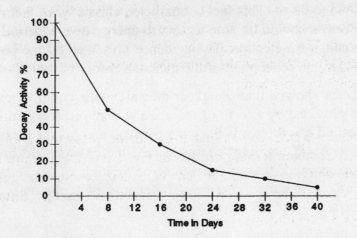

Figure 64

Radioactive Decay is not the only nuclear process. Other reactions may occur by the bombardment of one nucleus with another. One example is the bombardment of Beryllium with alpha particles,

$$^{9}_{4}Be + {}^{4}_{2}He \rightarrow {}^{12}_{6}C + {}^{1}_{0}n + energy$$

which produces carbon 12 and a free neutron as well as the release of the binding energy.

Nuclear Fission is another reaction that releases a great amount of energy. Fission occurs in some isotopes of atoms with large nuclei. Fission is the splitting of the nucleus into smaller nuclei. Uranium 235 is a common fission fuel for power plants. When a uranium 235 nucleus absorbs a neutron, the uranium nucleus will divide to produce any number of different element combinations. In any case, the energy released is very large and can be used for the production of electricity. The products produced most often by uranium 235 fission are Barium, Krypton, and free neutrons.

$$^{235}_{92}U + {}^{1}_{0}n \rightarrow {}^{138}_{56}Ba + {}^{95}_{36}Kr + 3{}^{1}_{0}n + energy$$

QUANTUM THEORY AND ATOMIC STRUCTURE

Around 1900, physicists were examining a phenomenon they called the Photoelectric Effect. The photoelectric effect is the emission of electrons by a substance when illuminated by electromagnetic radiation. If an electron on the surface of the substance could absorb enough energy, it would escape the crystal with a given velocity. Experiments showed that the photoelectrons are ejected only when they can instantly absorb the energy required to do so. This fact contradicted classic wave theory which shows the electron should be able to absorb energy over a period of time until it has enough for ejection. The evidence presented by the photoelectric effect lead to the conception of the quantum theory of radiation.

Max Planck showed that the experimental results could be explained if the energy provided by a form of radiation was an integral multiple of a quantity he called hf, where h is Planck's constant and f is the frequency of the radiation wave. Thus, light energy is radiated or absorbed in indivisible bundles containing energy equal to some multiple of hf. Today, these quantum bundles are called photons. The energy of a photon is $E = hf$. Planck's constant, h, is 6.63×10^{-34} J·s.

Eventually, Einstein used the photon to explain the photoelectric effect. The maximum kinetic energy possessed by a photoelectron is

$$\tfrac{1}{2}\,mv^2 = hf - w$$

where m and v are the mass and velocity of the photoelectron, h is Planck's constant, f is the frequency, and w is the energy needed or the work done for the electron to escape the surface. If the photon's energy was just enough to free it with a zero velocity, that is $hf = w$, then f is called the cut off frequency. This means that any photons with a frequency below cut off cannot cause photoemission regardless of exposure time. Thus, the earlier problems faced by wave theory are solved by the quantized photon theory.

The concept of quantized energy led to new theories regarding atomic structure. Neils Bohr theorized that the electron around the nucleus of an atom must exist in distinct or quantized orbitals since they do not radiate energy. Also, the closer the orbital is to the nucleus, the lower the energy is for that orbital.

If an electron in an atomic orbital can absorb a photon with the exact amount of energy so as to land in a higher level, it will do so. Similarly, if an excited electron emits a photon, it will fall to a lower orbital and the energy of the photon will be equal to the energy difference between the orbitals. This is shown by Figure 65.

Before absorption, we have an electron in level one which absorbs a 5eV photon. Since the difference between level 1 and level 3 is 5eV, the electron will jump to level 3. Once in level 3, there are two possible results. The first is that the electron could emit a 5eV photon and return to level 1. The second possibility is that the electron would emit a 3eV

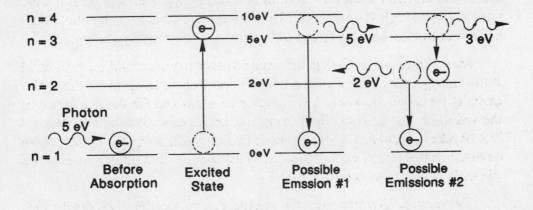

Figure 65

photon and fall to level 2, then emit a second photon with 2eV energy as it falls to level 1.

Bohr's idea has since been modified to incorporate such ideas as electron spin, magnetic effects, and angular momentum factors which he did not include in his atomic explanations.

LIST OF UNITS AND MEASUREMENTS

	Dimension	Units
	Length	Meter
	Time	Second
	Mass	Kilogram
Derived Dimensions	Acceleration	m/s^2
	Velocity	m/s
	Force	$kg \cdot m/s^2$
	Momentum	$kg \cdot m/s$
	Torque	$kg \cdot m^2/s^2$
	Angular Momentum	$kg \cdot m^2/s^2$
	Electrostatic Charge	Coulomb (C)
	Energy/Work	Joule ($kg \cdot m^2/s^2$)
	Power	Watt ($kg \cdot m^2/s^3$)
	Potential Difference	Volt ($kg \cdot m^2/c \cdot s^2$)
	Current	Ampere (c/s)

SAT II:
PHYSICS

Test 1

SAT II IN PHYSICS
TEST 1
ANSWER SHEET

1. Ⓐ Ⓑ Ⓒ Ⓓ Ⓔ	26. Ⓐ Ⓑ Ⓒ Ⓓ Ⓔ	51. Ⓐ Ⓑ Ⓒ Ⓓ Ⓔ
2. Ⓐ Ⓑ Ⓒ Ⓓ Ⓔ	27. Ⓐ Ⓑ Ⓒ Ⓓ Ⓔ	52. Ⓐ Ⓑ Ⓒ Ⓓ Ⓔ
3. Ⓐ Ⓑ Ⓒ Ⓓ Ⓔ	28. Ⓐ Ⓑ Ⓒ Ⓓ Ⓔ	53. Ⓐ Ⓑ Ⓒ Ⓓ Ⓔ
4. Ⓐ Ⓑ Ⓒ Ⓓ Ⓔ	29. Ⓐ Ⓑ Ⓒ Ⓓ Ⓔ	54. Ⓐ Ⓑ Ⓒ Ⓓ Ⓔ
5. Ⓐ Ⓑ Ⓒ Ⓓ Ⓔ	30. Ⓐ Ⓑ Ⓒ Ⓓ Ⓔ	55. Ⓐ Ⓑ Ⓒ Ⓓ Ⓔ
6. Ⓐ Ⓑ Ⓒ Ⓓ Ⓔ	31. Ⓐ Ⓑ Ⓒ Ⓓ Ⓔ	56. Ⓐ Ⓑ Ⓒ Ⓓ Ⓔ
7. Ⓐ Ⓑ Ⓒ Ⓓ Ⓔ	32. Ⓐ Ⓑ Ⓒ Ⓓ Ⓔ	57. Ⓐ Ⓑ Ⓒ Ⓓ Ⓔ
8. Ⓐ Ⓑ Ⓒ Ⓓ Ⓔ	33. Ⓐ Ⓑ Ⓒ Ⓓ Ⓔ	58. Ⓐ Ⓑ Ⓒ Ⓓ Ⓔ
9. Ⓐ Ⓑ Ⓒ Ⓓ Ⓔ	34. Ⓐ Ⓑ Ⓒ Ⓓ Ⓔ	59. Ⓐ Ⓑ Ⓒ Ⓓ Ⓔ
10. Ⓐ Ⓑ Ⓒ Ⓓ Ⓔ	35. Ⓐ Ⓑ Ⓒ Ⓓ Ⓔ	60. Ⓐ Ⓑ Ⓒ Ⓓ Ⓔ
11. Ⓐ Ⓑ Ⓒ Ⓓ Ⓔ	36. Ⓐ Ⓑ Ⓒ Ⓓ Ⓔ	61. Ⓐ Ⓑ Ⓒ Ⓓ Ⓔ
12. Ⓐ Ⓑ Ⓒ Ⓓ Ⓔ	37. Ⓐ Ⓑ Ⓒ Ⓓ Ⓔ	62. Ⓐ Ⓑ Ⓒ Ⓓ Ⓔ
13. Ⓐ Ⓑ Ⓒ Ⓓ Ⓔ	38. Ⓐ Ⓑ Ⓒ Ⓓ Ⓔ	63. Ⓐ Ⓑ Ⓒ Ⓓ Ⓔ
14. Ⓐ Ⓑ Ⓒ Ⓓ Ⓔ	39. Ⓐ Ⓑ Ⓒ Ⓓ Ⓔ	64. Ⓐ Ⓑ Ⓒ Ⓓ Ⓔ
15. Ⓐ Ⓑ Ⓒ Ⓓ Ⓔ	40. Ⓐ Ⓑ Ⓒ Ⓓ Ⓔ	65. Ⓐ Ⓑ Ⓒ Ⓓ Ⓔ
16. Ⓐ Ⓑ Ⓒ Ⓓ Ⓔ	41. Ⓐ Ⓑ Ⓒ Ⓓ Ⓔ	66. Ⓐ Ⓑ Ⓒ Ⓓ Ⓔ
17. Ⓐ Ⓑ Ⓒ Ⓓ Ⓔ	42. Ⓐ Ⓑ Ⓒ Ⓓ Ⓔ	67. Ⓐ Ⓑ Ⓒ Ⓓ Ⓔ
18. Ⓐ Ⓑ Ⓒ Ⓓ Ⓔ	43. Ⓐ Ⓑ Ⓒ Ⓓ Ⓔ	68. Ⓐ Ⓑ Ⓒ Ⓓ Ⓔ
19. Ⓐ Ⓑ Ⓒ Ⓓ Ⓔ	44. Ⓐ Ⓑ Ⓒ Ⓓ Ⓔ	69. Ⓐ Ⓑ Ⓒ Ⓓ Ⓔ
20. Ⓐ Ⓑ Ⓒ Ⓓ Ⓔ	45. Ⓐ Ⓑ Ⓒ Ⓓ Ⓔ	70. Ⓐ Ⓑ Ⓒ Ⓓ Ⓔ
21. Ⓐ Ⓑ Ⓒ Ⓓ Ⓔ	46. Ⓐ Ⓑ Ⓒ Ⓓ Ⓔ	71. Ⓐ Ⓑ Ⓒ Ⓓ Ⓔ
22. Ⓐ Ⓑ Ⓒ Ⓓ Ⓔ	47. Ⓐ Ⓑ Ⓒ Ⓓ Ⓔ	72. Ⓐ Ⓑ Ⓒ Ⓓ Ⓔ
23. Ⓐ Ⓑ Ⓒ Ⓓ Ⓔ	48. Ⓐ Ⓑ Ⓒ Ⓓ Ⓔ	73. Ⓐ Ⓑ Ⓒ Ⓓ Ⓔ
24. Ⓐ Ⓑ Ⓒ Ⓓ Ⓔ	49. Ⓐ Ⓑ Ⓒ Ⓓ Ⓔ	74. Ⓐ Ⓑ Ⓒ Ⓓ Ⓔ
25. Ⓐ Ⓑ Ⓒ Ⓓ Ⓔ	50. Ⓐ Ⓑ Ⓒ Ⓓ Ⓔ	75. Ⓐ Ⓑ Ⓒ Ⓓ Ⓔ

SAT II IN

PHYSICS

TEST 1

TIME: 170 Minutes
75 Questions

DIRECTIONS: Each of the questions or incomplete statements below is followed by five answer choices or completions. Choose the best answer to each question.

---

1. Light falls on a photoelectric material and no electrons are emitted. Electrons may be emitted if which of the following is increased?

   I.   Intensity of the light

   II. Frequency of the light

   III Wavelength of the light

   (A) I only   (B) II only

   (C) III only   (D) I and II

   (E) I and III

QUESTIONS 2-4 are related to the following diagram.

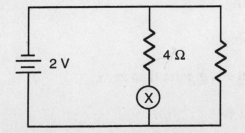

2. What is the total equivalent resistance of the circuit?

(A) 1/4   (B) 1/2

(C) 2   (D) 4

(E) 8

3. How many total volts are dropped in the circuit?

(A) 1/4   (B) 1/2

(C) 2   (D) 4

(E) 8

4. How many amps flow through the amp meter (X)?

(A) 1/4   (B) 1/2

(C) 2   (D) 4

(E) 8

5. A graph of displacement vs. time for an object moving in a straight line is shown below. The acceleration of the object must be

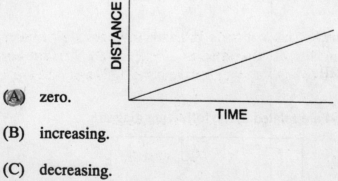

(A) zero.

(B) increasing.

(C) decreasing.

(D) constant and greater than zero.

(E) equal to g.

6. When an alpha particle is emitted from a parent nucleus, which of the following happens to the parent nucleus?

    (A) The atomic number and mass number increases.

    (B) The atomic number and mass number decreases.

    (C) The atomic number decreases and the mass number increases.

    (D) The atomic number increases and the mass number increases.

    (E) The atomic number and mass number remain the same.

QUESTIONS 7 and 8 refer to the following diagram.

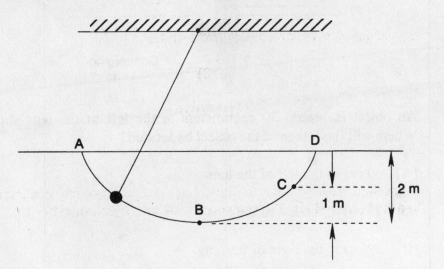

A mass swings freely back and forth in an arc from point A to point D, as shown above. Point B is the lowest point, C is located 1.0 meters above B, and D is 2.0 meters above B. Air resistance is negligible. $g = 10$ m/s².

7. The velocity of the mass at point B is closest to

    (A) 10 m/s.   (B) 40 m/s.

    (C) 20 m/s.   (D) 6 m/s.

    (E) 15 m/s.

$$\sqrt{f^2} = v_i^2 + 2ad$$

$$v_f^2 = 0 + 2(10)2$$

$$\sqrt{v_f^2} = \sqrt{40}$$

$$\sqrt{f} = 6$$

PE

75

8. If the potential energy of the mass is zero at point B, where will the kinetic and potential energies of the ball be equal?

    (A) Point B (B) Points B and C

    (C) Point C (D) Points C and D

    (E) Point D

QUESTIONS 9 and 10 refer to the following diagram.

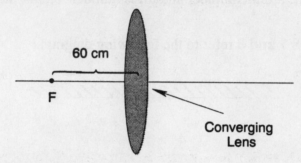

9. An object is placed 30 centimeters to the left of the lens shown. Where will the image of the object be located?

    (A) 60 cm to the left of the lens

    (B) 20 cm to the left of the lens

    (C) 20 cm to the right of the lens

    (D) 30 cm to the right of the lens

    (E) 60 cm to the right of the lens

10. The image formed will be

    (A) virtual and reduced.   (B) virtual and enlarged.

    (C) real and reduced.   (D) real and enlarged.

    (E) real and inverted.

QUESTIONS 11-13 refer to the following diagram.
The diagram below shows a 10 newton force pulling an object up a hill at a constant rate of 4 meters per second.

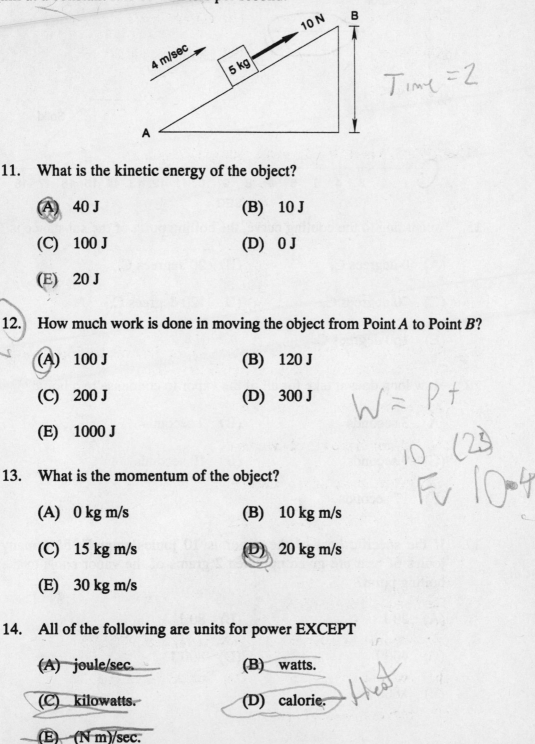

11. What is the kinetic energy of the object?

(A) 40 J   (B) 10 J

(C) 100 J   (D) 0 J

(E) 20 J

12. How much work is done in moving the object from Point *A* to Point *B*?

(A) 100 J   (B) 120 J

(C) 200 J   (D) 300 J

(E) 1000 J

13. What is the momentum of the object?

(A) 0 kg m/s   (B) 10 kg m/s

(C) 15 kg m/s   (D) 20 kg m/s

(E) 30 kg m/s

14. All of the following are units for power EXCEPT

(A) joule/sec.   (B) watts.

(C) kilowatts.   (D) calorie.

(E) (N m)/sec.

QUESTIONS 15-17 refer to the following cooling curve of a substance.

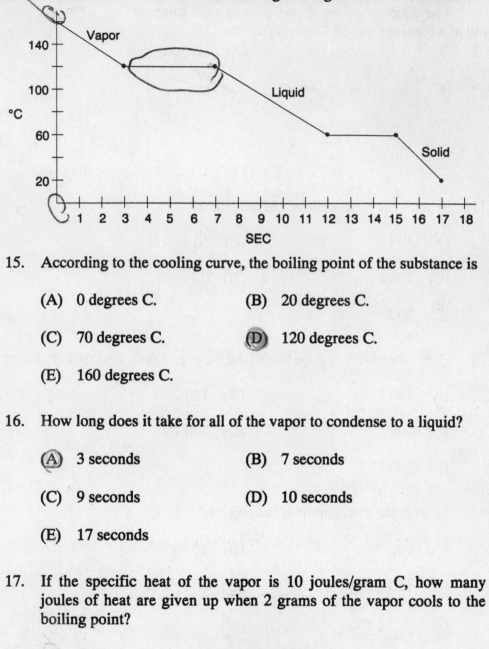

15. According to the cooling curve, the boiling point of the substance is

   (A) 0 degrees C.   (B) 20 degrees C.

   (C) 70 degrees C.   (D) 120 degrees C.

   (E) 160 degrees C.

16. How long does it take for all of the vapor to condense to a liquid?

   (A) 3 seconds   (B) 7 seconds

   (C) 9 seconds   (D) 10 seconds

   (E) 17 seconds

17. If the specific heat of the vapor is 10 joules/gram C, how many joules of heat are given up when 2 grams of the vapor cools to the boiling point?

   (A) 20 J   (B) 80 J

   (C) 400 J   (D) 800 J

   (E) 1800 J

18. The frequency of infrared radiation is less than all of the following EXCEPT

    (A) visible light.   (B) radio waves.

    (C) ultraviolet waves.   (D) X-rays.

    (E) gamma rays.

19. If the speed of light in a vacuum is c, then the speed of light in a medium with an index of refraction of 2 will be

    (A) $c/2$.   (B) $2c$.

    (C) $c/4$.   (D) $4c$.

    (E) $8c$.

20. When a positively charged conductor touches a neutral conductor, the neutral conductor will

    (A) gain protons.   (B) gain electrons.

    (C) lose protons.   (D) lose electrons.

    (E) stay neutral.

QUESTIONS 21 and 22 refer to the following equation and list of atomic particles.

$$^{27}_{13}\text{Al} + {}^{4}_{2}\text{He} \longrightarrow {}^{30}_{15}\text{P} + X + \text{energy}$$

    (A) Neutrons   (B) Positrons

    (C) Alpha particles   (D) Protons

    (E) Helium atoms

21. According to the equation, phosphorus is produced by bombarding aluminum atoms with what type of atomic particle?

(A) Neutrons   (B) Positrons

(C) Alpha particles   (D) Protons

(E) Helium atoms

22. According to the equation, particle X is which atomic particle?

(A) Neutrons   (B) Positrons

(C) Alpha particles   (D) Protons

(E) Helium atoms

23. Two objects of equal mass are a fixed distance apart. If the mass of each object could be tripled, the gravitational force between the objects would

(A) decrease by one-third.

(B) decrease by one-ninth.

(C) triple.

(D) increase by nine times.

(E) decrease by nine times.

24. All of the following phenomena can be explained if light is a wave EXCEPT

(A) reflection.   (B) refraction.

(C) photoelectric effect.   (D) diffraction.

(E) interference.

QUESTIONS 25-27 refer to the following diagram.

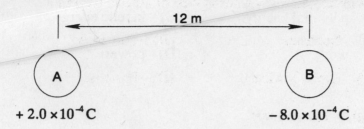

25. According to the diagram, what is the electrostatic force exerted on sphere *A*?

    $k = 9 \times 10^9$

    (A) 1.1×10^{-9} N   (B) 1.3×10^{-8} N

    (C) 120 N   (D) 10 N

    (E) 100 N

26. Compared to the force exerted on *B* at a separation of 12 meters, the force exerted on sphere *B* at a separation of 6 meters would be

    (A) 1/2 as great.   (B) 2 times as great.

    (C) 1/4 as great.   (D) 4 times as great.

    (E) 9 times as great.

27. If the two spheres are touched and then separated, the charge on sphere *A* would be

    (A) -6.0×10^{-4} C.   (B) 2.0×10^{-4} C.

    (C) -3.0×10^{-4} C.   (D) -8.0×10^{-4} C.

    (E) 8.0×10^{-4} C.

28. All of the following can be measured in joules except

    (A) potential energy.   (B) kinetic energy.

    (C) work.   (D) power.

    (E) heat.

QUESTIONS 29-31 relate to the following wave phenomena.

    I.   Diffraction

    II.   Interference

    III. Reflection

29. Occurs when two or more waves pass through the same region.

    (A) I   (B) II

    (C) III   (D) I and III

    (E) II and III

30. Standing waves are produced when periodic waves experience this phenomenon.

    (A) I   (B) II

    (C) III   (D) I and III

    (E) II and III

31. The spreading of a wave into a region behind an object is said to experience this phenomenon.

    (A) I   (B) II

    (C) III   (D) I and III

    (E) II and III

32. Compared to a 10 eV photon, a 2 eV photon has

   (A) higher frequency.   (B) lower frequency.

   (C) higher speed.   (D) lower speed.

   (E) lower wavelength.

QUESTIONS 33 and 34 refer to the following specific heats of some common substances.

   I.   Lead — 0.03 calories/gram C

   II.   Silver — 0.06 calories/gram C

   III. Iron — 0.11 calories/gram C

   IV.   Aluminum — 0.21 calories/gram C

   V.   Water — 1.0 calories/gram C

33. Ten calories of heat are added to 1 gram of each of the substances. Which substance experiences the greatest temperature increase?

   (A) I   (B) II

   (C) III   (D) IV

   (E) V

34. Ten grams of each substance is cooled ten degrees. Which substance gives up the greatest number of calories?

   (A) I   (B) II

   (C) III   (D) IV

   (E) V

35. All of the following are mechanical waves EXCEPT

    (A) water waves.   (B) sound waves.

    (C) light waves.   (D) waves on a rope.

    (E) human waves at a sporting event.

36. Images produced by a plane mirror are

    (A) virtual, erect, and the same size.

    (B) virtual, inverted, and larger.

    (C) virtual, inverted, and smaller.

    (D) real, inverted, and larger.

    (E) real, erect, and smaller.

37. The ratio of an object's weight to its mass is equal to the object's

    (A) momentum.

    (B) inertia.

    (C) gravitational force.

    (D) gravitational acceleration.

    (E) velocity.

38. When alpha particles are directed at a thin metallic foil, it can be observed that most of the particles

    (A) pass through with virtually no deflection.

    (B) bounce backwards.

    (C) are absorbed.

(D)   are widely scattered.

(E)   change into protons.

QUESTIONS 39-41 refer to the following units.

    I.   Joule

    II.   Hertz

    III. Meter

    IV. Newton

    V.   Gauss

39.   A fundamental unit.

    (A)   I   (B)   II

    (C)   III   (D)   IV

    (E)   V

40.   A derived unit equal to newtons times meters.

    (A)   I   (B)   II

    (C)   III   (D)   IV

    (E)   V

41.   A unit of frequency.

    (A)   I   (B)   II

    (C)   III   (D)   IV

    (E)   V

42. Two unequal masses falling freely from the same point above the earth's surface would experience the same

    (A) acceleration.

    (B) decrease in potential energy.

    (C) increase in kinetic energy.

    (D) increase in momentum.

    (E) change in mass.

QUESTIONS 43 and 44 refer to the following diagram and list of possible changes.

    I.   Decreases

    II. Increases

    III. Remains the same

    IV. Equals zero

    V. None of the above

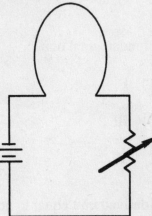

43. As the voltage across the coil is increased, the magnetic field around the coil

    (A) I   (B) II

    (C) III   (D) IV

    (E) V

44. If the coil is rotated in an external magnetic field and the voltage across the coil is decreased, the external force required to rotate the coil at a constant velocity

(A) I   (B) II

(C) III   (D) IV

(E) V

QUESTIONS 45-47 refer to the following list of names.

   I.   J.J. Thompson

   II.   Thales

   III. Ernest Rutherford

   IV. John Dalton

   V.   Niels Bohr

45.   This scientist discovered the electron.

   (A) I   (B) II

   (C) III   (D) IV

   (E) V

46.   This scientist's model of the atom contained electrons in a "pudding" of positive charge.

   (A) I   (B) II

   (C) III   (D) IV

   (E) V

47.   This scientist theorized that electrons could only be located in "quantized" energy levels.

   (A) I   (B) II

(C) III   (D) IV

(E) V

48. All of the following are vector quantities EXCEPT

(A) mass.   (B) an electrical field.

(C) a magnetic field.   (D) velocity.

(D) acceleration.

QUESTIONS 49 and 50 refer to the following diagram and list of angles.

I.   0 degrees

II.   45 degrees

III. 90 degrees

IV.   180 degrees

V.   200 degrees

49. The resultant of the two force vectors acting on a point at the same time has its smallest value when the angle between them is

(A) I.   (B) II.

(C) III.   (D) IV.

(E) V.

50. If the resultant of the two forces is 5 newtons, then the angle between them must be

(A) I.   (B) II.

(C) III.   (D) IV.

(E) V.

QUESTIONS 51-54 refer to the following graphs.

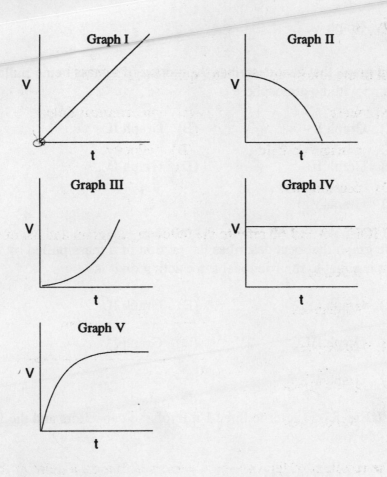

51. A graph that best describes the motion of a mass at rest and pulled by a constant force is

    (A) Graph I.   (B) Graph II.

    (C) Graph III.   (D) Graph IV.

    (E) Graph V.

52. The graph that best describes the vertical velocity of a mass falling from an airplane through air is

    (A) Graph I.   (B) Graph II.

(C) Graph III.   (D) Graph IV.

(E) Graph V.

53. The graph that best describes the motion of a mass being pulled by a planet with no atmosphere is

(A) Graph I.   (B) Graph II.

(C) Graph III.   (D) Graph IV.

(E) Graph V.

54. The graph that best describes the motion of a mass pulled by a force that is equal to the frictional force acting on it is

(A) Graph I.   (B) Graph II.

(C) Graph III.   (D) Graph IV.

(E) Graph V.

QUESTIONS 55-57 refer to three 1 microfarad capacitors and the following possible results.

I.   0.33 microfarad

II.   1.0 microfarad

III.   0.55 microfarad

IV.   3.0 microfarad

V.   6.0 microfarad

55. If the three capacitors are connected in parallel, their total capacitance will be

(A) I.   (B) II.

(C) III.   (D) IV.

(E) V.

56. If the three capacitors are connected in series, their capacitance will
be

(A) I.   (B) II.

(C) III.   (D) IV.

(E) V.

57. If the dielectric ($K = 1.0$) in each capacitor is replaced with a dielectric ($K = 3.0$), the capacitance of each capacitor will be

(A) I.   (B) II.

(C) III.   (D) IV.

(E) V.

58. The energy required to operate a 100 watt lamp 5 hours a day for 30
days is

(A) 1.5 kw hr.   (B) 15 kw hr.

(C) 150 kw hr.   (D) 1500 kw hr.

(E) 150 megawatt hr.

59. An object that can't be seen in a dark room can appear to be red in a
lighted room because it

(A) transmits red light.   (B) refracts red light.

(C) reflects red light.   (D) diffuses red light.

(E) absorbs red light.

60. Which of the following units measure the same quantity?

    I.   Electron Volt

    II. Kilocalorie

    III. Watt

    IV. Joule

    (A) I and II.   (B) I and III.

    (C) II and IV.   (D) I, II, and III.

    (E) I, II, and IV.

61. As the ball rolls down the hill as shown, its

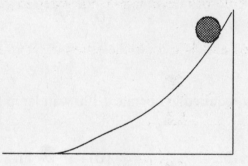

    (A) speed increases and acceleration decreases.

    (B) speed decreases and acceleration increases.

    (C) speed increases and acceleration increases.

    (D) speed decreases and acceleration decreases.

    (E) Both remain constant.

62. A battery is connected to a light bulb through a switch and trans-
    former as shown. Which of the following statements best describes
    what happens when the switch is opened and closed?

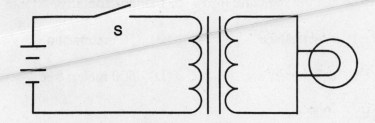

(A) As long as the switch is closed the bulb will light.

(B) The bulb will light momentarily when the switch is closing and then go out.

(C) The bulb will light momentarily when the switch is opened.

(D) The bulb will light momentarily when the switch is closing and momentarily again when it's opened.

(E) The bulb will never light while wired in this arrangement.

QUESTIONS 63 and 64 refer to the following diagram.

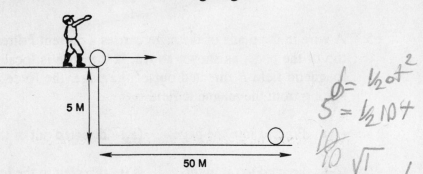

63. A child throws a baseball horizontally from an elevated position 5 meters above the ground as shown. The rock travels a horizontal distance of 50 meters. How much time passes before the baseball hits the ground?

(A) 1 second

(B) 2 seconds

(C) 5 seconds

(D) 1/2 second

(E) 10 seconds

64. How fast did the child throw the ball horizontally?

(A) 5 meters/sec   (B) 50 meters/sec

(C) 100 meters/sec   (D) 500 meters/sec

(E) 1000 meters/sec

QUESTION 65 refers to the following diagram.

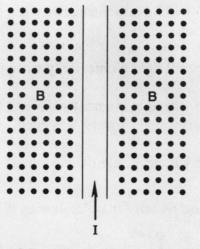

I

65. A wire in the plane of the page carries a current *I* directed toward the top of the page, as shown above. If the wire is located in a uniform magnetic field *B* directed out of the page, the force on the wire resulting from the magnetic field is

(A) directed into the page.   (B) directed out of the page.

(C) directed to the right.   (D) directed to the left.

(E) zero.

QUESTION 66 refers to the following diagram.

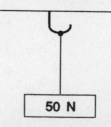

50 N

66. A uniform rope of weight 100 newtons hangs from a hook as shown above. A box of 50 newtons hangs from the rope. What is the tension in the rope?

(A) 50 N throughout the rope

(B) 75 N throughout the rope

(C) 100 N throughout the rope

(D) 150 N throughout the rope

(E) It varies from 100 N at the bottom of the rope to 150 N at the top.

QUESTION 67 refers to the following diagram.

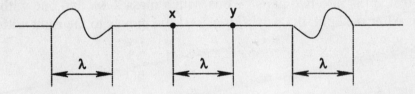

67. Two wave pulses, each of wavelength λ are traveling toward each other along a rope as shown above. When both pulses are in the region between points *X* and *Y* and which are a distance λ apart, the shape of the rope will be which of the following?

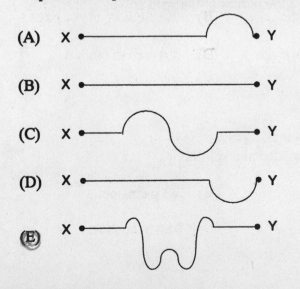

68. A gas at atmospheric pressure and room temperature is contained in a cylinder which is sealed on one end, and contains a frictionless movable cylinder at the other end. If the gas expands adiabatically, the piston is pushed out. Increasing the volume,

   (A) the pressure remains the same.

   (B) the temperature increases.

   (C) the temperature may increase or decrease, depending on the gas.

   (D) the temperature decreases.

   (E) there is no change in temperature.

PROBLEMS 69-72 refer to the following before and after diagram. Mass m at rest splits into two parts — one with a mass $2/3m$ and one with mass $1/3m$. After the split, the part with mass $1/3m$ moves to the right with a velocity v.

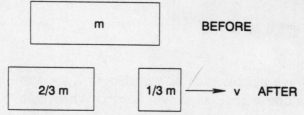

69. The velocity of the $2/3m$ part after the split is

   (A) $1/3\ v$.   (B) $1/2\ v$.

   (C) $2/3\ v$.   (D) $2\ v$.

   (E) $3\ v$.

70. The total momentum after the split is

   (A) 0 g cm/sec.   (B) 2/3 g cm/sec.

   (C) mv g cm/sec.   (D) $2\ mv$ g cm/sec.

   (E) $4\ mv$ g cm/sec.

71. During the split, the forces acting on the two parts

    (A) are in the ratio 1:3.   (B) are in the ratio 1:4.

    (C) are in the ratio 1:9.   (D) are in the ratio 1:2.

    (E) are equal.

72. If the original mass had been moving to the right with a velocity of W, the velocity of the $1/3\ m$ part after the split is

    (A) $1/3v + W$.   (B) $v + W$.

    (C) $v - W$.   (D) $W - 1/3\ v$.

    (E) $2\ W$.

73. The internal energy of water is determined by which of the following?

    I.   Temperature

    II.   Phase

    III. Mass

    (A) I only   (B) II only

    (C) III only   (D) I and II

    (E) I, II, and III

74. Two waves have amplitudes in the ratio 1:4. The energies of the waves are in the ratio

    (A) 1:4.   (B) 4:1.

    (C) 1:16.   (D) 1:8.

    (E) 8:1.

75. A block of weight W is pulled along a horizontal surface at a constant speed V by a force F, which acts at an angle θ with the horizontal, as shown above. The normal force exerted on the block by the surface is equal to

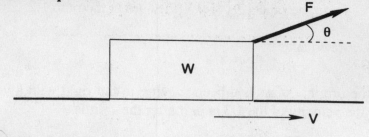

(A) $W - F \sin \theta$.

(B) $W - F \cos \theta$.

(C) $W + F \sin \theta$.

(D) $W + F \cos \theta$.

(E) W.

STOP

If time still remains, you may review work only on this test.
You may not work on any other test in this book until time has elapsed.

TEST 1

ANSWER KEY

1.	(B)	21.	(C)	41.	(B)	61.	(A)
2.	(C)	22.	(A)	42.	(A)	62.	(D)
3.	(C)	23.	(D)	43.	(B)	63.	(A)
4.	(B)	24.	(C)	44.	(E)	64.	(B)
5.	(A)	25.	(D)	45.	(A)	65.	(C)
6.	(B)	26.	(D)	46.	(A)	66.	(E)
7.	(D)	27.	(C)	47.	(E)	67.	(B)
8.	(C)	28.	(D)	48.	(A)	68.	(D)
9.	(A)	29.	(B)	49.	(D)	69.	(B)
10.	(B)	30.	(E)	50.	(C)	70.	(A)
11.	(A)	31.	(A)	51.	(A)	71.	(E)
12.	(A)	32.	(B)	52.	(E)	72.	(B)
13.	(D)	33.	(A)	53.	(C)	73.	(E)
14.	(D)	34.	(E)	54.	(D)	74.	(C)
15.	(D)	35.	(C)	55.	(D)	75.	(A)
16.	(B)	36.	(A)	56.	(A)		
17.	(D)	37.	(D)	57.	(D)		
18.	(B)	38.	(A)	58.	(B)		
19.	(A)	39.	(C)	59.	(C)		
20.	(D)	40.	(A)	60.	(E)		

DETAILED EXPLANATIONS
OF ANSWERS

TEST 1

1.   **(B)**

Not all frequencies of light cause photoelectric emission from a given material. Instead each photoelectric material exhibits a threshold frequency necessary to dislodge electrons.

Increasing this threshold frequency increases the number of electrons. Increasing the wavelength decreases the frequency and no electrons will be emitted. Increasing the intensity will increase the number of light particles, photons, hitting the material, but if these photons are not emitted at the threshold frequency then they will not dislodge any electrons. Thus choice II is the only parameter that, when increased, will cause emission of an electron.

2.   **(C)**

The equivalent resistance of resistors in parallel is found by taking the sum of the reciprocal of the resistors and then taking the reciprocal of the answer.

$$1/Rt = 1/R_1 + 1/R_2 = 1/4 + 1/4 = 2/4$$

$$Rt = 2.$$

3.   **(C)**

The total voltage in any DC circuit is equal to the voltage applied.

4.   **(B)**

Since the two resistors are of equal value, the total current splits equally between them. The total current equals the total voltage divided by the total resistance, i.e.,

$$I = 2 \text{ volts} / 2 \text{ ohms} = 1 \text{ amp.}$$

$$I_x = 1 \text{ amp} / 2.$$

5.   **(A)**

The slope of the line is constant, indicating that the distance covered per time is constant. An object traveling in a straight line must be traveling at a constant velocity to cover the same distance in the same time. Acceleration is a measure of the change in velocity per time. No change in velocity results in zero acceleration.

6.   **(B)**

An alpha particle is comprised of two protons and two neutrons, therefore a parent nucleus loses two protons (a decrease in atomic number) and a total of four nucleons (two protons and two neutrons, which decreases the atomic mass).

7.   **(D)**

Question 7 can be answered easily if you realize that the potential energy of at Point A equals the kinetic energy at Point B. Knowing the mass is not necessary since it is constant and cancels out when PE is set equal to KE. The velocity is then easily calculated.

$$PE = KE$$
$$mgh = \frac{1}{2}mv^2$$
$$\sqrt{2gh} = v$$
$$\sqrt{2(10m/s^2)2m} = v$$
$$6.3m/s = v$$

8.   **(C)**

In Question 8, at Point D (a vertical displacement of 2 meters) the potential energy of the mass is at a maximum and kinetic energy is zero. Since at Point C the mass has dropped 1 meter, its potential energy has decreased by $1/2$. The mass is now moving, and has gained kinetic energy, which according to the energy conservation law equals the decrease in potential energy.

9.   **(A)**

This problem is easily solved if you are familiar with the thin lens equation

$$\frac{1}{F} = \frac{1}{o} + \frac{1}{i};$$

where F is the focal length, o is the distance of the object from the lens, and i is the distance of the image from the lens. Therefore

$$\frac{1}{60} = \frac{1}{30} + \frac{1}{i};$$

and $i = -60$. Therefore the image is 60 cm to the left of the lens.

Note: It must also be remembered that the sign of F for a converging lens is positive, and the signs of o and i are negative if the image is virtual. (See Question 10.)

10. **(B)**

There are two approaches to solving this problem — one is to do a simple ray tracing diagram, and the other is to remember that the image of an object placed between F and a thin lens will be virtual and enlarged. A simple magnifying glass works this way.

11. **(A)**

Any mass that is moving has KE, regardless of its location. It is easily calculated by

$$KE = \frac{1}{2} mv^2$$

$$KE = \frac{1}{2} (5 \text{ kg}) \ (4 \text{m} / \text{s})^2 = 40 \text{ J}.$$

12. **(A)**

The work done is equal to the increase in potential energy of the mass from Point A to Point B; or

$$PE = mgh = 5 \text{ kg} (10 \text{ m/sec}^2) \ 2 \text{ m} = 100 \text{ J}.$$

13. **(D)**

To solve this problem you must know that the momentum of a mass is equal to its mass times its velocity

$$P = mv = 5 \text{ kg} (4 \text{ m/sec}) = 20 \text{ kg m/sec}.$$

14. **(D)**

Power is work or energy per time.

Watts = joule/sec.

Therefore, all of the choices have these units except (D), which is a unit for energy only.

15. **(D)**
   The temperature at which a substance goes from the vapor state to the liquid state is its boiling point. On the cooling curve shown, this occurs along the horizontal line between three seconds and seven seconds at a temperature of 120 degrees.

16. **(B)**
   From the diagram it can be determined that the substance is a vapor at zero seconds and 160 degrees. It remains a vapor for 3 seconds but cools to its boiling point of 120 degrees. At 3 seconds the substance begins condensing from a vapor state into a liquid, and at 7 seconds it is entirely a liquid.

17. **(D)**
   Question 17 can be answered using a calorimetry equation that should be familiar:

   Q = mass (Specific Heat) (change in temperature).

The mass (2 grams) and the specific heat (10 J/gram C) are given. The change in temperature between 0 and 3 seconds is read directly from the graph:

   160 C – 120 C = 40 C.

Substituting these into the equation gives the correct answer.

$$Q = \text{mass (specific heat)} \, \Delta t$$
$$= 2 \text{ g } (10 \text{ J/gC}) \, 40 \text{ C}$$
$$= 800 \text{ J}$$

18. **(B)**
   Question 18 requires that you know the sequence of electromagnetic energies in the electromagnetic spectrum, and their relative frequencies. In order of increasing frequency, the energies are as follows —

   radio waves < infrared < visible < ultraviolet < x-rays < gamma rays.

19. **(A)**
   The index of refraction of a medium is defined as the ratio of the speed of light in a vacuum to the speed of light in the medium. Thus

   $I.R.$ = c/speed in medium;

   2 = c/speed in medium;

   speed in medium = $c/2$.

20. **(D)**

All protons are contained in the nucleus of atoms and are quite immobile. Therefore answers (A) and (C) are unreasonable. Electrons, on the other hand, tend to distribute themselves uniformly on the surface of conductors. A positively charged conductor has lost some electrons, and will attract some of the electrons away from the neutral conductor, causing it to lose electrons, leaving it positively charged.

21. **(C)**

This question requires you to be able to recognize the symbol for an alpha particle:

He.

22. **(A)**

In Question 22, the rules for the conservation of charge and mass in nuclear reactions must be utilized. On the left-hand side of the equation, there are represented a total of 15 protons (2 + 13), and there are also 15 represented on the right side. On the left side, a total mass number of 31 (neutrons and protons) is represented, while on the right only 30 are represented. Since protons are conserved from right to left, and the mass number of P is 30, X must be a neutron.

23. **(D)**

Problem 23 can be solved if you are familiar with the relationship which states that the gravitational force between two objects is directly proportional to the product of their masses, and inversely proportional to the square of the distance between them.

$$F = \frac{GM_1 m_2}{r^2}$$

G = gravitational constant

M_1 = mass of object 1

m_1 = mass of object 2

r = distance between objects

If the distance between two objects is held constant, then the force is directly proportional to any change in the mass of the objects or

$$F \propto M_1 M_2.$$

This means that if the mass of one of the objects is tripled, then the force triples and if the mass of both of them is tripled the force will increase by nine times.

24. **(C)**
  Waves and particles have both been shown to undergo reflection and refraction, which eliminates answers (A) and (B). Only waves exhibit the capability of being refracted and interfere with each other, which eliminates answers (D) and (E). Albert Einstein won the Nobel Prize for proving that for the photoelectric effect to occur, light must have the properties of particles.

25. **(D)**
  Solving this problem requires the use of Coulomb's inverse square law of electrical interaction.

$$Fe = k\, qQ\, /\, r^2$$

Substitution into this equation gives 10 N.

$$Fe = 9.0 \times 10^9\, (2.0 \times 10^{-4})\, (-8.0 \times 10^{-4})\, /\, 12^2) = 10 \text{ N}$$

26. **(D)**
  If Coulomb's equation is considered (see explanation 25) it can be reasoned that if the charges on A and B remain the same, and the distance between them is halved and then squared, then the denominator is reduced by four times. Since the denominator r^2 is four times smaller, the quotient

$$kqQ/r^2$$

will be four times greater.

27. **(C)**
  To determine the correct answer requires an understanding of how electrical charge distributes itself on conductors. If A is touched to $B, - 2.0 \times 10^{-4}$ C of charge will flow from B onto A, neutralizing all of the positive charge on A. This would leave $- 6.0 \times 10^{-4}$ C charge on B. This charge would distribute itself equally between A and B, giving each a charge of $- 3.0 \times 10^{-4}$ C.

28. **(D)**
  Question 28 is a straightforward question to determine your familiarity with certain physics terms and the units used with them. A unit analysis of answers (A), (B), (C), and (E) shows them all to be measured in newtons times meters or joules.

  (A)   potential energy $= mgh = \text{kg(m/s}^2)\, m = \text{Nm} = \text{J}$

  (B) $E = 1/2\ \text{kg (m/s)}^2 = \text{kg (m/s}^2)\, m = \text{Nm} = \text{J}$

  (C) $W = Fd = \text{Nm} = \text{J}$

(E)   1 calorie = 4.19 J

However, power is found to have units of *N* times meters divided by time, which is J/s or a "watt."

29. (B)

Two waves passing through the same region can constructively or destructively add together. This phenomenon is called interference.

30. (E)

At certain frequencies, a string may be made to vibrate in several natural modes. Each direct wave is reflected at the end of the string and upon its return meets an ongoing wave. Regions of constructive and destructive *interference* occur at fixed positions, and a standing wave is produced.

31. (A)

Diffraction is that property of waves that allows them to bend around an obstacle.

32. (B)

The energy of a photon is directly proportional to its frequency

$$E = hf.$$

Thus answer (A) is incorrect when compared to (B). All light travels at the same speed in a vacuum, which eliminates (C) and (D). A 2eV photon has a higher wavelength than a 10 eV photon, therefore (E) is also incorrect. Where wavelength is determined by

$$c = \lambda f,$$

c = speed of light and λ = wavelength.

33. (A)

A specific heat value, if read like a sentence, explains the number of calories required to raise one gram of a substance one degree centigrade. Therefore, the substance in the table with the lowest specific heat will experience the greatest temperature increase, when equal numbers of calories are added to an equal mass of each substance.

34. (E)

If an equal mass of each substance is cooled the same number of degrees, the substance with the largest specific heat will give up the greatest number of calories.

35. **(C)**

Mechanical waves are vibrating matter, whereas light waves are electromagnetic and can travel through a vacuum. All of the choices, except light, involve some type of vibrating matter.

36. **(A)**

The images formed by a plane mirror are reflections of real objects. The images themselves are not real because no light passes through them. These images, which appear to be formed by rays, are actually a projection by the eye and are called virtual images. A real image is formed when light rays converge. Real images cannot be formed by a plane mirror because the light reflected from a plane surface diverges. The eye and the brain project the rays back behind the mirror where they "appear" to converge, and the eye then uses the principle of refraction to reconverge the reflected rays which appear to come from the virtual image. These properties of the image created by a plane mirror are described by option (A).

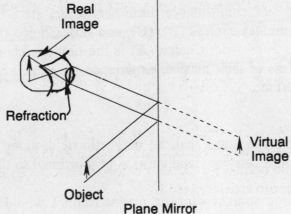

37. **(D)**

The weight of an object equals its mass times the acceleration due to gravity; or

Weight = mg.

Rearranging this expression gives

g = Weight/m,

or a ratio of weight to mass.

38. **(A)**

When he conducted his famous alpha particle scattering experiment, Dr. Ernest Rutherford found that most of the alpha particles fired at a thin piece of gold foil passed through virtually unaffected. This supported the hypothesis that an atom is predominantly space.

39. **(C)**

To answer this question requires an understanding of the difference between a fundamental unit and a derived unit. All of these responses can be expressed in terms of other units, except the meter.

40. **(A)**

To answer this question requires an understanding of derived units. A "joule" is defined as a newton times a meter.

41. **(B)**

A Hertz is defined as the number of waves that occur in one second.

42. **(A)**

Two unequal masses will have different kinetic energies, potential energies, and momentums since these parameters are a function of mass. This fact eliminates choices (B), (C), and (D). Choice (E) is nonsensical since mass is conserved. Choice (A) is the obvious choice, since all objects, regardless of their masses, experience the same acceleration g near the earth's surface.

43. **(B)**

Ampere's law states that the magnetic field, along any closed loop around a current carrying conductor, is proportional to the current in that conductor.

For a long straight wire the magnetic lines would trace out circles around the wire. The strength of this magnetic field would be proportional to the current in the wire. If the resistance of the wire is constant the magnetic field will also be proportional to the voltage applied across the wire. This is shown from Ohm's law

$$I = E/R,$$

if R is constant and V is increased, then I must be increased, and from Ampere's law the magnetic field must increase.

44. **(E)**

Lentz's law states that the direction of an induced current is such that its own magnetic field opposes the original change in the flux that induced the current. In the situation described above, the coil rotates through a magnetic field at a constant velocity, and the magnetic lines "cut" by the coil continuously vary from zero to a maximum. The current induced in the coil therefore varies from zero to a maximum causing a magnetic field around the coil. This induced magnetic field will therefore vary from zero to a maximum and thus the external force required to rotate it against the external magnetic field at a constant velocity will have to vary from zero to a maximum.

45. **(A)**

J.J. Thompson is credited with discovering the electron while performing his famous cathode ray tube experiments.

46. **(A)**

J.J. Thompson, after discovering the electron, described the structure of the atom as being "electrons immersed in a sea of positive charge." Some textbook writers describe it as the "raisin in pudding model."

47. **(E)**

The quantum model of the atom is credited to the Danish physicist Niels Bohr.

48. **(A)**

A vector has both magnitude and direction. All of the responses for this question require both a magnitude and a direction to describe them, except "mass," which requires only a magnitude.

49. **(D)**

Two vectors acting 180 degrees to each other have no y component. The x components act directly opposite to each other and are added algebraically, giving the smallest resultant possible between the two vectors.

50. **(C)**

If the two vectors are added vectorially and result in a force of 5 newtons, they form a 3-4-5 right triangle, and therefore must be acting at 90 degree angles to each other.

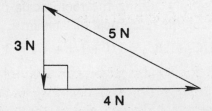

51. **(A)**

A mass at rest being acted on by a constant force will accelerate constantly, or its change in velocity per unit time will be a constant (with a beginning velocity of zero). Thus, a plot of velocity versus time for this mass would be a straight diagonal line passing through the origin.

52. **(E)**

An object dropped from an airplane has an initial vertical velocity of zero. As it falls through the air, its vertical acceleration will decrease due to air resistance. (The faster it gets, the greater the force upward due to the air.) Therefore the change in velocity will get less and less, and the object may reach a constant "terminal velocity."

53. **(C)**

As the mass moves towards the planet, the distance between the planet and the mass decreases. The inverse gravitational equation states that as the distance between two masses decreases, the force between them increases by the square of this decrease. Since the force is increasing, the acceleration (change in velocity/time) increases.

54. **(D)**

If the force pulling on a mass equals the force of friction between the mass and the surface it is sitting on, then the net force on the mass is zero. According to Newton's first law, if the net force is zero, an object will move at a constant velocity, or remain motionless. Graph IV describes a mass moving with a constant velocity.

55. **(D)**

The effective capacitance of capacitors connected in a parallel circuit can be calculated by simply adding the individual capacitances.

$Ct = C_1 + C_2 + C_3 = 1 + 1 + 1 = 3$ microfarads.

56. **(A)**

The effective capacitance of capacitors connected in a series circuit can be calculated by simply adding the reciprocals of the individual capacitances and then taking the reciprocal of the sum

$1/Ct = 1/C_1 + 1/C_2 + 1/C_3 = 1/1 + 1/1 + 1/1 = 3;$

$Ct = 1/3 = .33.$

57. **(D)**

The capacitance of a capacitor is directly proportional to the dielectric constant of the material separating the plates of the capacitor. Therefore for $K = 3.0$, the capacitance will be increased by a factor of 3.

$$C = \frac{\varepsilon A}{d}$$

ε = dielectric constant

A = area of plates

d = distance between plates

With A/d remaining constant $C = 1\mu f \cdot 3 = 3 \; \mu f$.

58. (B)

A kw hr is an amount of energy and can be calculated by multiplying "power" (in kw) times "time" (in hours). Therefore for this problem

kw hrs = .1 kilowatt × 150 hours = 15 kw hr.

59. (C)

An object appears red in a lighted room because it absorbs all colors but red, which it reflects.

60. (E)

Choices I, II, and IV are all units of energy. Choice III is a unit of power or energy per time.

61. (A)

A ball dropped vertically will accelerate with an acceleration a equal to g. A ball placed on a horizontal surface will not accelerate at all due to gravity. A ball released on a circular surface, as shown, initially has an acceleration equal to g, but as its motion becomes more and more horizontal, its acceleration due to gravity approaches zero. The velocity of the ball changes continually until it is traveling horizontally (assuming no friction), at which time it becomes constant.

62. (D)

For a current to flow in the coil connected to the light bulb, magnetic lines must cut across the coil. This occurs when the switch is closing (magnetic lines build up and cut across the bulb coil), or when the switch is opened (magnetic lines collapse across the bulb coil).

63. (A)

The time it takes for the rock to travel 50 meters horizontally is exactly equal to the time it takes for the rock to reach the ground

(5 meters); or

$$d = 1/2\ gt^2;$$

solving for t gives 1 second, i.e.,

$$t = \sqrt{2d/g} = \sqrt{2(5M)/10m/\sec/\sec} = 1\sec$$

64. (B)

The time it takes for the rock to travel 50 meters horizontally is exactly equal to the time it takes for the rock to travel 5 meters to the ground. From problem 63, this time is shown to be one second. For an object to travel 50 meters in one second, it must be traveling at a velocity of 50 meters per second.

65. (C)

The direction of the magnetic force on a current-carrying wire is perpendicular for both the current flow and the magnetic field strength B. When a right hand is held so that the fingers can be curled from the direction of I into the direction of B, the thumb points in the direction of the force.

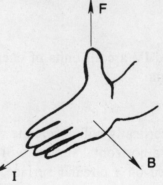

66. (E)

Newton's Third Law states that forces occur in pairs. The tension in the rope is the force which the hook has to "pull back with," or the total force "transmitted" to the hook by the rope in order to keep the rope and whatever is connected to it from accelerating downward. If the 100 newton rope did not have a mass attached to it, the hook would have to exert a force upward of 100 newtons, and if only half the rope were attached it would exert 50 N, etc. Therefore the hook must support the weight of a certain length of the rope plus the 50 newton mass.

67. (B)

Both pulses have a wavelength equal to the distance between x and y, but are 180 degrees out of phase. Therefore, when both pulses are between *x* and *y* simultaneously, they will destructively interfere to give no dis-placement from the horizontal.

68. **(D)**

Because work is done by the gas on the piston (it exerts a force in the direction the piston moves), and no heat is allowed to enter or leave, the internal energy of the gas decreases, and therefore the temperature must decrease. In an adiabatic process, a system does not exchange heat with the surroundings, and the change in internal energy is the negative of the work done. Mathematically

$$\Delta U = Q - W;$$

for adiabatic processes $Q = 0$; thus

$$\Delta U = - W.$$

69. **(B)**

Since momentum is conserved,

$$1/3 \, v = 2/3X;$$

$$X = 1/2 \, v.$$

70. **(A)**

Momentum is always conserved. The momentum of the mass before separation is equal to the sum of the momentums of each piece. The momentum before is zero since the mass had a velocity of zero. Therefore after separation occurs, the vector sum of the momentums of the pieces must also equal zero.

$$\text{Momentum after} = 1/2 \, v \, 2/3 \, m - 1 \, v \, 1/3 \, m = 0.$$

71. **(E)**

Since 1/3 of the mass received a velocity *v*, and 2/3 of the mass (twice as much) receive a velocity of 1/2 *v*, the amount of force on each piece is equal.

72. **(B)**

The 1/3 *m* piece would have a velocity equal to $(v + W)$ and the 2/3*m* piece would have a velocity equal to $(1/2v - W)$. The momentum of *m* before would now be *mW*, which is just equal to

$$1/3m \, (v + W) - 2/3m(1/2v - W)$$

$$= 1/3mv + 1/3mW - 1/3mv + 2/3mW$$

$$= 1/3mW + 2/3mW = mW.$$

73. **(E)**

Each of the three stated factors requires energy to change them. (I) To change the temperature of a substance requires that energy be added or subtracted. (II) To change the phase or state at which a substance exists requires that it be melted, vaporized, condensed, or fused. Either of these changes requires an increase or decrease in energy. (III) It is also true that the more mass you have at certain temperature, the more energy it contains (i.e., a swimming pool full or water at 30 C contains more energy than a tea cup full of water at 30 C).

74. **(C)**

The energy of a wave is directly proportioanl to its amplitude squared

$$1 \times 1 = 1; 4 \times 4 = 16.$$

75. **(A)**

The normal force is the net force pushing the block against the horizontal surface. The force pulling the block downward is its weight. The vertical component of F tends to lift the block away from the surface and is equal to $F \sin \theta$. Therefore the net force pushing the two surfaces together is

$$W - F \sin \theta.$$

SAT II:
PHYSICS

Test 2

SAT II IN PHYSICS
TEST 2
ANSWER SHEET

1. Ⓐ Ⓑ Ⓒ Ⓓ Ⓔ	26. Ⓐ Ⓑ Ⓒ Ⓓ Ⓔ	51. Ⓐ Ⓑ Ⓒ Ⓓ Ⓔ
2. Ⓐ Ⓑ Ⓒ Ⓓ Ⓔ	27. Ⓐ Ⓑ Ⓒ Ⓓ Ⓔ	52. Ⓐ Ⓑ Ⓒ Ⓓ Ⓔ
3. Ⓐ Ⓑ Ⓒ Ⓓ Ⓔ	28. Ⓐ Ⓑ Ⓒ Ⓓ Ⓔ	53. Ⓐ Ⓑ Ⓒ Ⓓ Ⓔ
4. Ⓐ Ⓑ Ⓒ Ⓓ Ⓔ	29. Ⓐ Ⓑ Ⓒ Ⓓ Ⓔ	54. Ⓐ Ⓑ Ⓒ Ⓓ Ⓔ
5. Ⓐ Ⓑ Ⓒ Ⓓ Ⓔ	30. Ⓐ Ⓑ Ⓒ Ⓓ Ⓔ	55. Ⓐ Ⓑ Ⓒ Ⓓ Ⓔ
6. Ⓐ Ⓑ Ⓒ Ⓓ Ⓔ	31. Ⓐ Ⓑ Ⓒ Ⓓ Ⓔ	56. Ⓐ Ⓑ Ⓒ Ⓓ Ⓔ
7. Ⓐ Ⓑ Ⓒ Ⓓ Ⓔ	32. Ⓐ Ⓑ Ⓒ Ⓓ Ⓔ	57. Ⓐ Ⓑ Ⓒ Ⓓ Ⓔ
8. Ⓐ Ⓑ Ⓒ Ⓓ Ⓔ	33. Ⓐ Ⓑ Ⓒ Ⓓ Ⓔ	58. Ⓐ Ⓑ Ⓒ Ⓓ Ⓔ
9. Ⓐ Ⓑ Ⓒ Ⓓ Ⓔ	34. Ⓐ Ⓑ Ⓒ Ⓓ Ⓔ	59. Ⓐ Ⓑ Ⓒ Ⓓ Ⓔ
10. Ⓐ Ⓑ Ⓒ Ⓓ Ⓔ	35. Ⓐ Ⓑ Ⓒ Ⓓ Ⓔ	60. Ⓐ Ⓑ Ⓒ Ⓓ Ⓔ
11. Ⓐ Ⓑ Ⓒ Ⓓ Ⓔ	36. Ⓐ Ⓑ Ⓒ Ⓓ Ⓔ	61. Ⓐ Ⓑ Ⓒ Ⓓ Ⓔ
12. Ⓐ Ⓑ Ⓒ Ⓓ Ⓔ	37. Ⓐ Ⓑ Ⓒ Ⓓ Ⓔ	62. Ⓐ Ⓑ Ⓒ Ⓓ Ⓔ
13. Ⓐ Ⓑ Ⓒ Ⓓ Ⓔ	38. Ⓐ Ⓑ Ⓒ Ⓓ Ⓔ	63. Ⓐ Ⓑ Ⓒ Ⓓ Ⓔ
14. Ⓐ Ⓑ Ⓒ Ⓓ Ⓔ	39. Ⓐ Ⓑ Ⓒ Ⓓ Ⓔ	64. Ⓐ Ⓑ Ⓒ Ⓓ Ⓔ
15. Ⓐ Ⓑ Ⓒ Ⓓ Ⓔ	40. Ⓐ Ⓑ Ⓒ Ⓓ Ⓔ	65. Ⓐ Ⓑ Ⓒ Ⓓ Ⓔ
16. Ⓐ Ⓑ Ⓒ Ⓓ Ⓔ	41. Ⓐ Ⓑ Ⓒ Ⓓ Ⓔ	66. Ⓐ Ⓑ Ⓒ Ⓓ Ⓔ
17. Ⓐ Ⓑ Ⓒ Ⓓ Ⓔ	42. Ⓐ Ⓑ Ⓒ Ⓓ Ⓔ	67. Ⓐ Ⓑ Ⓒ Ⓓ Ⓔ
18. Ⓐ Ⓑ Ⓒ Ⓓ Ⓔ	43. Ⓐ Ⓑ Ⓒ Ⓓ Ⓔ	68. Ⓐ Ⓑ Ⓒ Ⓓ Ⓔ
19. Ⓐ Ⓑ Ⓒ Ⓓ Ⓔ	44. Ⓐ Ⓑ Ⓒ Ⓓ Ⓔ	69. Ⓐ Ⓑ Ⓒ Ⓓ Ⓔ
20. Ⓐ Ⓑ Ⓒ Ⓓ Ⓔ	45. Ⓐ Ⓑ Ⓒ Ⓓ Ⓔ	70. Ⓐ Ⓑ Ⓒ Ⓓ Ⓔ
21. Ⓐ Ⓑ Ⓒ Ⓓ Ⓔ	46. Ⓐ Ⓑ Ⓒ Ⓓ Ⓔ	71. Ⓐ Ⓑ Ⓒ Ⓓ Ⓔ
22. Ⓐ Ⓑ Ⓒ Ⓓ Ⓔ	47. Ⓐ Ⓑ Ⓒ Ⓓ Ⓔ	72. Ⓐ Ⓑ Ⓒ Ⓓ Ⓔ
23. Ⓐ Ⓑ Ⓒ Ⓓ Ⓔ	48. Ⓐ Ⓑ Ⓒ Ⓓ Ⓔ	73. Ⓐ Ⓑ Ⓒ Ⓓ Ⓔ
24. Ⓐ Ⓑ Ⓒ Ⓓ Ⓔ	49. Ⓐ Ⓑ Ⓒ Ⓓ Ⓔ	74. Ⓐ Ⓑ Ⓒ Ⓓ Ⓔ
25. Ⓐ Ⓑ Ⓒ Ⓓ Ⓔ	50. Ⓐ Ⓑ Ⓒ Ⓓ Ⓔ	75. Ⓐ Ⓑ Ⓒ Ⓓ Ⓔ

SAT II IN

PHYSICS

TEST 2

TIME: 170 Minutes
75 Questions

DIRECTIONS: Each of the questions or incomplete statements below is followed by five answer choices or completions. Choose the best answer to each question.

QUESTIONS 1 and 2 refer to the following list of scientists' names.

   I.   Bohr

   II. Rutherford

   III. Millikan

   IV. Thompson

   V. Jones

1.   Suggested a model of the atom in which electrons can exist only in specified energy levels.

   (A) I   (B) II

   (C) III   (D) IV

   (E) V

2. Determined the charge on an electron.

(A) I   (B) II

(C) III   (D) IV

(E) V

QUESTIONS 3 and 4 relate to the following graph of distance vs. time for a motion along a straight line.

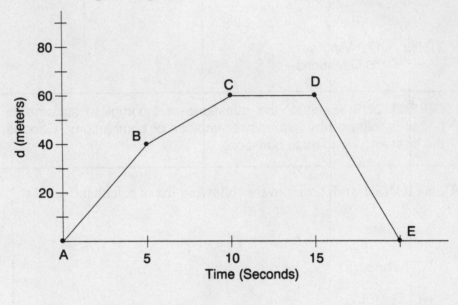

3. What is the velocity from *A* to *B*?

(A) 20 m/sec   (B) 8 m/sec

(C) 200 m/sec   (D) .125 m/sec

(E) None of the above.

4. What distance is traveled from *C* to *D*?

(A) 60 meters   (B) 30 meters

(C) 80 meters   (D) 600 meters

(E) 0 meters

QUESTIONS 5 and 6. Mass *M* slides down the incline shown with a constant velocity. Consider the following for the system.

I.   Tangent θ

II.   *mg*

III. *mg* sin θ

IV.   *mg* cos θ

V.   *mg* tan θ

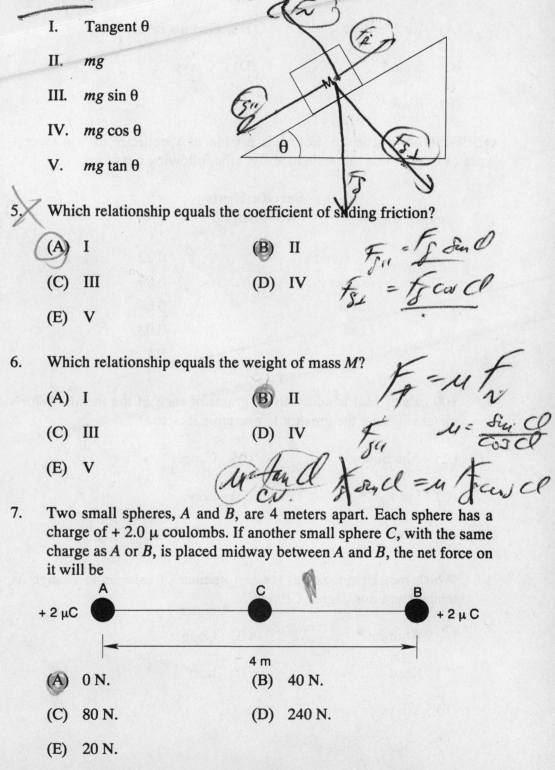

5. Which relationship equals the coefficient of sliding friction?

(A) I   (B) II

(C) III   (D) IV

(E) V

6. Which relationship equals the weight of mass *M*?

(A) I   (B) II

(C) III   (D) IV

(E) V

7. Two small spheres, *A* and *B*, are 4 meters apart. Each sphere has a charge of + 2.0 μ coulombs. If another small sphere *C*, with the same charge as *A* or *B*, is placed midway between *A* and *B*, the net force on it will be

(A) 0 N.   (B) 40 N.

(C) 80 N.   (D) 240 N.

(E) 20 N.

8. The interaction of electric and magnetic fields will not propagate which of the following?

(A) Visible light (B) Gamma rays

(C) Sound (D) X-rays

(E) Radio

QUESTIONS 9 and 10. Below is a table of specific heats for several types of matter. Use this table to answer the following questions.

Specific Heats
(cal/gram C)

Aluminum	0.22
Copper	0.09
Silver	0.06
Lead	0.03
Iron	0.1

9. 100 cals of heat is added to 10 grams of each of the metals. Which metal will have the greatest temperature increase?

(A) Aluminum (B) Copper

(C) Lead (D) Iron

(E) Silver

10. Which metal requires the greatest number of calories to change its temperature one degree Celsius?

(A) Aluminum (B) Copper

(C) Lead (D) Iron

(E) Silver

QUESTIONS 11 and 12 refer to the following diagrams. Imagine that a mass attached to a string is twirling clockwise in a vertical circle. When the ball reaches the points shown in the diagrams, the string breaks.

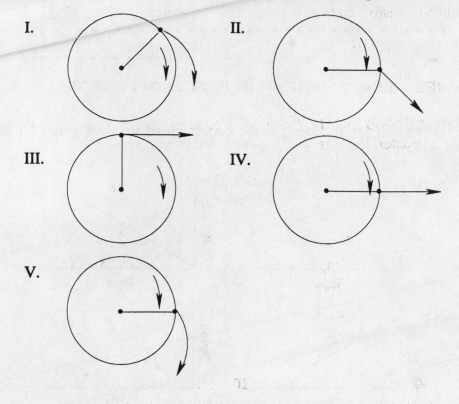

I.

II.

III.

IV.

V.

11. Which diagram shows the correct path followed by the mass when the string breaks?

(A) I

(B) II

(C) III

(D) IV

(E) V

12. The speed of the mass is doubled and the string breaks. Which diagram illustrates the correct path followed by the mass?

(A) I

(B) II

(C) III

(D) IV

(E) V

QUESTIONS 13 and 14 refer to the following figure.

The diagram shows the motion of an object moving from left to right. The dots are recorded at equal time intervals along the path of the motion.

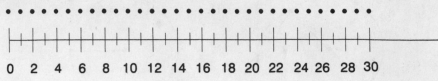

13. Which of the following is the correct speed vs. time graph for the motion?

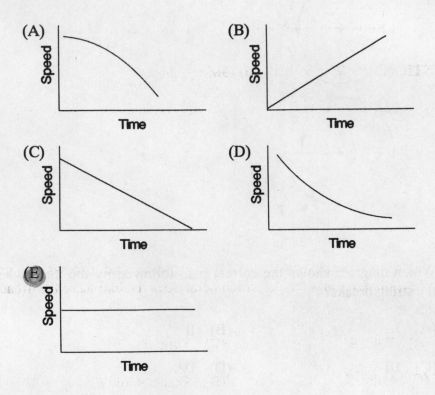

14. Which of the following is the correct acceleration vs. time graph for this motion?

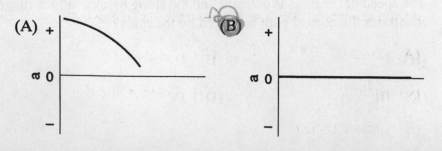

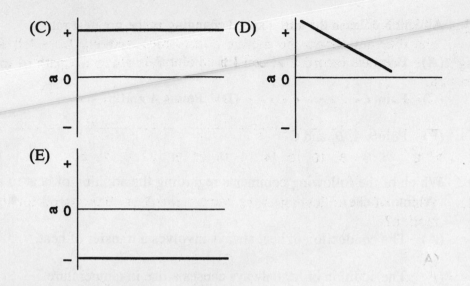

QUESTIONS 15-17 refer to the following figure.

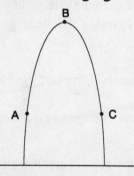

15. A ball is thrown upwards from the ground and follows the path shown in the diagram. At which point does the ball have the greatest speed?

    (A) Point A (B) Point B

    (C) Point C (D) Points A and B

    (E) Points A and C

16. At which point(s) does the ball have the slowest speed?

    (A) Point A (B) Point B

    (C) Point C (D) Points A and B

    (E) Points A and C

17. At which point is the ball's speed changing at the greatest rate?

(A) Point A

(B) Point B

(C) Point C

(D) Points A and B

(E) Points A, B, and C

18. Which of the following comments regarding the addition of heat to a system is false?

(A) The conduction of heat always involves a transfer of heat.

(B) The addition of heat always causes a rise in temperature.

(C) In a perfectly isolated system, any heat lost by one part of the system always equals the heat gained by another part of the same system.

(D) Heat and temperature are not the same thing.

(E) Temperature can change even though no heat is lost or gained.

19. Two 15 ohm resistors are connected in series to a 120 volt source. The current flowing in the resistors is

(A) 6 amps

(B) 4 amps

(C) 8 amps

(D) 0.25 amp

(E) 3 amps

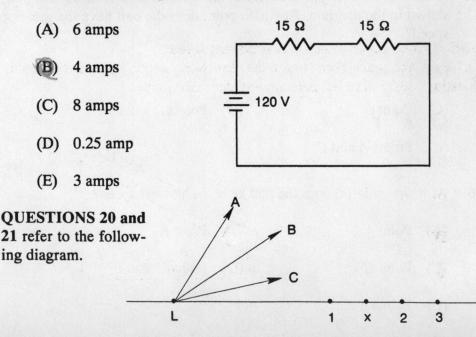

QUESTIONS 20 and 21 refer to the following diagram.

20. Projectile B is launched at an angle of 45° with the horizontal, and lands at point x. Where did projectiles A and C land if they were launched with the same velocity as projectile B?

    (A) Between L and x (B) Between x and 3

    (C) Between x and 2   (D) Between 2 and 3

    (E) Cannot be determined.

21. Which projectile(s) rose to the highest altitude?

    (A) A (B) B

    (C) C (D) All the same.

    (E) Cannot be determined.

22. If L is the wavelength of two waves producing a standing wave on a string, then the distance between two adjacent nodes is equal to

    (A) $1/4 L$.   (B) $1/2 L$.

    (C) L.   (D) $2 L$.

    (E) $4 L$.

QUESTIONS 23-25 refer to the following figure.

Select the letter that shows the direction of the force described in Questions 23-25. The block is moving down the plane.

I. A

II. B

III. C

IV. D

V. E

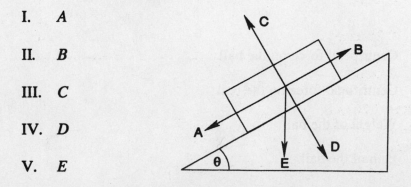

23. The frictional force.

   (A) I   (B) II

   (C) II   (D) IV

   (E) V

24. The force exerted by the surface.

   (A) I   (B) II

   (C) II   (D) IV

   (E) V

25. The weight of the block.

   (A) I   (B) II

   (C) II   (D) IV

   (E) V

QUESTIONS 26-29 relate to the following properties and diagram of a ball being twirled vertically by a string.

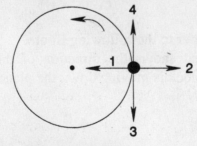

   I.   Centripetal force on the ball

   II. Centrifugal force on the ball

   III. Weight of the ball

   IV. Path of the ball

   V.   Velocity of the ball

26. Which property is described by vector #1?

    (A) I   (B) II

    (C) III   (D) IV

    (E) V

27. Which property is described by vector #2?

    (A) I   (B) II

    (C) III   (D) IV

    (E) V

28. Which property is described by vector #3?

    (A) I   (B) II

    (C) III   (D) IV

    (E) V

29. Which property is described by vector #4?

    (A) I   (B) II

    (C) III   (D) IV

    (E) V

QUESTIONS 30-32 refer to the following diagram.

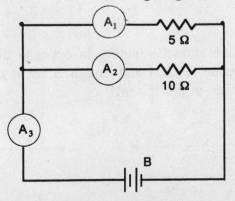

30. If ammeter A_3 reads 6 amps, ammeter A_1 will read how many amps?

(A) 2 amps   (B) 3 amps

(C) 4 amps   (D) 5 amps

(E) 6 amps

31. If the ammeter has zero resistance, how much voltage is dropped across the 5 ohm resistor?

(A) 30 volts   (B) 20 volts

(C) 9 volts   (D) 15 volts

(E) 1.2 volts

32. What is the voltage of Battery B?

(A) 40 volts   (B) 20 volts

(C) 90 volts   (D) 6.2 volts

(E) 15 volts

QUESTIONS 33 and 34 refer to the following diagrams.

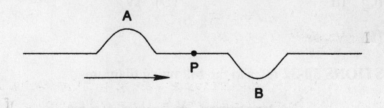

33. Two pulses are shown traveling in opposite directions on a rope. After one second, crest A and trough B are at point P. What is the shape of the rope at this instant?

(A)   (B)

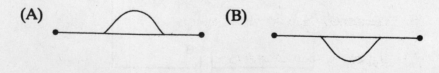

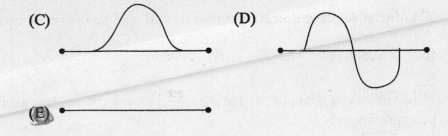

(C)   (D)

(E)

34. What is the shape of the rope at the end of two seconds?

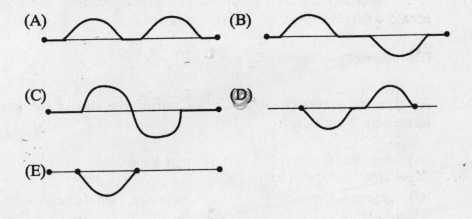

(A)   (B)

(C)   (D)

(E)

QUESTIONS 35 and 36. Use the following table of refractive indices to answer questions 35 and 36.

1. Air   ($N = 1.00$)
2. Water   ($N = 1.22$)
3. Glass   ($N = 1.50$)
4. Oil   ($N = 2.00$)
5. Diamond   ($N = 2.40$)

35. A ray of light passes through air, glass, and then water. Select the answer that best describes what happens to the velocity of the ray of light shown as it passes from air into glass and then out of glass into water.

(A) Decreases, then increases

(B) Decreases, then decreases again

(C) Increases, then decreases

(D) Increases, then decreases again

(E) No change

36. If the velocity of light in air is 3×10^8 m/sec, its velocity in glass would be approximately

(A) 3×10^8.

(B) 4.5×10^8.

(C) 2×10^8.

(D) 6×10^8.

(E) Cannot be determined.

37. As a person moves closer to a plane mirror, the size of the image formed by the mirror

(A) remains the same.

(B) gets larger.

(C) gets smaller.

(D) increases, then decreases.

(E) cannot be determined from information given.

38. Two capacitors having capacitances of 3 and 6 farads respectively are connected in parallel. The total capacitance in farads is

(A) 9.

(B) 2.

(C) 18.

(D) .5.

(E) 45.

QUESTIONS 39 and 40 refer to the following figure.

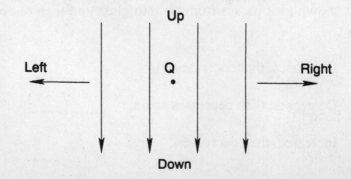

39. A positive charge Q is held at rest in uniform electric field E. When released (neglecting gravity), its motion will be

    (A) up.   (B) down.

    (C) left.   (D) right.

    (E) out of range.

40. If the charge on Q is doubled, the electrical force acting on it

    (A) remains constant.   (B) is twice as large.

    (C) is 1/2 as much.   (D) is 4 times larger.

    (E) is 1/4 as much.

41. A negative charge Q is fired into a uniform magnetic field B shown pointing into the page (by the x's). Which answer best describes its motion in the field?

    (A) Straight

    (B) Parabolic

    (C) Circular

    (D) Vibrates

    (E) Stops

QUESTIONS 42-44 refer to the following figure and information.

    I. Y_0

    II. Y_1

    III. Y_2

    IV. Y_1 and Y_2

    V. Y_0 and Y_1

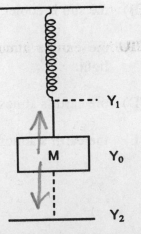

42. Where is the velocity of the mass M zero?

    (A) I   (B) II

    (C) III   (D) IV

    (E) V

43. Where is the net force on mass M a minimum?

    (A) I   (B) II

    (C) III   (D) IV

    (E) V

44. Where is the acceleration of mass M a maximum?

    (A) I   (B) II

    (C) III   (D) IV

    (E) V

45. When the sun is low on the horizon in the evening, it appears "redder." The best explanation for this is that

    (A) the sun is further away from the earth.

    (B) the sun is cooler in the evening.

    (C) the earth's atmosphere scatters the shorter wavelength, blue light.

    (D) the earth's atmosphere absorbs blue and green wavelengths.

    (E) the earth's atmosphere diffracts the light from the sun.

QUESTIONS 46 and 47 refer to the following figure.

The graph shows the decay of 10 grams of a radioactive substance for 10 days.

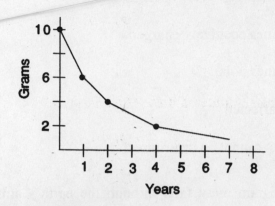

46. How much of the radioactive substance remains at the end of four years?

    (A) 10 grams   (B) 8 grams

    (C) 6 grams   (D) 4 grams

    (E) 2 grams

47. The half-life of this substance is between

    (A) 1 and 2 years.   (B) 2 and 3 years.

    (C) 3 and 4 years.   (D) 4 and 5 years.

    (E) 5 and 6 years.

48. A force of 50 newtons acts on a 1 kg mass for 2 seconds moving it 10 meters. What is the impulse applied to the block?

    (A) 1000   (B) 100

    (C) 500   (D) 50

    (E) 10

49. If a negatively charged rod is held near an uncharged metal ball, the metal ball

(A) becomes negatively charged.

(B) becomes positively charged.

(C) becomes polar.

(D) is unaffected.

(E) Affect cannot be determined.

50. If a 1 kilogram mass falls through the earth's atmosphere with a constant velocity, the retarding force of the atmosphere must be equal to

(A) 1 newton.

(B) 10 newtons.

(C) 100 newtons.

(D) 1000 newtons.

(E) None of the above.

51. In a circuit with a current flow of I, which of the following expressions for the power dissipated by a resistance R is incorrect?

(A) $W = R/E$

(B) $W = EI$

(C) $W = E^2/R$

(D) $W = I^2R$

(E) None of the above.

52. If 50 newtons are required to slide a 100 kg mass up the incline shown in the diagram, what is the efficiency?

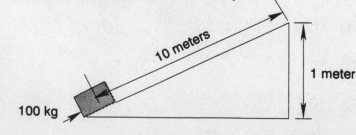

(A) 20%   (B) 30%

(C) 50%   (D) 75%

(E) 100%

QUESTIONS 53 and 54.
The figure below shows an object at 12 cm from a convex lens with a focal length of 4 cm. Draw an appropriate ray diagram, and answer the following questions concerning the image.

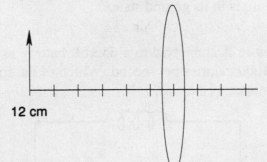

12 cm

53. What is the location of the image?

(A) 6 cm to the left of the lens

(B) 6 cm to the right of the lens

(C) 10 cm to the right of the lens

(D) 12 cm to the left of the lens

(E) 8 cm to the right of the lens

54. How would the image be best described?

(A) Real, inverted, and enlarged

(B) Real, upright, and reduced

(C) Real, inverted, and reduced

(D) Virtual, inverted, and reduced

(E) Virtual, upright, and enlarged

55. In the Bohr model of the atom, energy is radiated when

    (A) an electron falls from an outer energy level to an inner level.

    (B) an electron is stripped from an atom.

    (C) an ion is formed.

    (D) light shines on an atom.

    (E) an atom is in its ground state.

56. A coil of wire is connected to a 65 volt battery as shown. The wire produces 1000 calories per second. Which of the following is *closest* to the resistance of the coil?

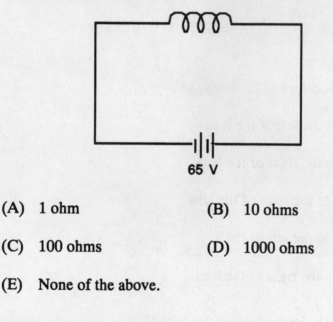

65 V

    (A) 1 ohm   (B) 10 ohms

    (C) 100 ohms   (D) 1000 ohms

    (E) None of the above.

57. Heat can be transferred through a vacuum

    (A) by convection.   (B) by radiation.

    (C) by conduction.   (D) by osmosis.

    (E) None of the above.

QUESTIONS 58-63 are based on the below heating curve for 10 grams of a substance.

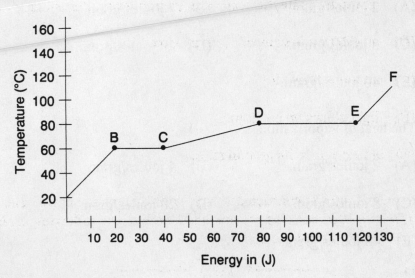

58. The freezing point is

(A) 40 degrees.   (B) 60 degrees.

(C) 80 degrees.   (D) 0 degrees.

(E) None of the above.

59. The substance is in the liquid state between

(A) *A* and *B*.   (B) *B* and *C*.

(C) *C* and *D*.   (D) *D* and *E*.

(E) *E* and *F*.

60. The boiling point is

(A) 40 degrees.   (B) 60 degrees.

(C) 80 degrees.   (D) 0 degrees.

(E) None of the above.

61. The heat of fusion is

    (A) 2 joules/gram.   (B) 4 joules/gram.

    (C) 8 joules/gram.   (D) 20 joules/gram.

    (E) 40 joules/gram.

62. The heat of vaporization is

    (A) 2 joules/gram.   (B) 4 joules/gram.

    (C) 8 joules/gram.   (D) 20 joules/gram.

    (E) 40 joules/gram.

63. Entropy is increasing between

    (A) *A* and *B*.   (B) *B* and *C*.

    (C) *C* and *D*.   (D) All of the above.

    (E) None of the above.

QUESTIONS 64-67 refer to the following figures.

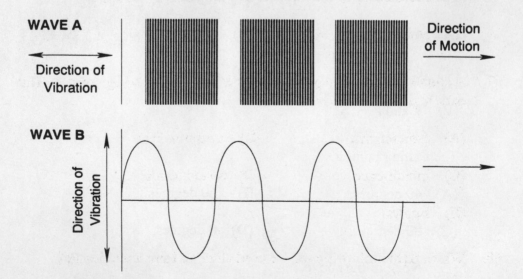

64. Wave *A* is known as a

    (A) torsional wave.   (B) circular wave.

    (C) longitudinal wave.   (D) transverse wave.

    (E) standing wave.

65. The wavelength of wave *A* is

    (A) equal to the wavelength of wave *B*.

    (B) twice the wavelength of wave *B*.

    (C) one-half the wavelength of wave *B*.

    (D) four times the wavelength of wave *B*.

    (E) Cannot be determined from the figures.

66. If the wavelength of wave *B* is doubled and its velocity remains constant, its period *T* will

    (A) remain constant.   (B) double.

    (C) decrease by 1/2.   (D) increases by 4 times.

    (E) None of the above.

67. A sound wave traveling through air is best described by wave *A*. The dark regions in the wave are called

    (A) rarefactions.   (B) compressions.

    (C) interference.   (D) sound bands.

    (E) ripples.

68. Which of the following can be used alone to form a real image?

    (A) Concave lens   (B) Convex mirror

(C)   Convex lens   (D)   Plane mirror

(E)   All can be used.

69.   X-rays striking a piece of gold foil may cause

(A)   electrons to be emitted.

(B)   isotopes of gold to form.

(C)   addition of protons to gold atoms.

(D)   addition of neutrons to gold atoms.

(E)   nuclear transmutation of gold into another element.

70.   The strength of a static charge on a glass rod can be determined using which of the following?

(A)   An electroscope   (B)   A voltmeter

(C)   An ammeter   (D)   A hygrometer

(E)   An ohm meter

QUESTIONS 71-74 refer to an atom with an atomic number of 26 and a mass number of 56.

71.   The number of electrons in the atom are

(A)   26.   (B)   13.

(C)   30.   (D)   56.

(E)   None of the above.

72.   The number of neutrons in the nucleus is

(A)   26.   (B)   13.

(C) 30.   (D) 56.

(E) None of the above.

73. The number of protons in the nucleus is

(A) 26.   (B) 13.

(C) 30.   (D) 56.

(E) None of the above.

74. The net charge on the atom is

(A) + 26.   (B) – 26.

(C) + 56.   (D) – 30.

(E) 0.

75. The unit of luminous flux is the

(A) lumen.   (B) steradian.

(C) lumen/cm.   (D) candle.

(E) All of the above.

STOP

If time still remains, you may review work only on this test.
You may not work on any other test in this book until time has elapsed.

TEST 2

ANSWER KEY

1.	(A)	21.	(A)	41.	(C)	61.	(A)
2.	(C)	22.	(B)	42.	(D)	62.	(B)
3.	(B)	23.	(B)	43.	(A)	63.	(D)
4.	(E)	24.	(C)	44.	(D)	64.	(C)
5.	(A)	25.	(E)	45.	(C)	65.	(A)
6.	(B)	26.	(A)	46.	(E)	66.	(B)
7.	(A)	27.	(B)	47.	(A)	67.	(B)
8.	(C)	28.	(C)	48.	(B)	68.	(C)
9.	(C)	29.	(E)	49.	(C)	69.	(A)
10.	(A)	30.	(C)	50.	(B)	70.	(A)
11.	(C)	31.	(B)	51.	(A)	71.	(A)
12.	(C)	32.	(B)	52.	(C)	72.	(C)
13.	(E)	33.	(E)	53.	(A)	73.	(A)
14.	(B)	34.	(D)	54.	(C)	74.	(E)
15.	(E)	35.	(A)	55.	(A)	75.	(A)
16.	(B)	36.	(C)	56.	(A)		
17.	(E)	37.	(A)	57.	(B)		
18.	(B)	38.	(A)	58.	(B)		
19.	(B)	39.	(B)	59.	(C)		
20.	(A)	40.	(B)	60.	(C)		

DETAILED EXPLANATIONS
OF ANSWERS

TEST 2

1.　**(A)**
The quantum model of the atom is credited to the Danish physicist Niels Bohr.

2.　**(C)**
Robert Millikan determined the charge on the electron.

3.　**(B)**
The slope of a distance vs. time graph is equal to the velocity. The slope of the graph from Point A to Point B is

$$(40 \text{ m} - 0 \text{ m}) / (5 \text{ sec} - 0 \text{ sec}) = 8 \text{ m/sec}.$$

4.　**(E)**
Reading directly from the graph at 10 (Point C) seconds the distance traveled is 60 meters and at 15 seconds (Point D) the distance traveled is still 60 meters. Therefore the distance traveled from Point C to Point D is 0 meters. In addition the slope of the line between C and D is zero which means the objects velocity is 0. Thus, it is not moving in the time between C and D.

5.　**(A)**
If the mass is moving with a constant velocity, the forces acting up the plane (friction) must equal the forces acting down the plane (those due to gravity). If can be shown that the coefficient of sliding friction

$$= mg \sin \theta / mg \cos \theta$$
$$= \sin \theta / \cos \theta$$
$$= \tan \theta.$$

6. **(B)**

The weight of an object on the planet earth equals its mass times g. The fact that the object is sitting on an incline has no effect on its weight.

7. **(A)**

Since spheres A and B have the same charge, and since sphere C is located an equal distance from A and B, the repulsive force of A and B on C will have the same magnitude. However since these two repulsive forces are acting in opposite directions, the net force on sphere C will be zero.

8. **(C)**

Sound waves are not produced electromagnetically. Sound waves are mechanical waves and require some sort of matter to travel through.

9. **(C)**

Lead has a specific heat of 0.03 cal/gram degree C. This means that if 0.03 calorie is added to one gram of lead its temperature will increase one degree C. Since all of the other materials require a greater number of calories to cause the same change, if the same number of calories is added to an equal mass of each, their temperature increase would be less than lead.

10. **(A)**

One gram of aluminum requires 0.22 calories to change the temperature one degree. The other substances require fewer calories.

11. **(C)**

When the string breaks, the net force acting on the ball is zero, and according to Newton's First Law, it will move in a straight line.

12. **(C)**

The path of a moving object, regardless of its speed, is always a straight line if the net force acting on it is zero.

13. **(E)**

Since the object is traveling the same distance in the same amount of time, it is moving with a constant velocity.

14. **(B)**

Acceleration is the measure of how the speed of an object is changing per time. The object's speed is not changing, therefore its acceleration is zero.

15. **(E)**

When the ball is at Point *A* the force of gravity has had less time to slow the ball down than at Point *B*. When the ball is at Point *C* it has been accelerated for the same length of time by the force of gravity as it was decelerated by gravity from Point *A* to Point *B*. Therefore the velocity at Point *A* *and* Point *C* is the same magnitude and reaches a maximum.

16. **(B)**

At Point *A* gravity has been slowing the ball down for the least amount of time. At Point *B* gravity has decreased the ball's speed to zero, before it begins to increase again as it moves to Point *C*.

17. **(E)**

The ball's speed changes due to the earth's gravitational attraction. This change is *g* 9.8 m/sec/sec during the entire trip.

18. **(B)**

Heat added that causes a state change does not result in a temperature change, (i.e., the melting of a solid).

19. **(B)**

Resistors in series behave electrically the same as one resistor with a resistance equal to the sum of the resistors connected in series. Thus two 15 ohm resistors behave as one 30 ohm resistor. Ohm's Law states that the current in a circuit equals the applied voltage divided by the total resistance.

$$I = E/R$$
$$= 120/30$$
$$= 4 \text{ amps}$$

20. **(A)**

Projectiles travel the maximum attainable horizontal distance when launched at 45 degrees. Since *B* traveled to location *x* when launched at 45 degrees, all other projectiles launched with the same velocity will travel distances between L and x.

21. **(A)**

Projectiles reach their maximum vertical distance when launched at 90 degrees. Projectile A is launched at an angle closer to 90 degrees with the others.

22. **(B)**

Standing waves occur when the multiples of one half the wavelengths will "fit" on the string.

23. **(B)**

The frictional force acts opposite to the direction of the motion.

24. **(C)**

The force exerted by the surface is opposite and equal to the component of the weight pushing against the surface.

25. **(E)**

The weight acts through the center of mass perpendicular to the base of the incline.

26. **(A)**

The force acting towards the center of the circular path is the centripetal force.

27. **(B)**

The pseudo-force created to describe the mass's response to the centripetal force is called the centrifugal force.

28. **(C)**

The weight of the mass.

29. **(E)**

The velocity vector acts tangent to the circle in the direction of its motion.

30. **(C)**

Since the current through the 5 ohm resistor must flow through A_1, and since 5 ohms is 1/2 as large as the 10 ohm resistor, then twice as much current will flow through it. Therefore, 4 of the 6 amps flows through the 5 ohm resistor, and 2 amps flows through the 10 ohm resistor.

31. **(B)**

Since 4 amps flow through the 5 ohm resistor, according to Ohm's Law

$$E = IR$$
$$= 4 \text{ amps (5 ohms)}$$
$$= 20 \text{ volts.}$$

32. **(B)**

According to Ohm's Law the total resistance of the two resistors is

$$1/R = 1/5 + 1/10 = 3/10;$$
$$R = 10/3.$$

Since the total applied voltage will be dropped across 10/3 ohms, then

$$E = IR$$
$$= 6 \text{ amps (10/3 ohms)}$$
$$= 20 \text{ volts.}$$

Note this is the same voltage dropped across each resistor since they are connected in parallel.

33. **(E)**

When crest A is directly over trough B, the two pulses add together destructively, and cancel each other at that instant.

34. **(D)**

After two seconds the pulses move past each other and continue moving in their respective directions.

35. **(A)**

As light passes from a less dense medium to a more dense medium it slows down (air to glass), and speeds up as it goes from more dense to less dense (glass to water). Since the refractive index is the ratio of the speed of light in a medium to the speed of light in a vacuum, the higher the value, the more dense the medium.

36. **(C)**

The speed of light cannot exceed 3×10^8 m/sec, but it can slow down as it passes through a medium.

37. **(A)**

For a plane mirror the image distance is always equal to the object's distance from the mirror. Also,

$$\frac{\text{size of image}}{\text{size of object}} = \frac{\text{image distance from mirror}}{\text{object distance from mirror}} = 1.$$

Therefore the size of the image remains constant as a person approaches a plane mirror.

38. **(A)**

If C is the total capacitance then

$$C = C_1 + C_2$$
$$= 3 \text{ farads} + 6 \text{ farads}$$
$$= 9 \text{ farads}.$$

39. **(B)**

By agreement the direction of an electric field is the direction a positive charge moves when placed in the field. Since the field is shown directed downward, then the positive charge will move in this direction.

40. **(B)**

The force experienced by a charged particle in an electrical field is found by multiplying the charge on the particle by the magnitude of the electrical field;

$$F = EQ.$$

Therefore if Q is doubled, the force it experiences is doubled.

41. **(C)**

A negative charge moving to the right will be deflected downward due to a force perpendicular to its velocity. Since the direction of motion is now changed, and since the force always acts perpendicular to the particle's velocity, the particle moves in a clockwise circular path. A positive charge would travel in a counterclockwise direction.

42. **(D)**

To set the mass oscillating it must be pulled or pushed to position Y_2, where its velocity is zero before it is released. The mass moves through position Y_0 and begins to slow down reaching a velocity of zero at position Y_1.

43. **(A)**

If the mass is allowed to hang freely it will position itself at position Y_0. The net force at this point is zero. (Force up equals force down.)

44. **(D)**

The acceleration reaches a maximum when the force acting on the mass is maximum. This occurs at Y_1 and Y_2.

45. **(C)**

The dust, water particles, etc., in the earth's atmosphere scatter the shorter wavelengths, blue and green light waves. When the sun is on the horizon, the light from the sun must travel a longer distance through the earth's atmosphere, decreasing the amount of blue and green wavelengths reaching the earth's surface.

46. **(E)**

Reading directly from the graph, the amount remaining at the end of four years is 2 grams.

47. **(A)**

The half-life is the time at which one half of the original amount of material remains. Reading directly from the graph, there are 5 grams remaining between 1 and 2 years.

48. **(B)**

$$\text{Impulse} = \text{Force} \times \text{Times}$$
$$= 50 \text{ N} \times 2 \text{ sec}$$
$$= 100 \text{ N sec.}$$

The mass and distance are irrelevant, because impulse only depends on the external forces applied.

49. **(C)**

The electrons in the ball are repelled away from the rod and move to the far side of the ball, leaving the side nearest the rod positive. Even though the net charge on the ball is zero, the separation of the charges cause the ball to become polar.

50. **(B)**

The force acting on the mass is 9.8 newtons (1 kg × 9.8 m/sec/sec), therefore if it is falling at a constant velocity, the retarding force must be 9.8 newtons up.

51. **(A)**

All of the expressions except this one give an answer of joules/time or watts.

52. **(C)**

Work input = 50 newtons × 10 m = 500 J
Work output = 100 kg g (1 meter) = 1000 J
Efficiency = Work in / Work out × 100 = 500/1000 × 100 = 50%

53. **(A)**

A properly constructed ray diagram places the image 6 cm to the right of the lens.

Also by using the thin lens equation,

$$\frac{1}{f} = \frac{1}{i} + \frac{1}{o}.$$

Remember the focal length is positive for a convex lens and negative for a concave lens.

$$\frac{1}{4} - \frac{1}{12} = \frac{1}{o}$$
$$6 \text{ cm} = o$$

The positive 6 means the image is real and thus to the right of the lens.

54. **(C)**

The ray diagram shows the image to be real, inverted, and reduced.

55. **(A)**

In the Bohr model, an atom radiates energy when an electron moves from an outer energy level to an inner energy level.

56. **(A)**

$$1000 \text{ calories/sec} = 4190 \text{ joules/sec} = 4190 \text{ Watts}$$

$$P = V^2 / R$$

then $\quad R = V^2 / P$

$$= (65 \times 65) / 4190$$

$$= 4225/4190 \text{ ohm}$$

57. **(B)**

Conduction and convection require matter. Osmosis is not an energy transfer process. Only radiation is correct.

58. **(B)**

The freezing point is the temperature at which the substance goes from a solid to a liquid (or liquid to a solid). This occurs between B and C.

59. **(C)**

Between C and D the liquid state is being heated from 60 degrees to 80 degrees.

60. **(C)**

The boiling point is the temperature at which the substance goes from a liquid to a gas (or gas to a liquid). This occurs between D and E.

61. **(A)**

The heat of fusion is the heat required to melt 1 gram of the substance. Twenty joules are used between B and C to melt the 10 grams. Thus

$$20 \text{ j} / \text{grams} = 2 \text{ joules} / \text{gram}.$$

62. **(B)**

The heat of vaporization is the heat required to vaporize 1 gram of the substance. Forty joules are used between D and E to vaporize the 10 grams. Thus

40 j / 10 grams = 4 joules/gram.

63. **(D)**

Disorder increases during each of the segments.

64. **(C)**

Waves formed by vibrations parallel to the direction of motion of the waves are called longitudinal waves.

65. **(A)**

The wavelength of a wave is equal to the distance between any two recurring points on the wave. The distance between compressions or rarefactions on wave A is the same as the distance between "peaks" or "valleys" on wave B. Therefore they have the same wavelength.

66. **(B)**

The velocity of a wave is equal to its wavelength divided by its period.

$$v = \lambda/T$$

Therefore the period is equal to the wavelength divided by the velocity.

$$T = \lambda/v$$

Then if the wavelength is doubled and the velocity is unchanged, the Period T must also double.

67. **(B)**

The air particles are "compressed" in the dark regions, thus the term compression is used to describe these regions. The lighter regions are called rarefactions. Interference occurs between two waves. Sound bands and ripples are nonsensical.

68. **(C)**

A convex lens is the only one of these items that can be used to form a real image. The other three form virtual images.

69. **(A)**

X-rays are not energetic enough to affect the nucleus of atoms. Choices (B), (C), (D), and (E) involved changes in the nucleus.

70. **(A)**

The distance that the leaves on an electroscope separate is determined by the magnitude of the charge brought near them.

71. **(A)**

The atomic number is the number of protons in the nucleus of an atom. The number of electrons in a neutral atom equals the number of protons.

72. **(C)**

The number of neutrons equals the mass number minus the number of protons.

73. **(A)**

The number of protons in an atom is equal to its atomic number.

74. **(E)**

Since the number of protons equals the number of electrons, the net charge is zero.

75. **(A)**

The MKS standard unit for luminous flux is the lumen. A lumen (lm) is the luminous flux (radiant power) emitted from a 1/60 sq. cm opening on a standard source and included within a solid angle of 1 steradian (sr).

A steradian (B) is the solid angle subtended at the center of a sphere by an area A on its surface that is equal to the square of its radius R. (C) A nonsense unit equivalent to power per volume. (D) An outdated international unit of luminous intensity equivalent to the quantity of light emitted by the flame of a certain make of candle.

SAT II: PHYSICS

Test 3

SAT II IN PHYSICS
TEST 3
ANSWER SHEET

1. Ⓐ Ⓑ Ⓒ Ⓓ Ⓔ
2. Ⓐ Ⓑ Ⓒ Ⓓ Ⓔ
3. Ⓐ Ⓑ Ⓒ Ⓓ Ⓔ
4. Ⓐ Ⓑ Ⓒ Ⓓ Ⓔ
5. Ⓐ Ⓑ Ⓒ Ⓓ Ⓔ
6. Ⓐ Ⓑ Ⓒ Ⓓ Ⓔ
7. Ⓐ Ⓑ Ⓒ Ⓓ Ⓔ
8. Ⓐ Ⓑ Ⓒ Ⓓ Ⓔ
9. Ⓐ Ⓑ Ⓒ Ⓓ Ⓔ
10. Ⓐ Ⓑ Ⓒ Ⓓ Ⓔ
11. Ⓐ Ⓑ Ⓒ Ⓓ Ⓔ
12. Ⓐ Ⓑ Ⓒ Ⓓ Ⓔ
13. Ⓐ Ⓑ Ⓒ Ⓓ Ⓔ
14. Ⓐ Ⓑ Ⓒ Ⓓ Ⓔ
15. Ⓐ Ⓑ Ⓒ Ⓓ Ⓔ
16. Ⓐ Ⓑ Ⓒ Ⓓ Ⓔ
17. Ⓐ Ⓑ Ⓒ Ⓓ Ⓔ
18. Ⓐ Ⓑ Ⓒ Ⓓ Ⓔ
19. Ⓐ Ⓑ Ⓒ Ⓓ Ⓔ
20. Ⓐ Ⓑ Ⓒ Ⓓ Ⓔ
21. Ⓐ Ⓑ Ⓒ Ⓓ Ⓔ
22. Ⓐ Ⓑ Ⓒ Ⓓ Ⓔ
23. Ⓐ Ⓑ Ⓒ Ⓓ Ⓔ
24. Ⓐ Ⓑ Ⓒ Ⓓ Ⓔ
25. Ⓐ Ⓑ Ⓒ Ⓓ Ⓔ

26. Ⓐ Ⓑ Ⓒ Ⓓ Ⓔ
27. Ⓐ Ⓑ Ⓒ Ⓓ Ⓔ
28. Ⓐ Ⓑ Ⓒ Ⓓ Ⓔ
29. Ⓐ Ⓑ Ⓒ Ⓓ Ⓔ
30. Ⓐ Ⓑ Ⓒ Ⓓ Ⓔ
31. Ⓐ Ⓑ Ⓒ Ⓓ Ⓔ
32. Ⓐ Ⓑ Ⓒ Ⓓ Ⓔ
33. Ⓐ Ⓑ Ⓒ Ⓓ Ⓔ
34. Ⓐ Ⓑ Ⓒ Ⓓ Ⓔ
35. Ⓐ Ⓑ Ⓒ Ⓓ Ⓔ
36. Ⓐ Ⓑ Ⓒ Ⓓ Ⓔ
37. Ⓐ Ⓑ Ⓒ Ⓓ Ⓔ
38. Ⓐ Ⓑ Ⓒ Ⓓ Ⓔ
39. Ⓐ Ⓑ Ⓒ Ⓓ Ⓔ
40. Ⓐ Ⓑ Ⓒ Ⓓ Ⓔ
41. Ⓐ Ⓑ Ⓒ Ⓓ Ⓔ
42. Ⓐ Ⓑ Ⓒ Ⓓ Ⓔ
43. Ⓐ Ⓑ Ⓒ Ⓓ Ⓔ
44. Ⓐ Ⓑ Ⓒ Ⓓ Ⓔ
45. Ⓐ Ⓑ Ⓒ Ⓓ Ⓔ
46. Ⓐ Ⓑ Ⓒ Ⓓ Ⓔ
47. Ⓐ Ⓑ Ⓒ Ⓓ Ⓔ
48. Ⓐ Ⓑ Ⓒ Ⓓ Ⓔ
49. Ⓐ Ⓑ Ⓒ Ⓓ Ⓔ
50. Ⓐ Ⓑ Ⓒ Ⓓ Ⓔ

51. Ⓐ Ⓑ Ⓒ Ⓓ Ⓔ
52. Ⓐ Ⓑ Ⓒ Ⓓ Ⓔ
53. Ⓐ Ⓑ Ⓒ Ⓓ Ⓔ
54. Ⓐ Ⓑ Ⓒ Ⓓ Ⓔ
55. Ⓐ Ⓑ Ⓒ Ⓓ Ⓔ
56. Ⓐ Ⓑ Ⓒ Ⓓ Ⓔ
57. Ⓐ Ⓑ Ⓒ Ⓓ Ⓔ
58. Ⓐ Ⓑ Ⓒ Ⓓ Ⓔ
59. Ⓐ Ⓑ Ⓒ Ⓓ Ⓔ
60. Ⓐ Ⓑ Ⓒ Ⓓ Ⓔ
61. Ⓐ Ⓑ Ⓒ Ⓓ Ⓔ
62. Ⓐ Ⓑ Ⓒ Ⓓ Ⓔ
63. Ⓐ Ⓑ Ⓒ Ⓓ Ⓔ
64. Ⓐ Ⓑ Ⓒ Ⓓ Ⓔ
65. Ⓐ Ⓑ Ⓒ Ⓓ Ⓔ
66. Ⓐ Ⓑ Ⓒ Ⓓ Ⓔ
67. Ⓐ Ⓑ Ⓒ Ⓓ Ⓔ
68. Ⓐ Ⓑ Ⓒ Ⓓ Ⓔ
69. Ⓐ Ⓑ Ⓒ Ⓓ Ⓔ
70. Ⓐ Ⓑ Ⓒ Ⓓ Ⓔ
71. Ⓐ Ⓑ Ⓒ Ⓓ Ⓔ
72. Ⓐ Ⓑ Ⓒ Ⓓ Ⓔ
73. Ⓐ Ⓑ Ⓒ Ⓓ Ⓔ
74. Ⓐ Ⓑ Ⓒ Ⓓ Ⓔ
75. Ⓐ Ⓑ Ⓒ Ⓓ Ⓔ

SAT II IN

PHYSICS

TEST 3

TIME: 170 Minutes
75 Questions

DIRECTIONS: Each of the questions or incomplete statements below is followed by five answer choices or completions. Choose the best answer to each question.

1. A laser pulse is sent from the earth to the moon and is reflected back. The signal takes 2.7 s to complete the trip. If light travels at a speed of 3×10^8 m/s, the approximate distance from the earth to the moon is

(A) 4×10^8 m.

(B) 8×10^8 m.

(C) 10×10^8 m.

(D) 1.2×10^9 m.

(E) 2.7×10^9 m.

2. The graph shows the speed of an object as a function of time. The average speed of the object during the time interval shown is

(A) 3 m/s.

(B) 5 m/s.

(C) 7 m/s.

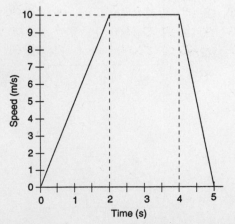

(D) 8 m/s.   (E) 10 m/s.

3. The time it takes for a plane to change its speed from 100 m/s to 500 m/s with a uniform acceleration in a distance of 1200 m is

(A) 1 s.   (B) 2 s.

(C) 3 s.   (D) 4 s.

(E) 5 s.

(handwritten) $500 = 100 + a$ $\frac{100}{2400} = \frac{2400}{2400}$

$500^2 = 100^2 + 2a1200$

$250000 \quad 10000 + 2400a$

4. Uniform acceleration may be determined by any of the following methods EXCEPT

(handwritten) $\frac{Vf - Vi}{t}$

(A) the change of velocity/time to change velocity.

(B) speed/time.

(C) constant force/mass.

(D) the slope of a velocity vs. time graph.

(E) the distance an object travels from rest/the time it travels squared.

5. Which velocity vs. time graph best represents the speed of a falling styrofoam ball as a function of time, taking air resistance into account?

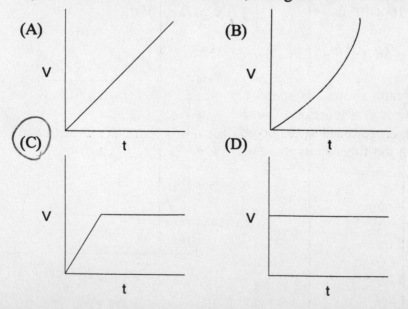

(E)

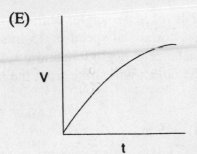

V

t

QUESTIONS 6 and 7 refer to the following diagram, passage and choices.
An object is fired horizontally from the top of a building *A* and follows a free-fall trajectory as shown (to *B*). Neglecting air friction, consider
the five vectors shown.

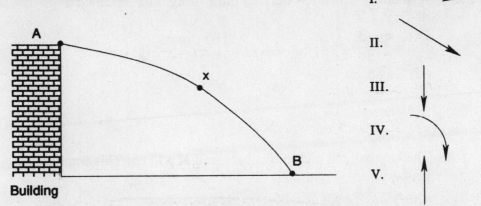

6. Which vector best represents the direction of the object's velocity at
   X?

   (A) I   (B) II

   (C) III   (D) IV

   (E) V

7. Which vector best represents the direction of the object's acceleration at *X*?

   (A) I   (B) II

   (C) III   (D) IV

   (E) V

8. A projectile is fired from ground level at an angle, with an initial vertical speed of 30 m/s and initial horizontal speed of 15 m/s. Assuming the ground is level, air resistance is negligible and $g = 10$ m/s^2, the distance horizontally that the object will strike from the initial point is

(A) 30 m.   (B) 45 m.

(C) 90 m.   (D) 150 m.

(E) 450 m.

9. A quantity which has derived units of kg. m/s^2 is called a

(A) speed.   (B) mass.

(C) watt.   (D) joule.

(E) newton.

10. The baseball bat pictured is balanced at point x. This implies that

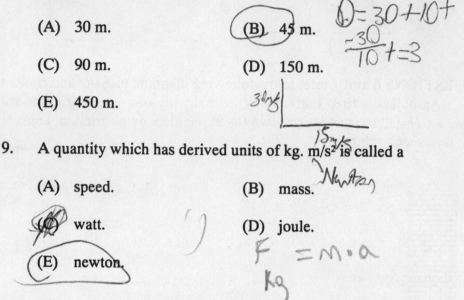

(A) side L weighs the same as side R.

(B) side L has a mass which is the same as the mass of side R.

(C) the torque of side L equals the torque of side R.

(D) the density of the wood on side L is less than the density of side R.

(E) None of the above.

11. A plane is travelling in the air at constant velocity. Which diagram best represents the component vectors of the forces acting on the plane at X travelling toward the right?

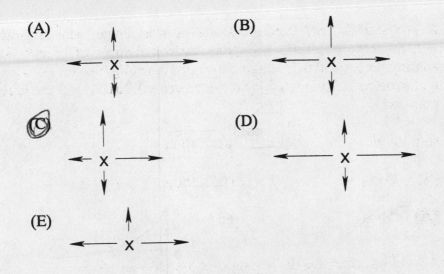

(A)

(B)

(C)

(D)

(E)

12. A billiard ball, while coasting to a stop on a pool table, must have a net external force which is

(A) zero.

(B) backward.

(C) forward.

(D) downward.

(E) upward.

13. The moon is in a nearly circular orbit above the earth's atmosphere. Which statement is true?

(A) It is in equilibrium and has no net force.

(B) It has constant velocity.

(C) It continues to use up its energy rapidly like a space ship and is falling back to earth.

(D) It is accelerating toward the earth.

(E) Its acceleration is in the same direction as its velocity.

14. In the diagram, a mass on a spring is pulled down a distance, $-x$, from its equilibrium position, P, and released. As the object moves back to P and up an additional distance, $+x$, its acceleration graph looks as follows (assume upward acceleration is positive).

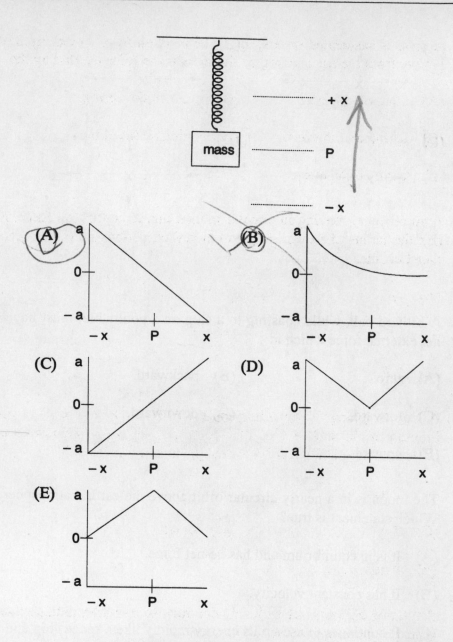

15. A .1 kg ball travelling 20 m/s is caught by a catcher. In bringing the ball to rest, the mitt recoils for .01 second. The absolute value of average force applied to the ball by the glove is

(A) 20 N.

(B) 100 N.

(C) 200 N.

(D) 1000 N.

(E) 2000 N.

16. A mass is suspended on a spring. The reaction force to the force of gravity from the earth acting on the mass is the force exerted by the

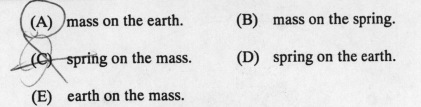

(A) mass on the earth.   (B) mass on the spring.

(C) spring on the mass.   (D) spring on the earth.

(E) earth on the mass.

17. If an object is moving in circular motion due to centripetal force, F, and the radius of its circular motion is then doubled, the new force then becomes

(A) $2F$.   (B) F.

(C) $F/2$.   (E) F^2.

(E) $1/F$.

18. A boy weighing 20 kg riding on a 10 kg cart travelling at 3 m/s jumped off in such a way that he landed on the ground with no horizontal speed. What was the change of speed of the cart?

(A) 1 m/s   (B) 2 m/s

(C) 3 m/s   (D) 6 m/s

(E) 9 m/s

19. A rotating object which suddenly contracts to a smaller radius rotates with a higher angular velocity because

(A) smaller objects turn more quickly than larger ones.

(B) the object's density must increase.

(C) the rotational inertia of smaller objects is greater.

(D) the angular velocity of rotating objects must remain the same.

(E) angular momentum must be conserved.

20. In the accompanying diagram of a planet orbiting the sun, at what position does the planet have maximum kinetic energy?

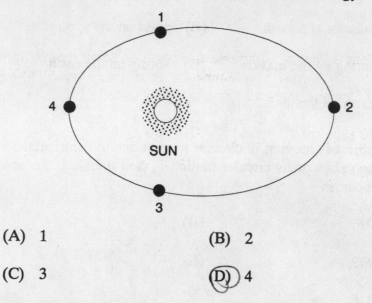

(A) 1   (B) 2

(C) 3   (D) 4

(E) None. Kinetic energy is always conserved.

21. A person standing with two feet on a bathroom scale reads a weight of 500 N on the dial. When he lifts one foot into the air, thereby only supporting himself on half the area compared to before, the new scale reading

(A) is cut in half since only half the area is now pressing on the scale.

(B) stays the same since the same entire person is still being supported on the scale.

(C) is doubled since the same weight now presses on half the area, thereby doubling the pressure.

(D) depends on how heavy the person is.

(E) None of the above.

22. Which of the following is a vector quantity?

(A) Volume   (B) Energy

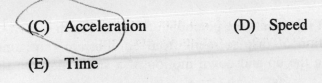

(C)   Acceleration   (D)   Speed

(E)   Time

23.   A student pushes a 10 kg box horizontally down a hallway with a force of 200 N, just overcoming the force of friction. If the box is pushed 5 meters, the work done against friction is

(A)   200 Joules.   (B)   400 Joules. $F \cdot d = W$

(C)   500 Joules.   (D)   1000 Joules.

(E)   2000 Joules.

QUESTIONS 24 and 25 refer to the following graphs.

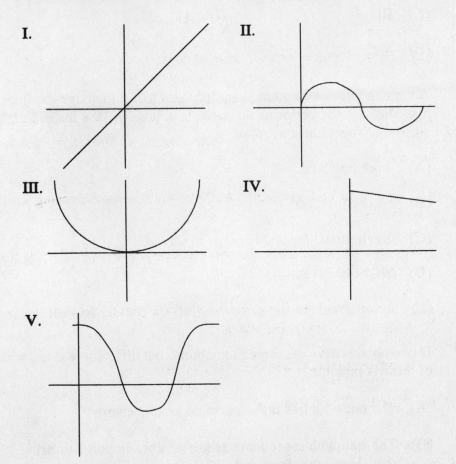

24. Which graph best represents the potential energy in a spring (vertical scale) as a function of displacement from equilibrium (horizontal scale) considering the up and down motion of a small mass on that spring?

(A) I

(B) II

(C) III

(D) IV

(E) V

25. Which graph best represents the total energy (vertical) versus time (horizontal) of a small mass on a spring oscillating up and down?

(A) I

(B) II

(C) III

(D) IV

(E) V

26. A woman raises a 2 kg box from the floor to 1.5 m above the floor in 5 seconds. If she performs the same task later in 10 s instead of 5 s, she has changed the amount of

(A) work involved.

(B) energy involved.

(C) gravitational potential energy involved.

(D) height involved.

(E) power involved.

27. If two objects have the same momentum, but different masses, which of these is possible?

(A) The one with less mass has more kinetic energy.

(B) The one with more mass requires more impulse to bring it to that momentum from rest.

(C) The same work is done to each to accelerate it from rest.

166

(D)   They each have the same velocity.

(E)   None of the above.

28.   Whenever an object strikes a stationary object of equal mass what must always occur?

(A)   The collision must be elastic.

(B)   The two bodies must stick together.

(C)   The body that was moving must stop.

(D)   Momentum will not be conserved.

(E)   Total energy of all kinds is conserved.

29.   A 1.0 kg pendulum is released at a height of 3.2 m vertically from a reference level. Assuming $g = 10$ m/s^2, and neglecting air resistance, at the bottom of its swing its speed will be

(A)   8 m/s.   (B)   6 m/s.

(C)   4 m/s.   (D)   2 m/s.

(E)   1 m/s.

30.   The friction force between two surfaces depends appreciably on all of the following factors EXCEPT

(A)   the normal force between the two surfaces.

(B)   the physical and chemical natures of the two surfaces.

(C)   whether the two surfaces are static or kinetic with respect to each other.

(D)   the surface area in contact between the two surfaces.

(E)   whether one surface is rolling or sliding with respect to the other.

31. The smallest directly detectable charge has the magnitude of 1.6 × 10^{-19} coulomb and is the same charge as the charge of

(A) a neutron.

(B) an alpha particle.

(C) an electron.

(D) a neutrino.

(E) a gamma ray.

32. Two charges are separated by 2.0 m. The force of attraction between them is 4 N. If the distance between them is doubled, the new force between them is

(A) .5 N.

(B) 1 N.

(C) 2 N.

(D) 4 N.

(E) 8 N.

33. The electric field at a point near a charged object, P, is

(A) the force on a unit negative charge at that point.

(B) the force on a unit positive charge at that point.

(C) the direction of the electric potential at that point.

(D) the acceleration of an electron at that point.

(E) the energy contained in the field at that point.

34. The conventional representation of electric field lines surrounding a negatively charged object shows arrows

(A) surrounding a charged object.

(B) emanating from the poles of the charged object.

(C) in the direction to the nearest positive charge.

(D) emanating radially outward from the charge.

(E) emanating radially inward toward the charge.

35. The potential energy change a unit charge experiences in moving from one point to another is called the

(A) voltage.   (B) current.

(C) resistance.   (D) field.

(E) charge.

36. The usual symbol for the electrical circuit component called a capacitor is

(A)   (B)

(C)   (D)

(E)

37. Consider the following circuit.

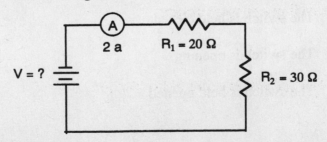

What is the potential difference across the voltage source?

(A) 20 V

(B) 25 V

(C) 50 V

(D) 80 V

(E) 100 V

38. Consider the following circuit.

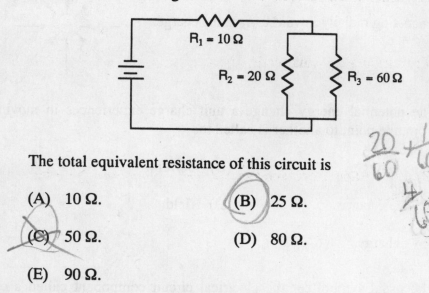

The total equivalent resistance of this circuit is

(A) 10 Ω.

(B) 25 Ω.

(C) 50 Ω.

(D) 80 Ω.

(E) 90 Ω.

39. The primary coil of an induction coil has a battery and switch in series with it. The secondary coil has a galvanometer in series with it as shown. Consider the following situations.

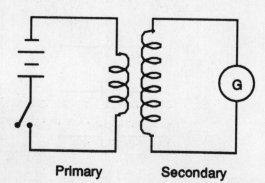

I. The switch is closing.

II. The switch is held closed.

III. The switch is opening.

IV. The switch is held opened.

During which situation(s) will the galvanometer read?

(A) II only

(B) III only

(C) II and IV

(D) I only

(E) I and III only

40. Conventional representation of magnetic field lines shows arrows

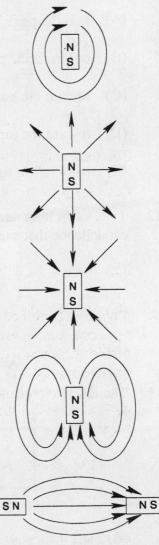

(A) surrounding a magnetic object.

(B) emanating from a magnetic object.

(C) directed into a magnetic object.

(D) emanating from one pole of a magnetic object reaching around to another pole.

(E) pointing from one pole on a magnetic object to the same pole on the nearest magnetic object.

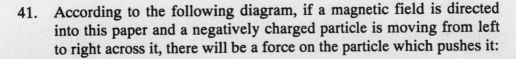

41. According to the following diagram, if a magnetic field is directed into this paper and a negatively charged particle is moving from left to right across it, there will be a force on the particle which pushes it:

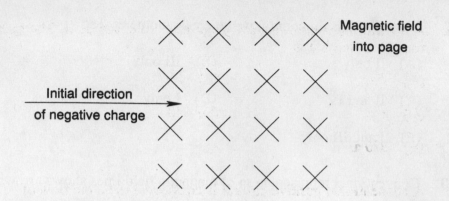

Initial direction of negative charge

Magnetic field into page

(A) into the page.

(B) out from the page.

(C) toward the bottom of the page.

(D) toward the top of the page.

(E) from left to right across the page.

42. Two capacitors arranged in a parallel connection have equivalent capacitance that can be calculated by the formula $C_{equiv.} =$

(A) $1/C_1 + 1/C_2$ (B) $C_1 + C_2$

(C) $(C_1 + C_2)/2$ (D) $C_1 \times C_2$

(E) C_1/C_2

43. The total voltage of the system between A and B in the circuit below is

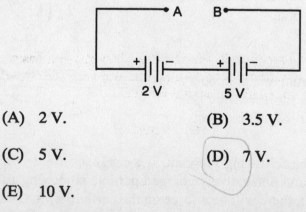

2 V   5 V

(A) 2 V.   (B) 3.5 V.

(C) 5 V.   (D) 7 V.

(E) 10 V.

44. A 40 watt light bulb has a voltage of 8 volts across it. The current running through it is

    (A) 1 a.   (B) 5 a.

    (C) 8 a.   (D) 40 a.

    (E) 320 a.

45. A conventional positive current is considered to be the flow of

    (A) positive charges.   (B) negative electrons.

    (C) neutrons.   (D) volts.

    (E) negative ions.

46. As a wave moves along a string, the property which decreases is its

    (A) wavelength.   (B) speed.

    (C) frequency.   (D) amplitude.

    (E) tone.

47. If the frequency of a wave source is 5 Hz and the wave speed is 10 m/s, then the distance between successive wave crests is

    (A) 1 m.   (B) 2 m.

    (C) 5 m.   (D) 10 m.

    (E) 50 m.

48. A wave leaves one medium in which it travels 6 m/s and has a wavelength of 2 m and enters a second medium in which the wavelength is 3 m. The wave speed in the second wave is

    (A) 1.5 m/s.   (B) 5 m/s.

    (C) 6 m/s.   (D) 9 m/s.

    (E) 18 m/s.

49. For waves of frequency, f, wavelength, λ, and velocity, v, propagated in a certain medium, if the frequency is doubled, then

(A) λ is doubled and v remains the same.

(B) λ is doubled and v is halved.

(C) λ is the same and v is doubled.

(D) λ is the same and v is halved.

(E) λ is halved and v is the same.

50. Which ray in the diagram below best predicts the new direction of the wave in medium II, a medium in which the velocity of the wave is slower than in medium I?

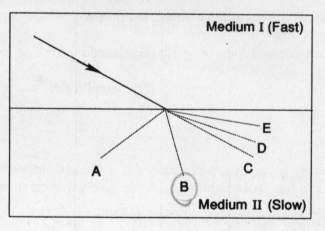

51. As the wavelength of a wave increases, the amount of diffraction the wave experiences in going around a barrier

(A) increases.   (B) decreases.

(C) remains the same.   (D) cancels.

(E) interferes.

52. If a segment, the distance between two nodes in a standing wave, is 20 cm long, the wavelength of the original travelling wave used to create the standing wave is

(A) 10 cm.　　　　　　(B) 20 cm.

(C) 30 cm.　　　　　　(D) 40 cm.

(E) 50 cm.

53. The index of refraction, n, of material is the relationship of

(A) the speed of light in the material to the speed of light in a vacuum, v/c.

(B) the speed of light in a vacuum to the speed of light in the material, c/v.

(C) the mass times the speed of light squared, mc^2.

(D) the speed of light in the material to the speed of light in air, v/v_a.

(E) the speed of light in the material to the speed of light in water, v/v_w.

54. The reflected image of an object in front of a plane mirror always appears

(A) smaller than the object.

(B) the same size as the object and inverted.

(C) as far behind the mirror as the object is in front of the mirror.

(D) distorted.

(E) diffuse.

55. A convex lens which converges parallel light rays creates an image which is real when the object is

(A) at the focal length of the lens.

(B) beyond the focal length of the lens.

(C)   on the same side of the lens as the image.

(D)   between the focal length of the lens and the lens.

(E)   virtual.

56.   As applied to visible light, the doppler effect causes a light wave of a given frequency approaching the viewer to be perceived by objective instruments as being

(A)   bluer.

(B)   redder.

(C)   darker.

(E)   brighter.

(E)   faster.

57.   Polarization is a wave phenomenon which applies only to

(A)   sound.

(B)   light.

(C)   radio waves.

(D)   transverse waves.

(E)   longitudinal waves.

58.   A point source light which has an intensity level of 10 candle power at a distance of 2 m, will have an intensity at 4 m of

(A)   .5 cp.

(B)   1 cp.

(C)   2.5 cp.

(D)   5 cp.

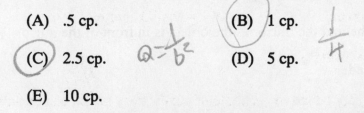

(E)   10 cp.

59.   Two sounds close in frequency, f_1 and f_2, will produce a third sound (or beating) having a frequency determined by

(A) $f_2 - f_1$.

(B) $f_1 + f_2$.

(C) $f_1 \times f_2$.

(D) f_1 / f_2.

(E) f_1, the lower pitched sound.

60. When the frequency of a forced vibration approaches the natural frequency of a particular vibrating object, the vibration in the object increases its

    (A) pitch.   (B) frequency.

    (C) wavelength.   (D) speed.

    (E) amplitude.

61. Absolute temperature is best described as a measure of the

    (A) speed of molecules.

    (B) mass of molecules.

    (C) pressure between molecules.

    (D) number of molecules.

    (E) average translational kinetic energy of molecules.

62. The amount of energy that must be added to a unit quantity of a material to raise its temperature by one degree is called the

    (A) specific heat.   (B) internal energy.

    (C) heat content.   (D) potential energy.

    (E) thermal energy.

63. Thermal energy added to a sample of a substance which changes the phase of the substance is called

    (A) heat of formation.   (B) calorimetry.

    (C) latent heat.   (D) heat of reaction.

    (E) heat content.

64. A typical liquid-filled thermometer works due to the fact that as the thermometer heats up, its

   (A) liquid molecules grow larger.

   (B) liquid molecules require more space between themselves.

   (C) liquid molecules multiply.

   (D) outer tube contracts and squeezes liquid to the thermometer.

   (E) Both (B) and (D).

65. The relationship between the pressure and volume of an ideal gas when temperature is held constant is

   (A) logarithmic.   (B) geometric.

   (C) inverse.   (D) direct.

   (E) ratio.

66. As gas is released into the atmosphere from the high pressure inside an aerosol can, it cools. This is due mainly to

   (A) the first law of thermodynamics.

   (B) the second law of thermodynamics.

   (C) the law of entropy.

   (D) Boyle's law.

   (E) the ideal gas law.

67. The second law of thermodynamics, the law of entropy, would not be violated if a ball were to bounce higher and higher with each bounce and if the internal energy (temperature) dropped to compensate for its gain of kinetic energy. This unlikely event does not violate the second law of thermodynamics because

(A)   the second law is an approximate law.

(B)   the second law is not really a valid law.

(C)   the second law is a statistical law.

(D)   the second law is a misconception.

(E)   it violates the first law of thermodynamics.

68.   The ratio of useable work produced by a device to the work input required by that device is called

(A)   latent heat.   (B)   work output.

(C)   capacity.   (D)   thermodynamics.

(E)   efficiency.

69.   This table illustrates the energy levels of an atom of element X in a gaseous state:

E_0	0
E_1	7.0 eV
E_2	13.0 eV
E_3	17.4 eV
Ionization	21.4 eV

If an electron having 15.0 eV collided with an atom of X, which one of the following energies could the electron remain with?

(A)   0 eV   (B)   2.0 eV

(C)   4.4 eV   (D)   14.0 eV

(E)   16.0 eV

70.   The fact that electrons in atoms could only absorb discrete amounts of energy was first part of the

(A) kinetic theory.

(B) Heisenberg uncertainty principle.

(C) DeBroglie wave model of the atom.

(D) Bohr theory of the atom.

(E) photoelectric effect.

71. If a particular metal in a photo cell releases a current when blue light shines on it, it must also release a current when it is struck with

(A) ultraviolet light.   (B) infrared light.

(C) microwaves.   (D) radio waves.

(E) red light.

72. A particle was ejected from the nucleus of an atom in a radioactive decay and the atomic number of the atom increased. The particle was probably

(A) a quark.   (B) a neutron.

(C) a proton.   (D) an alpha particle.

(E) a beta particle.

73. When uranium undergoes fission according to the following reaction

$$^{235}_{92}U + ^{1}_{0}n \rightarrow ^{141}_{56}Ba + X + 3^{1}_{0}n$$

The X stands for

(A) $^{92}_{51}Sb$ (B) $^{43}_{51}Sb$

(C) $^{90}_{36}Kr$ (D) $^{92}_{36}Kr$

(E) $^{145}_{55}Ba$

74. The law of conservation of energy needed to be redefined as the law of conservation of matter and energy as a result of Einstein's formulation of

    (A) $1 - v^2 / c^2$.

    (B) $E = mc^2$.

    (C) $l = l_0 \gamma$.

    (D) $KE_{max} = \varepsilon V_0$.

    (E) $E = hf$.

75. What were thought to be four fundamental forces of nature — Gravity, Electromagnetism, Weak Nuclear, and Strong Nuclear — have recently been shown to be three forces by the unification of the

    (A) Electromagnetic and Strong Nuclear.

    (B) Strong Nuclear and Weak Nuclear.

    (C) Gravitational and Electromagnetic.

    (D) Gravitational and Strong Nuclear.

    (E) Electromagnetic and Weak Nuclear.

STOP

If time still remains, you may review work only on this test.
You may not work on any other test in this book until time has elapsed.

TEST 3

ANSWER KEY

1.	(A)	21.	(B)	41.	(C)	61.	(E)
2.	(C)	22.	(C)	42.	(B)	62.	(A)
3.	(D)	23.	(D)	43.	(D)	63.	(C)
4.	(B)	24.	(C)	44.	(B)	64.	(B)
5.	(E)	25.	(D)	45.	(A)	65.	(C)
6.	(B)	26.	(E)	46.	(D)	66.	(A)
7.	(C)	27.	(A)	47.	(B)	67.	(C)
8.	(C)	28.	(E)	48.	(D)	68.	(E)
9.	(E)	29.	(A)	49.	(E)	69.	(B)
10.	(C)	30.	(D)	50.	(B)	70.	(D)
11.	(D)	31.	(C)	51.	(A)	71.	(A)
12.	(B)	32.	(B)	52.	(D)	72.	(E)
13.	(D)	33.	(B)	53.	(B)	73.	(D)
14.	(A)	34.	(E)	54.	(C)	74.	(B)
15.	(C)	35.	(A)	55.	(B)	75.	(E)
16.	(A)	36.	(A)	56.	(A)		
17.	(C)	37.	(E)	57.	(D)		
18.	(D)	38.	(B)	58.	(C)		
19.	(E)	39.	(E)	59.	(A)		
20.	(D)	40.	(D)	60.	(E)		

DETAILED EXPLANATIONS
OF ANSWERS

TEST 3

1. **(A)**
    Distance equals velocity times time, thus 3×10^8 m/s times 1.35 s (one way) is approximately 4×10^8 m. Therefore, choice (A) is correct. Choice (B) does not take into account that 2.7 s is the round trip time. Choices (C), (D), and (E) are not related to any calculation.

2. **(C)**
    The average speed for each second during which the speed is either constant or changes uniformly may be calculated.

    $0-1$ s $V_{av} = 2.5$ m/s;

    $1-2$ s, $V_{av} = 7.5$ m/s;

    $2-3$ s, $V_{av} = 10$ m/s;

    $3-4$ s, $V_{av} = 10$ m/s;

    $4-5$ s, $V_{av} = 5$ m/s.

These average speeds may in turn be averaged:

$(2.5 + 7.5 + 10 + 10 + 5) / 5 = 35/5 = 7$ m/s.

Thus the average speed is 7 m/s and the correct choice is (C).

3. **(D)**
    Time equals distance divided by average velocity if the acceleration is uniform. The average velocity is

    $(100$ m/s $+ 500$ m/s$) / 2$ or 300 m/s.

1200 m / 300 m/s = 4 s and the correct choice is (D).

4. **(B)**
    The exception is (B), which determines distance. (A), (C), or (E) can

be used to determine acceleration with the appropriate information. (D) is a graphical method of determining acceleration.

5.   **(E)**
A falling object has increasing air resistance as it speeds up, eventually reaching terminal speed as the air resistance equals the force of gravity. (A) would be true without air resistance. (B) would imply an increasing (non-uniform) acceleration. (C) would imply an abrupt appearance of air resistance and (D) would imply no acceleration.

6.   **(B)**
The direction of the velocity vector is indicated by the direction of a tangent line to its trajectory at that point x. Thus (B) is correct. A tangent line is not curved as in (D).

7.   **(C)**
The acceleration of a freely falling object is that due to gravity and is always directed downward, toward the center of mass of the earth. Though it maintains a component of horizontal speed, it has no horizontal component of acceleration; thus (C) is correct.

8.   **(C)**
Since the object is fired vertically at 30 m/s and g is 10 m/s, it loses 10 m/s each second and reaches the top of its path in 3 seconds. Symmetrically, it falls for an additional 3 seconds. During these six seconds, it independently moves horizontally at 15 m/s for a total of 90 m. Considering only the up or down movement of its path, one would incorrectly arrive at 45 m, choice (B).

9.   **(E)**
Kg m/s^2 are the SI dimensions of a force unit called the newton. (A) is m/s. (B) is kg. (C) is kg m^2/s^3, and (D) is kg m^2/s^2.

10.   **(C)**
If the object were unbalanced, the object would rotate. Rotation involves torque which is calculated by the product of force perpendicular to rotation and distance from rotation that the force is applied. Because side L is longer than R, yet it supplies equal torque, side L must weigh less than side R, thus eliminating (A) and (B). While (D) could be true, the situation does not imply it.

11. **(D)**

The upward and downward forces cancel and the left and right forces cancel leaving no net force acting on the plane, a necessary condition for constant velocity in accordance with Newton's laws. Other choices all have a non-zero net force.

12. **(B)**

A change in speed requires a net force according to Newton's second law. Since it is slowing down, its change of speed is negative and the force must be backwards. Also, frictional forces always act in a direction opposite to motion; therefore choice (B) is correct. Choice (A) would imply no change of speed. Choice (C) would imply speeding up. Choice (D) would imply that the ball would be pushed into the surface of the table. While this would increase friction, the friction would still act backwards. Choice (E) implies that the ball would leave the table.

13. **(D)**

The gravitational force between the earth and the moon produces a centripetal acceleration. Since the moon is not moving in a straight line, there must be a net force, eliminating (A). Since it is changing direction, it does not have a constant velocity (though it has a near constant speed) eliminating (B). Though there may be insignificant energy losses, *Conservation of Angular Momentum and Energy* are dominant factors and do not allow the moon to slow down appreciably or fall back to the earth, thus eliminating choice (C). Its velocity is always tangent to its path at any moment while its acceleration is always directed toward the earth, nearly perpendicular to its path at any moment, thus choice (E) is incorrect.

14. **(A)**

(A) varies with the restoring force of the spring which varies linearly and directly with x according to Hooke's Law. Since it accelerates upwards at first the answer must start with positive a, eliminating (C) and (E). Since it decelerates after the equilibrium point we can eliminate (B) and (D).

15. **(C)**

Impulse, $F\Delta t$ is calculated by determining the change of an object's momentum, $M\Delta V$. Therefore,

$$F = M\Delta V / \Delta T = .1 \text{ kg} \times (0 \text{ m/s} - 20 \text{ m/s}) / .01 \text{ s} = -200 \text{ N}$$

and its absolute value is 200 N.

16. **(A)**

In Newton's Third Law, action/reaction pairs must apply their equal and opposite forces on each other. Thus, if the earth pulls on the mass, the mass must pull on the earth as a reaction. There are other action/reaction pairs here as well, e.g., spring on mass/mass on spring, but these are not the object of the question.

17. **(C)**
Since

$$F = mv^2 / R,$$

if R is doubled, the equation becomes

$$mv^2 / 2R \quad \text{and/or} \quad (mv^2 / R) / 2 = F / 2.$$

18. **(D)**

Conservation of momentum requires that the forward momentum lost by the boy be gained by the cart. Thus, 3 m/s × 20 kg, 60 kg m/s must be gained by the cart. And 60 kg m/s divided by the mass of the cart, 10 kg, necessitates a change in speed of 6 m/s. Since a change of speed was asked for, one need not add the original cart speed of 3 m/s to the 6 m/s.

19. **(E)**

Angular momentum is a product of factors which include mass, velocity, and radius and is conserved. As one is reduced, another must increase to compensate. Therefore, as radius is reduced, velocity must increase (assuming the mass of the object does not change).

An object's speed is not inherently determined by its size, eliminating (A). When a rotating object withdraws its mass into a smaller radius about the axis of rotation, it does not mean that its density necessarily changes (e.g., a figure skater rotating with extended arms can pull her arms in but her density would not change). This eliminates (B). The rotational inertia of smaller objects is generally less, due to their smaller radius, thus eliminating (C). An object cannot both increase its angular velocity and keep its angular velocity the same, so (D) must be eliminated.

20. **(D)**

Kinetic energy, as determined here by highest speed, is a maximum when the planet is closest to the sun, and a minimum when furthest as in 2. It is intermediate when at 1 and 3.

21. **(B)**
    The pressure is doubled, (C), but the scale reads force, not pressure. The mass is the same and the force of gravity on the mass remains constant.

22. **(C)**
    Acceleration involves a direction which makes it a vector quantity. The others are scalar values independent of direction. Do not confuse speed (D) with velocity, which is a vector quantity.

23. **(D)**
    Work is calculated by taking the product of force and distance, Thus

    $$200 \text{ N} \times 5 \text{ m} = 1000 \text{ J}.$$

The 10 kg mass of the box is an unneeded term.

24. **(C)**
    Hooke's Law refers to the energy in a spring as

    $$\text{PE} = 1/2 \, kx^2,$$

where k is the spring constant and x is the displacement. This function has a parabolic shape.

25. **(D)**
    Total energy remains constant but slowly some escapes the mass-spring system in the form of thermal energy to the environment.

26. **(E)**
    Power is the time rate of doing work.

    $$P = mgh \, / \text{ time}.$$

Doubling the time halves the power. The other choices remain constant in this situation.

27. **(A)**
    Momentum is the product of mass and velocity; less mass means more velocity. The one with more velocity has more KE because KE involves the square of the velocity, but the first power of the mass. Impulse is a change of momentum. Two objects starting from rest and attaining the same momentum must have the same impulse. This eliminates (B). Work can be equated to the KE acquired by an object in changing its speed. Since the lesser mass has more KE, it must have had more work done on it

in bringing it up to the same momentum. This eliminates (C). Since momentum is the product of mass and velocity, mass and velocity must be inversely proportional, if momentum remains constant. So less mass means more velocity, eliminating (D). Since (A) is correct, (E) cannot be.

28. **(E)**   Total energy of a closed system is always conserved, as well as the total momentum. Thus (D) is incorrect. Choices (A), (B), and (C) may or may not occur.

29. **(A)**

Conservation of Energy requires that gravitational potential energy, *mgh*, be converted to kinetic energy 1/2 *mv²*. Therefore,

$$mgh = \frac{1}{2}mv^2 \quad \text{and}$$

$$V = \sqrt{2gh} = \sqrt{2 \times 10 \times 3.2} = \sqrt{64} = 8 \text{ m / s}.$$

30. **(D)**

Friction, in part, depends on the force normal to the surfaces in contact. While changing the area in contact does change the pressure (force per unit area) it does not change the total force, e.g.,

pressure × area = force.

So if area increases, pressure decreases proportionally, and the force between the two surfaces remains the same, and so does friction.

31. **(C)**

The change on the electron is found to be the elementary charge. Smaller charges are thought to exist in quarks, though these have not yet been directly detected.

32. **(B)**

Force varies inversely with the square of the distance. By doubling the distance, the force becomes one-fourth as large (1/2²), 1 N.

33. **(B)**

The electric field, *E*, is the force on a unit positive charge to a point.

34. **(E)**

By convention, electric field lines point in toward negative charges, and out from positive charges.

35. **(A)**
Voltage is another name for electric potential difference.

36. **(A)**
(B) refers to a resistor, (C) refers to a battery, (D) refers to a ground, and (E) refers to a diode.

37. **(E)**
Ohm's law states

$V = IR.$

The current, I, is 2 amps, the total resistance is 50 Ω since series resistances add directly,

30 Ω + 20 Ω = 50 Ω.

Substituting, $V = 100$ volts.

38. **(B)**
The equivalent resistance of the parallel resistors, R_1 and R_2, can be found by adding their reciprocals as

1/20 + 1/60 = 1/r

r parallel = 15 Ω.

This, then, must be added to R_1 which is in series with the parallel branch. Thus 15 Ω + 10 Ω produces a total equivalent resistance of 25 Ω.

39. **(E)**
Induction occurs only when the electromagnetic field is changing (I and III) not while it is constant (II and IV).

40. **(D)**
By convention, magnetic lines leave N magnetic poles and enter S magnetic poles. Unlike charged objects, magnets always come as N – S, bipolar entities, though magnetic monopoles are theorized to exist.

41. **(C)**
The left-hand rule which governs negative particles indicates that the magnetic field, the direction of motion of the charge and the force on the charge are mutually perpendicular. With your left hand, point your finger into the page (magnetic field), and point your thumb toward the right side of the paper (direction of charge); your palm then points in the direction of the force on the charge.

The right-hand rule can also be used and you reverse the direction of the force because the charge is negative.

42. **(B)**

Parallel capacitances are added directly to obtain equivalent capacitance. Series capacitances are added according to (A) for $1/C_{equiv}$.

43. **(D)**

Series voltages add directly.

44. **(B)**

Current is watts/volts. Thus

40 watts / 8 volts = 5 amps.

45. **(A)**

Historically, standard circuits were thought to carry positive charges. Later, discoveries showed that negative electrons were the common particles involved in currents. But the convention held.

46. **(D)**

The displacement from equilibrium, or amplitude, decreases due to energy losses to the environment. Wavelength, (A), frequency, (C), and speed, (B) all remain constant and tone, (E), refers to frequency of a sound wave.

47. **(B)**

Wave speed divided by frequency is wavelength.

48. **(D)**

As a wave passes the boundary between two media, its frequency must remain unchanged. Therefore,

$$V_1 / X_1 = V_2 / X_2$$

and substituting, we find $V_2 = 9$ m/s where V is wave speed and X is wavelength.

49. **(E)**

V always remains the same in a given medium of constant quality under normal circumstances of λ or f thus eliminating choices (B), (C), and (D). f is inversely proportional to λ in a given medium, eliminating (A).

50. **(B)**

   When a wave enters a new, slower medium at an angle, the new direction of its ray is more toward the perpendicular to the boundary surface. We must eliminate choice (A), since it would imply that the light beam, in reversing its left to right direction in the diagram, is actually reflecting instead of diffracting at the point of entry into medium II. Choice (C) would imply no change in speed. Choice (D) would imply an increase in speed, and choice (E) would imply an even greater increase in speed than in (D). These must all be eliminated. The index of refraction, n, of a faster medium is a smaller number and therefore

$$\frac{n \text{ medium I}}{n \text{ medium II}}$$

must be less than 1. According to Snell's law,

$$\frac{n \text{ medium I}}{n \text{ medium II}} = \frac{\sin \theta_{II}}{\sin \theta_I}$$

(See figure below.) For this to be less than 1, θ_{II} must be less than θ_I. This eliminates choices (C), (D), and (E).

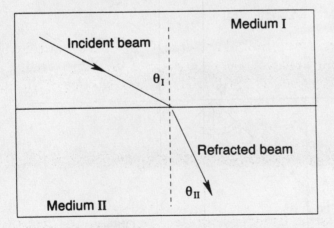

$$\frac{n \text{ medium I}}{n \text{ medium II}} = \frac{\sin \theta_{II}}{\sin \theta_I}$$

51. **(A)**

   Diffraction is a wavelength-dependent phenomenon, directly dependent on wavelength. As wavelength increases, diffraction increases (e.g., for sound, low tones [long waves] go around corners [diffract] better than high tones). Choices (B) and (C) are contrary to (A) and must be eliminated. Cancellation and interferences are other wave phenomena not pertinent to the question, thus eliminating (D) and (E).

52. **(D)**

A segment, between two nodes, is half a wavelength long.

53. **(B)**

The index of refraction, n, is the ratio of the speed of light in a vacuum to the speed of light in a material, c/v.

54. **(C)**

The law of reflection states the angle of incidence equals the angle of reflection. The geometry of the light rays from the object to the mirror to the image has a symmetry which makes the image appear as far behind the mirror as the object is in front of the mirror and erect. Since the light beam leaving the object, travelling to the mirror, reflecting, and striking the eye travels as far as the light beam from the image appears to travel to the eye, the size perspective of the object and image appear the same, eliminating (A) (see the figure below). Since plane images produce erect images, choice (B) can be eliminated. The nature of a plane mirror also creates images which are not distorted and non-diffuse.

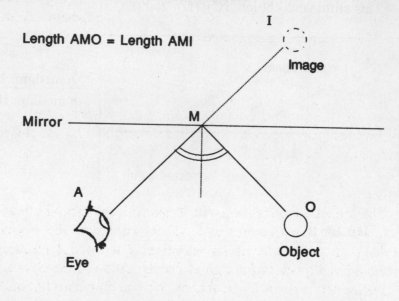

55. **(B)**

The thin lens equation,

1/object distance + 1/image distance = 1/focal length,

will produce a positive image distance (a real image) if the object distance is greater than the focal length for a converging lens. When the object distance is the focal length, 1/image distance must be zero and hence an image is produced at infinity (meaning never), eliminating (A). When the image is on the same side of the lens as the object, it is not a real image, it is virtual. This eliminates both (C) and (E). The image is virtual when the object is between the focal length and the lens, eliminating choice (D).

56. (A)
Any approaching wave source is perceived as having a higher frequency. Therefore, light is bluer (not necessarily blue) (i.e., closer to the blue end of the spectrum — higher frequency).

57. (D)
Polarization occurs in transverse waves, not longitudinal waves, eliminating (E). Sound is a longitudinal wave eliminating (A). While polarization does occur in light and radiowaves, (B) and (C), it does not occur exclusively in either. Since the question includes the word "only," we can eliminate (B) and (C) since choosing either of them would eliminate the other and be incorrect.

58. (C)
Since a point source of light sends photons spreading out spherically, the intensity falls off inversely as the square of the distance from the light source. Thus a doubling of the distance produces one-fourth of the intensity.

59. (A)
"Beats" are produced as the two original waves come in and out of phase with each other and interfere, as determined by the difference between the two frequencies.

60. (E)
The forced vibration, when in phase with the natural vibration of the object, will be able to repeatedly add its energy to the object, thereby increasing the amplitude of its vibration. The natural frequency of an object is a fixed quantity for a given configuration of the object. Since the pitch of a sound wave is its frequency, we can eliminate (A) and (B). The wavelength of a wave in a given medium is inversely proportional to its frequency. Thus if its natural frequency is fixed its wavelength is fixed, eliminating (C). The speed of a wave in a given medium is constant, eliminating (D).

61. (E)
Absolute temperature is described in the kinetic theory as a constant times $1/2 \ mv^2$, the average kinetic energy of the molecules. While the

speed and mass are both factors, in the kinetic energy of a molecule, it would be incorrect to say that either alone would be a measure of temperature, thus eliminating (A) and (B). While the pressure between molecules can be affected by their temperatures, other factors can also affect the pressure, such as volume, eliminating (C). While more molecules add to the kinetic energy of a sample, they do not add to the average of the sample, thus eliminating (D).

62. **(A)**
The number of joules of energy required to raise one kilogram of a substance by one degree Kelvin is the specific heat of that substance at that temperature in the SI system.

63. **(C)**
Latent heat is the amount of thermal energy required to charge the phase of a unit quantity of a substance.

64. **(B)**
The kinetic theory states that as the molecules heat up, they gain energy and move faster, increasing their mean free path between collisions.

65. **(C)**
The ideal gas law states as P increases, V decreases and vice versa, to the first power of each variable. Thus V is proportional to $1/P$.

$$PV = nRT$$

where n is amount in moles and R is the universal gas constant.

66. **(A)**
The first law of thermodynamics is a statement of the law of conservation of energy. If the gas must do work in pushing the molecules of the atmosphere further aside, that work must come from the internal energy of the gas, hence the temperature drops.

67. **(C)**
The second law is a statistical law and only predicts events based on their probability. It does not "outlaw" possible but very improbable events as long as no other prohibitive law is violated. If the ball did not cool as it bounced higher, the first law, conservation of energy, would be violated.

68. **(E)**
     Efficiency is work output/work input and statistically governed to be less than 100% by the second law of thermodynamics.

69. **(B)**
     An atom can only absorb discrete amounts of energy, as shown by Franck and Hertz. In this case, 13.0 eV may be absorbed (13.0 eV − 0 eV), leaving 2 eV for the electron (15.0 eV − 13.0 eV).

70. **(D)**
     Bohr first "quantized" the electron in the atom through Plank and Einstein first "quantized" energy in heated solids.

71. **(A)**
     The photo effect states that electrons will not be ejected from an atom unless incident electromagnetic radiation has at least a minimum frequency value. The only EM radiation having a greater frequency than blue light is ultraviolet.

72. **(E)**
     When a β is emitted from a nucleus, the number of neutrons decreases by one and the number of protons increases by one thereby increasing its atomic number by one but not appreciably changing its mass.

73. **(D)**
     Conservation of mass requires X to have a mass of 92 and an atomic number of 36.

74. **(B)**
     Einstein formulated the relationship

$$E = mc^2$$

to describe the convertibility of matter into energy and vice versa. The two quantities are not thought of as different forms of the same property.

75. **(E)**
     In the mid 1980s, the Electromagnetic and Weak Nuclear forces were found to be different manifestations of the same force, now called the Electroweak force.

SAT II: PHYSICS

Test 4

SAT II IN PHYSICS
TEST 4
ANSWER SHEET

1. Ⓐ Ⓑ Ⓒ Ⓓ Ⓔ	26. Ⓐ Ⓑ Ⓒ Ⓓ Ⓔ	51. Ⓐ Ⓑ Ⓒ Ⓓ Ⓔ
2. Ⓐ Ⓑ Ⓒ Ⓓ Ⓔ	27. Ⓐ Ⓑ Ⓒ Ⓓ Ⓔ	52. Ⓐ Ⓑ Ⓒ Ⓓ Ⓔ
3. Ⓐ Ⓑ Ⓒ Ⓓ Ⓔ	28. Ⓐ Ⓑ Ⓒ Ⓓ Ⓔ	53. Ⓐ Ⓑ Ⓒ Ⓓ Ⓔ
4. Ⓐ Ⓑ Ⓒ Ⓓ Ⓔ	29. Ⓐ Ⓑ Ⓒ Ⓓ Ⓔ	54. Ⓐ Ⓑ Ⓒ Ⓓ Ⓔ
5. Ⓐ Ⓑ Ⓒ Ⓓ Ⓔ	30. Ⓐ Ⓑ Ⓒ Ⓓ Ⓔ	55. Ⓐ Ⓑ Ⓒ Ⓓ Ⓔ
6. Ⓐ Ⓑ Ⓒ Ⓓ Ⓔ	31. Ⓐ Ⓑ Ⓒ Ⓓ Ⓔ	56. Ⓐ Ⓑ Ⓒ Ⓓ Ⓔ
7. Ⓐ Ⓑ Ⓒ Ⓓ Ⓔ	32. Ⓐ Ⓑ Ⓒ Ⓓ Ⓔ	57. Ⓐ Ⓑ Ⓒ Ⓓ Ⓔ
8. Ⓐ Ⓑ Ⓒ Ⓓ Ⓔ	33. Ⓐ Ⓑ Ⓒ Ⓓ Ⓔ	58. Ⓐ Ⓑ Ⓒ Ⓓ Ⓔ
9. Ⓐ Ⓑ Ⓒ Ⓓ Ⓔ	34. Ⓐ Ⓑ Ⓒ Ⓓ Ⓔ	59. Ⓐ Ⓑ Ⓒ Ⓓ Ⓔ
10. Ⓐ Ⓑ Ⓒ Ⓓ Ⓔ	35. Ⓐ Ⓑ Ⓒ Ⓓ Ⓔ	60. Ⓐ Ⓑ Ⓒ Ⓓ Ⓔ
11. Ⓐ Ⓑ Ⓒ Ⓓ Ⓔ	36. Ⓐ Ⓑ Ⓒ Ⓓ Ⓔ	61. Ⓐ Ⓑ Ⓒ Ⓓ Ⓔ
12. Ⓐ Ⓑ Ⓒ Ⓓ Ⓔ	37. Ⓐ Ⓑ Ⓒ Ⓓ Ⓔ	62. Ⓐ Ⓑ Ⓒ Ⓓ Ⓔ
13. Ⓐ Ⓑ Ⓒ Ⓓ Ⓔ	38. Ⓐ Ⓑ Ⓒ Ⓓ Ⓔ	63. Ⓐ Ⓑ Ⓒ Ⓓ Ⓔ
14. Ⓐ Ⓑ Ⓒ Ⓓ Ⓔ	39. Ⓐ Ⓑ Ⓒ Ⓓ Ⓔ	64. Ⓐ Ⓑ Ⓒ Ⓓ Ⓔ
15. Ⓐ Ⓑ Ⓒ Ⓓ Ⓔ	40. Ⓐ Ⓑ Ⓒ Ⓓ Ⓔ	65. Ⓐ Ⓑ Ⓒ Ⓓ Ⓔ
16. Ⓐ Ⓑ Ⓒ Ⓓ Ⓔ	41. Ⓐ Ⓑ Ⓒ Ⓓ Ⓔ	66. Ⓐ Ⓑ Ⓒ Ⓓ Ⓔ
17. Ⓐ Ⓑ Ⓒ Ⓓ Ⓔ	42. Ⓐ Ⓑ Ⓒ Ⓓ Ⓔ	67. Ⓐ Ⓑ Ⓒ Ⓓ Ⓔ
18. Ⓐ Ⓑ Ⓒ Ⓓ Ⓔ	43. Ⓐ Ⓑ Ⓒ Ⓓ Ⓔ	68. Ⓐ Ⓑ Ⓒ Ⓓ Ⓔ
19. Ⓐ Ⓑ Ⓒ Ⓓ Ⓔ	44. Ⓐ Ⓑ Ⓒ Ⓓ Ⓔ	69. Ⓐ Ⓑ Ⓒ Ⓓ Ⓔ
20. Ⓐ Ⓑ Ⓒ Ⓓ Ⓔ	45. Ⓐ Ⓑ Ⓒ Ⓓ Ⓔ	70. Ⓐ Ⓑ Ⓒ Ⓓ Ⓔ
21. Ⓐ Ⓑ Ⓒ Ⓓ Ⓔ	46. Ⓐ Ⓑ Ⓒ Ⓓ Ⓔ	71. Ⓐ Ⓑ Ⓒ Ⓓ Ⓔ
22. Ⓐ Ⓑ Ⓒ Ⓓ Ⓔ	47. Ⓐ Ⓑ Ⓒ Ⓓ Ⓔ	72. Ⓐ Ⓑ Ⓒ Ⓓ Ⓔ
23. Ⓐ Ⓑ Ⓒ Ⓓ Ⓔ	48. Ⓐ Ⓑ Ⓒ Ⓓ Ⓔ	73. Ⓐ Ⓑ Ⓒ Ⓓ Ⓔ
24. Ⓐ Ⓑ Ⓒ Ⓓ Ⓔ	49. Ⓐ Ⓑ Ⓒ Ⓓ Ⓔ	74. Ⓐ Ⓑ Ⓒ Ⓓ Ⓔ
25. Ⓐ Ⓑ Ⓒ Ⓓ Ⓔ	50. Ⓐ Ⓑ Ⓒ Ⓓ Ⓔ	75. Ⓐ Ⓑ Ⓒ Ⓓ Ⓔ

SAT II IN

PHYSICS

TEST 4

TIME: 170 Minutes
75 Questions

DIRECTIONS: Each of the questions or incomplete statements below is followed by five answer choices or completions. Choose the best answer to each question.

---

1. Centripetal force accelerates you

    (A) toward the center because your velocity is changing in magnitude.

    (B) toward the center because your velocity is changing in direction.

    (C) tangentially because your velocity is changing in magnitude.

    (D) away from the center because your velocity is changing in magnitude.

    (E) away from the center because your velocity is changing direction.

2. Which statement is NOT true about a projectile fired at an angle (not 90°) from the ground if you disregard air resistance?

    (A) Time to reach the highest point is the same as the time to fall back to earth.

(B) The initial vertical velocity component is the same as the final vertical velocity component just before landing, but in the opposite direction.

(C) The horizontal velocity component doesn't change.

(D) The maximum horizontal distance occurs when fired at a 45-degree angle.

(E) At the highest point in the flight the horizontal and vertical velocity components are both zero.

QUESTIONS 3-6 refer to the answer choice that best describes the type of collision given.

I. One-dimensional, perfectly elastic

II. One-dimensional, elastic

III. One-dimensional, inelastic

IV. One-, two-, or three-dimensional, perfectly elastic

V. Two- or three-dimensional, inelastic

3. Collisions between molecules according to kinetic theory.

(A) I   (B) II

(C) III   (D) IV

(E) V

4. A boxcar rolls into another boxcar at rest and connects to it.

(A) I   (B) II

(C) III   (D) IV

(E) V

5. Hitting a billiard ball with the cue ball head on.

   (A) I   (B) II

   (C) III   (D) IV

   (E) V

6. Shooting a target as it crosses your line of sight.

   (A) I   (B) II

   (C) III   (D) IV

   (E) V

QUESTIONS 7-11. Choose the answer that most commonly describes the type of graph needed.

    I.   Distance vs. Time

    II.   Velocity vs. Time

    III. Acceleration vs. Time

    IV. Force vs. Distance

    V.   Force vs. Acceleration

7. The slope of the tangent to a point on this graph would tell you the instantaneous velocity.

   (A) I   (B) II

   (C) III   (D) IV

   (E) V

8. A zero slope line on this graph would indicate constant velocity.

   (A) I   (B) II

(C) III   (D) IV

(E) V

9.   The area under this curve determines displacement.

(A) I   (B) II

(C) III   (D) IV

(E) V

10. The area under this curve determines work.

(A) I   (B) II

(C) III   (D) IV

(E) V

11. The slope of this curve determines mass.

(A) I   (B) II

(C) III   (D) IV

(E) V

QUESTIONS 12-16 can best be described as an application of which of the following laws?

I.   Newton's First Law

II.   Newton's Second Law

III. Newton's Third Law

IV.   Newton's Law of Gravitation

V.   Hooke's Law

12. Cavendish's Experiment.

    (A) I   (B) II

    (C) III   (D) IV

    (E) V

13. Stepping out of a boat over to a dock.

    (A) I   (B) II

    (C) III   (D) IV

    (E) V

14. Voyager Probe after leaving Neptune.

    (A) I   (B) II

    (C) III   (D) IV

    (E) V

15. A baseball player sliding into second base.

    (A) I   (B) II

    (C) III   (D) IV

    (E) V

16. A person walking to the end of a diving board.

    (A) I   (B) II

    (C) III   (D) IV

    (E) V

17. Four light bulbs of equal wattage are in a series circuit connected to a battery that has some amount of internal resistance. The circuit is rewired to contain only three bulbs in series. Which statement accurately describes a change that will take place?

(A) The total resistance of the circuit will increase.

(B) The total current in the circuit will decrease.

(C) The external voltage drop in the circuit outside the battery will increase.

(D) The internal voltage drop within the battery will increase.

(E) The power delivered to each bulb will remain the same.

18. According to the laws of resistance, doubling the thickness of a given wire and making it ten times longer will cause its resistance to be

(A) 40 times greater.   (B) 20 times greater.

(C) 5 times greater.   (D) 2.5 times greater.

(E) 0.05 as much as before.

QUESTIONS 19 and 20. Select the one choice that best describes each item.

    I.   Inductors

    II.   Conductors

    III. Insulators

    IV. Capacitors

    V.   Transformers

19. A substance that inhibits the flow of charge.

(A) I   (B) II

(C) III   (D) IV

(E) V

20. Changes voltage without changing frequency.

(A) I   (B) II

(C) III   (D) IV

(E) V

21. The laws of photoelectric emission

(A) completely support Newton's particle theory of light.

(B) state that emission is inversely proportional to the intensity of the incident light.

(C) state that increasing the intensity of the incident light increases the kinetic energy of the photoelectrons.

(D) state that increasing the frequency of the incident light increases the kinetic energy of the photoelectrons.

(E) state that the maximum energy to release the electron from a surface is the work function.

22. A blackbody radiator

(A) does not absorb thermal radiation.

(B) is a perfectly reflecting surface.

(C) is used in newer automobile engines.

(D) has an emissivity of 1.

(E) emits radiation only in the visible light region.

QUESTIONS 23 and 24 refer to the following six diagrams.

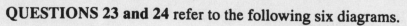

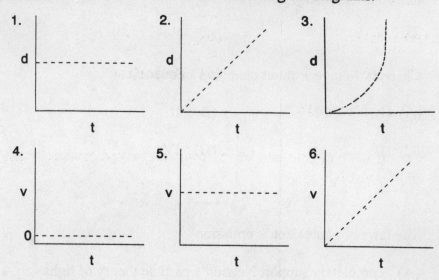

23. Which two graphs describe an object at rest?

(A) 1 and 2   (B) 4 and 5

(C) 2 and 5   (D) 1 and 4

(E) 3 and 6

24. Which two graphs describe positive acceleration?

(A) 1 and 2   (B) 4 and 5

(C) 2 and 5   (D) 1 and 4

(E) 3 and 6

25. Which is not an equivalent unit of work?

(A) joule   (B) newton meter

(C) kilowatt-hour   (D) ft-lb

(E) gram-sec

26. Machines can multiply

(A) energy.   (B) force.

(C) speed.   (D) Both (B) and (C).

(E) (A), (B), and (C).

27. The critical velocity needed to complete a vertical circle can be computed using

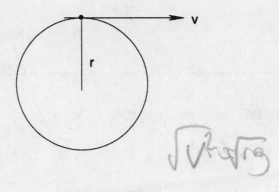

(A) $\sqrt{rg}$.   (B) $\sqrt{2rg}$.

(C) $\sqrt{rg}\,/\,2$.   (D) $2\sqrt{rg}$.

(E) rg.

28. If you find yourself sitting atop a Ferris wheel facing north and rotating forward, the direction of the torque according to the right hand rule is

(A) south.   (B) up.

(C) west.   (D) east.

(E) down.

29. Which statement is NOT true about Simple Harmonic Motion?

(A) The acceleration is proportional to the displacement.

(B) The acceleration is always directed toward the equilibrium point.

(C) Damping will occur unless energy is continuously supplied.

(D) It is the same as periodic motion.

(E) Velocity at maximum displacement is zero.

QUESTIONS 30 and 31 refer to the following five vector diagrams.

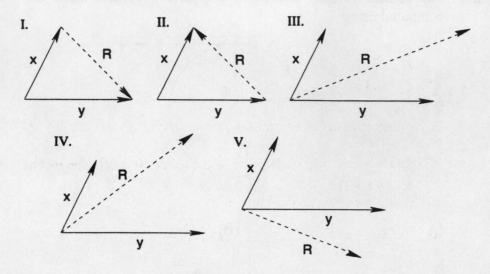

30. Which vector diagram correctly demonstrates $x + y$?

(A) I   (B) II

(C) III   (D) IV

(E) V

31. Which vector diagram correctly demonstrates $x - y$?

(A) I   (B) II

(C) III   (D) IV

(E) V

QUESTIONS 32-35 refer to the figure and answer choices below.

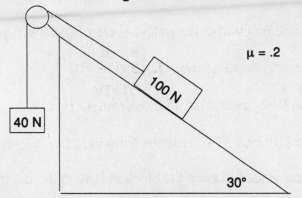

I.   7.3 newtons down the incline

II.   greater than 7.3 newtons down the incline

III. between 7.3 newtons down and 27.3 newtons up the incline

IV.   27.3 newtons up the incline

V.   greater than 27.3 newtons up the incline

32. The force needed to allow the 100 N block to go down the incline at constant speed.

(A) I   (B) II

(C) III   (D) IV

(E) V

33. The force needed to make the block accelerate down the incline.

(A) I   (B) II

(C) III   (D) IV

(E) V

34. The force needed to allow the block to go up the incline at constant speed.

   (A) I   (B) II

   (C) III   (D) IV

   (E) V

35. The force needed to keep the block at rest on the incline.

   (A) I   (B) II

   (C) III   (D) IV

   (E) V

36. The gravitational force of attraction between any two objects is

   (A) directly proportional to the product of the two masses.

   (B) directly proportional to the square of the distance between their centers.

   (C) inversely proportional to the product of the two masses.

   (D) indirectly proportional to the distance between their centers.

   (E) does not depend on the distance.

37. When a wave enters a new medium, its velocity will increase if

   (A) the wavelength decreases.

   (B) the impedance decreases.

   (C) the force needed to produce a wave in the new medium is greater than the old medium.

(D)   it comes in only at an angle.

(E)   None of the above.

38.   As a train sounds its horn and moves at constant speed toward a stationary listener, the listener will hear

(A)   the pitch gradually get higher.

(B)   a constantly higher pitch.

(C)   the same pitch as the engineer.

(D)   a constantly lower pitch.

(E)   the pitch gradually getting lower.

39.   A transverse wave

(A)   displaces the medium perpendicular to the wave velocity.

(B)   displaces the medium parallel to the wave velocity.

(C)   transmits sound.

(D)   Both (A) and (C).

(E)   Both (B) and (C).

40.   Refraction occurs when

(A)   a wave enters a new medium at some angle.

(B)   a wave bends around a barrier.

(C)   a wave bounces back on itself.

(D)   a wave runs into another wave.

(E)   a wave changes speed at a boundary of a new medium.

QUESTIONS 41-43 refer to the following five wave diagrams.

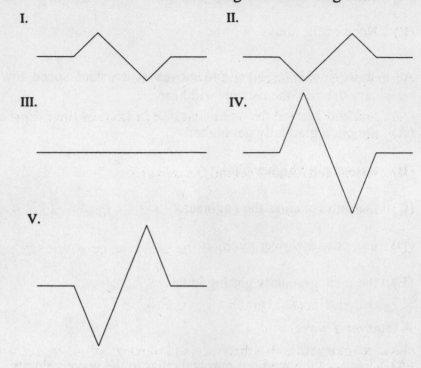

I.

II.

III.

IV.

V.

41. An example of destructive interference by adding I + II is

(A) I.   (B) II.

(C) III.   (D) IV.

(E) V.

42. The superpositioning of II + II would look most like

(A) I.   (B) II.

(C) III.   (D) IV.

(E) V.

43. The superpositioning of V + I would look most like

(A) I.   (B) II.

(C) III.   (D) IV.

(E) V.

44. An image that is enlarged and inverted must be

(A) real and located the same distance in front of the mirror as the object.

(B) virtual and located behind the mirror.

(C) real and located on the opposite side of a lens from the object.

(D) virtual and located beyond the center of curvature of the mirror.

(E) real and located behind the mirror.

45. What relationship exists between illumination of an object and the distance from the source to the object?

(A) Direct proportion

(B) Indirect proportion

(C) Inverse proportion

(D) Inverse squared proportion

(E) Squared proportion

46. The distance from a compression in a sound wave to the nearby rarefaction is 5 m. The frequency of the sound is 33 hertz. The temperature is most near

$v = f\lambda$

(A) 0 degrees K.   (B) 135 degrees K.

(C) 273 degrees K.   (D) 548 degrees K.

(E) Temperature is not related to the speed of sound.

47. When monochromatic light passes through a double slit, a bright fringe is formed due to a path difference of

(A) 1/4 λ.

(B) 1/2 λ.

(C) 3/4 λ.

(D) 7/8 λ.

(E) 1 λ.

48. In order for two beams to produce an interference pattern, they must have their planes of polarization

(A) parallel to one another.

(B) perpendicular to one another.

(C) in phase with each other.

(D) Both (A) and (C).

(E) Both (B) and (C).

49. The image in a convex mirror is always

(A) virtual.

(B) larger than the object.

(C) inverted.

(D) farther from the mirror than the object.

(E) the same as a concave mirror.

50. In order for total internal reflection to occur,

(A) light must originate in the medium of lower index of refraction.

(B) light must originate in the medium in which light travels fastest.

(C) light must be at an angle less than the critical angle.

(D) light must be at an angle greater than or equal to the critical angle.

(E) light must be perpendicular to the boundaries of the mediums.

51. The index of refraction for an unknown substance is 1.2. The critical angle for total internal reflection to occur in the substance if going from the substance to air is found by

(A) $\sin (1.2) = \theta$.

(B) $\sin (.8) = \theta$.

(C) $\sin \theta = 1.2$.

(D) $\sin \theta = .8$.

(E) $1/\sin (1.2) = \theta$.

52. An optically active substance

(A) produces many colors.

(B) produces fluorescent effects.

(C) produces phosphorescent effects.

(D) shows strain patterns when placed between polarizer and analyzer.

(E) rotates the plane of polarization of polarized light.

53. According to the theory of relativity, as an object approaches the speed of light

(A) time, space, and mass contract.

(B) time, space, and mass expand.

(C) time and space contract, and mass increases.

(D) time and mass contract, and space expands.

(E) mass and space contract, and time increases.

54. Which statement is NOT true of a beta particle?

(A) It is a very energetic electron.

(B) It is a fundamental particle.

(C) It is the result of the conversion of a neutron into a proton.

(D) It is a negatively charged particle.

(E) It is not deflected by a magnetic field.

55. A nuclide with a half-life of 2 days is tested after 6 days. What fraction of the sample has decayed?

(A) 1/2   (B) 1/4

(C) 3/8   (D) 3/4

(E) 7/8

56. Natural radioactive decay produces

(A) alpha particles.   (B) beta particles.

(C) gamma particles.   (D) Both (A) and (B).

(E) (A), (B), and (C).

57. Through this reaction,

$$_6C^{12} + {_1}H^2 - {_7}N^{13}$$

what else is produced?

(A) β^+ (B) $_1H^1$

(C) $_0n^1$ (D) α

(E) γ

58. A large square sheet of copper with a small hole in it is heated from 30 degrees C to 130 degrees C. Which of the following will occur?

(A) The area of the sheet increases and the diameter of the hole increases.

(B) The area of the sheet increases and the diameter of the hole decreases.

(C) The area of the sheet decreases and the diameter of the hole increases.

(D) The area of the sheet decreases and the diameter of the hole decreases.

(E) The area of the sheet increases and the diameter of the hole remains constant.

QUESTIONS 59-62 refer to the following temperature–thermal energy graph of a pure substance.

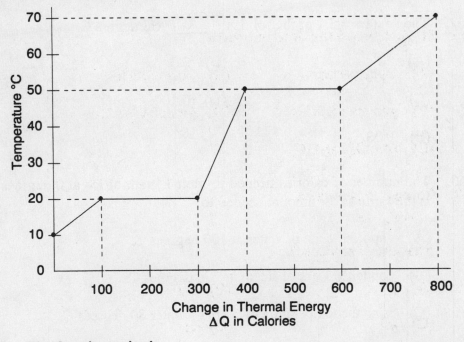

59. The freezing point is

(A) 0 degrees C.   (B) 10 degrees C.

(C) 20 degrees C.   (D) 30 degrees C.

(E) 50 degrees C.

60. The boiling point is

(A) 0 degrees C.   (B) 10 degrees C.

(C) 20 degrees C.   (D) 30 degrees C.

(E) 50 degrees C.

61. The ratio of the heat of vaporization to the heat of fusion is

(A) 1:1.   (B) 2:1.

(C) 1:2.   (D) 3:1.

(E) 1:3.

62. The heat capacity of the solid is _____ cal/degree C.

(A) 10   (B) 3.3

(C) 1   (D) 0.1

(E) 0.33

63. The number of calories needed to melt 1 gram of ice at 0 degrees C is the same as the amount needed to

(A) vaporize 1 gm of water at 100 degrees C.

(B) condense 1 gm of steam at 100 degrees C.

(C) raise the temperature of 1 gm of water 80 degrees C.

(D) melt 1 gm of copper at 0 degrees C.

(E) melt 5 gm of ice at 0 degrees C.

64. What is the ideal efficiency of a steam engine that takes steam from the boiler at 200 degrees C and exhausts it at 100 degrees C?

(A) 50%

(B) 25%

(C) 21%

(D) 11%

(E) 2%

65. The force between two charges is NOT

(A) dependent on a constant $k = 9,000,000,000$.

(B) dependent on the product of the charges.

(C) dependent on the inverse square of the distance from the centers of the charges.

(D) indicated by lines of force.

(E) dependent on mass of the charged objects.

66. Three capacitors of 2 farads each are connected in parallel. The equivalent capacitance is

(A) 2.0 farads.

(B) 1.5 farads.

(C) 0.667 farads.

(D) 6.0 farads.

(E) 8.0 farads.

67. The same three capacitors connected in series would be

(A) 2.0 farads.

(B) 1.5 farads.

(C) 0.667 farads.

(D) 6.0 farads.

(E) 8.0 farads.

68. The magnitude of the magnetic deflecting force F does NOT depend on

   (A) the size of the charge, q.

   (B) the velocity of the charge, v.

   (C) the strength of the magnetic field, B.

   (D) the angle between the velocity and B field, θ.

   (E) a potential difference, V.

QUESTIONS 69 and 70 refer to the following information.

A lamp is connected to a 12-volt battery. An ammeter indicates a current of 5 amps.

69. The wattage of the lamp is

   (A) 2.4 watts.   (B) 5/12 watts.

   (C) 60 watts.   (D) 120 watts.

   (E) 300 watts.

70. The resistance of the lamp is

   (A) 30 ohms.   (B) 2.4 ohms.

   (C) .42 ohms.   (D) 12 ohms.

   (E) 60 ohms.

QUESTIONS 71-73 refer to the following.

   I.   watt

   II.   coul/sec

   III.   joule/coul

IV. coul/volt

V. volt/amp

71. Which statement is true about power?

(A) I is a unit of power.

(B) II × III produces a correct unit of power.

(C) II × II × V produces a correct unit of power.

(D) Both (A) and (B).

(E) (A), (B), and (C).

72. How could you produce the units for an RC circuit?

(A) (I × II) – III.   (B) II × III.

(C) (III × IV) + II.   (D) (II × V) + q/IV.

(E) V × (I – q).

73. How could you express Ohm's Law?

(A) III = II × V.   (B) I = II × III.

(C) V = II × III.   (D) V = IV × I.

(E) III = II × I.

74. In order for the torque on a current-carrying loop in a magnetic field to be at a minimum, the angle between the plane of the loop and the magnetic field must be

(A) 0°.   (B) 30°.

(C) 45°.   (D) 60°.

(E) 90°.

75. Appropriate units for the *B* field are

    I.   Weber.

    II. Newton.

    III. Amp.

    IV. Coul.

    V. Meter.

(A) I/V.

(B) II/(III × V).

(C) I.

(D) III × IV.

(E) I × V.

STOP

If time still remains, you may review work only on this test.
You may not work on any other test in this book until time has elapsed.

TEST 4

ANSWER KEY

1.	(B)	21.	(D)	41.	(C)	61.	(A)
2.	(E)	22.	(D)	42.	(E)	62.	(A)
3.	(D)	23.	(D)	43.	(B)	63.	(C)
4.	(C)	24.	(E)	44.	(C)	64.	(C)
5.	(B)	25.	(E)	45.	(D)	65.	(E)
6.	(E)	26.	(D)	46.	(C)	66.	(D)
7.	(A)	27.	(A)	47.	(E)	67.	(C)
8.	(B)	28.	(C)	48.	(D)	68.	(E)
9.	(B)	29.	(D)	49.	(A)	69.	(C)
10.	(D)	30.	(C)	50.	(D)	70.	(B)
11.	(E)	31.	(B)	51.	(D)	71.	(E)
12.	(D)	32.	(A)	52.	(E)	72.	(D)
13.	(C)	33.	(B)	53.	(C)	73.	(A)
14.	(A)	34.	(D)	54.	(E)	74.	(E)
15.	(B)	35.	(C)	55.	(E)	75.	(B)
16.	(E)	36.	(A)	56.	(E)		
17.	(D)	37.	(B)	57.	(C)		
18.	(D)	38.	(B)	58.	(A)		
19.	(C)	39.	(A)	59.	(C)		
20.	(E)	40.	(E)	60.	(E)		

DETAILED EXPLANATIONS OF ANSWERS

TEST 4

1.   **(B)**
Centripetal force is a force directed toward the center of the circle, so answers (C), (D), and (E) are incorrect. It is perpendicular to the velocity of the object, causing it to change its direction, not its speed. Hence answer (A) is also incorrect.

2.   **(E)**
At the highest point in the projectile's flight, only the vertical velocity reaches zero. As indicated by (C), the horizontal velocity doesn't change and is not zero as long as the projectile is fired at some angle other than 90 degrees.

3.   **(D)**
According to kinetic theory, the molecules must undergo perfectly elastic collisions or energy would be lost and temperature would drop. Answers II, III, and V do not conserve energy, and answer I limits the collisions to one dimensional only.

4.   **(C)**
When a boxcar connects with another boxcar at rest, their combined mass describes an inelastic collision, so answers I, II, and IV are incorrect. Moving in a straight line on the tracks constrains the motion to one dimension only, so answer V is also incorrect.

5.   **(B)**
The billiard balls do not stick together, so they are not inelastic collisions as described by answers III and V. Since energy is lost in this collision, it is not a perfectly elastic collision as stated in answers I and IV. The head-on collision thus produces a one-dimensional elastic collision.

6. **(E)**
Since the target is crossing the path of the bullet, this two-dimensional problem eliminates answers I, II, and III. It is not perfectly elastic as described by IV, because energy is not conserved. It could be elastic if the bullet passes through or inelastic if the bullet lodges in the target and their combined mass moves off together.

7. **(A)**
The tangent to the distance time graph gives instantaneous velocity. The tangent to the velocity time graph gives acceleration II. The tangent to the acceleration time graph III indicates the change in acceleration. IV is used for work and V is used for Newton's Law.

8. **(B)**
Zero slope on the velocity time graph shows that velocity doesn't change. A zero slope on graph I would indicate no motion, and a zero slope on III would indicate increasing velocity. A zero slope on IV or V would indicate a constant force causing accelerated motion.

9. **(B)**
Area under graph II indicates displacement as in multiplying velocity times time to get distance. The area under III gives velocity, the area under IV gives work, and the other two—I and V—are undefined quantities.

10. **(D)**
Same as 9.

11. **(E)**
For a given mass this graph should be a direct proportion resulting in a straight line whose slope would indicate different size masses. The other graphs may be affected by the mass of an object but do not indicate in any way what the mass of the object may be. As explained in Questions 7 and 8, the slopes of answers I, II, III, and IV deal with motion that is unrelated to mass, but Newton's Law relates force and acceleration dependent on mass.

12. **(D)**
Cavendish's Experiment was to verify Newton's Law of Gravitation and determine G. It depends on the mass of two objects and the distance between their centers. It is not an application of Newton's Laws of Motion, so answers I, II, and III are incorrect. Answer IV is also incorrect,

since it deals with forces proportional to distance under stress or bending.

13.   **(C)**

As you step toward the dock, the boat moves out from under you in the opposite direction, an example of action and reaction, or Newton's Third Law. For each force applied by an object, there is an opposite force applied on the object.

14.   **(A)**

Voyager is now moving through space in a straight line with no net force acting on it, according to Newton's First Law. Since there is no net force, an object at rest remains at rest or one moving in a straight line will continue to move at constant speed in a straight line.

15.   **(B)**

A baseball player sliding into second base requires a net force due to friction proportional to his mass to produce the necessary deceleration according to Newton's Second Law.

16.   **(E)**

A person standing on a diving board displaces the diving board from its equilibrium position an amount proportional to his or her weight. This is an example of Hooke's Law,

$$F = kx,$$

which states that the displacement from an equilibrium position is proportional to the force applied.

17.   **(D)**

Since there are now fewer bulbs in series, the total resistance drops. The total current increases since the EMF remains constant. The internal resistance will be a greater percentage of the total, thereby increasing the internal voltage drop but decreasing the external voltage drop, causing a change in power delivered.

18.   **(D)**

According to the laws of resistance,

$$R = \frac{\rho L}{A} = \frac{\rho L}{\pi r^2}$$

resistance is directly proportional to the length but inversely proportional to the cross-sectional area. Doubling the thickness of the wire increases the area by a factor of 4, since area depends on the square of the radius. This by itself would decrease the resistance by a factor of 4, making answers (A) and (B) incorrect. Increasing the length by a factor of 10 makes the resistance 10 times greater; thus answer (E) is incorrect. The net effect then is 10/4 greater, or 2.5 times as great. Thus answer (E) is incorrect.

19. **(C)**
An insulator is a material that used in a resistor to inhibit the flow of charge. An inductor is a solenoid of low resistance. A conductor is a material that conducts electric charge. A capacitor stores charge, and a transformer changes voltage without changing frequency.

20. **(E)**
Same as 19.

21. **(D)**
The first law of photoelectric emission states that the emission of photoelectrons is directly proportional to the intensity of the incident light, so (B) is incorrect. The second law states that the kinetic energy is independent of the intensity of the light, so (C) is incorrect. The third law states that within the range of effective frequencies the kinetic energy varies directly with the difference between the frequency of the incident light and the cutoff frequency, which is why (D) is the correct answer. The work function is the minimum energy needed to release an electron, so (E) is false, and, although the wave theory could not explain the photoelectric effect, it did not support the particle theory, so (A) is also incorrect.

22. **(D)**
A blackbody radiator does absorb thermal radiation, so (A) is incorrect. It does not reflect it, so (B) is incorrect. It is not a radiator of a car, so (C) is also incorrect. But it does have an emissivity of 1, which emits radiation well beyond the visible light region and which makes (D) correct and (E) incorrect.

23. **(D)**
In graph 1 your position is not changing, and in graph 4 your velocity is zero, so you are not moving. In graphs 2 and 5 you are traveling at some constant speed, thus making answers (A), (B), and (C) incorrect. In graphs 3 and 6 you are accelerating, so answer (E) is incorrect.

24. **(E)**
Same as 23.

25. **(E)**
Mass times time is not work. Force times distance, as indicated by answers (B) and (D), indicates work, and (A) is a unit for work equal to a newton meter, whereas (C) is power times time, which is equal to work.

26. **(D)**
Machines may be used to multiply a force (B) or speed (C), which are both correct, making the answer (D). But energy cannot be multiplied, since you must get out less work than you put in, thus making (A) and (E) incorrect.

27. **(A)**
At the top of a vertical circle the centripetal force

$$f_s = \frac{mv^2}{r}$$

must equal the weight *mg*.

$$\frac{mv^2}{r} = mg.$$

Solving for *v*,

$$v = \sqrt{rg}.$$

28. **(C)**
If you curl the fingers of your right hand in the circular direction in which the Ferris wheel is turning in a vertical circle, your thumb will point at a right angle to the north, toward the west. The torque must be at a right angle to the north, so (A) is incorrect. Answers (B) and (E) could be possible only if you were on a merry-go-round instead of a Ferris wheel, and answer (D) would be obtained if you used your left hand instead of your right.

29. **(D)**
By definition, SHM is accelerated motion proportional to its displacement (A), but in the opposite direction (B) of its displacement. Its velocity is zero at its maximum displacement (E), and damping or dying out of the motion will occur unless continuously supplied (C). Periodic

motion simply is back and forth over the same path in equal periods of time so that SHM is periodic, but not all periodic is SHM. Thus answer (D) is not a true statement.

30. **(C)**
    Using the head to tail method or parallelogram method determines the correct diagonal. I and II do not start at the correct corner of the parallelogram, so they are incorrect. IV has too long a resultant, and V is − $X + Y$ or $Y − X$, thus they too are incorrect.

31. **(B)**
    $X − Y$ or $X + −Y$ by the head to tail method is determined by going from the head of the one you are subtracting to the head of the first vector or drawing the opposite of Y and using the parallelogram method. Again, V and I are $Y − X$, so they are incorrect. III is $X + Y$, so it is incorrect, and IV has too long a resultant even for $X + Y$, so it is incorrect.

QUESTIONS 32-35 require you to first calculate the parallel force component Fp, the normal force component F_n, and the amount of friction F_f.

$$F_p = F_w \sin \theta = 100 \sin 30 = 50 \text{ N}$$
$$F_n = F_w \cos \theta = 100 \cos 30 = 86.6 \text{ N}$$
$$F_p = F_n \text{ (coefficient of friction)} = 86.6 \,(.2) = 17.3 \text{ N}$$

32. **(A)**
    The 40 N pulling up the incline plus the friction of 17.3 N is 7.3 N greater than the 50 N pulling down the incline. The additional 7.3 N down the incline would make the net force zero so that it could slide at a constant speed down the incline. In summing up the forces in the direction of motion

$$F_p + F_{\text{applied}} − 40 \text{ N} − F_f = 0$$

for constant speed down the incline

$$50 \text{ N} + F_{\text{applied}} − (40 \text{ N} + 17.3 \text{ N}) = 0$$

$$F_{\text{applied}} = 7.3.$$

33. **(B)**
    Any additional force greater than 7.3 N down the incline would cause a net force greater than zero down the incline, forcing the entire system to accelerate in that direction.

34. **(D)**

If the block is to go up the incline, then the F_f would be directed down the incline with F_p for a total of 67.3 N down. When added to the 40 N up the incline we need 27.3 N up the incline to make the net force zero in order to go at constant speed up the incline.

$$40 \text{ N} + F_{\text{applied}} - F_p - F_f = 0$$

for constant speed up the incline

$$40 \text{ N} + F_{\text{applied}} - 50 \text{ N} - 17.3 \text{ N} = 0$$

$$F_{\text{applied}} = 27.3 \text{ N}$$

up the incline.

35. **(C)**

Since F_f is a reaction force, it acts only as much as it is acted upon. Since anything greater than the 7.3 N down accelerates it down, and anything greater than the 27.3 N up would accelerate it up, anything in-between would simply cause the block to remain stationary on the incline.

36. **(A)**

Gravitational Force

$$F = \frac{GMm}{r^2}$$

is directly, not inversely, proportional to the product of the masses, so (C) is incorrect and inversely not directly or indirectly proportional to the square of the distance between their centers, so (B) and (D) are incorrect. It does depend on the distance, so (E) is incorrect.

37. **(B)**

When the impedance decreases, the wave increases in speed as the force needed to produce the wave is less not more, as stated in answer (C), and the wavelength increases instead of decreases as stated in answer (A). The speed changes whether it comes in at an angle or straight in, so answer (D) is incorrect. Since (B) is true then (E) is also incorrect.

38. **(B)**

The Doppler effect as it is used here will cause a wave to be compressed shorter, causing a higher pitch that stays constant until the velocity of the train changes relative to the listener. Since it is a higher pitch, answers (D) and (E) are incorrect, and since it is a constantly higher pitch, answers (A) and (C) are incorrect.

39. **(A)**
A transverse wave is movement of the medium perpendicular, not parallel, to the velocity of the wave, so answers (B) and (E) are incorrect. Sound is transmitted longitudinally, or in parallel disturbances to the velocity, so both answers (C) and (D) are incorrect.

40. **(E)**
The refraction of a wave is due to a change in speed at a boundary of a new medium and does not depend on the angle, so answer (A) is incorrect. (B) is diffraction, (C) is reflection, and (D) is interference, so they are all incorrect.

41. **(C)**
Since 1 and 2 are of equal amplitude and wavelength, when added together they will wipe each other out in totally destructive interference.

42. **(E)**
If (B) were superimposed on itself and all points added together, the trough and trough and the crest plus crest would produce (E). (D) is the sum of $(A + A)$, and (C) is $(A + B)$, so they are both incorrect.

43. **(B)**
The large trough of (E) plus the small crest of (A) would result in the small trough of (B). The large crest of (E) plus the small trough of (A) results in the small crest of (A), so it is incorrect. They cannot totally destruct, so (C) is incorrect. (E) plus (A) cannot equal (E), so (E) is incorrect. (D) has too large a crest first followed by too large a trough, so it too is incorrect.

44. **(C)**
An inverted image must be real, and virtual images are always erect, so (B) and (D) are incorrect. To be enlarged it must be beyond the center of curvature of a mirror or on the opposite side of a lens beyond twice the focal length, with the object located between the focus and twice the focal length, so (A) and (E) are incorrect.

45. **(D)**
The illumination of an object drops off with the square of the distance, also known as the inverse square law. If the distance increases by a factor of, for example, 3, then the amount of illumination drops to 1/9, as long as the surface is perpendicular to the light.

46. **(C)**

A compression to a rarefaction is 1/2 of a wavelength, so doubling 5 m means

$$10 \text{ m} \times 33 \text{ Hz} = 330 \text{ m/s},$$

which is the approximate speed of sound at 0°C, since $v = 331 + .6$ (C). (A) is −273 C, (B) is obtained by not doubling 5 m, (D) is twice the temperature difference, and (E) is not true, since the speed does not depend on temperature.

47. **(E)**

Since

$$d \sin \theta = m\lambda$$

for a maximum only, an integral number of wavelengths will produce bright fringes. Since no fractional amounts are allowed, (A), (B), (C), and (D) are incorrect.

48. **(D)**

Waves must be both parallel (A) and in phase with each other (C) to produce interference. Since being perpendicular to one another will not cause interference, both (B) and (E) are incorrect.

49. **(A)**

A convex mirror produces an image behind the mirror that is always erect, not inverted, so (C) is incorrect. It always produces a reduced image, so (B) is incorrect. The image is closer, not farther, than the object, so (D) is incorrect. The light appears to be coming from behind the mirror, making it a virtual image. A concave mirror can produce real and virtual, both enlarged and reduced, both erect and inverted images, thus making answer (E) incorrect.

50. **(D)**

For total internal reflection to occur, light must be at an angle greater than or equal to the critical angle determined by

$$\sin i = n_2/n_1$$

in the slower medium or the one of higher index of refraction. Since the light must originate in the slower, not the faster, medium, answer (B) is incorrect. Since the slower medium is of a higher index of refraction than (A), (A) is also incorrect. Because the angle must be greater than or equal to the critical angle for total internal reflection to occur, both answers (C) and (E) are incorrect.

51. **(D)**

Since you are going from the substance to air,

$$\sin i = 1/n,$$

or $\sin \theta = 1/(6/5),$

or $\sin \theta = 5/6 = .8.$

You do not take the sin of the index, which is why (A) and (B) are incorrect. It is not the reciprocal of the sin of 6/5, which is why (E) is incorrect. And you do not set sin θ = (6/5)/1, which is why (C) is incorrect.

52. **(E)**

An optically active substance like sugar rotates the plane of polarization so that light emerging from it is still plane polarized but not vertically, so if the analyzer is horizontal, some light will get through. It does not produce colors or fluorescent or phosphorescent effects, so (A), (B), and (C) are incorrect. Strain patterns are due to diametrical compression, so (D) is incorrect.

53. **(C)**

As you approach the speed of light, time slows down, so answers (B) and (E) are incorrect. Length decreases, so answer (D) is incorrect. Mass increases as you approach the speed of light, so answer (A) is incorrect.

54. **(E)**

A beta particle is one of the fundamental particles, so (B) is a true statement. It is a high-energy, negatively charged electron, so answers (A) and (D) are true statements. And it may result from the conversion of a neutron into a proton, so answer (C) is correct. But it would be affected by a magnetic field, so answer (E) is not true.

55. **(E)**

After only 2 days, 1/2 the sample has decayed and 1/2 remains, so answer (A) is incorrect. After 4 days, 1/2 of the 1/2, or 1/4, remains, so 3/4 has decayed. Thus answers (B), (C), and (D) are not possible. After 6 days, 1/2 of the 1/4, or 1/8, remains, which means 7/8 of the original amount has decayed.

56. **(E)**

Some unstable nuclei emit alpha particles, some emit beta particles, and gamma particles usually accompany both types of emission. Thus (A), (B), and (C) are correct, making the answer (E).

57. **(C)**

Since the nucleon number is reduced by one, answers (A), (D), and (E) are incorrect, and since the charge number doesn't change, answer (B) is also incorrect, leaving as the only possibility the production of a neutron.

58. **(A)**

The area of the copper expands, so answers (C) and (D) are incorrect. The linear circumference of the hole also expands, leaving the sheet larger and the hole larger, so answers (B) and (E) are also incorrect.

59. **(C)**

The freezing point is the temperature at which the slope of the line is zero, since no change in temperature occurs during freezing. This eliminates answers (A), (B), and (D). Although answer (E) has a slope of zero, it is the second such area where the slope is zero, which indicates the second phase change, not freezing, which is the first to occur.

60. **(E)**

Like question 59, the boiling point occurs when the slope is zero, since no temperature change occurs during boiling. This again eliminates answers (A), (B), and (D). Since it is the second phase change possible, (C) is incorrect, because it is the temperature at which freezing occurs.

61. **(A)**

The amount of heat needed to melt the substance and to vaporize it is the same: 200 calories per gram. Thus the ratio is 1:1.

62. **(A)**

During the solid phase, from 10 to 20 degrees, the substance absorbs 100 calories, making the heat capacity Q/T equal to 100/10, or 10 cal/C degree.

63. **(C)**

Since the heat of fusion of ice is about 80 cal/g, then to melt 1 gram of ice would require 80 calories, which is just enough to raise the temperature of 1 gram of water 80°, since the specific heat of water is 1 cal/g °C. It takes 540 calories to vaporize or condense a gram of water, so answers (A) and (B) are incorrect. Copper doesn't melt at 0°C, so answer (D) is incorrect. And it would take about 400 calories to melt 5 grams of ice, so answer (E) is also incorrect.

64. **(C)**
First you must change the temperatures to Kelvin, which becomes 473 and 373. Then you use

$$\{T_1 - T_2\} / T_1$$

to get .21, or 21%. Answer (A) is often incorrectly attained when you forget to change the temperatures to Kelvin.

65. **(E)**
The Coulomb's Law force between two charges is equal to the constant k times the product of the two charges divided by the square of the distance from their centers and is indicated by lines of force, thus making statements (A), (B), (C), and (D) all true. But in no way is the force dependent upon the mass of a charged object, so answer (E) is the false statement.

66. **(D)**
In parallel circuits the total capacitance is simply the sum of the individual capacitors, so

$$2 + 2 + 2 = 6 \text{ farads.}$$

67. **(C)**
In series circuits the reciprocal of the sum of the reciprocals is the total capacitance, so

$$1/C_T = 1/C_1 + 1/C_2 + 1/C_3,$$

or $1/2 + 1/2 + 1/2 = 3/2,$

which becomes 2/3 farads.

68. **(E)**
Since

$$F = qvB \sin \theta,$$

it depends on all quantities except the potential difference in volts, answer (E).

69. **(C)**
    The wattage can be computed easily by

    $$P = IV,$$

so   50 amps × 12 volts = 60 watts.

Answer (A) derives from incorrectly dividing volts by amps, answer (B) from incorrectly dividing amps by volts, and answer (E) is from squaring amps and then multiplying times volts. Answer (D) derives from doubling amps and then multiplying by volts.

70. **(B)**
    The resistance can be computed easily by solving Ohm's Law for R,

    $$R = V/I,$$

so   12 volts/5 amps = 2.4 ohms.

Another possible way to reach the same solution would be to use

    $$P = I^2R.$$

Solving for R,

    $$R = P/I^2,$$

so   60 watts/25 amps^2 = 2.4 ohms.

71. **(E)**
    A watt is a joule/sec, which is a unit of power, so answer (A) is correct. You achieve the same result when multiplying a coul/sec times a joule/coul so answer (B) is also correct.

    $$I^2 \times R,$$

where I = amp = coul/sec,

and R = volt/amp,

for power, results in answer (C) also being correct. Thus (E) is the correct answer.

72. **(D)**
    Since

    $$V = iR + q/C$$

in an RC circuit we need two quantities added together that both produce volts. Answers (A), (B), and (E) do not produce the correct units and are not added together. Answer (C) adds joule/volt to coul/sec. Only answer

(D) correctly adds coul/sec × volt/amp, which equals volts to coul divided by coul/volt, which also equals volts.

73.   **(A)**
Ohm's Law states that
$$V = IR,$$
so the first term must be equal to volts or joule/coul, the units that make up volts. This eliminates answers (B), (C), and (D). The other two terms must be a product that will produce volts such as current (coul/sec) times resistance (volts/amp). This is done in answer (A), but answer (E) multiplies amps times watts, which is incorrect.

74.   **(E)**
As a current-carrying loop rotates in a magnetic field, the torque changes from a maximum when the plane of the loop is parallel to a minimum when it is perpendicular to the direction of the B field. Thus an angle of 0 degrees, answer (A), between the plane of the loop and the magnetic field would produce a maximum torque that would decrease as the angle increases to 90 degrees, answer (E), to produce the minimum torque.

75.   **(B)**
The B field can be measured in webers/meter^2 or, since
$$F = qvB,$$
$$B = \frac{F}{qv} = \frac{\text{force}}{(\text{charge} / \text{velocity})} \quad \text{or in units} \quad \frac{\text{N}}{\text{coul}(\text{meter} / \text{sec})}$$

rearranging the units
$$\frac{\text{N}}{(\text{coul} / \text{sec})\text{meter}} \quad \text{or} \quad \frac{\text{N}}{(\text{amp})\text{meter}},$$

which is also known as a tesla. This eliminates answers (A), (C), and (E), because, although they contain webers, none of them are divided by m^2. Answer (D) is also incorrect, as it would produce only an amp (meter).

SAT II:
PHYSICS

Test 5

SAT II IN PHYSICS
TEST 5
ANSWER SHEET

1. Ⓐ Ⓑ Ⓒ Ⓓ Ⓔ	26. Ⓐ Ⓑ Ⓒ Ⓓ Ⓔ	51. Ⓐ Ⓑ Ⓒ Ⓓ Ⓔ
2. Ⓐ Ⓑ Ⓒ Ⓓ Ⓔ	27. Ⓐ Ⓑ Ⓒ Ⓓ Ⓔ	52. Ⓐ Ⓑ Ⓒ Ⓓ Ⓔ
3. Ⓐ Ⓑ Ⓒ Ⓓ Ⓔ	28. Ⓐ Ⓑ Ⓒ Ⓓ Ⓔ	53. Ⓐ Ⓑ Ⓒ Ⓓ Ⓔ
4. Ⓐ Ⓑ Ⓒ Ⓓ Ⓔ	29. Ⓐ Ⓑ Ⓒ Ⓓ Ⓔ	54. Ⓐ Ⓑ Ⓒ Ⓓ Ⓔ
5. Ⓐ Ⓑ Ⓒ Ⓓ Ⓔ	30. Ⓐ Ⓑ Ⓒ Ⓓ Ⓔ	55. Ⓐ Ⓑ Ⓒ Ⓓ Ⓔ
6. Ⓐ Ⓑ Ⓒ Ⓓ Ⓔ	31. Ⓐ Ⓑ Ⓒ Ⓓ Ⓔ	56. Ⓐ Ⓑ Ⓒ Ⓓ Ⓔ
7. Ⓐ Ⓑ Ⓒ Ⓓ Ⓔ	32. Ⓐ Ⓑ Ⓒ Ⓓ Ⓔ	57. Ⓐ Ⓑ Ⓒ Ⓓ Ⓔ
8. Ⓐ Ⓑ Ⓒ Ⓓ Ⓔ	33. Ⓐ Ⓑ Ⓒ Ⓓ Ⓔ	58. Ⓐ Ⓑ Ⓒ Ⓓ Ⓔ
9. Ⓐ Ⓑ Ⓒ Ⓓ Ⓔ	34. Ⓐ Ⓑ Ⓒ Ⓓ Ⓔ	59. Ⓐ Ⓑ Ⓒ Ⓓ Ⓔ
10. Ⓐ Ⓑ Ⓒ Ⓓ Ⓔ	35. Ⓐ Ⓑ Ⓒ Ⓓ Ⓔ	60. Ⓐ Ⓑ Ⓒ Ⓓ Ⓔ
11. Ⓐ Ⓑ Ⓒ Ⓓ Ⓔ	36. Ⓐ Ⓑ Ⓒ Ⓓ Ⓔ	61. Ⓐ Ⓑ Ⓒ Ⓓ Ⓔ
12. Ⓐ Ⓑ Ⓒ Ⓓ Ⓔ	37. Ⓐ Ⓑ Ⓒ Ⓓ Ⓔ	62. Ⓐ Ⓑ Ⓒ Ⓓ Ⓔ
13. Ⓐ Ⓑ Ⓒ Ⓓ Ⓔ	38. Ⓐ Ⓑ Ⓒ Ⓓ Ⓔ	63. Ⓐ Ⓑ Ⓒ Ⓓ Ⓔ
14. Ⓐ Ⓑ Ⓒ Ⓓ Ⓔ	39. Ⓐ Ⓑ Ⓒ Ⓓ Ⓔ	64. Ⓐ Ⓑ Ⓒ Ⓓ Ⓔ
15. Ⓐ Ⓑ Ⓒ Ⓓ Ⓔ	40. Ⓐ Ⓑ Ⓒ Ⓓ Ⓔ	65. Ⓐ Ⓑ Ⓒ Ⓓ Ⓔ
16. Ⓐ Ⓑ Ⓒ Ⓓ Ⓔ	41. Ⓐ Ⓑ Ⓒ Ⓓ Ⓔ	66. Ⓐ Ⓑ Ⓒ Ⓓ Ⓔ
17. Ⓐ Ⓑ Ⓒ Ⓓ Ⓔ	42. Ⓐ Ⓑ Ⓒ Ⓓ Ⓔ	67. Ⓐ Ⓑ Ⓒ Ⓓ Ⓔ
18. Ⓐ Ⓑ Ⓒ Ⓓ Ⓔ	43. Ⓐ Ⓑ Ⓒ Ⓓ Ⓔ	68. Ⓐ Ⓑ Ⓒ Ⓓ Ⓔ
19. Ⓐ Ⓑ Ⓒ Ⓓ Ⓔ	44. Ⓐ Ⓑ Ⓒ Ⓓ Ⓔ	69. Ⓐ Ⓑ Ⓒ Ⓓ Ⓔ
20. Ⓐ Ⓑ Ⓒ Ⓓ Ⓔ	45. Ⓐ Ⓑ Ⓒ Ⓓ Ⓔ	70. Ⓐ Ⓑ Ⓒ Ⓓ Ⓔ
21. Ⓐ Ⓑ Ⓒ Ⓓ Ⓔ	46. Ⓐ Ⓑ Ⓒ Ⓓ Ⓔ	71. Ⓐ Ⓑ Ⓒ Ⓓ Ⓔ
22. Ⓐ Ⓑ Ⓒ Ⓓ Ⓔ	47. Ⓐ Ⓑ Ⓒ Ⓓ Ⓔ	72. Ⓐ Ⓑ Ⓒ Ⓓ Ⓔ
23. Ⓐ Ⓑ Ⓒ Ⓓ Ⓔ	48. Ⓐ Ⓑ Ⓒ Ⓓ Ⓔ	73. Ⓐ Ⓑ Ⓒ Ⓓ Ⓔ
24. Ⓐ Ⓑ Ⓒ Ⓓ Ⓔ	49. Ⓐ Ⓑ Ⓒ Ⓓ Ⓔ	74. Ⓐ Ⓑ Ⓒ Ⓓ Ⓔ
25. Ⓐ Ⓑ Ⓒ Ⓓ Ⓔ	50. Ⓐ Ⓑ Ⓒ Ⓓ Ⓔ	75. Ⓐ Ⓑ Ⓒ Ⓓ Ⓔ

SAT II IN

PHYSICS

TEST 5

TIME: 170 Minutes
75 Questions

DIRECTIONS: Each of the questions or incomplete statements below is followed by five answer choices or completions. Choose the best answer to each question.

---

1. A graph of the distance traveled, plotted against the elapsed time for the case of a car which is accelerated at a constant 7 miles per hour per second, would be similar to the graph of

   (A) an inverse proportion.

   (B) a direct proportion.

   (C) an inverse square function.

   (D) a direct square function.

   (E) an indirect function.

2. A car decelerates from 60 m/s to rest in a distance of 240 m. The deceleration is _____ m/s^2.

   (A) 120   (B) 40

   (C) 15   (D) 10

   (E) 7.5

3. According to the diagram, the x component of A is

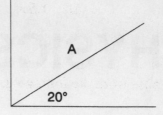

(A) A tan 20°.   (B) A cos 20°.

(C) A sin 20°.   (D) 0.

(E) A.

4. For a force system to come into equilibrium it must be balanced by

(A) an equilibriant.   (B) a torque.

(C) a joule.   (D) a watt.

(E) None of the above.

5. A balloon is seen to fall with constant speed. This constant speed is best explained by

(A) gravity supplies a constant pull.

(B) the retarding force of air friction exceeds the force of gravity allowing zero acceleration.

(C) the net force upon it is zero.

(D) the buoyant force is exceeded by the force of gravity.

(E) the acceleration is constant.

6. If a force F causes mass M to accelerate at a rate A, then a force of $3F$ will cause a mass of $1/2$ M to accelerate at a rate

(A) 2 *A*.   (B) 2/3 *A*.

(C) 3 *A*.   (D) 1.5 *A*.

(E) 6 *A*.

For **QUESTIONS 7-9** choose from the following:

   I.   Reflection

   II.   Refraction

   III. Diffraction

   IV. Interference

   V.   Regelation

7.   Term not associated with light.

   (A) I   (B) II

   (C) III   (D) IV

   (E) V

8.   Bending of a wave around a barrier or through a small opening.

   (A) I   (B) II

   (C) III   (D) IV

   (E) V

9.   Used to produce beats with sound waves.

   (A) I   (B) II

   (C) III   (D) IV

   (E) V

10. The ratio of an object's weight to its mass is equal to the object's

   (A) acceleration due to gravity.

   (B) gravitational mass.

   (C) inertial mass.

   (D) velocity.

   (E) gravitational force.

11. As an object falls, its potential energy

   (A) decreases.

   (B) increases.

   (C) remains the same.

   (D) is converted to chemical energy.

   (E) creates energy.

12. A 5 kg cart accelerates at 3 m/s^2 for 4 seconds. After this time, what is its kinetic energy?

   (A) 22.5 J   (B) 60 J

   (C) 180 J   (D) 360 J

   (E) 720 J

13. A change in momentum is NOT equal to which of the following?

   (A) Kinetic energy

   (B) Impulse

   (C) Force × change in time

(D)   Mass × change in velocity

(E)   kg m/s

14.   In order to change the momentum of an object there must be

(A)   a change in time.

(B)   a change in distance.

(C)   a force applied.

(D)   a change in temperature.

(E)   a voltage applied.

15.   Ball bearings are used much like wheels to

(A)   reduce noise.

(B)   add weight for equilibrium.

(C)   reduce friction.

(D)   decrease cost of machine.

(E)   allow for expansion.

16.   When an object slides at constant speed down an incline, the coefficient of friction may be approximated by

(A)   sin θ.

(B)   cos θ.

(C)   tan θ.

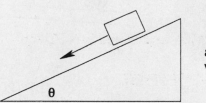

a = 0
v = constant

(D)   cot θ.

(E)   inverse sin θ.

17. Two equal forces will be in equilibrium when the angle between them is

(A) 0°.   (B) 45°.

(C) 90°.   (D) 135°.

(E) 180°.

18. What force is required to accelerate a block up an incline?

(A) Force weight component parallel to incline

(B) Force of friction

(C) Mass of block × net acceleration

(D) All of the above.

(E) None of the above.

19. If a force of 5 pounds is applied 5 inches from the hinge of a nut-cracker, the resistance offered by a nut placed one inch from the hinge is

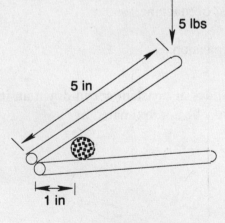

(A) 15 lbs.   (B) 20 lbs.

(C) 25 lbs.   (D) 30 lbs.

(E) 50 lbs.

20. Torque is measured in

    (A) pounds.   (B) joules.

    (C) newtons.   (D) ft-lbs.

    (E) kilograms.

21. The value for the Universal Gravitation constant is

    (A) 3×10^8 m/s.   (B) 9×10^9 N-m.

    (C) 6.67×10^{-11} N-m^2/kg^2.   (D) 100 kg.

    (E) 7.2.

For **QUESTIONS 22-24** choose from the following:

    I.   Lines of force

    II.   Dielectric

    III. Potential gradient

    IV.   Permitivity of free space

    V.   Equipotential surface.

22. Insulating materials used in capacitors

    (A) I   (B) II

    (C) III   (D) IV

    (E) V

23. A constant equal to 8.854×10^{-12} F/m.

    (A) I   (B) II

(C) III

(D) IV

(E) V

24. Numerically equal to the electrical field strength.

(A) I

(B) II

(C) III

(D) IV

(E) V

25. Hooke's Law is used to explain

(A) expansion of gases.

(B) pressure of a gas.

(C) pressure of liquids.

(D) ratio between stress and strain of a spring.

(E) thermodynamics.

26. Which of the following will cause the period of a pendulum to be doubled?

(A) Doubling the length

(B) Doubling the mass

(C) Doubling the acceleration of gravity

(D) Increasing the mass by a factor of 4

(E) Increasing the length by a factor of 4

27. One of the implications of the formula for calculating relativistic mass is that

(A) the mass of an object decreases when its velocity increases.

(B) the mass of an object increases when its velocity increases.

(C) some of the mass can be changed into velocity.

(D) some of the velocity can be changed into mass.

(E) mass and velocity are synonymous.

28. As the angle between two concurrent forces of 16 and 12 newtons increases from 90° to 180°, the magnitude of the resultant changes from

(A) 28 to 4.   (B) 28 to 20.

(C) 20 to 4.   (D) 4 to 28.

(E) 4 to 20.

29. The number of calories required to melt 15 grams of ice at 0°C is

(A) 100.   (B) 400.

(C) 800.   (D) 1200.

(E) 2000.

30. The heat from a radiator is spread throughout the room by

(A) convection.   (B) absorption.

(C) conduction.   (D) radiation.

(E) sublimation.

31. If the velocity of electromagnetic waves is 300,000,000 meters per second, the frequency of a 6 meter radio wave is

(A) 50 million hertz.   (B) 500 million hertz.

(C)   100 million hertz.   (D)   33 hertz.

(E)   .33 hertz.

For **QUESTIONS 32-34** choose from the following:

I.   Radio waves

II.   Light waves

III.   X-rays

IV.   Ultraviolet

V.   Sound waves

32.   Which are NOT electromagnetic waves?

(A) I   (B) II

(C) III   (D) IV

(E) V

33.   Region that contains microwaves.

(A) I   (B) II

(C) III   (D) IV

(E) V

34.   High energy electrons.

(A) I   (B) II

(C) III   (D) IV

(E) V

35. The speed of sound is fastest in

    (A) steel.   (B) water.

    (C) air.   (D) vacuum.

    (E) Same in all materials.

36. When an object is between the principal focus and a concave mirror the image is

    (A) virtual.

    (B) inverted.

    (C) reduced in size.

    (D) located in front of the mirror.

    (E) located at the focus.

37. An example of the polarization of light can be seen in

    (A) cameras.   (B) sunlamps.

    (C) sunglasses.   (D) eclipses.

    (E) colors.

38. The acceleration of the 5 kg mass (in m/s^2) is

    (A) 4.2.

    (B) 3.92.

    (C) 2.33.

    (D) .428.

    (E) .4.

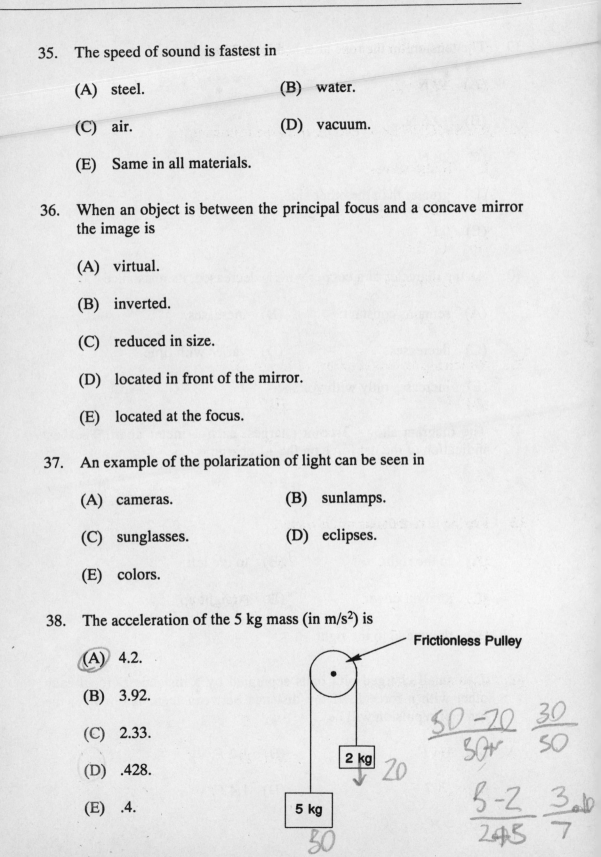

Frictionless Pulley

$$\frac{50 - 70}{30+} \quad \frac{30}{50}$$

2 kg 20

5 kg 50

$$\frac{5-2}{2+5} \quad \frac{3}{7}$$

39. The tension on the rope attached to the 5 kg mass is

(A) 49 N.

(B) 19.6 N.

(C) 28 N.

(D) greater than the other side.

(E) 0 N.

40. As the diameter of a copper wire is decreased, its resistance

(A) remains constant.   (B) increases.

(C) decreases.   (D) varies with time.

(E) increases only with voltage.

41. The diagram shows 3 point charges, each 1 meter apart. The best indication of the net force on the +1 charge is

0 + 1

+ 2 0   0 + 2

(A) to the right.   (B) to the left.

(C) straight down.   (D) straight up.

(E) down and to the right.

42. Two small charged pith balls separated by a distance D repel each other with a force F. If the distance between them is doubled, the force of repulsion will be

(A) 1/4 F.   (B) 1/2 F.

(C) .707 F.   (D) 1.4 F.

(E) 4 F.

For **QUESTIONS 43-45** choose from the following:

I. Rheostat

II. Capacitor

III. Resistor

IV. Solenoid

V. Motor

43. The opposite of a generator.

(A) I   (B) II

(C) III   (D) IV

(E) V

44. A conducting loop in the form of a helix.

(A) I   (B) II

(C) III   (D) IV

(E) V

45. A dimmer control is an example.

(A) I   (B) II

(C) III   (D) IV

(E) V

46. The magnitude of an induced EMF is dependent on

(A) mass and charge.   (B) velocity.

(C) gravity. (D) temperature and area.

(E) magnetic flux and time.

47. The discovery of Millikan's determination of the charge on an electron used

(A) glass beads. (B) mathematical theory.

(C) oil drops. (D) gamma rays.

(E) photons.

For **QUESTIONS 48-50** choose from the following:

I. Conduction

II. Convection

III. Radiation

IV. Thermal conductivity

V. Stefan's Law

48. Rate of heat flow to cross sectional area and temperature gradient.

(A) I (B) II

(C) III (D) IV

(E) V

49. Transfer of thermal energy without the use of a material medium.

(A) I (B) II

(C) III (D) IV

(E) V

50. Transfer of thermal energy without the flow of a material medium, but a medium is required.

    (A) I

    (B) II

    (C) III

    (D) IV

    (E) V

51. Which is NOT true of radioactive elements?

    (A) Cause special physiological effects

    (B) Undergo decay

    (C) Produce an electric charge

    (D) Affect emulsion on photographic film

    (E) Are all artificially made

52. Which unit is NOT used with radioactivity?

    (A) Roentgen

    (B) Rad

    (C) Barn

    (D) Weber

    (E) Curie

53. Which is NOT true of fission?

    (A) Neutron bombardment

    (B) Graphite, water, and beryllium moderators

    (C) High temperature plasma

    (D) First reactor built in Chicago in 1942

    (E) Uranium fuel pellets

For **QUESTIONS 54-57** choose the best answer from the following choices.

    I.   Isobaric

    II.   Isometric

    III. Isothermal

    IV. Adiabatic

    V.   Carnot cycle

54. A process through which pressure is inversely proportional to volume.

    (A) I   (B) II

    (C) III   (D) IV

    (E) V

55. A process in which P, V, and T all change but no heat flows into or out of the system.

    (A) I   (B) II

    (C) III   (D) IV

    (E) V

56. A process through which temperature and volume remain directly proportional.

    (A) I   (B) II

    (C) III   (D) IV

    (E) V

57. A process through which temperature and pressure remain directly proportional.

(A) I (B) II

(C) III (D) IV

(E) V

For **QUESTIONS 58-60** choose the best answer that identifies the particle or process involved.

I. α

II. $\beta -$

III. $\beta +$

IV. γ

V. Electron capture

58. A radioactive decay mode in which a photon is emitted.

(A) I (B) II

(C) III (D) IV

(E) V

59. A radioactive decay mode in which an electron is emitted.

(A) I (B) II

(C) III (D) IV

(E) V

60. A radioactive decay mode in which an electron is absorbed.

(A) I (B) II

(C) III   (D) IV

(E) V

61. An object weighing 100 N at the earth's surface is moved to a distance of 3 earth radii from the surface of the earth. It's new weight will be

(A) 25 N.   (B) 33.3 N.

(C) 11.1 N.   (D) 6.25 N.

(E) 400 N.

62. Which is NOT true of a longitudinal wave?

(A) Displaces the medium parallel to the wave velocity

(B) Has a series of compressions and rarefactions

(C) Transmits sound

(D) May interfere with other longitudinal waves

(E) Can be seen by plucking a guitar string

For **QUESTIONS 63-65** choose the best answer that identifies the application of the following devices.

I.   Camera

II. Telescope

III. Microscope

IV. Slide Projector

V.   Dish Antenna

63. A mirror-like object that focuses the image at a point at the focus.

    (A) I   (B) II

    (C) III   (D) IV

    (E) V

64. Uses a single lens to produce inverted and reduced images.

    (A) I   (B) II

    (C) III   (D) IV

    (E) V

65. Uses a single lens to produce an inverted and enlarged image.

    (A) I   (B) II

    (C) III   (D) IV

    (E) V

For **QUESTIONS 66 and 67** choose the best answer from the following.

    I.   Conservation of momentum

    II. Conservation of energy

    III. Conservation of velocity

66. Always conserved in all collisions.

    (A) I   (B) II

    (C) III   (D) Both I and II.

    (E) Both II and III.

67. Conserved in perfectly elastic collisions.

(A) I

(B) II

(C) III

(D) Both I and II.

(E) Both II and III.

For **QUESTIONS 68-70** identify the quantity or combination of quantities that best answers the question.

I.   Mass

II.   Distance

III. Displacement

IV.   Speed

V.   Velocity

68. Which are vector quantities?

(A) I, II, and IV.

(B) III and V.

(C) IV and V.

(D) All of the above.

(E) None of the above.

69. Fundamental quantities besides time.

(A) I and IV.

(B) II and V.

(C) I and II.

(D) III and V.

(E) III and IV.

70. Equal to momentum.

(A) I × II.

(B) II × V.

(C) III × V.   (D) I × V.

(E) V × V.

For **QUESTIONS 71 and 72** choose from the following.

   I.   Real, inverted, reduced

   II.   Real, inverted, same size

   III. Real, inverted, enlarged

   IV. Virtual, erect, enlarged

   V.   Virtual, erect, reduced

71. What would best describe the image of an object 18 cm in front of a concave mirror with a focal length of 15 cm?

   (A) I   (B) II

   (C) III   (D) IV

   (E) V

72. What would best describe the image of an object placed 10 cm in front of a concave lens of focal length 15 cm?

   (A) I   (B) II

   (C) III   (D) IV

   (E) V

73. In a step-up transformer, if there are 20 turns on the secondary for each turn on the primary, then a primary voltage of 110 volts becomes

(A) 5.5 V.

(B) 110 V.

(C) 130 V.

(D) 2200 V.

(E) 11,000 V.

For **QUESTIONS 74 and 75** choose from the five circuit diagrams of 4 resistors of 10 ohms each wired in 5 of the possible combinations.

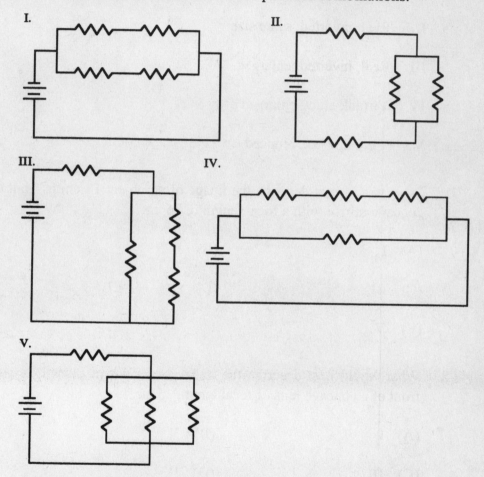

I.

II.

III.

IV.

V.

74. Which of the five combinations shown produces the least total resistance?

(A) I

(B) II

(C) III

(D) IV

(E) V

75. Which of the five possible combinations produces the largest total resistance?

(A) I

(B) II

(C) III

(D) IV

(E) V

STOP

If time still remains, you may review work only on this test.
You may not work on any other test in this book until time has elapsed.

TEST 5

ANSWER KEY

1.	(D)	21.	(C)	41.	(D)	61.	(D)
2.	(E)	22.	(B)	42.	(A)	62.	(E)
3.	(B)	23.	(D)	43.	(E)	63.	(E)
4.	(A)	24.	(C)	44.	(D)	64.	(A)
5.	(C)	25.	(D)	45.	(A)	65.	(D)
6.	(E)	26.	(E)	46.	(E)	66.	(A)
7.	(E)	27.	(B)	47.	(C)	67.	(D)
8.	(C)	28.	(C)	48.	(D)	68.	(B)
9.	(D)	29.	(D)	49.	(C)	69.	(C)
10.	(A)	30.	(A)	50.	(A)	70.	(D)
11.	(A)	31.	(A)	51.	(E)	71.	(C)
12.	(D)	32.	(E)	52.	(D)	72.	(E)
13.	(A)	33.	(A)	53.	(C)	73.	(D)
14.	(C)	34.	(C)	54.	(C)	74.	(D)
15.	(C)	35.	(A)	55.	(D)	75.	(B)
16.	(C)	36.	(A)	56.	(A)		
17.	(E)	37.	(C)	57.	(B)		
18.	(D)	38.	(A)	58.	(D)		
19.	(C)	39.	(C)	59.	(B)		
20.	(D)	40.	(B)	60.	(E)		

DETAILED EXPLANATIONS
OF ANSWERS

TEST 5

1. **(D)**
    If you were plotting velocity vs. time, the graph would be a direct proportion (B) or indirect (E) if the acceleration had been negative. Since time is not multiplied by distance it cannot be an inverse function, thus answers (A) and (C) are incorrect, but the constant acceleration is proportional to the ratio of distance to time squared.

2. **(E)**
    One way to solve this problem is to determine the average velocity first.

    $$v_{Avg} = (v_f + v_i)/2 = (0 + 60 \text{ m/s})/2 = 30 \text{ m/s},$$

    Then to determine the time needed to go 240 m using

    $$d = vt$$

    $$t = d/v = 240 \text{ m} / 30\text{m/s} = 8 \text{ sec}$$

    Finally to get the acceleration

    $$a = (v_f - v_i) / t = (0 - 60 \text{ m/s}) / 8 \text{ sec} = 7.5 \text{ m/s}^2$$

3. **(B)**
    In calculating the x component by dropping a perpendicular to the x axis and creating a right triangle and using the cosine function such that

    $$\text{cosine } 20 = x/A,$$

    you may then solve for x and get

    $$x = A \cos 20.$$

4. **(A)**
    An equilibrant is the single force needed to bring an unbalanced system into equilibrium such that the net force is zero. A torque (B) is a

force times a perpendicular distance, a joule (C) is a unit of work, and a watt (D) is a unit of power.

5. **(C)**

All of the other answers express a net force or some acceleration, not constant velocity, which is accomplished with no net force or zero acceleration.

6. **(E)**

Acceleration is directly proportional to force, so a force of $3\,F$ on a mass M would cause an acceleration $3A$. Acceleration is also inversely proportional to mass so that cutting the mass in half would double the acceleration. The combination of the two then produces 6 times the amount of acceleration.

7. **(E)**

Reflection (I) is the bouncing back of a beam of light or a wave at a barrier. Refraction (II) is the changing speed upon entering a new medium. Diffraction (III) is the bending of a wave around a barrier or through a small opening. Interference (IV) is the superimposing of one wave on another, but regelation is a term for melting under pressure.

8. **(C)**
See explanation 7.

9. **(D)**
See explanation 7. Beats are produced by the interference of two waves of slightly different frequency.

10. **(A)**

$$W/m = g.$$

By definition a newton is 1 kg accelerated at 1 m/s^2 so N/kg gives you units for acceleration. In this case the force is the weight and when divided by its mass the acceleration is that due to gravity. Answers (B) and (C) are incorrect because they are mass not acceleration. Answer (D) is incorrect because it is velocity (m/s) not acceleration (m/s^2) and answer (E) is incorrect because gravitational force is the weight of the object.

11. **(A)**

Potential energy, mgh, decreases with height, thus answer (A) is true and answers (B) and (C) are false. Energy cannot be created so answer (E) is incorrect, but some is converted to overcome friction and to kinetic energy but not chemical energy as described in answer (D).

12. **(D)**
    In order to use the equation for kinetic energy of one half mass times velocity squared you must determine the velocity to be acceleration times time

$$v = at = 3m/s/s(4s) = 12 \text{ m/s}$$

therefore, kinetic energy is

$$1/2 \ mv^2 = 1/2 \ (5 \text{ kg}) (12 \text{ m/s})^2 = 360 \text{ joules}.$$

13. **(A)**
    Impulse (B) which is force × time (C) is numerically equal to the change in momentum which is mass × change in velocity (D) and measured in units of kg m/s (E). Kinetic energy, however, is measured in joules according to one half mass times velocity squared.

14. **(C)**
    To change its momentum, mv, an object must change mass or velocity. According to Newton's second law a net force must be applied in order to accelerate, that is a change in velocity. A different place (B) or interval of time (A), or a different temperature (D), or an applied voltage (E) would not change its mass or velocity.

15. **(C)**
    The smoothness of the surface and the ability to roll rather than slide allows ball bearings to greatly reduce friction. Adding weight would not help equilibrium so answer (B) is incorrect. The other three answers (A), (D), and (E) may be a beneficial by-product, but the main reason is the reduction in friction.

16. **(C)**
    Since the coefficient of friction is the force of friction divided by the force normal to the surface, if it is sliding down at constant speed with no outside forces acting on it, then the force parallel component, $mg \sin \theta$, is equal to the force of friction and the force normal component is $mg \cos \theta$. Dividing the two to get the coefficient of friction causes mg to cancel leaving $\sin \theta / \cos \theta$ which is $\tan \theta$, therefore $\tan \theta$ is equal to the coefficient of friction in this special case.

17. **(E)**

For two equal forces to produce equilibrium they must be in opposite directions or 180 degrees apart, so that their sum is zero.

18. **(D)**

In order to go up even a frictionless incline at constant speed, you need a force equal to the force weight component parallel to the incline, answer (A). Added to that then must be any frictional force that must be overcome, that is answer (A) + (B) and you are still only going at constant speed. Some additional force determined by the mass and the desired acceleration must be included to accelerate up the incline. So the correct answer must contain (A) + (B) + (C).

19. **(C)**

In balancing the torques as measured from the hinge, then 5 pounds times 5 inches would ideally balance 25 pounds at one inch.

20. **(D)**

Torque or moments as mentioned in some texts is determined by the product of a force perpendicularly applied and some distance from an axis of rotation. Although joules are N × m, they are defined as units of work and the force is parallel to the distance, thus answer (B) is incorrect. The only correct answer then is ft-lbs. Answers (A) and (C) are measurements of force only and answer (E) is mass only.

21. **(C)**

This number, verified by Cavendish, is the only one containing the appropriate units to produce the proper units in the equation for gravitational force. (I) is the speed of light, (II) is the number used in Coulomb's Law but the units are entirely wrong, (IV) is a quantity of mass and (V) is a constant with no units.

22. **(B)**

The name given for different materials used to store charge in a capacitor.

23. **(D)**

The constant used in conjunction with 4π to determine the constant k in Coulomb's Law.

24. **(C)**
    The potential gradient in volts/meter is numerically the same as the electrical field strength in newtons/coulomb. Lines of force (A) indicate the direction of the electric field and are perpendicular to the equipotential surfaces. An equipotential surface (E) is an area where the voltage is the same.

25. **(D)**
    Hooke's Law,

    $$F = kx$$

    states that the greater the force applied the more it stretches or bends, so the ratio of stress, F/A to strain, change in length/length, would be an example. Answers (A) and (B) are incorrect because the expansion and pressure of a gas deals with gas laws like Charles and Boyle's. A liquid is almost incompressible, but pressure is dealt with in Bernoulli's Equation and the Laws of Thermodynamics deal with heat engines, thus answers (C) and (E) are incorrect.

26. **(E)**
    Since the period of a pendulum is proportional to the square root of the length, the square root of 4 would double the period so the length would have to be increased by a factor of four. The mass has no effect except determining the distance to where the center of mass is located so answers (B) and (D) are incorrect. Doubling the acceleration due to gravity would decrease the period, thus making answer (C) incorrect. Doubling the length would only increase the period by the square root of 2 so answer (A) is also incorrect.

27. **(B)**
    Indeed we have shown in particle accelerators that mass does in fact increase as we approach the speed of light, thus answer (A) is incorrect. Mass can be changed into energy, but it is not equivalent to velocity, which makes answers (C), (D), and (E) incorrect.

28. **(C)**
    At 90 degrees the resultant would be a 20 by pythagoras theorem and would decrease to 4 by addition of a positive 16 with a negative 12 at 180 degrees. (A) goes from 0 to 180 degrees. (B) goes from 0 to 90 degrees. (D) goes from 180 to 0 degrees and (E) goes from 180 to 90 degrees.

29. **(D)**

Q, the quantity of heat needed, equals the mass times the latent heat of fusion.

$$Q = m L_f$$
$$= 15 \text{ g} \times 80 \text{ cal/g}$$
$$= 1200 \text{ calories}$$

30. **(A)**

Convection uses currents of air of a fluid to transport the heat throughout the room. Conduction (C) is direct contact to the heat source, absorption (B) deals with radiant energy, (D) is heat without a medium to transport it, and (E) is a phase change.

31. **(A)**

Using $v = f$(wavelength), then

$$f = v/\text{wavelength}$$
$$= 300,000,000 \text{ m/s} / 6 \text{ m}$$
$$= 50,000,000 \text{ hertz}$$

32. **(E)**

Sound waves are longitudinal compression waves that require a medium and are therefore not electromagnetic waves.

33. **(A)**

Microwaves lie in the radio wave region.

34. **(C)**

High energy electrons describe the x-ray region, (B) contains visible light from 4000 to 7600 angstroms, and ultraviolet is just above the visible spectrum.

35. **(A)**

Sound travels fastest in solids, slower in liquids, which makes answer (B) incorrect and slowest in gases, which eliminates answers (C), (D), and (E).

36. **(A)**

Since you are inside the focal length the image is virtual, erect, enlarged, and located behind the mirror. Thus answers (B), (C), (D), and (E) are incorrect.

37. **(C)**
Sunglasses that help to cut the glare are advertised as polarized when they only allow light from one plane to pass through them. (A) takes in all the light, (B) emits light, (D) partially blocks light, and (E) is different wavelengths of light.

38. **(A)**
First you must solve for the net force

$$5(9.8) - 2(9.8) = 49 - 19.6 = 29.4 \text{ N}$$

This net force is that accelerates the entire 7 kg. Using

$$F = ma$$
$$a = F/m$$
$$= 29.4 \text{ N} / 7 \text{ kg}$$
$$= 4.2 \text{ m/s/s}$$

39. **(C)**
The tension on the rope may be calculated a number of ways. By summing the individual forces on each block then,

$$49 \text{ N} - T = 5 \text{ kg} \times 4.2 \text{ m/s/s}$$

or $\quad T - 19.6 \text{ N} = 2 \text{ kg} \times 4.2 \text{ m/s/s}$

Each results in the solution $T = 28$ N.

40. **(B)**
According to the laws of resistance, the resistance of a wire is inversely proportional to the cross sectional area. Since the diameter is decreasing, then the resistance would increase thus making answers (A) and (C) incorrect. Resistance is not affected by time or the amount of voltage so answers (D) and (E) are also incorrect.

41. **(D)**
Both charges will repel the + 1 charge in a direction opposite of the line going through the + 1 charge and each + 2 charge. Since the quantity of charge and the distance to the charges are the same, the force of repulsion by each are equal. These two forces when added together will be directed upward perpendicular to a line through the two + 2 charges.

42. **(A)**

Due to the inverse square law, it is easily determined that by doubling the distance, the inverse square of 2 becomes 1/4 so the force drops to $(1/4)F$.

43. **(E)**

A motor uses electrical energy current in a magnetic field to deliver work while a generator takes in mechanical work on a magnetic field to generate electrical current.

44. **(D)**

A solenoid is a long wire wound in a close-packed helix and carries a current setting up a magnetic field.

45. **(A)**

A variable resistor or rheostat is used in a circuit to control the current and thus the power delivered to part of the circuit, as in the example of a dimmer switch to control the brightness of a light. A capacitor (II) is used to store a charge and a resistor (III) is used to determine the current flow and to work done on it.

46. **(E)**

Faraday's Law of Induction says that the induced EMF in a circuit is equal to the negative rate at which the magnetic flux through the circuit is changing. Mass (A), velocity (B), gravity (C), or temperature (D) have nothing to do with it.

47. **(C)**

Millikan's oil drop experiment used bursts of x-rays to charge drops of oil which were placed in an electric field to be balanced by adjusting the field until the force was equal and opposite the weight of the oil drop. He did this experimentally so answer (B) is incorrect. He used oil drops not glass beads so answer (A) is incorrect. And he used x-rays not gamma rays or photons so answers (D) and (E) are incorrect.

48. **(D)**

Thermal conductivity is a constant for a material which measures the amount of heat flow through a cross sectional area depending on the temperature difference on both sides.

49. **(C)**
Radiation is the transfer of thermal energy through a vacuum without need for a medium.

50. **(A)**
Conduction is the transfer of heat through a substance without the material itself moving. Convection (B) is the transfer of thermal energy by currents or movement of the material itself. (E) Stefan's Law deals with the energy radiated by a blackbody radiator.

51. **(E)**
Radioactivity was first discovered as it occurred naturally around us. Elements do undergo decay as in answer (B). They can cause physiological effects as in answer (A). They can be seen because of what they do to photographic plates as in answer (D), and can be used to produce a charge as in answer (C).

52. **(D)**
The weber, answer (D) is used in connection with magnetic effects. All of the other answers are units directly related to radioactivity. Roentgen, answer (A), is an exposure unit of absorbed dose of X or Gamma radiation. A rad, answer (B), is the standard unit of absorbed dose. The barn, answer (C), is used to specify nuclear cross sections and the curie, answer (E), is a unit of radioactivity disintegrations per second.

53. **(C)**
High temperature plasmas, answer (C), are used in nuclear fusion, not fission.

54. **(C)**
In an isothermal process the temperature remains constant and the pressure varies inversely with the volume as their product must remain constant.

55. **(D)**
An adiabatic process does not allow heat to transfer into or out of the system, but work is added or removed by a change in P, V, and T.

56. **(A)**
In an isobaric process the pressure is held constant allowing the volume to vary directly with the absolute temperature.

57. **(B)**

   In an isometric or isochoric process the volume is held fixed allowing the pressure to vary directly with the absolute temperature. The carnot cycle, choice (V), is a hypothetical cycle of four reversible processes in succession.

58. **(D)**

   A gamma ray is a high energy photon emitted by a nucleus in a transition between two energy levels.

59. **(B)**

   A beta particle if negative is an electron. If the beta particle had been positive as in answer (III) then it would be a positron.

60. **(E)**

   Electron capture is a process in which an atom or ions passing through a material medium either loses or gains one or more orbital electrons. An alpha particle, answer (I), is a low energy positively charged particle.

61. **(D)**

   Using the inverse square law as it applies to universal gravitation, by increasing the distance to 3 earth radii above the surface, the new distance is 4 earth radii from the center of the earth. The inverse square of 4 is 1/16. This would cause the new weight to be 1/16 of what it was on earth.

62. **(E)**

   A longitudinal wave is a back and forth wave where the motion of the medium is parallel to the velocity of the wave. But in answer (E), a vibrating guitar string, the motion of the string is perpendicular to the velocity and is therefore a transverse wave.

63. **(E)**

   A dish antenna takes a signal from a great distance and brings it into focus at the focal point.

64. **(A)**

   A camera produces an inverted and reduced image on the film.

65. **(D)**

A slide projector requires you to place the slide in upside down since it inverts the image and enlarges it if placed at a point in front of the lens between *f* and 2*f*. A telescope, answer (II), and a microscope, answer (III), both use a combination of lenses or mirrors to produce the desired image.

66. **(A)**

Momentum is always conserved, but energy is only conserved in perfectly elastic collisions, thus making answers (B) and (D) incorrect. Velocity is not conserved so answers (C) and (E) are also incorrect.

67. **(D)**

As stated in explanation 66, momentum is always conserved and energy is also conserved in perfectly elastic collisions.

68. **(B)**

Vector quantities are those having both magnitude and direction. Mass, distance, and speed have magnitude only. This eliminates answers (A), (C), and (D). Displacement is distance in a particular direction and velocity is speed in a particular direction making them both vector quantities.

69. **(C)**

The three fundamental physical quantities are mass, length, and time. Answers (A), (B), (D), and (E) are all incorrect because they include either speed or velocity which are both measured as a rate using a combination of length and time.

70. **(D)**

Momentum is determined by mass times velocity, answer (D). The other answers produce undefined quantities.

71. **(C)**

The object is located between the focus and center of curvature so the image would be located beyond the center of curvature thereby enlarging it. This eliminates answers (A), (B), and (E). The image could be projected on a screen since it is formed by actual rays of light so that it is a real image. Thus answer (D) is incorrect.

72. **(E)**

A concave lens, like a convex mirror, only has one case possible. It always produces a virtual image. This by itself eliminates answers (A), (B), and (C). The divergence of the rays make the light from the image appear to be coming from the same side of the lens as the object at a distance closer to the lens, which means the image is reduced. This also eliminates answer (D).

73.   **(D)**

The ratio of the number of turns is the same ratio as the voltage. The primary of 110 volts is to one turn as the new voltage is to 20 turns. Thus 20 times 110 produces 2200 volts on the secondary.

74.   **(D)**

In choice (I) two resistors in series (20) plus the other two in series (20), are in parallel for a total of 10 ohms. In answer (II) one in series (10), plus two in parallel (5), plus one in series (10), would give the largest of the combinations described, a total of 25 ohms. In answer (III) two in series (20), with one in parallel (10), would be equivalent to 20/3 or 6 and 2/3 plus one more in series (10) would produce a total of 16 2/3. For answer (IV) three in series (30), plus one (10) in parallel, would add up to produce 30/4 or 7.5 ohms. Finally, answer (V) with one in series (10), with three in parallel 10/3 or 3.33 would produce an equivalent resistance of 13.33 ohms.

75.   **(B)**

See explanation 74.

REA's Problem Solvers

The "PROBLEM SOLVERS" are comprehensive supplemental text-books designed to save time in finding solutions to problems. Each "PROBLEM SOLVER" is the first of its kind ever produced in its field. It is the product of a massive effort to illustrate almost any imaginable problem in exceptional depth, detail, and clarity. Each problem is worked out in detail with a step-by-step solution, and the problems are arranged in order of complexity from elementary to advanced. Each book is fully indexed for locating problems rapidly.

ACCOUNTING
ADVANCED CALCULUS
ALGEBRA & TRIGONOMETRY
AUTOMATIC CONTROL
    SYSTEMS/ROBOTICS
BIOLOGY
BUSINESS, ACCOUNTING, & FINANCE
CALCULUS
CHEMISTRY
COMPLEX VARIABLES
COMPUTER SCIENCE
DIFFERENTIAL EQUATIONS
ECONOMICS
ELECTRICAL MACHINES
ELECTRIC CIRCUITS
ELECTROMAGNETICS
ELECTRONIC COMMUNICATIONS
ELECTRONICS
FINITE & DISCRETE MATH
FLUID MECHANICS/DYNAMICS
GENETICS
GEOMETRY

HEAT TRANSFER
LINEAR ALGEBRA
MACHINE DESIGN
MATHEMATICS for ENGINEERS
MECHANICS
NUMERICAL ANALYSIS
OPERATIONS RESEARCH
OPTICS
ORGANIC CHEMISTRY
PHYSICAL CHEMISTRY
PHYSICS
PRE-CALCULUS
PROBABILITY
PSYCHOLOGY
STATISTICS
STRENGTH OF MATERIALS &
    MECHANICS OF SOLIDS
TECHNICAL DESIGN GRAPHICS
THERMODYNAMICS
TOPOLOGY
TRANSPORT PHENOMENA
VECTOR ANALYSIS

If you would like more information about any of these books,
complete the coupon below and return it to us, or visit your local bookstore.

RESEARCH & EDUCATION ASSOCIATION
61 Ethel Road W. • Piscataway, New Jersey 08854
Phone: (732) 819-8880

Please send me more information about your Problem Solver books

Name _____

Address _____

City _____ State _____ Zip _____

Praise for Diana Palmer

'Nobody does it better.'
—*New York Times* bestselling author Linda Howard

'Ms Palmer masterfully weaves a tale that entices on many levels, blending adventure and strong human emotion into a great read.'
—*RT Book Reviews*

'Nobody tops Diana Palmer when it comes to delivering pure, undiluted romance. I love her stories.'
—*New York Times* bestselling author Jayne Ann Krentz

'Palmer knows how to make the sparks fly... heartwarming.'
—*Publishers Weekly* on *Renegade*

'A compelling tale...[that packs] an emotional wallop'
—*Publishers Weekly* on *Renegade*

'This story is a thrill a minute—one of Palmer's best.'
—*Rendezvous* on *Lord of the Desert*

Novels by **Diana Palmer**

DESPERADO
LAWLESS
AFTER MIDNIGHT
ONCE IN PARIS
DANGEROUS
PAPER ROSE
MIDNIGHT RIDER
NIGHT FEVER
ONE NIGHT IN NEW YORK
BEFORE SUNRISE
OUTSIDER
LAWMAN
HARD TO HANDLE
FEARLESS
DIAMOND SPUR
TRUE COLOURS
HEARTLESS
MERCILESS
COURAGEOUS
ROUGH DIAMONDS

Coming soon:

CHRISTMAS WITH THE RANCHER
WYOMING FIERCE
PROTECTOR
WYOMING BOLD

DIANA PALMER

ROUGH DIAMONDS

MILLS & BOON

First published in Great Britain 2013
by Mills & Boon, an imprint of Harlequin (UK) Limited, Eton House,
18-24 Paradise Road, Richmond, Surrey TW9 1SR

ROUGH DIAMONDS © Harlequin Enterprises II B.V./S.à.r.l. 2013

Wyoming Tough © Diana Palmer 2011
Diamond in the Rough © Diana Palmer 2009

ISBN: 978 0 263 91008 7

009-0813

Harlequin (UK) policy is to use papers that are natural, renewable and recyclable products and made from wood grown in sustainable forests. The logging and manufacturing processes conform to the legal environmental regulations of the country of origin.

Printed and bound by
CPI Group (UK) Ltd, Croydon, CR0 4YY

Wyoming Tough

CHAPTER ONE

EDITH DANIELLE MORENA BRANNT was not impressed with her new boss. The head honcho of the Rancho Real, or Royal Ranch in Spanish, near Catelow, Wyoming, was big and domineering and had a formidable bad attitude that he shared with all his hired hands.

Morie, as she was known to her friends, had a hard time holding back her fiery temper when Mallory Dawson Kirk raised his voice. He was impatient and hot-tempered and opinionated. Just like Morie's father, who'd opposed her decision to become a working cowgirl. Her dad opposed everything. She'd just told him she was going to find a job, packed her bags and left. She was twenty-three. He couldn't really stop her legally. Her mother, Shelby, had tried gentle reason. Her brother, Cort, had tried, too, with even less luck. She loved her family, but she was tired of being chased for who she was related to instead of who she was inside. Being a stranger on somebody else's property was an enchanting proposition.

Even with Mallory's temper, she was happy being accepted for a poor, struggling female on her own in the harsh world. Besides that, she wanted to learn ranch work and her father refused to let her so much as lift a rope on his ranch. He didn't want her near his cattle.

"And another thing," Mallory said harshly, turning to Morie with a cold glare, "there's a place to hang keys when you're through with them. You never take a key out of the stable and leave it in your pocket. Is that clear?"

Morie, who'd actually transported the key to the main tack room off the property in her pocket at a time it was desperately needed, flushed. "Sorry, sir," she said stiffly. "Won't happen again."

"It won't if you expect to keep working here," he assured her.

"My fault," the foreman, old Darby Hanes, chimed in, smiling. "I forgot to tell her."

Mallory considered that and nodded finally. "That's what I always liked most about you, Darb, you're honest." He turned to Morie. "An example I'll expect you to follow, as our newest hire, by the way."

Her face reddened. "Sir, I've never taken anything that didn't belong to me."

He looked at her cheap clothes, the ragged hem of her jeans, her worn boots. But he didn't judge. He just nodded.

He had thick black hair, parted on one side and a little shaggy around the ears. He had big ears and a big nose, deep-set brown eyes under a jutting brow, thick eyebrows and a mouth so sensuous that Morie hadn't been able to take her eyes off it at first. That mouth made up for his lack of conventional good looks. He had big, well-manicured hands and a voice like deep velvet, as well as big feet, in old, rugged, dirt-caked boots. He was the boss, and nobody ever forgot it, but he got down in the mud and blood with his men and worked as if he was just an employee himself.

In fact, all three Kirk brothers were like that. Mallory was the oldest, at thirty-six. The second brother, Cane—a coincidence if there ever was one, considering Morie's mother's maiden name, even if hers was spelled with a *K*—was thirty-four, a veteran of the Second Gulf War, and he was missing an arm from being in the front lines in combat. He was confronting a drinking problem and undergoing therapy, which his brothers were trying to address.

The youngest brother, at thirty-one, was Dalton. He was a former border agent with the department of immigration, and his nickname was, for some odd reason, Tank. He'd been confronted by a gang of narco-smugglers on the Arizona border, all alone. He was shot to pieces and hospitalized for weeks, during which most of the physicians had given him up for dead because of the extent of his injuries. He confounded them all by living. Nevertheless, he quit the job and came home to the family ranch in Wyoming. He never spoke of the experience. But once Morie had seen him react to the backfire of an old ranch truck by diving to the ground. She'd laughed, but old Darby Hanes had silenced her and told her about Dalton's past as a border agent. She'd never laughed at his odd behaviors again. She supposed that both he and Cane had mental and emotional scars, as well as physical ones, from their past experiences. She'd never been shot at, or had anything happen to her. She'd been as sheltered as a hothouse orchid, both by her parents and her brother. This was her first taste of real life. She wasn't certain yet if she was going to like it.

She'd lived on her father's enormous ranch all her life. She could ride anything—her father had taught her himself. But she wasn't accustomed to the backbreaking work that daily ranch chores required, because she hadn't been permitted to do them at home, and she'd been slow her first couple of days.

Darby Hanes had taken her in hand and shown her how to manage the big bales of hay that the brothers still packed into the barn—refusing the more modern rolled bales as being inefficient and wasteful—so that she didn't hurt herself when she lifted them. He'd taught her how to shoe horses, even though the ranch had a farrier, and how to doctor sick calves. In less than two weeks, she'd learned things that nothing in her college education had addressed.

"You've never done this work before," Darby accused, but he was smiling.

She grimaced. "No. But I needed a job, badly," she said, and it was almost the truth. "You've been great, Mr. Hanes. I owe you a lot for not giving me away. For teaching me what I needed to know here." And what a good thing it was, she thought privately, that her father didn't know. He'd have skinned Hanes alive for letting his sheltered little girl shoe a horse.

He waved a hand dismissively. "Not a problem. You make sure you wear those gloves," he added, nodding toward her back pocket. "You have beautiful hands. Like my wife used to," he added with a faraway look in his eyes and a faint smile. "She played the piano in a restaurant when I met her. We went on two dates and got married. Never had kids. She passed two years ago, from cancer." He stopped for a minute and took a long breath. "Still miss her," he added stiffly.

"I'm sorry," she said.

"I'll see her again," he replied. "Won't be too many years, either. It's part of the cycle, you see.

Life and death. We all go through it. Nobody es-
capes."

That was true. How odd to be in a philosophi-
cal discussion on a ranch.

He lifted an eyebrow. "You think ranch hands
are high-school dropouts, do you?" he mused. "I
have a degree from MIT. I was their most prom-
ising student in theoretical physics, but my wife
had a lung condition and they wanted her to come
west to a drier climate. Her dad had a ranch...."
He stopped, chuckling. "Sorry. I tend to run on.
Anyway, I worked on the ranch and preferred it to
a lab. After she died, I came here to work. So here
I am. But I'm not the only degreed geek around
here. We have three part-timers who are going to
college on scholarships the Kirk brothers set up
for them."

"What a nice bunch of guys!" she exclaimed.

"They really are. All of them seem tough as
nails, and they mostly are, but they'll help anyone
in need." He shifted. "Paid my wife's hospital bill
after the insurance lapsed. A small fortune, and
they didn't even blink."

Her throat got tight. What a generous thing to
do. Her family had done the same for people, but
she didn't dare mention that. "That was good of
them," she said with genuine feeling.

"Yes. I'll work here until I die, if they'll keep
me. They're great people."

They heard a noise and turned around. The boss was standing behind them.

"Thanks for the testimonial, but I believe there are cattle waiting to be dipped in the south pasture...." Mallory commented with pursed lips and twinkling dark eyes.

Darby chuckled. "Yes, there are. Sorry, boss, I was just lauding you to the young lady. She was surprised to find out that I studied philosophy."

"Not to mention theoretical physics," the boss added drily.

"Yes, well, I won't mention your degree in biochemistry if you like," Darby said outrageously.

Mallory quirked an eyebrow. "Thanks."

Darby winked at Morie and left them alone.

Mallory towered over the slight brunette. "Your name is unusual. Morie...?"

She laughed. "My full name is Edith Danielle Morena Brannt," she replied. "My mother knew I'd be a brunette, because both my parents are, so they added *morena,* which means *brunette* in Spanish. I had, uh, Spanish great-grandparents," she stuttered, having almost given away the fact that they were titled Spanish royalty. That would never do. She wanted to be perceived as a poor, but honest, cowgirl. Her last name wasn't uncommon in South Texas, and Mallory wasn't likely to connect it with King Brannt, who was a true cattle baron.

He cocked his head. "Morie," he said. "Nice."

"I'm really sorry, about the key," she said.

He shrugged. "I did the same thing last month, but I'm the boss," he added firmly. "I don't make mistakes. You remember that."

She gave him an open smile. "Yes, sir."

He studied her curiously. She was small and nicely rounded, with black hair that was obviously long and pulled into a bun atop her head. She wasn't beautiful, but she was pleasant to look at, with those big brown eyes and that pretty mouth and perfect skin. She didn't seem the sort to do physical labor on a ranch.

"Sir?" she asked, uncomfortable from the scrutiny.

"Sorry. I was just thinking that you don't look like the usual sort we hire for ranch hands."

"I do have a college degree," she defended herself.

"You do? What was your major?"

"History," she said, and looked defensive. "Yes, it's dates. Yes, it's about the past. Yes, some of it can be boring. But I love it."

He looked at her thoughtfully. "You should talk to Cane. His degree is in anthropology. Pity it wasn't paleontology, because we're close to Fossil Lake. That's part of the Green River Formation, and there are all sorts of fossils there. Cane loved to dig." His face hardened. "He won't talk about going back to it."

"Because of his arm?" she asked bluntly. "That wouldn't stop him. He could do administrative work on a dig." She flushed. "I minored in anthropology," she confessed.

He burst out laughing. "No wonder you like ranch work. Did you go on digs?" He knew, as some people didn't, that archaeology was one of four subfields of anthropology.

"I did. Drove my mother mad. My clothes were always full of mud and I looked like a street child most of the time." She didn't dare tell him that she'd come to dinner in her dig clothing when a famous visiting politician from Europe was at the table, along with some members of a royal family. Her father had been eloquent. "There were some incidents when I came home muddy," she added with a chuckle.

"I can imagine." He sighed. "Cane hasn't adjusted to the physical changes. He's stopped going to therapy and he won't join in any family outings. He stays in his room playing online video games." He stopped. "Good Lord, I can't believe I'm telling you these things."

"I'm as quiet as a clam," she pointed out. "I never tell anything I know."

"You're a good listener. Most people aren't."

She smiled. "You are."

He chuckled. "I'm the boss. I have to listen to people."

"Good point."

"I'll just finish getting those bales of hay stacked," she said. She stopped and glanced up at him. "You know, most ranchers these days use the big bales...."

"Stop right there," he said curtly. "I don't like a lot of the so-called improvements. I run this ranch the way my dad did, and his dad before him. We rotate crops, and cattle, avoid unnecessary supplements, and maintain organic crops and grass strains. And we don't allow oil extraction anywhere on this ranch. Lots of fracking farther south in Wyoming to extract oil from shale deposits, but we won't sell land for that, or lease it."

She knew they were environmentally sensitive. The family had been featured in a small northwestern cattlemen's newspaper that she'd seen lying on a table in the bunkhouse.

"What's fracking?" she asked curiously.

"They inject liquids at high speed into shale rock to fracture it and allow access to oil and gas deposits. It can contaminate the water table if it isn't done right, and some people say it causes earthquakes." His dark eyes were serious. "I'm not taking any chances with our water. It's precious."

"Yes, sir," she replied.

He shrugged. "No offense. I've had the lectures

on the joys of using genetically modified crops and cloning." He leaned down. "Over my dead body."

She laughed in spite of herself. Her elfin face radiated joy. Her dark eyes twinkled with it. He looked at her for a long moment, smiling quizzically. She was pretty. Not only pretty, she had a sense of humor. She was unlike his current girlfriend, a suave eastern sophisticate named Gelly Bruner, whose family had moved to Wyoming a few years previously and bought a small ranch near the Kirks. They met at a cocktail party in Denver, where her father was a speaker at a conference Mallory had attended. He and Gelly went around together, but he had no real interest in a passionate relationship. Not at the moment anyway. He'd had a bad experience in the past that had soured him on relationships. He knew instinctively that Gelly would only be around as long as he had money to spend on her. He had no illusions about his lack of good looks. He got women because he was rich. Period.

"Deep thoughts, sir?" she teased.

He laughed curtly. "Too deep to share. Get to work, kid. If you need anything, Darby's nearby."

"Yes, sir," she replied, and wondered for a moment if she was somehow in the military. It seemed right to give him that form of address. She'd heard cowboys use it with her father since she was a child. Some men radiated authority and resolve. Her father was one. So was this man.

"Now you're doing the deep-thinking thing," he challenged.

She laughed. "Just stray thoughts. Nothing interesting."

His dark eyes narrowed. "What was your favorite period? In history," he added.

"Oh! Well, actually, it was the Tudor period."

Both thick, dark eyebrows went up. "Really. And which Tudor was your favorite?"

"Mary."

His eyebrows levered up a fraction. "Bloody Mary?"

She glared at him. "All the Tudor monarchs burned people. Is it less offensive to burn just a few rather than a few hundred? Elizabeth burned people, and so did her father and her brother. They were all tarred with the same brush, but Elizabeth lived longer and had better PR than the rest of her family."

He burst out laughing.

"Well, it's true," she persisted. "She was elevated to mystic status by her supporters."

"Indeed she was." He grimaced. "I hated history."

"Shame."

He laughed again. "I suppose so. I'll have to

read up on the Tudors so that we can have discussions about their virtues and flaws."

"I'd enjoy that. I like debate."

"So do I, as long as I win."

She gave him a wicked grin and turned back to her work.

The bunkhouse was quiet at night. She had a small room of her own, which was maintained for female hires. It was rough and sparsely accommodated, but she loved it. She'd brought her iPad along, and she surfed the internet on the ranch's wireless network and watched films and television shows on it. She also read a lot. She hadn't been joking about her passion for history. She still indulged it, out of college, by seeking out transcripts of Spanish manuscripts that pertained to Mary Tudor and her five-year reign in England. She found the writings in all sorts of odd places. It was fascinating to her to walk around virtual libraries and sample the history that had been painstakingly translated into digital images. What a dedicated group librarians must be, she marveled, to offer so much knowledge to the public at such a cost of time and skill. And what incredible scholarship that gave someone the skills to read Latin and Greek and translate it into modern English, for the benefit of historians who couldn't read the ancient languages.

She marveled at the tech that was so new and

so powerful. She fell asleep imagining what the future of electronics might hold. It was entrancing.

JUST AT DAWN, HER CELL PHONE rang. She answered it in a sleepy tone.

"Sleepyhead" came a soft, teasing voice.

She rolled over onto her back and smiled. "Hi, Mom. How's it going at home?"

"I miss you," Shelby said with a sigh. "Your father is so bad-tempered that even the old hands are hiding from him. He wants to know where you are."

"Don't you dare tell him," Morie replied.

She sighed again. "I won't. But he's threatening to hire a private detective to sniff you out." She laughed. "He can't believe his little girl went off to work for wages."

"He's just mad that he hasn't got me to advise him on his breeding program and work out the kinks in his spreadsheets." She laughed. "I'll come home soon enough."

"In time for the production sale, I hope," Shelby added. The event was three weeks down the road, but King Brannt had already made arrangements for a gala event on the ranch during the showing of his prize Santa Gertrudis cattle on Skylance, the family ranch near San Antonio. It would be a party of epic proportions, with a guest list that included famous entertainers, sports figures, politicians and even royalty, and he'd want his whole family there. Especially Morie, who was essential to the hostessing. It would be too much for Shelby alone.

"I'll come back even if it's just for the night," Morie promised. "Tell Dad, so he doesn't self-destruct." She laughed.

"I'll tell him. You're like him, you know," she added.

"Cort's a lot more like him. What a temper!"

"Cort will calm right down when he finally finds a woman who can put up with him."

"Well, Dad found you," Morie noted. "So there's hope for Cort."

"You think so? He won't even go on dates anymore after that entertainment rep tried to seduce him in a movie theater. He was shocked to the back teeth when she said she'd done it in all sorts of fancy theaters back home." She laughed. "Your brother doesn't live in the real world. He thinks women are delicate treasures that need nourishing and protecting." She paused for a moment, then continued. "He really needs to stop watching old movies."

"Have him watch some old Bette Davis movies," Morie advised. "She's the most modern actress I ever saw, for all that her heyday was in the 1940s!"

"I loved those movies," Shelby said.

"Me, too." Morie hesitated. "I like Grandma's old movies."

Maria Kane had been a famous movie star, but she and Shelby had never been close and theirs had been a turbulent and sad relationship. It was still a painful topic for Shelby.

"I like them, too," Shelby said, surprisingly. "I never really knew my mother. I was farmed out to housekeepers at first and then to my aunt. My mother never grew up," she added, remembering something Maria's last husband, Brad, had said during the funeral preparations in Hollywood.

Morie heard that sad note in her mother's voice and changed the subject. "I miss your baked fish."

Shelby laughed. "What a thing to say."

"Well, nobody makes it like you do, Mom. And they're not keen on fish around here, so we don't have it much. I dream of cod fillets, gently baked with fresh herbs and fresh butter… Darn, I have to stop drooling on my pillow!"

"When you come home, I'll make you some. You really need to learn to make them yourself. If you do move out and live apart from us, you have to be able to cook."

"I can always order out."

"Yes, but fresh food is so much nicer."

"Yours certainly is." She glanced at her watch.

"Got to go, Mom. We're dipping cattle today. Nasty business."

"You should know. You were always in the thick of it here during the spring."

"I miss you."

"I miss you, too, sweetheart."

"Love you."

"Love you, too. Bye."

She hung up, then got out of bed and dressed. Her mother was one in a million, beautiful and talented, but equally able to whip up exotic meals or hostess a dinner party for royalty. Morie admired her tremendously.

She admired her dad, too, but she was heartily sick of men who took her out only with one end in mind—a marriage that would secure their financial futures. It was surprising how many of them saw her as a ticket to independent wealth. The last one had been disconcertingly frank about how his father advised him to marry an heiress, and that Morie was at least more pleasant to look at than some of the other rich men's daughters he'd escorted.

She was cursing him in three languages when her father came in, listened to her accusations and promptly escorted the young man off the property.

Morie had been crushed. She'd really liked the young man, an accountant named Bart Harrison, who'd come to town to audit a local business for his firm. It hadn't occurred to her at first that he'd searched her out deliberately at a local fiesta. He'd known who she was and who her family was, and he'd pursued her coldly, but with exquisite manners, made her feel beautiful, made her hungry for the small attentions he gave with such flair.

She'd been very attracted to him. But when he started talking about money, she backed away and ran. She wanted something more than to be the daughter of one of the richest Texas ranchers. She wanted a man who loved her for who she really was.

Now, helping to work cattle through the smell-iest, nastiest pool of dip that she'd ever experienced in her life, she wondered if she'd gone mad to come here. May had arrived. Calving was in full swing, and so was the dipping process necessary to keep cattle pest-free.

"It smells like some of that fancy perfume, don't it?" Red Davis asked with a chuckle. He was in his late thirties, with red hair and freckles, blue eyes and a mischievous personality. He'd worked ranches most of his life, but he never stayed in one place too long. Morie vaguely remembered hearing her father say that Red had worked for a former mercenary named Cord Romero up near Houston.

She gave him a speaking look. "I'll never get the smell out of my clothes," she wailed.

"Why, sure you can," the lean, redheaded cowboy assured her, grinning in the shade of his wide-brimmed straw hat. "Here's what you do, Miss Morie. You go out in the woods late at night and wait till you see a skunk. Then you go jump at him. That's when he'll start stamping his front paws to warn you before he turns around and lifts his tail...."

"Red!" she groaned.

"Wait, wait, listen," he said earnestly. "After he sprays you and you have to bury your clothes and bathe in tomato juice, you'll forget all about how this old dipping-pool smells. See? It would solve your problem!"

"I'll show you a problem," she threatened.

He laughed. "You have to have a sense of humor to work around cattle," he told her.

"I totally agree, but there is nothing at all funny about a pond full of... Aaahhhhh!"

As she spoke, a calf bumped into her and knocked her over. She landed on her breasts in the pool of dip, getting it in her mouth and her eyes and her hair. She got to her knees and brought her hands down on the surface of the liquid in an eloquent display of furious anger. Which only made the situation worse, and gave Red the opportunity to display his sense of humor to its true depth.

"Will you stop laughing?" she wailed.

"Good God, are we dipping people now?" Mallory wanted to know.

Morie didn't think about what she was doing; she was too mad. She hit the liquid with her hand and sent a spray of it right at Mallory. It landed on his spotless white shirt and splattered up into his face.

She sat frozen as she realized what she'd just done. She'd thrown pest dip on her boss. He'd fire her for sure. She was now history. She'd have to go home in disgrace…!

Mallory wiped his face with a handkerchief and gave her a long, speaking look. "Now that's why I never wear white shirts around this place," he commented with a dry look at Red, who was still doubled over laughing. "God knows what Mavie will say when she has to deal with this, and it's your fault," he added, pointing his finger at Morie. "You can explain it to her while you duck plates, bowls, knives or whatever else she can get to hand to throw at you!"

Mavie was the housekeeper and she had a red temper. Everybody was terrified of her.

"You aren't going to fire me?" Morie asked with unusual timidity.

He pursed his sensuous lips and his dark eyes twinkled. "Not a lot of modern people want to run cattle through foul-smelling pest-control substances," he mused. "It's easier to take a bath than to find somebody to replace you."

She swallowed hard. The awful-smelling stuff was in her nostrils. She wiped at it with the handkerchief. "At least I won't attract mosquitoes now." She sighed.

"Want to bet?" Red asked. "They love this stuff! If you rub it on your arms, they'll attack you in droves…. Where are you going, boss?"

Mallory just chuckled as he walked away. He didn't even answer Red.

Morie let out a sigh of relief as she wiped harder at her face. She shook her head and gave Red a rueful wince. "Well, that was a surprise," she murmured drily. "Thought I was going to be an ex-employee for sure."

"Naw," Red replied. "The boss is a good sport. Cane got into it with him one time over a woman who kept calling and harassing him. Boss put her through, just for fun. Cane tossed him headfirst into one of the watering troughs."

She laughed with surprise. "Good grief!"

"Shocked the boss. It was the first time Cane did anything really physical since he got out of the military. He thinks having one arm slows him down, limits him. But he's already adjusting to it. The boss ain't no lightweight," he added. "Cane picked him up over one shoulder and threw him."

"Wow."

He sobered. "You know, they've all got problems of one sort or another. But they're decent, honest, hardworking men. We'd do anything for them. They take care of us, and they're not judgmental." Red grimaced at some bad memory. "If they were, I'd sure be out on my ear."

"Slipped up, did you?" She gave him a quizzical look. "You, uh, didn't throw pesticide on the boss?"

He shook his head. "Something much worse, I'm afraid. All I got was a little jail time and a lecture from the boss." He smiled. "Closest call I've had in recent years."

"Most people mess up once in a while," she said kindly.

"That's true. The only thing that will get you fired here is stealing," he added. "I don't know why it's such an issue with the boss, but he let a guy go last year for taking an expensive drill that didn't belong to him. He said he wouldn't abide a thief on the place. Cane, now, almost jumped the guy." He shook his head. "Odd, odd people in some respects."

"I suppose there's something that happened to them in the past," she conjectured.

"Could be." He made a face. "That girl, Gelly, that the boss goes around with has a shifty look," he added in a lowered tone. "There was some talk about her when she and her dad first moved here, about how they got the old Barnes property they're living on." He grimaced. "She's a looker, I'll give her that, but I think the boss is out of his noggin for letting her hang around. Funny thing about that drill going missing," he added with narrowed, thoughtful eyes. "She didn't like the cowboy because he mouthed off to her. She was in the bunkhouse just before the boss found the missing drill in the guy's satchel, and the cowboy cussed a blue streak about being innocent. It didn't do any good. He was let go on the spot."

She felt cold chills down her spine. She'd only seen the boss's current love interest once, and it had been quite enough to convince her that the woman was putting on airs and pretending a sophistication she didn't really have. Most men weren't up on current fashions in high social circles, but Morie was, and she knew at first glance that Gelly Bruner was wearing last year's colors and fads. Morie had been to Fashion Week and subscribed, at home, to several magazines featuring the best in couture, both in English and French. Her wardrobe reflected the newer innovations. Her mother, Shelby, had been a top model in her younger days, and she knew many famous designers who were happy to outfit her daughter.

She didn't dare mention her fashion sense here, of course. It would take away her one chance to live like a normal, young single woman.

"You went to college recently, didn't you?" Red asked. He grinned at her surprise. "There's no secrets on a ranch. It's like a big family...we know everything."

"Yes, I did," she agreed, not taking offense.

"You live in them coed dorms, with men and women living together?" he asked, and seemed interested in her answer.

"No, I didn't," she said curtly. "My parents raised me very strictly. I guess I have old attitudes because of it, but I wasn't living in a dorm with single men." She shrugged. "I lived off campus with a girlfriend."

He raised both eyebrows. "Well, aren't you a dinosaur!" he exclaimed, but with twinkling eyes and obvious approval.

"That's right—I should live in a zoo." She made a wry face. "I don't fit in with modern society. That's why I'm out here," she added.

He nodded. "That's why most of us are out here. We're insulated from what people call civilization." He leaned down. "I love it here."

"So do I, Red," she agreed.

He glanced at the cattle and grimaced. "We'd better get this finished," he said, looking up at the sky. "They're predicting rain again. On top of all that snowmelt, we'll be lucky if we don't get some more bad flooding this year."

"Or more snow," she said, tongue-in-cheek.

Wyoming weather was unpredictable; she'd already learned that. Some of the local ranchers had been forced to live in town when the snow piled up so that they couldn't even get to the cattle. Government agencies had come in to airlift food to starving animals.

Now the snowmelt was a problem. But so were mosquitoes in the unnaturally warm weather. People didn't think mosquitoes lived in places like Wyoming and Montana, but they thrived everywhere, it seemed. Along with other pests that could damage the health of cattle.

"You come from down south of here, don't you?" Red asked. "Where?"

She pursed her lips. "One of the other states," she said. "I'm not telling which one."

"Texas."

Her eyebrows shot up. He laughed. "Boss had a copy of your driver's license for the files. I just happened to notice it when I hacked into his personnel files."

"Red!"

"Hey, at least I stopped hacking CIA files," he protested. "And darn, I was enjoying that until they caught me."

She was shocked.

He shrugged. "Most men have a hobby of some sort. At least they didn't keep me locked up for long. Even offered me a job in their cybercrime unit." He laughed. "I may take them up on it one day. But for now, I'm happy being a ranch hand."

"You are full of surprises," she exclaimed.

"You ain't seen nothing yet," he teased. "Let's get back to work."

CHAPTER TWO

THE SMALL TOWN NEAR THE RANCH was called Catelow, named after a settler who came out west for his health in the early 1800s. He and his family, and some friends who were merchants, petitioned for and got a railhead established so that he could ship cattle east from his ranch property. A few of his descendants still lived locally, but more and more of the younger citizens went out of state to big cities for high-tech jobs that paid better wages.

Still, the town had all the necessary amenities. Catelow had a good police force, a fire department, a shopping mall, numerous ethnic restaurants, a scattering of Protestant churches and a Catholic one, a city manager from California who was a whiz at making a sickly city government thrive, and a big feed store next to an even bigger hardware store.

There was also a tractor dealership. From her childhood, following her father around various vendors, she'd been fascinated with heavy machinery. Once, while she was in college, for her birthday present King Brannt had actually rented a Caterpillar earthmover and had the driver teach her how to operate it. She'd had her brother, Cort, do home movies of the event. The rat wouldn't edit out the part where she drove the machine into a ditch and got it stuck in the mud, however. Cort had a wicked sense of humor, like King's younger brother, Danny, who was now a superior court judge, happily married to his former secretary, redheaded Edie Jackson. They had two sons.

She walked down the rows of tractors, sighing over a big green one that could probably have done everything short of cook a meal. It even had a cab to keep the sun off the driver.

"This is how you spend your day off, looking at tractors?" a sarcastic feminine voice asked from behind her.

Startled, she turned to find Mallory with Gelly Bruner clinging to his arm.

"I like tractors," Morie said simply. She glared at the other woman, whose obviously tinted blond hair was worn loose, with gem clips holding it back. She was dressed in a clinging silk dress with high, spiky heels and a sweater. It was barely May, and some days were still chilly. "Something wrong with that?"

"It's not very womanly, is it?" Gelly sighed. She shifted in a deliberate way that emphasized her slender curves. She moved closer to Mallory and beamed up at him. "I'd much rather browse in a Victoria's Secret shop," she purred.

"Oh, yes, I can certainly see myself dipping cattle wearing one of those camisole sets," Morie replied with a rueful grin.

"I can't see you wearing anything...feminine, myself," Gelly returned. Her smile had an ugly edge to it. "You aren't really a girlie girl, are you?"

Morie, remembering how she'd turned heads in a particularly exquisite oyster-colored gown from a famous French designer, only stared at Gelly without speaking. The look was unanswerable, and it made the other woman furious.

"I hate tractors, and it's chilly out here," Gelly told Mallory, tugging at his arm. "Can't we get a cappuccino in that new shop next to the florist?"

Mallory shrugged. "Suits me." He glanced at Morie. "Want to come?" he asked.

Morie was shocked and pleased by the request. The boss, taking the hired help out for coffee? She pondered doing it, just to make the other woman even madder. Gelly was flushed with anger by now.

"Thanks," she said. "But I'm having fun looking at the equipment."

Gelly relaxed and Mallory seemed perplexed.

"I'm buying," he added.

Which indicated that he thought Morie couldn't afford the expensive coffee and was declining for that reason. She felt vaguely offended. Of course, he knew nothing about her background. Her last name might be unusual, but she'd seen it in other states, even in other countries. He wasn't likely to connect a poor working girl with a famous cattleman, even if he might have met her father at some point. He ran Santa Gertrudis cattle, and her father's Santa Gertrudis seed bulls were famous, and much sought after at very high prices, for their bloodlines.

She cleared her throat. "Yes, well, thanks, but not today."

Mallory smiled oddly. "Okay. Have fun."

"Thanks."

They moved away, but not quickly enough for her to miss Gelly's muttered, "Very egalitarian of you to offer cappuccino to the hired help," she said in a tone that stung. "I bet she doesn't even know what it is."

Morie gritted her teeth. *One day, lady,* she thought, *you're going to get yours.*

She turned back to the tractors with a sigh.

A red, older-model sports car roared up at the office building and stopped in a near skid. The door opened and closed. A minute later, a pleasant tall man with light brown hair and dark eyes came up to her. He was wearing a suit, unusual in a rural town, except for bankers.

He glanced at her with a smile. "Looking to buy something?"

"Me? Oh, no, I work on a ranch. I just like heavy equipment."

His eyebrows arched. "You do?"

She laughed. "I guess it sounds odd."

"Not really," he replied. "My mom always said she married my dad because he surrounded himself with backhoes and earthmovers. She likes to drive them."

"Really!"

"My dad owns this." He waved his hand at the tractors. "I'm sales and marketing," he added with a grimace. "I'd rather work in advertising, but Dad doesn't have anybody else. I'm an only child."

"Still, it's not a bad job, is it?" she asked pleasantly.

He chuckled. "Not bad at all, on some days." He extended a well-manicured hand. "Clark Edmondson," he introduced himself.

She shook it. "Morie Brannt."

"Very nice to meet you, Miss…Ms.….Mrs.…?" he fished.

"Ms.," she said, laughing. "But I'm single."

"What a coincidence. So am I!"

"Imagine that."

"Are you really just looking, or scouting out a good deal for your boss?"

"I'm sure my boss can do his own deals," she

replied. "I work for Mallory Kirk at the Rancho Real," she added.

"Oh. Him." He didn't look impressed.

"You know him."

"I know him, all right. We've had words a time or two on equipment repairs. He used to buy from us. Now he buys from a dealer in Casper." He shrugged. "Well, that's old news. A lot of locals work for him, and he doesn't have a large turnover. So I guess he's good to his employees even if he's a pain in the neck to vendors."

She laughed. "I suppose."

He cocked his head and looked down at her with both hands in his pockets. "You date?"

She laughed, surprised. "Well, sort of. I mean, I haven't recently."

"Like movies?"

"What sort?"

"Horror," he said.

"I like the vampire trilogy that's been popular." He made a face.

"I like all the new cartoon movies, the Harry Potter ones, the Narnia films and anything to do with *Star Trek* or *Star Wars*," she told him.

"Well!"

"How about you?"

"I'm not keen on science fiction, but I haven't seen that new werewolf movie." He pursed his lips. "Want to go see it with me? There's a community theater. It doesn't have a lot of the stuff the big complexes do, but it's not bad. There's a Chinese restaurant right next door that stays open late."

She hesitated. She wasn't sure this was a good idea. He looked like a nice man. But her new boss seemed to be a fair judge of character and he wouldn't do business here. It was a red flag.

"I'm mostly harmless," he replied. "I have good teeth, I only swear when really provoked, I wear size-eleven shoes and I've only had five speeding tickets. Oh, and I can speak Norwegian."

She stared at him, speechless. "I've never known anyone who could speak Norwegian."

"It will come in handy if I ever go to Norway," he replied with a chuckle. "God knows why I studied it. Spanish or French or even German would have made more sense."

"I think you should learn what you want to learn."

"So. How about the movie?"

She glanced at her watch. "I have to help with calving, so I'm mostly on call for the rest of the weekend. It's already past time I was back at work. I only have a half day on Saturdays."

"Darn. Well, how about next Friday night? If calving permits?"

"I'll ask the boss," she said.

He raised an eyebrow.

"I have to," she replied. "I'm a new hire. I don't want to risk losing my job for being AWOL."

"Sounds like the military," he suggested.

"I guess so. It sort of feels like it, on the ranch, too."

"All three of the brothers fought overseas," he said. "Two of them didn't fare so well. Mallory, though, he's hard to dent."

"I noticed." She hadn't known that Mallory had been in the military, but it made sense, considering his air of authority. He was probably an officer, as well, when he'd been on active duty.

She saw him staring, waiting. She grimaced. "If I can get the time off, I'd like to see the film."

He beamed. "Great!"

She sighed. "I've forgotten how to go on a date. I'll have to go in jeans and a shirt. I didn't bring a dress or even a skirt to the ranch when I hired on. All my stuff is back home with my folks."

"You're noticing the suit. I wear it to impress potential customers," he said with a grin. "Around town, I mostly wear slacks and sport shirts, so jeans will be fine. We aren't exactly going to a ball, Cinderella," he added with twinkling eyes. "And I'm no prince."

"I think they're rewriting that fairy tale so that Cinderella is CEO of a corporation and she rescues a poor dockworker from his evil stepbrothers," she said, tongue-in-cheek.

"God forbid!" he exclaimed. "Don't women want to be women anymore?"

"Apparently not, if you watch television or films much." She sighed. She looked down at her own clothing. "Modern life requires us to work for a living, and there are only so many jobs available. Not much economically viable stuff for girls who lounge around in eyelet and lace and drink tea in parlors." Her dark eyes smiled.

"Did I sound sarcastic? I didn't mean to. I like feminine women, but I think lady wrestlers are exciting when they do it in mud."

She laughed explosively. "Sexist!"

"Hey, I'd watch two men wrestle in mud, too. I like mud."

She remembered being covered in that, and pesticide, on the ranch and winced. "You wouldn't if you had to dip cattle around it," she promised him.

"Good thing I don't know anything about the cattle business, then," he said lightly. "So ask your boss if you can have three hours off next Friday and we'll see the werewolf movie."

She hesitated. "Won't it be kind of gory?"

He sighed. "There's always that cartoon movie that Johnny Depp does the voice-over for, the chameleon Western."

She laughed. He was pleasant, nice to look at and had a sense of humor. And she hadn't been on a date in months. It just might be fun.

"Okay, then," she told him. "I like Johnny Depp in anything, even if it's only his voice. That's a date."

He smiled back. "That's a date," he agreed.

THERE WAS A LOT TO DO around a ranch during calving season, and most of the cowboys—and cowgirl—didn't plan on getting much sleep.

Heifers who were calving for the first time were watched carefully. There was also an old mama cow who was known for wandering off and hiding in thickets to calve. Nobody knew why; she just did it. Morie named her Bessy and devoted herself to keeping a careful eye on the old girl.

"Now don't go following that old cow around and forget to watch the others," Darby cautioned. "She can't hide where we won't be able to find her."

"I know that, but she's getting some age on her and there's snow being forecast again," she said worriedly. "What if she got stuck in a drift? If we had a repeat of the last storm, we might not even be able to hunt for her. Hard to ride a horse through snow that's over his head," she added, with a straight face.

He laughed. "I see your point. But you have to consider that this is a big spread, and we've got dozens of mama cows around here. Not to mention, we've got a lot of replacement heifers who are dropping calves for the first time. That's a lot of profit in a recession. Can't afford to lose many."

"I know." Her father had cut his cattle herd because of the rising prices of grain, she recalled, and he was concentrating on a higher-quality bull herd rather than expanding into a cow-calf operation like the one his father, the late Jim Brannt, had built up.

"Dang, it's cold today," Darby said as he finished doctoring one of the seed bulls.

"I noticed." Morie chuckled, pulling her denim coat tighter and buttoning it. She had really good clothes back home, but she'd brought the oldest ones with her, so that she didn't raise any suspicions about her status.

"Better get back to riding that fence line," he added.

"I'm on my way. Just had to pick up my iPod," she said, displaying it in its case. "I can't live without my tunes."

He pursed his lips. "What sort of music do you like?"

"Let's see, country and western, classical, soundtracks, blues…"

"All of it, in other words."

She nodded. "I like world music, too. It's fun to listen to foreign artists, even if I mostly can't understand anything they sing."

He shook his head. "I'm just a straight John Denver man."

She lifted both eyebrows.

"He was a folk singer in the sixties," he told her. "Did this one song, 'Calypso,' about that ship that Jacques Cousteau used to drive around the world when he was diving." He smiled with nostalgia. "Dang, I must have spent a small fortune playing that one on jukeboxes." He looked at her. "Don't know what a jukebox is, I'll bet."

"I do so. My mom told me all about them."

He shook his head. "How the world has changed since I was a boy." He sighed. "Some changes are good. Most—" he glowered "—are not."

She laughed. "Well, I like my iPod, because it's portable music." She attached her earphones to the device, with which she could surf the internet, listen to music, even watch movies as long as she was within reach of the Wi-Fi system on the ranch. "I'll see you later."

"Got a gun?" he asked suddenly.

She gaped at him. "What am I going to do, shoot wolves? That's against the law."

"Everything's against the law where ranchers are concerned. No, I wasn't thinking about four-legged varmints. There's an escaped convict, a murderer. They think he's in the area."

She caught her breath. "Could he get onto the ranch?"

"No fence can keep out a determined man. He'll just go right over it," he told her. He went back into the bunkhouse and returned with a small handgun in a leather holster. "It's a .32 Smith & Wesson," he said, handing it up. He made a face when she hesitated. "You don't have to kill a man to scare him. Just shoot near him and run." He frowned. "Can you shoot a gun?"

"Oh, yes, my dad made sure of it," she told him. "He taught me and my brother to use anything from a peashooter to all four gauges of shotguns."

He nodded. "Then take it. Put it in your saddle-bag. I'll feel better."

She smiled at him. "You're nice, Darby."

"You bet I am," he replied. "Can't afford to lose someone who works as hard as you do."

She made a face at him. She mounted her horse, a chestnut gelding, and rode off.

The open country was so beautiful. In the distance she could see the Teton Mountains, rising like white spires against the gray, overcast sky. The fir trees were still a deep green, even in the last frantic clutches of fading winter. It was too soon for much tender vegetation to start pushing up out of the ground, but spring was close at hand.

Most ranchers bred their cattle to drop calves in early spring, just as the grass came out of hibernation and grain crops began growing. Lush, fresh grass would be nutritious to feed the cows while they nursed their offspring. By the time the calves were weaned, the grass would still be lush and green and tasty for them, if the rain cooperated.

She liked the way the Kirk boys worked at ecology, at natural systems. They had windmills everywhere to pump water into containers for the cattle. They grew natural grasses and were careful not to strain the delicate topsoil by overplanting. They used crop rotation to keep the soil fresh and productive, and they used natural fertilizer. They maintained ponds of cattle waste, which was used to produce methane that powered electricity for the calving barn and the other outbuildings. It was a high-tech, fascinating sort of place. Especially for a bunch of cattlemen who'd taken a dying ranch and made it grow and thrive. They weren't rich yet, but they were well-to-do and canny about the markets. Besides that, Mallory was something of a financial genius. The ranch was starting to make money. Big money.

Cane went to the cattle shows with their prize bulls, Darby had told her, when Cane stayed sober for a long-enough stretch. He was sort of intimidating to Morie, but he had a live-wire personality and he could charm buyers.

Dalton, whom they called, for some reason, Tank, was the marketing specialist. He drew up brochures for the production sales, traveled to conferences and conventions, attended political-action committee meetings for the county and state and even national cattlemen's associations, and devoted himself to publicizing the ranch's prize cattle. He worked tirelessly. But he was a haunted man, and it showed.

Mallory was the boss. He made all the big decisions, although he was democratic enough to give his brothers a voice. They were all opinionated. Darby said it was genetic; their parents had been the same.

Morie understood that. Her dad was one of the most opinionated men she'd ever known. Her mother was gentle and sweet, although she had a temper. Life at home had always been interesting. It was just that Morie had become an entrée for any money-hungry bachelor looking for financial stability. Somewhere there must be a man who'd want her for what she was, not what she had.

She rode the fence line, looking for breaks. It was one of the important chores around the ranch. A fence that was down invited cattle to cross over onto public lands, or even onto the long two-lane state highway that ran beside the ranch. One cow in the road could cause an accident that would result in a crippling lawsuit for the brothers.

Darby had been vocal about the sue-everybody mentality that had taken over the country in recent years. He told Morie that in his day, attorneys were held to a higher standard of behavior and weren't even allowed to advertise their services. Nobody had sued anybody that he knew of, when he was a boy. Now people sued over everything. He had little respect for the profession today. Morie had defended it. Her uncle was a superior court judge who'd been a practicing attorney for many years. He was honest to a fault and went out of his way to help people who'd been wronged and didn't have money for an attorney. Darby had conceded that perhaps there were some good lawyers. But he added that frivolous lawsuits were going to end civilization as it stood. She just smiled and went on about her business. They could agree to disagree. After all, tolerance was what made life bearable.

She halted at the creek long enough to let her gelding have a drink. She adjusted her earphones so that she could listen to Mark Mancina's exquisite soundtrack for the motion picture *August Rush*. There was an organ solo that sent chills of delight down her spine. She got the same feeling listening to Bach's Toccata and Fugue in D Minor played on a pipe organ. Music was a big part of her life. She could play classical piano, but she was rusty. College had robbed her of practice time. She'd noticed a big grand piano in the Kirks' living room. She wondered which of the brothers played. She'd never asked.

She stopped at a stretch of fence where the last snow-and-ice storm had brought a limb down. The ice was gone, but the limb was still resting on the fence, bending it down so that cattle could have walked over it. The limb was a big one, but she was strong. She dismounted, buttoned her coat pocket so that the iPod wouldn't fall out and went at the limb.

She had to break pieces off before she could ease it onto the ground. In the process, one of the sharp branches cut her cheek. She muttered as she felt blood on her fingers when she touched it. Well, it would mend.

She pushed the limb onto the ground with a grimace, but she was glad to see that the fence wasn't damaged, only a little bent from the collision. She wrangled it back into some sort of order and made a note on the iPod so that she could report its location to the brothers with the GPS device she always carried with her. They were pretty high-tech for a low-budget operation, she thought. They had laptops that they used during roundup to coordinate all the activity.

She paused as the crescendo built on the soundtrack, and closed her eyes to savor it. How wonderful it must be, she thought, to be a composer and be able to write scores that touched the very heart and soul of listeners. She was musical, but she had no such talent. She didn't compose.

She only interpreted the music of others when she played the piano or, less frequently, the guitar.

"Hurt yourself?" A deep, drawling voice came from behind.

She whirled, her heart racing, her eyes wide and shocked as she faced a stranger standing a few feet away. She looked like a doe in the sights of a hunter.

He was tall and lean, with dark eyes and hair under a wide-brimmed hat, wearing jeans and a weather-beaten black hat. He was smiling.

"Mr. Kirk," she stammered, as she finally recognized Dalton Kirk. She hadn't seen him often. He wasn't as familiar to her as Mallory was. "Sorry, I wasn't paying attention…"

He reached out and took one of the earphones, pursing his sensual lips as he listened. He handed it back. *"August Rush,"* he said.

Her eyebrows shot up. "You know the score?"

He smiled at her surprise. "Yes. It's one of my own favorites, especially that pipe-organ solo."

"That's my favorite, too," she agreed.

He glanced at the fence. "Make a note of the co-ordinates so we can replace that section of fence, will you?" he asked. "It will keep the cattle in for now, but not for long."

"I already did," she confirmed. She was still catching her breath.

"There's an escaped convict out here somewhere," he told her. "I don't think he's guilty, but he's desperate. I love music as much as anybody, but there's a time and place for listening to it, and this isn't it. If I'd been that man, and desperate enough to shoot somebody or take a hostage, you'd be dead or taken away by now."

She'd just realized that. She nodded.

"Now you see why it's against the law to listen with earphones when you're driving," he said. "You couldn't hear a siren with those on." He indicated the earphones.

"Yes. I mean, yes, sir."

He cocked his head. His dark eyes twinkled. "Call me Tank. Everybody does."

"Why?" she blurted out.

"We were facing down an Iraqi tank during the invasion of Iraq," he told her, "and we were taking substantial damage. We lost comms with the artillery unit that was covering us and we didn't have an antitank weapon with us." He shrugged. "I waded in with a grenade and the crew surrendered. Ever since, I've been Tank."

She laughed. He wasn't as intimidating as he'd once seemed.

"So keep those earphones in your pocket and listen to music when it's a little safer, will you?"

"I will," she promised, and put away the iPod.

He mounted the black gelding she hadn't heard

approaching and rode closer. "That thing isn't a phone, is it?"

"No, sir."

"Do you carry a cell phone?" he added, and his lean, strong face was solemn.

She pulled a little emergency one out of her pocket and showed it to him. "It's just for 911 calls, but it would do the job."

"It wouldn't. We'll get you one. It's essential here. I'll tell Darby—he'll arrange it for you."

"Thanks," she said, surprised. She should have been using her own phone, but she thought it might give her away. It was one of the very expensive models. The one she was carrying looked much more like something a poor cowgirl would own.

"Oh, we're nice," he told her with a straight face. "We have sterling characters, we never curse or complain, we're always easy to get along with…." He stopped because she was muffling laughter.

"Just because Cane can turn the air blue, and Mallory throws things is no reason to think we're not easygoing," he instructed.

"Yes, sir. I'll remember that."

He laughed. "If you need anything, you call," he said. "Keep your eyes open. The man who escaped was charged with killing a man in cold blood," he added solemnly. "Joe Bascomb. He was with me in Iraq. But desperate men can do desperate things. He might hurt a stranger, even a woman, if he thought she might turn him in to the law. He's sworn he'll never go back to jail." His eyes were sad. "I never thought he'd run. I'm sure he didn't mean to kill the other man, if in fact he did. But they're bound and determined to catch him, and he's determined not to be caught. So you watch your back."

"I'll be more careful."

"Please do. Good help is hard to find." He tipped his hat, and rode away.

Morie breathed a sigh of relief and got back on her horse.

CHAPTER THREE

THERE WAS SOME BIG SHINDIG planned for the following Friday, Morie heard. The housekeeper, Mavie Taylor, was vocal about the food the brothers wanted prepared for it.

"I can't make canapés," she groaned, pushing back a graying strand of hair that had escaped its bun. She propped her hands on her thin hips and glowered. "How am I supposed to come up with things like that when all they ever want is steak and potatoes?"

"Listen, canapés are easy," Morie said gently. "You can take a cocktail sausage and wrap it in bacon, secure it with a toothpick and bake it." She gave the temperature setting and cooking time. "Then you can make little cucumber sandwiches cut into triangles, tea cakes, cheese straws…"

"Wait a minute." She was writing frantically on a pad. "What else?"

Morie glowed. It was the first time the acid-tongued housekeeper had ever said anything halfway pleasant to her. She named several other small, easily prepared snacks that would be recognizable to any social animal as a canapé.

"How do you know all this?" the woman asked finally, and suspiciously.

"Last ranch I worked at, I had to help in the kitchen," Morie said, and it was no lie. She often helped Shelby when company was coming.

"This is nice," she replied. She tried to smile. It didn't quite work. Those facial muscles didn't get much exercise. "Thanks," she added stiffly.

Morie grinned. "You're welcome."

Her small eyes narrowed. "Okay, what about table linen and stuff?"

"Do you have a selection of those?"

"I hope so." The harassed woman sighed. "I only came to work here a couple of weeks before you did. I've never had to cook for a party and I don't have a clue about place settings. I'm no high-society chef! I mean, look at me!" she exclaimed, indicating her sweatpants and T-shirt that read Give Chickens the Vote!

Morie tried not to giggle. She'd never credited the Kirks' venomous housekeeper with a sense of humor. Perhaps she'd misjudged the woman.

"I cooked for a bunkhouse crew before this," Mavie muttered. "The brothers knew it…I told them so. Now here they come wanting me to cook for visiting politicians from Washington and figure out how to put priceless china and delicate crystal and silver utensils in some sort of recognizable pattern on an antique linen tablecloth!"

"It's all right," Morie said. "I'll help."

She blinked. "You will? They won't like it." She nodded toward the distant living room.

"They won't know," she promised.

The housekeeper shifted nervously. "Okay. Thanks. That Bruner woman's always in here complaining about how I cook," she added sourly.

"That's all right, she's always complaining about how I dress."

The other woman's eyes actually twinkled. Nothing made friends like a common enemy. "She thinks I'm not capable of catering a party. She wants to hire one of her society friends and let Mallory pay her a fortune to do it."

"We'll show her," Morie said.

There was a chuckle. "Okay. I'm game. What's next?"

MORIE SPENT A VERY ENJOYABLE hour of her free time laying out a menu for Mavie and diagramming the placement of the silver and crystal on the tablecloth. She advised buying and using a transparent plastic cover over the antique tablecloth to preserve it from spills of red wine, which, the housekeeper groaned, the brothers preferred.

"They'll never let me do that." She sighed.

"Well, I suppose not," Morie replied, trying to imagine her mother, that superhostess, putting plastic on her own priceless imported linen. "And I suppose we can find a dry cleaner who can get out stains if they're fresh."

"I don't guess I can wear sweats to serve at table," Mavie groaned.

"You could hire a caterer" came the suggestion.

"Nearest caterer I know of is in Jackson, ninety miles away," the housekeeper said. "Think they'll spring to fly him and his staff down here?"

Morie chuckled. No, not in the current economic environment. "Guess not."

"Then we'll have to manage." She frowned. "I do have one passable dress. I guess it will still fit. And I can get a couple of the cowboys' wives to come and help. But I don't know how to serve anything."

"I do," Morie said gently. "I'll coach you and the wives who help."

Mavie cocked her head. Her blue eyes narrowed. "You're not quite what you seem, are you?"

Morie tried to look innocent. "I just cooked for a big ranch," she replied.

The housekeeper pursed her lips. "Okay. If you say so."

Morie grinned. "I do. So, let's talk about entrées!"

MALLORY CAME IN WHILE Morie was sipping a cup of coffee with Mavie after their preparations.

Morie looked up, disturbed, when Mallory stared at her pointedly.

"It's my afternoon off," she blurted.

His thick eyebrows lifted. "Did I say anything?"

"You were thinking it," she shot back.

"Hard worker and reads minds." Mallory nodded. "Nice combination."

"She gave me some tips on canapés for that high-society party you're making me cook for," Mavie grumbled, glaring at him. "Never cooked for any darn politicians. I don't like politicians." She frowned. "I wonder what hemlock looks like…?"

"You stop that," Mallory said at once. "We're feeding them so we can push some agendas their way. We need a sympathetic ear in Washington for the cattlemen's lobby."

"They should keep buffalo in the park where they belong instead of letting them wander onto private land and infect cattle with brucellosis," Morie muttered. "And people who don't live here shouldn't make policy for people who do. They're trying to force out all the independent ranchers and farmers, it seems to me."

Mallory pulled up a chair and sat down. "Exactly," he said. "Mavie, can I have coffee, please?"

"Sure thing, boss." She jumped up to make more.

"Another thing is this biofuel," Mallory said. "Sure, it's good tech. It will make the environment better. We're already using wind and sun for power, even methane from animal waste. But we're growing so much corn for fuel that we're risking precious food stores. We've gone to natural, native grasses to feed our cattle because corn prices are killing our budget."

"Grass fed is better," Morie replied. "Especially for consumers who want lean cuts of beef."

He glowered at her. "We don't run beef cattle."

"You run herd bulls," she pointed out. "Same end result. You want a bull who breeds leaner beef calves."

Mallory shifted uncomfortably. "We don't raise veal."

"Neither do—" She stopped abruptly. She was about to say "we," because her father wouldn't raise it, either. "Neither do a lot of ranchers. You must have a good model for your breeding program."

"We do. I studied animal husbandry in school," he said. "I learned how to tweak the genetics of cattle to breed for certain traits."

"Like lower birth weight in calves and leaner conformation."

"Yes. And enlarged..." He stopped in midsentence and seemed uncomfortable. "Well, for larger, uh, seed storage in herd bulls."

She had to bite her tongue to keep from bursting out laughing. It was a common reference among cattlemen, but he was uncomfortable using the term with her. He was very old-world. She didn't laugh. He was protecting her, in a sense. She shouldn't like it. But she did.

He was studying her with open curiosity. "You know a lot about the cattle business."

"I pick up a lot, working ranches," she said. "I always listened when the boss talked about improving his herd."

"Was he a good boss?"

"Oh, yes," she said. Her dad had a very low turnover in his employees. He was fair to them, made sure they had insurance and every other benefit he could give them.

"Why did you leave, then?" he asked.

She shifted. Had to walk a careful line on this one, she thought. "I had a little trouble with an admirer," she said finally. It was true. The man hadn't been a ranch hand, but she insinuated that he was.

Mallory's eyes narrowed. "That won't ever happen here. You have problems with any of the cowboys, you just tell me. I'll handle it."

She beamed. "Thanks."

"No problem. Thanks, Mavie," he added when

the housekeeper put a cup of black coffee with just a little cream at his hand. "You make the best coffee in Wyoming."

"You're only saying that because you want an apple pie for supper."

His eyebrows shot up. "Hell, am I that obvious?"

"Absolutely," she declared.

He shrugged. "I love apple pie."

"I noticed. I suppose I can peel apples and listen while you two talk cattle," she said, and got up to retrieve fresh apples from the counter along with a big bowl and a paring knife.

"Uh, about men," Morie said, looking for an opening.

He scowled. "You are having problems here!"

"No!" She swallowed. "No, I'm not. There's this nice man in town who wants to go out with me. His father runs the local tractor store—"

"No!"

She gaped at him.

"Clark Edmondson has a bad reputation locally," he continued curtly. "He took out one of Jack Corrie's daughters and deserted her at a country bar when she wouldn't make out with him in his car. He was pretty drunk at the time."

"We're not going to a bar," she stammered uncharacteristically, "just to a movie in town."

He cocked his head. "What movie?"

"That cartoon one, about the chameleon. The lizard Western."

"Actually, that one's pretty good. I would have thought he'd prefer the werewolf movie, though."

She shifted in her chair. "That's the first one he suggested. I don't like gore. The reviewers said it had some in it, and it got bad reviews."

"You believe reviewers know what they're talking about?" he queried with a twinkle in his eyes. "They don't buy books or movie tickets, you know. They're just average people with average opinions. One opinion doesn't make or break a sale in the entertainment business."

"I never thought of it like that."

"I don't read reviews. I look at what a book is about, or a movie, and make up my own mind whether to read it or see it in a theater. In fact, the werewolf movie had exquisite cinematography and some of the best CGI I've seen in a long time. I liked it, especially that gorgeous blonde girl in that red, red cape in the white, snowy background," he recalled. "Film reviewers. What do they know?" he scoffed.

"Opinionated, is what he is," Mavie said from beside them, where she sat peeling apples. "And it was Bill Duvall who told you about the Corrie girl. He's sweet on her and she doesn't like Clark, so you take that into account when you hear the story." She looked down at her hands working on an apple. "Nothing wrong with Clark, except he's flighty. You don't understand flighty, because all three of you are rock-solid sort of people, full of opinions and attitude."

Mallory let out a short laugh as he sipped coffee. "I don't have an attitude."

"Oh, yes, you do," the housekeeper shot back.

He shrugged. "Maybe I do." He glanced at Morie and his eyes narrowed. "You take your cell phone with you, and if Clark gets out of hand, you call. Got that?"

"Oh...okay." It was like being back at home. He sounded just like her dad did when she'd dated a boy he didn't know in high school. "He wanted to take me to the movies on Saturday, but I'm supposed to be watching calving...."

"I'll get one of the part-timers to come in and cover for you. This time," he added curtly. "Don't expect concessions. We can't afford them."

She flushed. "Yes, sir. Thanks."

"She's over twenty-one, boss," Mavie said drily.

"She works for me," he replied. "I'm responsible for every hire I've got. Some more than others." He looked pointedly at Morie, and he didn't look away.

It was like being caught by a live wire when she met that searching stare. Her heart kicked into high gear. Her breath caught in her throat. She felt the intensity of the look right down to her toes.

She'd never felt such a surge of pleasure in her whole life.

Mallory appeared to forcibly drag his eyes away. He sipped coffee. "Well, you can go, but you be careful. I still think he's a risk. But it's your life."

"Yes, it is," she replied. Her throat felt tight, and she was flushed. She got to her feet. "Thanks for the coffee," she told the housekeeper. "It's time for me to get to work."

"Don't fall in the dipping pool," Mallory said with a straight face, but his dark eyes twinkled in a way that was new and exciting.

"Yes, sir, boss," she replied. She smiled and turned to move quickly out of the room before she embarrassed herself by staring at him. She wondered how she was going to conceal the sudden new delight she got from looking at her boss.

SHE HAD A NICE PAIR OF SLACKS and a pink-and-lime embroidered sweater. She wore those for her date, and let her long hair down. She brushed it until it shone. It was thick and black and beautiful, like her mother's. When she looked in the mirror, she saw many traces of her mother in her own face. She wasn't beautiful, but she wasn't plain, either. She had the same elfin features that had taken Shelby Kane Brannt to such fame in her modeling days. And Morie's grandmother, Maria Kane, had been a motion-picture star, quite famous for her acting ability. Morie hadn't inherited that trait. Her one taste of theater in college had convinced her that she was never meant for the stage.

She had a lightweight denim coat, and she wore that over her sweater, because it was cold outside. The weather was fluctuating madly. Typical Wyoming weather, she thought amusedly. The Texas climate was like that, too.

She heard a car drive up to the bunkhouse. She whipped her fanny pack into place and went out to meet Clark. He was sitting behind the wheel of the sports car, grinning.

She noted that he didn't get out to open her door. He leaned across and threw it open for her.

She climbed in. "Hi."

"Hi, back. Ready for a nice movie?"

"You bet."

He put the car in gear and roared out down the driveway.

"Don't do that," she groaned. "We have heifers calving in the barn!"

"Oops, sorry, didn't think," he said, but he didn't look concerned. "They'll get over it. Nice night. They said it might snow, but I don't believe the forecast. They're mostly wrong."

She was thinking about the nervous heifers being kept up because it was their first breeding season, and wondering how much flak she was going to get from her boss if anything happened because of Clark's thoughtlessness.

"Stop worrying," he teased. "It's just cows, for heaven's sake."

Just cows. She loved to stop and pet them when she was in the barn. She loved their big eyes and big noses, and the soft fur between their eyes. They were so gentle. And these little heifers, even if they were animals, must be so scared. She'd always had a terror of childbirth, for reasons she could never quite understand. It was one of many reasons that she was hesitant to marry at all.

"Do you know that Elizabeth the First never married and never had a child?" she remarked.

He made a face. "History. I hate that. Let's talk about who's leading the pack in *American Idol!*"

She gaped at him. She didn't watch television very much. "I watch the Weather Channel, the military channel and the science channels mostly," she remarked. "I've never watched any of those audience-participation shows."

"I can see that we're never going to meet in the middle on issues," he remarked. "Doesn't matter. You're cute and I like you. We can go from there."

Could they? She wondered.

THE MOVIE WAS FUN. It was clever and funny and both of them came out of the theater smiling.

"Now let's have some nice Chinese food," he said. "You hungry?"

"Starved. But we're going Dutch," she added firmly. "I bought my own movie ticket...I'll pay for my food, too."

His eyebrows arched. "I wouldn't expect you to owe me anything if I bought dinner."

She smiled. "Just the same, I like everything on an equal footing."

"You're a strange girl," he commented thoughtfully.

"Strange?" She shrugged. "I suppose I am."

"Let's eat."

He led the way into the restaurant and they followed the waitress to a table in a corner.

"This is beautiful," Morie remarked, loving the Asian decor, which featured nice copies of ancient statues and some wood carvings that were very expensive. Morie, who'd traveled Asia, appreciated the culture depicted. She'd loved the people she met in her travels.

"Junk," he told her casually. "Nothing valuable in here."

"I meant that it was pretty," she clarified.

"Oh." He glanced around. "I guess so. A little gaudy for my taste."

She was about to respond when her eye caught movement at the door. There, at the counter, was her boss, Mallory Kirk, with Gelly Bruner. He spoke to the waitress and let her seat them nearby.

He smiled coolly and nodded at Morie and Clark. She was thinking that it was an odd coincidence, having him show up here. Certainly he wouldn't have had any reason to be spying on her....

"Do you believe this?" Clark asked, shocked. "Does he do this every time you go out with a man? I've heard of possessive employers, but this takes the cake."

"He takes his date all over the place," she replied, trying to sound casual. "This is the only really good restaurant in town."

"I suppose so."

"He wouldn't have any reason to keep an eye on me," she pointed out. "I'm just the hired help."

He pursed his lips and studied her. "Sure."

MALLORY WAS LOOKING AT HER, too, his dark eyes on the long wealth of thick black hair that hung straight and shiny down her back almost to her waist.

"Why are you staring at her?" Gelly asked coldly. "She's just a common person. She works for you. And why are we here? You know I hate Chinese food!"

He didn't hear her. He was thinking that he'd never seen anything as beautiful as that long black hair. It brought to mind a poem. She'd probably be familiar with it, too—Bess, the landlord's black-eyed daughter, plaiting a dark red love knot into her long, black hair. "The Highwayman" by Alfred Noyes. It was a tragic poem, the heroine sacrificing herself for the hero. "'I'll come to thee by moonlight, though hell should bar the way...'"

"What?" Gelly asked blankly.

He hadn't realized that he'd spoken aloud. "Nothing. What would you like to order?" he added and forced himself to look at his date and not Morie.

MORIE WAS UNCOMFORTABLE. Clark wanted to talk about contestants on the television show, and she had no point of reference at all.

"That guy, you know, he really can't sing, but he's got a following and he's getting most of the votes," he muttered. "I like the girl. She's classy, she's got a great voice... Are you listening?"

She grimaced. "Sorry. I was thinking about the weather reports. They think we might have another snow, and we've got a lot of first-time mothers dropping calves."

"Cows," he groaned. "Morie, there's more to life than four-legged steaks."

Her eyes widened. "Mr. Kirk doesn't have a cow-calf operation. It's strictly a seed-bull ranch."

He blinked. "Seed bull."

"Yes. They produce industry-leading bulls for market." She leaned forward. "They don't eat them."

He shook his head. "You are the oddest girl I ever met."

She grinned. "Why, thank you!"

He picked up his wineglass and had a long sip. "Sure you don't want any wine?" he asked. "This is the only restaurant in town where you can buy single drinks legally."

"I can't drink," she said. "Bad stomach. I get very sick. Can't drink carbonated beverages, either. Just coffee or iced tea. Or, in this case—" she lifted the little cup with steaming green tea "—hot tea." She sipped it and closed her eyes. "Wonderful!"

He made a face. "You didn't put sugar in it."

"Oh, nobody puts sugar in it in Japan," she blurted out and then bit her tongue. "At least, from what I've read," she corrected quickly.

"I can't drink it straight. It tastes awful." He put the wineglass down. "They have good desserts here, sticky rice with mango or coconut ice cream."

"The ice cream," she said, laughing. "I love it."

"Me, too." He motioned to the waitress. "At least we both like one thing," he mused.

WHEN THEY GOT READY to leave, Mallory Kirk watched them through narrowed eyes. He got up while Morie was paying the bill and motioned Clark to one side.

Clark gave him a nervous look. "Mr. Kirk," he said pleasantly enough.

Mallory's dark eyes narrowed. "She's not young enough to be my daughter, but I'm responsible for her. If you do anything she doesn't like," he added with the coldest smile Clark had ever seen, "I'll pay you a visit."

"You can't threaten people," Clark began, flushed.

"Oh, it's no threat, son," Mallory said. His jaw tautened. "It's an ironclad, gold-edged promise."

He turned and walked off, pausing at his table to leave a tip and help Gelly to her feet.

Clark escorted an oblivious Morie out to his car. He was flushed from the wine and angry that one of the Kirk brothers had threatened him.

"I should call the police," he muttered as he started the car and roared off out of the parking lot.

"What for?" Morie asked, curious.

"Your boss made a threat," he said stiffly.

"My boss? What are you talking about?"

He started to tell her and then thought better of it. She was pretty and he liked her; he didn't want her to think there was a reason for her boss to warn him off.

He shrugged. "He just said I'd better look after you," he amended.

Her dark eyebrows arched. "Why in the world would he say something like that?" she asked, and tried not to look as flattered as she felt. No man interfered in a woman's life unless he liked her.

"Beats me." He glanced at her. "He's not stuck on you, is he?"

She burst out laughing. "Oh, sure, he likes me because I've got millions in a trust fund and I know all the best people," she said drily.

He laughed, too. He was out of his mind. She wasn't the sort of woman a cattle baron would want to marry. The Kirks had fabulous parties with all sorts of famous people attending them to sell those cattle she talked about. They had some incredibly well-known friends, apparently. But Morie dressed in old clothes, even for a date. She was clueless. He was overreacting. Maybe Mallory really did feel responsible for her. Maybe he knew her folks. He might be afraid of a lawsuit. It wasn't anything personal. Just good business.

"Well, I loved the movie," she said. "Thanks."

"Thank you. I don't get out as much as I'd like to," he added. "But we could see a movie once in a while and have dinner out, if you like."

She smiled. "I'll think about that."

He'd planned to take her to an overlook that doubled as the local lover's lane. But after Mallory's blunt speech, he wasn't keen to push the man. So instead, he drove her back to the ranch.

He even turned off the engine and walked her to the door of the bunkhouse.

"You live in there with all those men?" he asked curiously.

"I have my own room," she explained. "They're nice men."

"If you say so."

"Well, thanks again," she said, hesitating.

He smiled. He liked that little nervous laugh, the way her lips turned up at the corners, the faint dimple beside her mouth.

He bent and drew his lips gently against hers.

She tolerated the kiss. But she didn't react to it. She felt nothing. Nothing at all.

He noticed that. They were too different to settle in together. But she was cute and he liked company on a night out.

"We'll do it again soon," he said.

She smiled. "Sure."

She turned around and went into the bunkhouse. Darby was sitting by the door, his eyebrows arching as she walked in and closed the door behind her.

"Have fun?" he asked in a hushed tone, so he didn't wake the cowboys down the hall.

"Yes. I guess."

He tilted his head. "You guess?"

"Boss showed up at the restaurant," she said, and looked puzzled. "I didn't know he liked Chinese food."

Darby's eyes almost popped. "He hates it."

She hesitated. "Well, he had Ms. Bruner with him. Maybe she likes it."

"Maybe."

"You sleep good, Darby."

"You, too," he said gently.

"The heifers doing okay?" she asked.

"Doing fine. We'll just hope and pray that that the weatherman's wrong on that snow forecast."

"I'll agree with that. Good night."

"'Nite."

She went into her room and closed the door. Darby had seemed shocked that the boss went to the restaurant where Morie was eating. She was shocked, too, but also pleased and flattered and thrilled to death.

She slept, finally. And her dreams were sweet.

CHAPTER FOUR

THE LAST THING MORIE EXPECTED the next day was to find a seething Gelly Bruner on her doorstep. Well, at the bunkhouse when she went in for lunch.

"I hate Chinese food," Gelly said without a greeting.

"I'm sorry," Morie said. "In that case, perhaps you should avoid Chinese restaurants." She smiled.

"He went there because of you, didn't he?" she demanded. "To make sure your date knew he was watching out for you."

Morie looked innocent. "Why would he do that? He's not my dad."

Gelly frowned. "He's not your boyfriend, either, and you'd better not make eyes at him," she added coldly. "You won't last long here if you do."

"I work here," Morie pointed out. "That's all."

"You see how they live and you like it," the blonde said, giving Morie's clothing an even colder look. "You're poor and you'd like to have nice things and mingle with the right people."

"I do mingle with the right people," Morie said, offended.

"Cowboys" came the disparaging reply. "Smelly and stupid."

"They're neither."

"If you do anything to make Mallory notice you, I'll make sure it never happens again," she added, lowering her voice. "You won't be the first person I've helped off this ranch. It isn't wise to make an enemy of me."

"I work here," Morie said, growing angry. She had her mother's looks, but her father's fiery temper. "And nobody threatens me."

Gelly shifted. She wasn't used to people who fought back. "My people are well-to-do," she said stiffly. "And you won't like how I get even."

Morie raised an eyebrow. "Ditto."

"Well, you just stay away from Mallory," she said bluntly. "He's mine and I don't share!"

"Does he know?"

Gelly blinked. "Know what?"

"That he belongs to you? Perhaps I should ask him...."

"You shut up!" The blonde woman's fists balled at her sides and her face grew flushed with temper. "I'll get you!"

"Wind and water," Morie said philosophically. "Words."

Gelly drew back her hand and started to slap the younger woman, but Morie threw up her forearm instinctively and blocked the move.

"I have a brown belt in Tae Kwon Do," she told Gelly in a soft voice. Her dark eyes glittered. "Try that again, and you'll wish you hadn't."

Gelly let out a furious sound. "I'll tell Mallory!"

"Be my guest," Morie offered. "I can teach him a few moves, too, in case you try that with him."

Gelly stomped back off toward the house, muttering to herself.

Morie shook her head at the retreating figure.

"Unwise," Darby said, joining her. He watched Gelly walk away. "She makes a bad enemy. We lost a hand because she accused him of stealing. Told you about that."

"She'll think she's poked a hornet's nest if she tries it with me. Nobody warns me off people and gets away with it," she said curtly. "I don't have any designs on the boss, for God's sake! I don't even know him. I just work here!"

Darby patted her on the shoulder paternally. "There, there, don't let it get you down. Two nights' sleep and you'll forget why you argued with her. Come on in and eat. We've got chili and Mexican corn bread that Mavie made for us. She's a wonderful cook."

"Yes, she is," Morie agreed. She grimaced. "Sorry. I don't usually lose my temper, but she set me off. What a piece of work!"

"I do agree. But she's the boss's headache, not ours, thank God."

"I suppose so."

She followed him inside.

BUT THAT WASN'T THE END of it. Mallory called Morie up to the big house, and he wasn't smiling as he motioned her into the living room and closed the door.

"Sit down, please." He indicated a leather chair, not the cushy brocade-covered white sofa. Her jeans were stained with grass and mud from helping with calving. Probably he didn't want a brown-spotted couch, she thought wickedly.

She sat. "Yes, sir?"

He paced. "Gelly said that you threatened her."

"Did she?" She sounded amazed. "How odd."

He turned and stared down at her with piercing dark eyes. "I'd like to hear your side of the story before I decide what to do."

She cocked her head and studied him. "I'll tell you, if you're sure you want to know, boss. But I won't sugarcoat it, even though I need this job."

He seemed surprised. "Okay. That's a deal. Shoot."

"She warned me off you," she said simply.

"Then she threatened to have me fired. Finally, she tried to slap me and I blocked the move. She left and I went back to work."

"In between, there's some stuff missing," he pointed out. "Like what you said that made her try to slap you."

"She said that I was after you because you were rich and I was poor," she added. The words did sting, despite Morie's background. "She also said cowboys were smelly and stupid and that she could get me fired if she liked. I told her that I didn't like threats and that perhaps I should ask you if you were her personal property. That's when she tried to slap me."

He just stared at her. He didn't speak. God knew what Gelly had actually told him about the incident.

"I've never known her to get physical with anyone," he returned. "She was crying."

"Oh, gee, I'm sorry," Morie said with cutting sarcasm. "Start a fight and lose it and then go crying to some big, strong man to make it all right. That how it goes?"

His jaw tautened. "I'm the boss."

"Yes, you are, sir," she agreed. "So if you want to fire me, go right ahead. There are a few ranches where I haven't tried to get work yet. I'm willing to give them a try."

He let out an angry sigh. "You might just admit

that you were wrong and apologize to her," he said curtly.

"Apologize when I was defending myself from an attack?" she asked. "How does that work, exactly?"

"She said you started it."

"And I say that she did."

He looked even angrier. "She's a socialite. You're a hired hand on my ranch. That's what makes the difference."

"I get it." She nodded, trying to contain her temper. "It's the class thing, right? She's rich and I'm poor, so she's right."

"You work for me, damn it!" he shot back. "And you're that close—" he held up his forefinger and thumb a fraction apart "—to not working for me!"

Her small hands balled up at her sides. "Nobody throws a punch at me and gets away with it. I don't care who she is! If she'd landed that blow, I'd have had her prosecuted and I'd call every damned newspaper and television station in Wyoming to make sure everybody knew what she did!"

His eyes were glittering. "She said you told her that you wanted me and you were going to get me, and she'd be out in the cold!"

She rolled her eyes. "Good grief, you're almost old enough to be my father," she burst out. "What in the world was she thinking?"

He had been pacing while they talked, but

as she spoke her last sentence, he'd stopped and stared at her. Then he moved like greased lightning toward her.

His mouth came down on hers with a pressure and skill that shocked her speechless. While she was trying to decide on a course of action, he backed her up against the wall between two landscape paintings, lifted her and braced his body against hers. The kiss was, at first, a medium of his anger. And then, quite suddenly, it was something entirely different.

She felt one big, warm hand high on her hip, his long leg insinuating itself between both of hers. He shifted, so that she felt him intimately. He was aroused and apparently not shy about sharing the fact with her. His mouth eased and became persuasive, teasing her lips apart while his hand positioned her slender hips so that he could get even closer.

She shivered. No man had ever made such a sudden, sensual pass at her, and she'd never felt such a surge of utter and absolute pleasure at physical contact.

But when the contact grew even more intimate, and she felt her body urging her to help him with that zipper he was trying to undo, she came to her senses.

She dragged her mouth out from under his with reluctance. "No!" she whispered. "No, don't!"

She pushed at his chest weakly. If he insisted, she wasn't sure that she could stop him. She didn't want to stop him....

He was out of his mind with the pleasure. He hadn't felt it in years, certainly not with Gelly, who was something of a cold fish, despite her flirting. Morie had made a sharp remark about his age and it had hit him in a sore place. But this was insane. He was taking advantage of the hired help!

He dragged himself away from her and looked down. She was flushed and shaking. But it wasn't from fear. He knew women. She was as aroused as he was. She hadn't protested the kissing, but she wasn't willing to go further. She behaved as if she'd never had a man. He frowned. Could there be a virgin left in the world? Sometimes he doubted it.

"I'm not an old man," he said angrily.

She was still trying to get her breath. "Oh, no, you're definitely not old," she managed. She could taste him on her mouth, smell the woodsy cologne he wore on her clothing.

He averted his eyes. He didn't lose control of himself, ever. This was embarrassing. "Sorry," he said stiffly.

She swallowed. "It's okay. But I should go back to work now."

"Yes, you should."

She moved away from the wall, hoping she wasn't more disheveled than she felt, and that Mavie wouldn't be around to see her when she left.

He didn't say a word. He watched her go, stiff and uncomfortable, and pondered Gelly's remark that Morie was a rounder who was looking for a rich sugar daddy. He knew that wasn't true. She might be poor. She might even have designs on him for his wealth—it wouldn't be the first time. But she was innocent. He'd have bet the ranch on it.

MORIE AVOIDED THE OTHER cowboys when she went riding fence lines. She hoped she didn't look as disconcerted and unsettled as she felt. The boss had kissed her. No, she corrected, that hadn't been a kiss. That had been something a lot more overt and sensual. She'd been saucy and deliberately provocative. She'd taunted the sleeping bear, but she hadn't expected such a response.

Her mouth still tingled from the kiss. He might not be the handsomest man around, but he knew exactly what to do with a woman. She hadn't wanted him to stop. That would have been a disaster. He might have wanted her side of the story, but it was obvious that he believed part of Gelly's story. He wanted Morie to apologize to that blond shark, did he? Well, hell would freeze over first.

She was the injured party. Gelly should apologize, not her.

But Gelly was the woman in his life. She was wealthy and pretty and cultured. Morie had the same background, but she didn't dare admit it. She couldn't keep her job if the boss knew who her family was.

Which brought to mind another small problem. The boss was having a gala party on Saturday. Morie had been helping Mavie with recipes and tips on serving and place settings and even decorations. Mavie wanted her to help make the canapés. She'd even asked the boss, so Morie was in something of a spot.

As long as she could hide in the kitchen during the festivities, it would be all right. But her family traveled in the same social circles that the Kirk brothers did. It was possible, even probable, that there would be someone at that party who would recognize her. She couldn't let that happen. She'd gone to a lot of trouble to get this job, mainly because she wanted to prove to her parents and herself that she could make it in the world on her own, with no money and no influence. There was also the question of not being pursued for her wealth by some fortune-hunting male on the make.

She wasn't going to lose her job. She just had to stay out of sight in the kitchen. If she refused to help Mavie, that would lead to questions she couldn't answer. She agreed. But she was going to wear a kerchief over her hair and an overall and keep hidden. She only hoped none of the guests were comfortable enough to come in and speak to the cook. That wasn't likely, though. Of course it wasn't.

THE BIG HOUSE WAS ABLAZE with lights, inside and out. The weather was perfect. It was a beautiful spring night, the temperature was unusually comfortable and guests wandered around inside and out nibbling on canapés and drinking the best imported champagne.

Mavie was fascinated by the people she and her hired staff were feeding. "Did you see that movie star?" she exclaimed. "I just watched his last film, and now he's got a series on one of the pay-per-view channels. Isn't he gorgeous?"

Morie peered out and chuckled. She knew the man, who was sweet and unaffected by his great fame. "He's a doll," she said.

"There's that soccer star who's paid millions a year," Mavie continued. "And that's the president of one of those desert countries overseas!"

"Philippe Sabon," Morie blurted out without thinking. Her father knew the man, whose wife was from Texas.

Mavie glanced at her suspiciously.

"I read about him in the newspapers," Morie

covered quickly. "What a story! He's even more handsome in person!"

Mavie gave an emphatic nod. "Yes, he sure is."

"We'd better get back to work," Morie groaned. "Look at how fast those trays are going down!"

"Good thing we've got plenty of raw material in here." Mavie chuckled.

They worked steadily for the next hour, making and baking succulent treats for the guests. The band was playing some lazy blues tunes, and a few couples were dancing in the big family room by the patio door.

"You should be in there dancing and having fun," Mavie said. "You're young enough to enjoy these parties."

Morie gaped at her. "I'm the hired help."

"Baloney. The boss doesn't think like that."

"Want to bet?" Morie murmured under her breath. She'd already had an unforgettable taste of the boss's attitude toward the lower classes. It had a sting.

Mavie glanced her way. "You want to watch that Gelly person. She was raging to the boss about how you talked to her like a dog and said she was a useless person."

"I said no such thing!" Morie replied indignantly.

"Just telling you what she's saying" came the

soft reply. "I've seen women like her all my life. They purr when they're around the man in charge and claw when they're not. She isn't as wealthy as she makes herself out to be. One of my friends works for her folks, and gets paid nothing, not even minimum. She says they put on airs and pretend to be rich, but they're barely middle class. Gelly's hoping for a rich husband to prop up the family finances. She's got her eye on the boss."

"If he's nuts enough to marry her, he'll get what he deserves," Morie pointed out. "That woman has more sharp edges than a razor's blade."

She nodded in agreement. "I think she does, too."

It was almost ten o'clock. The staff would leave soon, and so would most of the guests. Morie would be glad to see her bed. She'd been on her feet since daylight. She was half-starved, as well, because she hadn't had a dinner break. Neither had Mavie.

"I'm so hungry." Morie sighed.

"Me, too. We'll save a few canapés for ourselves," she said, laughing. "I'll put some on a plate for you to take back to your room."

"Thanks, Mavie."

"No, thank you," she replied. "You're a wonderful little worker. I couldn't have managed this alone."

She grinned. "I like working in the kitchen."

"Me, too. Call me old-fashioned, but I love to cook...."

"WHERE'S THAT WONDERFUL cook?" came a familiar deep voice from the doorway. A minute later, Morie's uncle Danny Brannt came through the doorway, laughing. He stopped dead when he spotted Morie.

She put her finger to her lips, when Mavie's back was turned, and shook her head frantically.

"Who's the cook?" he repeated, beaming at Mavie. "I just had to thank you for those delicious canapés. It's been a long time since I've tasted anything that good."

"It was me—" Mavie laughed "—but my helper here came up with most of the recipes." She indicated Morie. "She's Morie," she added. "I'm Mavis, but everyone calls me Mavie."

"I'm happy to meet you," he said. "Both of you." But when he looked at Morie his eyebrows lifted. "Like working here, do you?" he asked her.

"Oh, yes, very much," she replied.

He pursed his lips. "Can I speak with you for a minute?" he added. "I want to ask you something about that little sausage canapé. For my housekeeper," he said.

"Sure," she replied.

He walked to the back door, held it open and let

her go out before him. She worried that it might make Mavie suspicious, but she had to make him understand. She explained what she was doing.

"What the devil are you up to?" he asked seriously. "Your dad would have a fit if he knew you were working for wages on a ranch!"

"You can't tell him," she replied firmly. "I'm going to show him that I can make it on my own. He doesn't have to like it. But if you tell him where I am, he'll come up here and make trouble. He'll be telling the boss what I can and can't be expected to do and it will ruin everything. You know how he is."

"I guess I do." He frowned. "How did you get a job way up here?"

"A friend of a friend told me they were hiring. And what are you doing here?" she exclaimed.

"I met Cane during a trial. He was a friend of the plaintiff, a land case I heard in superior court in Texas. We had lunch and became friends. Good heavens, I had no idea I'd come to his party and find my niece cooking for it!"

She laughed. "Well, somebody had to. Mavie had no clue about canapés and Mom makes the best I ever tasted. So does Aunt Edie and your housekeeper."

"If your dad ever finds out about this…"

"He won't. And if he ever does, I'll defend you," she promised confidently.

He shook his head. "You always were a handful, even when you were little."

"And you always loved me anyway, Uncle Danny."

"Yes, I did." He hugged her warmly. "Okay, I guess you know what you're doing. I won't tell Kingston. But there will be a dustup when the truth comes out. You'll have to protect me," he added with a grin.

"You know I will. Thanks."

"What are you doing out here instead of working, Miss Brannt?" Gelly's shrill, angry voice came from the doorway. "You are not to have private conversations with my guests, you little gold digger!"

Danny moved into the light. The woman's attitude toward his niece pricked his temper. He'd already formed an opinion of Gelly Bruner, and it wasn't a good one. "I'm not your guest," he pointed out coldly. "I came to see the Kirks."

She flushed and looked uncertain.

"Why don't you go back to the party and stop trying to micromanage your boyfriend's staff?" he drawled. "Perhaps I should have a word with him…."

"Sorry," Gelly said stiffly and managed a cool smile. "Excuse me, please."

She almost ran off.

Morie was stifling laughter. Her uncle could be

as intimidating as her father ever was, even if he was usually the easygoing one of the brothers.

Mavie had stepped over to the doorway after Gelly had raced away. She'd obviously heard every word of the exchange with Gelly. Now her eyes were dancing. "Want to stay? I'll cook for you anytime," she added.

He laughed. "Sorry. I have my own business to take care of. The canapés were really delicious. And thanks for the recipe," he told Morie. "I hope I'll see you again one day."

"Same here," she replied, smiling. "Thanks."

He shrugged. "My pleasure." He gave her a last wave before he went back into the family room.

"Who is he?" Mavie asked her.

"A superior court judge from Texas who's a friend of Cane's, apparently," Morie replied innocently. "He wanted me to tell him how to make those sausages so he could get his housekeeper to make them for a party he's having soon. Imagine that! I got to talk to a real judge!"

"He wasn't bad-looking, either," Mavie said with a grin. "Did you say something to Gelly?" she added worriedly.

"No, I didn't say anything. But you heard what the judge said," she added. "She came out to tell me to stop mingling with her guests and get to work. He said she needed to mind her own business."

"Ha!"

Morie's smile widened. "He's such a nice man. I wish we could keep him."

"Me, too." Mavie looked uneasy. "You'll be in trouble, though."

"I'm always in trouble. Let's clean up and then I want to go to bed."

"I'll just put some of those canapés on the plate for you."

"Thanks."

"You're a great little worker," Mavie returned. "I like having you around."

"That's the nicest thing anyone's said to me in a long time," Morie replied, touched.

Mavie just smiled.

MORIE SAT IN FRONT of her small television and watched an old black-and-white comedy while she ate her canapés. They'd turned out very well. What a surprise to have her uncle show up at the Kirks' party. She wasn't aware that he knew Cane. At least she'd been able to get him to keep her secret from her father. She shuddered to think what King would say to her boss.

She knew her mother hadn't told King Brannt where his daughter was working, or what she was doing. Shelby had mentioned that she'd said Morie had a nice job at a department store but she hadn't said where. What a joke. Morie couldn't have sold heaters to people living in the Yukon.

It had been several days since Mallory had kissed the breath out of her. He'd been avoiding her ever since. Or she'd been avoiding him. It had been unexpected and shocking, but a delicious little interlude that played over and over in Morie's mind. She'd loved it. But obviously the boss hadn't. It seemed that he wanted to make sure she didn't get any ideas about his interest. He'd made a point of being businesslike every time he spoke to her now. There was no more light teasing or pleasant conversation. It was strictly business.

She finished the last canapé and turned off the television. It was up at dawn for more calving and she was still achy and stiff from helping Darby pull two calves that simply weren't anxious to be born. Their reward was the soft bawling sound the calves made when they were delivered and stood up, wobbling away to be licked clean by their mothers.

It was incredible to help deliver a calf. The process of birth was fascinating to anyone who worked around livestock. The cycle of life and death was a never-ending one on a ranch.

Morie loved working outdoors, away from the city, away from traffic and regimented life. Here, the time clock was the sun. They got up with it and went to bed with it. They learned how to identify birds by their songs. They learned the subtle weather signs that were lost in electronic prognostication. They were of the earth. It was the most wonderful job going, Morie thought, even if the pay wasn't top scale and the work was mostly physical labor that came with mussed, stained clothing. She wouldn't have traded it to model Paris gowns, and she'd once been offered that opportunity. It had amused and pleased her mother, who wasn't surprised when Morie said she'd rather learn how to rope calves.

Her father would never teach her. Her brother, Cort, got the ranch training. Her primitive dad, who was living in the Stone Age, she often told him, wanted her to be a lady of leisure and do feminine things. She told him that she could work cattle every bit as well as her brother and she wanted to prove it. Her dad just laughed and walked off. Not on his ranch. Not ever.

So she found someone else's ranch to prove it on. She'd gotten her college degree. Her dad should be happy that she'd accomplished at least one thing he'd insisted upon. Now she was going to please herself.

She threw on a nightshirt and a pair of pajama bottoms and climbed into bed. She was asleep in seconds.

THE NEXT MORNING, the boss came down to the barn, where she was feeding out a calf whose mother had been attacked by a pack of wolves. The mother had died and state agencies had been called in to trap the wolves and relocate them.

Mallory looked down at her, with the calf on her knees, and something cold inside him started to melt. She had a tender heart. He loved the picture she made, nursing that calf. But he pulled himself up taut. That couldn't be allowed. He wasn't having any more embarrassing interludes with the hired help that could come back to bite him.

She looked up and saw him watching her. She averted her eyes. "Morning, boss," she said.

"Morning."

His tone wasn't reassuring. She sighed. "I'm in trouble again, I guess."

"Gelly said you put a visitor up to insulting her when she told you to get back to work in the kitchen," he said flatly.

Morie just sighed.

"Well?" he persisted.

"The guy was a superior court judge who wanted my canapé recipe for his housekeeper, so I went outside with him to give it to him," she replied wearily. "Miss Bruner interrupted us, and he was angry at the way she spoke to me. I didn't put him up to anything."

He frowned. "A judge?"

"Well, he said he was," she replied, flushing. She wasn't supposed to know the occupations of his guests.

"I see."

No, you don't, she fumed silently. *You don't see anything. Gelly leads you around by your temper, and you let her.*

He hesitated. "The canapés were very good."

"Thanks. Mavie and I worked hard."

"Yes." His dark eyes narrowed. "How is it," he continued suspiciously, "that you know so much about how to organize a high-society party? And just where did you learn it?"

CHAPTER FIVE

MORIE STARED UP AT HIM with wide eyes while she searched frantically for an answer that wouldn't give her away.

"The, uh, the last place I worked," she said. "The housekeeper knew all that stuff and the boss didn't like to hire staff, so I had to learn how to do those things to help her out."

"I see."

"It's just something I picked up, and, honestly, I'd rather feed calves than work in the kitchen," she added. "Just in case you had in mind to ask me to work with Mavie instead of out here."

"I didn't have that in mind."

She nodded. "Good."

He shoved his hands into the pockets of his jeans. "You don't like Gelly."

"It's not my place to like or dislike one of your friends, boss," she replied in a subdued tone. "I'm just the newest hire...that's all I am."

"Gelly feels threatened by you, God knows why," he added unconsciously. She might have been pretty if she did something to her hair and wore makeup and nice clothing. But she was scruffy and not very attractive most of the time. It still shook him that he'd kissed her and enjoyed it so much. He tried not to revisit that episode.

"Not my problem," she murmured, and hoped she didn't sound insolent.

"She said that the judge seemed to know you."

"Can't imagine why," she said, looking up innocently. "I sure don't travel in those circles. He might have seen me in the kitchen where I used to work, though."

"Where was that?" he asked. "The place you used to work?"

She stared at him blankly. She'd made up the name of the place, although she'd given the phone number of a friend's housekeeper who'd promised to sound convincing if anybody checked her out.

"Well?" he persisted.

She was flushed and the soy calf formula was leaking out of the oversize bottle she was using to feed him. Just when it seemed as if she was going to blow her own cover, a sudden loud noise came from outside the barn. It was followed by a barrage of range language that was even worse than what Morie had heard come out of her father during roundup.

Mallory rushed out. Morie, curious, put the calf

back in his stall, set the empty bottle on a nearby shelf and followed.

Cane was throwing things. A saddle was lying on the ground. In the distance, a horse was galloping away.

"Mud-brained, unshod son of a...!" he raged, until he spotted Morie and bit down hard on the last word.

"What in the world is the matter with you?" Mallory asked.

Cane glared at him. His thick, short black hair was in disorder all over his head. His dark brown eyes, large and cold, were glittery with bad temper. His sensuous mouth was pulled tight against his teeth.

"I was trying to put a saddle on Old Bill," he muttered. "I thought I could manage him. I haven't been on a horse since I came home. The damned outlaw knocked me down on the saddle and ran off."

The empty sleeve, pinned at the elbow where his arm had been amputated, was poignant. Cane was ultrasensitive about his injury. He never spoke of the circumstances under which he'd lost part of his arm, or about his military service. He drank, a lot, and kept to himself. He was avoided by most of the men, especially when he was turning the air blue, like now.

Morie sighed and went to the barn. She brought

out one of the other older saddle horses they kept for visitors. This one was quite gentle, like the one that had run away. She heard Mallory telling one of the men to go after it.

She picked up Cane's saddle, ignoring his outraged, indignant look. She turned the horse and draped the saddle over his back, pulling up the cinch and fastening it deftly.

"Don't fuss," she told Cane when she handed him the bridle. "Everybody needs a little help now and then. It's not demeaning to let someone do you a favor. Even the hired help."

He glared down at her for a few seconds, during which she thought he was probably going to storm away or dress her down for her insolence.

But finally he just shook his head. "Okay. Thanks."

"You're welcome." She handed him the reins.

He was looking at the horse dubiously. It was obvious that he hadn't tried to mount one since he was wounded.

"We have a friend back in Texas that we used to go riding with," she said, without giving away much. "He lost an arm doing merc work overseas. He mounted offside so that he could use his good hand on the pommel to spring up into the saddle. Worked like a charm."

His dark eyebrows went up under the wide brim

of his hat. "You don't let anybody intimidate you, do you?"

She smiled. "You're not intimidating. You're just a little scary sometimes."

He shook his head again. "Okay, I'll try it. But if I land on my face, you're fired."

"You can't fire her," Mallory pointed out. "Unless you hired her, and you didn't. Get on that horse and let's go search out straggling heifers. They really are right about snow this time."

Cane looked at his brother. "I'll give it a shot."

He fumbled the first time and almost fell. But he tried again, and again, until he got the rhythm just right. He sprang up into the saddle with a heavy sigh and took the reins in his hand. He wheeled the horse around and looked down at Morie. "Thanks."

She gave him an encouraging look. "You're welcome."

Mallory rode in between them. "Let's go. Daylight's burning."

"I'm right behind you."

Mallory glanced at Morie and he wasn't smiling. He didn't like Cane smiling at her. He didn't know why, and that made him even angrier.

"Get back to work," he told her. He rode off behind his brother without another word.

Morie glared after him. "I was going to," she

muttered. "What did you think, I had a date to go sailing on the Caribbean or something?"

"Talking to yourself," Darby teased. "Better watch that. They'll be sending men with nets after you."

"If they do, I'll tell them the boss drove me batty," she assured him.

"Nice, what you did for Cane," he said, sobering. "He hasn't tried to get on a horse since he came back. I thought he'd give up after Old Bill ran off. None of us would have dared to do what you did. Saw him punch a cowboy once for even offering, a few months ago."

"He's just hurting," she said. "He doesn't know how to cope, how to interact with people, how to go on doing normal things. I heard that he won't go to physical therapy or even talk to a psychologist. That's hurting him, too. It must be horrible, for a man so active and vital, to lose an arm."

"He was the rodeo champ," he replied solemnly. "Killed him when he had to stop competing."

"He'll adjust," she said softly. "It will take time, and help. Once he realizes that, and starts going back to the therapist, he'll learn to live with it. Like our friend did."

His eyes narrowed. "Odd friend. A mercenary."

"We have friends of all sorts." She laughed. "My dad likes renegades and odd people."

"Well, I suppose it takes all kinds to run the

world," he replied. His eyes sparkled. "And we had better get back to work. Bad time to lose a job, in this economy."

"Tell me about it!"

WHEN CANE AND THE BOSS came back, she was riding out to check the fence line.

"You keep that music box in your pocket and those earphones out of your ears while you're out alone, got that?" Mallory ordered abruptly.

She knew without asking that Tank had told him how he found her moving the broken tree limb. She grimaced. "Okay, boss."

"What sort of music do you like?" Cane asked conversationally.

"Every sort," she said with a grin. "Right now my favorite is the soundtrack from *August Rush*."

His eyebrows arched. "Nice. Tank loves it, too. He bought the score. He's still trying to master it."

"Dalton plays?" she blurted out. She flushed and laughed when Mallory stared at her. "I noticed the grand piano in the living room. I wondered who played it."

"Tank's good," Cane said, smiling. He nodded toward Mallory. "He plays, too. Of course, he's mostly tone-deaf, but that doesn't stop him from trying."

"I can play better than Tank," Mallory said, insulted.

"Not to hear him tell it," Cane observed.

"We got the fence fixed," Mallory told her. His eyes narrowed. "You should never have tried to move that limb by yourself." He was looking pointedly at the scratch on her cheek.

She touched it self-consciously. "It only grazed me. I heal quickly."

"Even I would have called somebody to help me," Mallory persisted.

Her eyebrows arched. "Aren't you the same man who tried to lift the front end of a parked car to move it when it was blocking the barn?" she asked with a bland smile.

He glared down at her. "I would usually have called somebody to help me. I'm the boss. You don't question what I do...you just do what I say."

"Oh, yes, sir," she replied.

"And stop giggling," he muttered.

Her eyebrows arched. "I wasn't!"

"You were, inside, where you thought I couldn't hear it. But I can hear it."

She pursed her lips. "Okay."

He shook his head. "Let's go," he told his brother.

But Cane didn't follow. He was still looking at Morie with eyes that saw more than Mallory's did. "You know, you look very familiar to me," he said, frowning slightly. "I think I've seen you before, somewhere."

She'd had that very same feeling when she first met Cane. But she didn't remember him from any of her father's gatherings. However, he might have been with one of the cattlemen's groups that frequently toured Skylance to view King Brannt's exquisite Santa Gerts. She wasn't sure. It made her nervous. She didn't want Cane to remember where he'd seen her, if he had.

"I just have that kind of face, I expect," she said, assuming an innocent expression. "They say we all have a counterpart somewhere, someone who looks just like us."

"That might be true." He paused for a moment. "What you did—getting the horse saddled for me—that was kind. I'm sorry I was so harsh."

"It was nothing. Besides, I'm used to harsh. I work for him." She pointed toward Mallory.

"One more word and you're a memory," Mallory retorted, but his lips twitched upward at the corners.

She laughed and went back to work.

THAT NIGHT, THEY HAD A SERIES of old movies on one of the classic channels, starring Morie's grandmother, Maria Kane. It was fascinating to watch her work, to see flashes of Shelby Kane and even herself in that beautiful, elfin face and exquisite posture.

"I wish I'd known you," she whispered to the television screen. But Maria had died even before Shelby married Kingston Brannt. In fact, her funeral had been the catalyst that convinced King he couldn't live without Shelby.

Morie had heard all about her parents' romance. King and Shelby had been enemies from their earliest acquaintance. She and his brother, Danny, had been good friends who went out together on a strictly platonic basis. Then Danny had asked Shelby to pretend to be engaged to him, and he'd taken her home to Skylance. King had been eloquent in his antagonism to the match. It had provoked him into truly indefensible treatment of Shelby, for which he was later very sorry. Shelby, remembering, said that King had treated her like a princess from the day they married, trying to make up to her for all his former harsh treatment and rough words. He'd changed so much that Shelby often wondered if he was the same man she'd known in the beginning, she told her daughter.

"I can't picture Dad being mean to you." Morie had laughed. "He brings you flowers and chocolates all the time, buys you something every time he goes out of town, lavishes you with beautiful jewelry, takes you to Paris shopping...."

"Yes, he's the most wonderful husband any

woman could ask for, now," Shelby had replied, smiling. "But you didn't know him before." She shook her head. "It was a very difficult courtship. He was hurt by another relationship and he took it out on me." She sighed, smiling at some secret memory. "I was showing a Western collection in New York during Fashion Week when he turned up in the audience. He picked me up and carried me out of the building. I was kicking and protesting, but he never missed a step."

Morie burst out laughing. "I can imagine Dad doing something like that," she remarked.

Shelby sighed, her eyes dreamy. "We had coffee and a misunderstanding. He took me back to my apartment, prepared to say goodbye for good."

"Then what happened?" Morie asked, fascinated by the fact that her parents had once been young like her. It was hard to think of them as a dating couple.

"I asked him to kiss me goodbye," she continued, and actually flushed. "We got engaged in the car and we were married three long days later." She shook her head. "You never really know somebody until you live with them, Morie," she added gently. "Your father always seemed to be the hardest, angriest, most untamable man on earth. But when we were alone..." She cleared her throat. The flush grew as she recalled their tempestu-

ous, passionate wedding night and the unbeliev-
able pleasure that had kept them in the hotel room
for two days and nights with only bottled water
and candy bars to sustain them through a mara-
thon of lovemaking that had produced their first
child, Cort. They were so hungry for each other
that precautions had never entered their minds.
But they'd both wanted children very much, so it
hadn't been a problem. The memory was so poignant that it could still turn her face red.

Morie laughed. "Mom, you're blushing."

Shelby chuckled self-consciously. "Yes, well,
your father is a class of his own in some ways, and
I won't discuss it. It's too personal. I just hope that
you're half as lucky as I've been in your choice of
husbands."

Morie grimaced. "If I don't get out of here, I'll
never get married. Everybody wants me because
I've got a rich father."

"Some man will want you just for yourself. The
traveling accountant was a bad choice. You were
vulnerable and he was a predator," Shelby said
with a flash of anger. "He was very lucky that
he got out of town before your father could get to
him."

"I'll say." She studied Shelby. "Why won't Dad
let me work on the ranch like Cort?"

"He and his father are very similar in some

ways," she replied. "Jim Brannt raised him to have a great respect for women and to understand that they are much too delicate for physical labor." She shook her head. "I suppose some of that is my fault, too. You know, I lived with my aunt, and she was much the same. She didn't want me to lift a finger because ladies didn't do that. On the other hand, she hated my mother. She didn't want me to turn out like her, either."

"They play some of Grandmother's movies on television," she said. "She really was a wonderful actress. They said she married four men."

Shelby nodded. "The last was the best...Brad. He died in a car crash just after I married King."

"Did Grandmother commit suicide or was that just malicious gossip?" she wondered aloud.

"I never knew," Shelby confided. "Brad said she overdosed because the studio fired her. But my aunt had often said she wasn't the suicidal kind at all. Maybe she just accidentally took too many pills to help her sleep. I'd like to believe that's the case."

"Perhaps it was."

Shelby had hugged her. "Anyway, you don't want to go around covered in mud and calf poop, really, do you?" she teased. "Even if you were muddy from archaeology, at least it was clean dirt."

Morie had burst out laughing.

Her father had come into the room during the conversation. He wore a satisfied expression as he bent to kiss Shelby and hug her close.

"I got tickets," he told her.

"To *The Firebird?*" Shelby exclaimed excitedly. "But they were sold out!"

"Old Doc Caldwell was persuaded to part with his. I thought his wife was going to kiss me to death since she hates Stravinsky," he said, and produced the tickets out of his shirt pocket. He handed them to Shelby.

"When are we going?" she asked.

"Tonight." He glanced at Morie and patted her cheek affectionately. "Sorry, kid, I couldn't get an extra ticket."

"Not a problem, Dad," she'd replied with a smile. "Debussy is more to my taste. Stravinsky is a little too experimental for my tastes."

"Want a new dress to wear to it?" King asked Shelby. "We can fly up to Dallas to Neiman Marcus."

"I have a wonderful new dress in the closet that I've been saving." She pressed close to him and was enfolded hungrily in his arms. "Thanks, sweetheart."

He kissed her hair. "Nothing's too good for my best girl."

Watching them, Morie was suddenly aware that

their love for each other had only intensified since they'd been married. They were still like newly-weds, often lost in each other and unaware of anything around them. She'd hoped for that sort of romance in her own life, and she'd never found it. Cort, too, remarked that their parents were exceptionally suited to each other and that he envied that relationship.

Cort, of course, was sweet on the daughter of King's neighbor and friend, Cole Everett, who had a son and a daughter and lived nearby on the Big Spur Ranch. They frequently traded seed bulls and went to conventions together. Odalie Everett was blonde and blue-eyed like her beautiful mother, and although she wasn't really pretty, she had a voice that was soulful and clear as a bell. She sounded just like her mother, except that Heather had been a famous contemporary singer before she married her stepbrother, Cole, and Odalie was being groomed for an operatic career. Her parents were dead set against her forming any sort of relationship with a man because of her musical aspirations. It would be difficult for her to pursue such a demanding career and have a family. She had a voice that had been hailed by critics from California to New York and she was training at the Met already. Cort, unsurprisingly, had never made his feelings for her known. In fact, he pretended that he had none. He'd been Odalie's enemy for years, for reasons that no one understood. Least of all poor Odalie, who adored him.

Morie snapped back to the present. She had her own worries. Her brother would have to find his way to love all by himself. She turned her attention back to the television as the commercial ended and her grandmother came back onto the screen, larger than life.

After the movie ended, Morie looked in the mirror and was surprised to see that she was almost the image of her grandmother. If she'd used makeup and had her hair styled properly, she could have been mistaken for Maria Kane. So it was just as well that she'd neglected her hair and packed away her cosmetics to work on the Rancho Real, she decided. It would never do for people who watched old classic movies to notice that resemblance and start asking questions.

DARBY PRESENTED HER with a cell phone the next morning. "Boss said to get that for you and make sure you carry it when you're out alone. Still got that pistol I gave you in your saddlebags?"

"I do," she replied. "Have they caught that escaped killer yet?"

He shook his head. "He's a hunter. Knows these woods like the back of his hand, and is able to live off the land. It will take them a long time to hunt him down. He's got kinfolk around here, too, and the sheriff thinks some of them may be helping him hide."

"I don't know that I'd help a killer escape the law," she remarked.

"What if it was your brother or your father?" he asked simply.

She sighed. "That's a harder choice."

"Killer's got a cousin that they think might help him. They've got his place staked out. They're sure Bascomb is getting food and shelter somewhere." He shook his head. "But the cousin's place is miles from here. I don't think Joe Bascomb would turn up on the ranch."

"He doesn't have anything against the Kirks, does he?" she asked a little worriedly.

"Not that I know of," Darby told her. "In fact, Tank testified as a character witness for him during the trial. Tank still thinks he's innocent."

"What did he do?"

"Killed a man that he said was beating up his girlfriend. Said he didn't mean to do it. He hit the man and he fell into a brick wall, hit his head and died. Would have probably been ruled accidental except the girlfriend suddenly testified that he banged the man's head against the wall and killed him deliberately."

"Why would she lie?" she asked.

"She was sweet on Bascomb, but he was in love with his late wife and didn't want anything to do with this girl. Story was, she called him to come help her because she was scared of her new boyfriend. He was fond of her, so he went. The boyfriend had hit her once or twice and Joe Bascomb intervened to save her." He sighed. "Noble effort. He saved her and he said she got even with him because he wouldn't get involved with her, although she denied it in court. It got him convicted. It's a capital offense, too. He slipped away from the transport deputy, handcuffs and leg irons and all, and hid out in the woods. They found the cuffs and irons later." He smiled. "Joe's a blacksmith. Wasn't hard for him to get free, I expect."

"He sounds like a decent man."

He nodded. "More than one decent man's gone to prison on the word of a spiteful woman, however." He checked his watch. "Best get going or you'll be late back for lunch."

"I'm on my way."

She saddled her horse and rode off.

AT LEAST SHE DIDN'T HAVE TO worry about the escaped killer so much, now that she knew why he'd been convicted. Of course, he'd be desperate and she didn't want to get in his way or threaten him.

But she could understand his plight. Sadly, there didn't seem to be any way to save him. He'd go to prison for life or die in the electric chair at a judge's pleasure. It didn't seem right.

She found no more breaks in the line. The weather was beautiful. The predicted snow didn't materialize. Everything was getting green and lush, and she finally took off her jacket because it was getting hot.

She paused by a stream and closed her eyes to listen to it gurgle along. She felt herself relax. A twig snapped. She whirled and looked around her, her hand tight on the bridle of her mount. A good thing, because the gelding jumped at the sound. Horses were nervous creatures, she thought, and usually with good reason. She'd seen one tear loose from a hitching post and go careening over a fence just from a pan being dropped in the kitchen.

"What is it, boy?" she asked softly, looking around with some unease.

Nothing stirred. But she cut her losses. She mounted, turned the horse and urged him into a gallop toward the ranch.

LATER, SHE TOLD MALLORY about it when he came home. She found him in the kitchen drinking coffee with Mavie. He was concerned.

"It's not unlikely that Joe might come here. Tank helped him in court and thinks he's innocent," Mallory said. "But the fact is that he's an escaped, convicted killer. If you help him or Tank helps him, there will be consequences. You remember that."

"I didn't see anybody," she protested. "I just heard a branch snap, like somebody stepped on it. I thought I should tell you, just the same. Could have been an animal, I expect."

"Could have been. Or could have been Joe Bascomb," he added. "You keep your eyes open. Darby give you that cell phone?"

She nodded and produced it.

His eyes narrowed as he looked at her. "Cane said he thought he'd seen you before. Now that he mentioned it, you do look familiar."

"I told him...I just have that sort of face." She laughed. She couldn't react to the remark. "I might look like somebody you remember."

He frowned. "Not really. Tank and I were watching this old movie on the classics channel. It starred that actress who killed herself—what was her name? Kane," he said finally. "Maria Kane. That's it. You remind me of her."

"I do?" She smiled broadly to hide her discomfort. "Thanks! I think she was gorgeous! I watched that movie myself. I like the old black-and-white ones."

He was diverted, as she'd meant him to be. "Me, too. I'm partial to Randolph Scott and Gary Cooper and John Wayne, myself."

She raised her hand. "Bette Davis."

He made a face. "Hard as nails. I like feminine women."

She shifted uncomfortably. He was making a statement. Probably Gelly Bruner was his ideal. He'd already said he liked the pretty blonde actress in the werewolf movie. Gelly was blonde and blue-eyed, and pretty, also. Morie, with her dark hair and eyes and olive complexion, would never be to his taste. He might like kissing her, but he wasn't looking at her as if he wanted anything more from her.

"Do you ever wear anything besides slacks and shirts with writing or pictures on them?" he asked suddenly.

She stared at him. "I'd have a real hard time pulling calves in a dress." She said it with a straight face.

He gave a sudden laugh. "Damn!"

"Well, I would, boss," she said reasonably.

He just sipped his coffee. "I guess you would."

Piano music was coming from the living room. It was soft and pretty at first, then there were fumbles and then a crash. "Damn it!" Tank groaned.

They heard him get up and soon he came into the kitchen. He glanced at Morie. "I can't get the rhythm of that coda. Do you have your iPod with you, with the soundtracks on it?"

"No," she replied. She'd left it in the bunkhouse. "But I can show you."

He frowned. "You can play a piano?"

She shifted as Mallory stared openly at her. "Sort of."

"Sort of." Tank caught her hand and pulled her along with him to the living room. He seated her at the grand piano. "Show me."

CHAPTER SIX

"I JUST PICKED UP a little piano playing at the last job I worked," Morie protested, denying her many years of piano lessons. "I probably can't even do an octave now."

"Can you read music?" Tank persisted.

She shifted. "Yes. A little."

"Come on, then. Play."

She couldn't figure a way out of it. They might ask all sorts of questions if they knew how well she played. She'd been offered a music scholarship in college, which she'd turned down. Her parents could well afford her tuition, and the scholarship might help some deserving student who had no such means.

After a minute's hesitation, she put her long-fingered hands on the keyboard and looked at the score before her.

She found the pedals with her foot, rested her hands on the keyboard and suddenly began to play.

Mallory, standing in the doorway, was shocked speechless. Tank, closer, smiled as he sank into an easy chair. A minute later, Cane heard the exquisite score and came into the room, as well, perching on the sofa.

Lost in the music, Morie played with utter joy. It had been weeks since she'd had access to a piano, and this one was top quality. It had been tuned recently, as well. The sounds that came from it were as exquisite as the score she was playing with such expression.

When the final, poignant crescendo was reached and she played the last notes, there was an utter stillness in the room and, then, exuberant applause.

She got up, embarrassed and flushed. "I only play a little," she protested. "Thanks."

Mallory was staring at her through narrowed eyes. "Aren't you full of surprises, for a poor cowgirl," he remarked with faint suspicion.

She bit her lower lip, hard. "All of us have natural talent of some sort. I always knew how to play. I played by ear for a long time, then this nice lady took me in and tutored me where I worked last." Actually, it had been Heather Everett, who played as well as she sang.

"And where was that, did you say?" Mallory persisted.

But this time he didn't catch her out. "The Story Ranch outside Billings." She happened to know that the ranch had been sold after the owner's death. There was nobody who could deny her story. And she could always give him the phone number of the housekeeper who'd promised to cover her allegations.

Mallory actually looked disappointed. "I see."

"He was a grand old fellow to work for," she elaborated. "He had a piano and he let me practice on it. I was heartbroken when he died." She was certain that she would have been, if she'd known him. Her father spoke of the old gentleman with great affection. He knew him from cattlemen's conventions.

"You have a real talent," Cane remarked. "Have you thought about a career using it?"

"Shut up," Mallory said at once, glaring at his brother. "I'm not looking for a new hire to look after my prize heifers because she—" he indicated her "—wants to go off looking for a recording contract!"

"She should use her talent," Cane argued hotly. "She's wasting her life working for pennies, using up her health lifting heavy limbs off fences! Down the road, she'll pay for all this physical labor. She's too slightly built to even be doing it!"

Mallory knew that, but it irritated him that his brother had pointed it out to him. "She asked for the job and was willing to do whatever it involved!" he shot back.

Cane stood up, dark eyes glittering. "And you're taking advantage of it!"

"You could send somebody with her to ride fences," Tank interjected, stepping between the brothers. He smiled at Morie, who was looking with stifled horror at the confrontation she'd provoked so innocently. "In fact, I could ride them with her. I've got enough time free."

"Or I could," Cane said shortly. "You need to work on marketing for the production sale. I'm the one with the most free time."

"She works for me, damn it!" Mallory ground out. "I tell her what to do. You don't hire and fire! Either of you! Personnel problems are my business!"

"I am not a problem!" Morie said, and stomped her foot at the three brothers. "Listen, I don't mind doing whatever my job calls for, honest I don't. I really appreciate your kindness. But I just work here. I'm a hired hand."

They stared at her.

"Your hands are precious," Cane said gently, and with feeling, because he only had one left and he knew better than any of the other brothers how precious they truly were. "You mustn't risk them on physical labor."

"I'll buy her a pair of damned gloves, then!" Mallory snapped. "Want me to hire a companion for her, to do the hard jobs, while I'm at it?"

Morie felt sick. She lowered her eyes and moved away. "I'll get back to work," she said in a faint tone. "I never meant to cause trouble. I'm really sorry."

She went out the door before they could stop her.

"Oh, you're a real prince," Cane shot at his older brother. "Now she's upset!"

"I should go after her," Tank agreed.

"I'll go after her," Cane replied curtly, starting for the door.

"What the hell is the matter with you two?" Mallory demanded hotly. "She's an employee! She's a hire!"

They glared at him.

"You've already forgotten Vanessa, have you?" he asked with a cold smile.

They sobered at once.

"She was handing our family heirlooms out the window to her lover, when we caught her," he reminded them. "She was sweet and caring, and the best cook in two counties. She pampered us. Brought hot chocolate and cookies out to the barn in the snow when we couldn't leave sick bulls. Made soup for us when we had to take turns staying in the line cabins, before market prices shot up. Treated us like princes. And all the while, she was pricing the stuff in the cabinets, the paintings, the silver services, the china, the crystal that was in our family for a hundred years."

They looked shamefaced.

"She came with excellent references, too," Mallory continued. "Except when I finally got around to checking them out, they were bogus. She lied even when we caught her red-handed. Her lover had made her do it. She was innocent. She loved working for us. She'd do anything if we'd forgive her and let her come back. She'd testify against her lover, even."

"But she had a record as long as my leg," Tank put in quietly.

"And a real talent for lying." Cane nodded.

"And we almost lost the ranch because she sued us for defamation of character and sexual harassment, of which we were totally innocent."

"Good thing the jury believed us," Cane replied.

"Good thing we had the best damned attorney in Wyoming," Mallory agreed. "We can't afford to trust people we don't know. Gelly is already suspicious of Morie, and she's come to me twice with stories that Morie denies and makes light of." He shifted. "I don't trust her." He didn't add that his own great physical attraction to her was one of his biggest issues. It made him vulnerable. He couldn't afford to trust his instincts, when they might be leading him down a dark road. "She knows how to make canapés and plan society dos, and play the piano like a professional. It doesn't jibe with her job description."

"Then what do you think is her real background?" Cane asked curtly.

"Think about it," Mallory replied. "A woman who wanted to insinuate herself into a rich household, without drawing attention to her background, would pretend to know nothing about wealthy people. But underneath, she'd be clued in about how they lived, what they did. She'd know their habits and their tastes. She'd have to, to play up to them. Then she'd bring out those talents, a little at a time, to deepen the mystery and make herself acceptable."

"You're reaching," Tank said shortly. "Gelly's poisoned you against Morie."

"I was already headed in that direction," Mallory replied. "She isn't telling us the truth about her background. I'm sure of it."

"That doesn't mean it's a shady background," Cane replied. "Vanessa poisoned all of us against women for a while. It's why we hired Mavie, who isn't young or beautiful or interested in us. But Morie might be the genuine article."

"And she might not be," Mallory said grimly. "I just think we need to keep an eye on her and not trust her too far. Just like any other new hire."

They had to agree. They'd gone in headfirst,

because she seemed sweet and helpful and kind. But it could be an act. They knew from experience how gullible all three of them could be.

"I guess you're right," Cane said solemnly.

"I'm always right," Mallory said, tongue-in-cheek. "I'm the eldest."

Tank glared at him. "Only by two years. Don't get conceited."

Mallory chuckled. "Better get back to work."

MORIE WAS DISCONCERTED by the argument. She was preoccupied when she went to the tack room to get her bridle and saddle to ride fence. There was a lot of fence on the ranch. She'd never seen so many acres, except on her father's spread. This was a huge tract of land that made up the ranch property, and it was cross-fenced for miles and miles and miles.

Darby glanced at her as she came out. "Trouble?" he asked gently.

She hesitated. She nodded.

"Mallory again?"

"I started a fight. I didn't mean to. I was just playing the piano."

His eyebrows arched. "That was you?" he exclaimed. "I thought it was a record they'd put on!"

She looked down shyly. "I took piano for almost ten years," she said. "I love to play. Tank, I mean Mr. Kirk, had the score from that movie, *August*

Rush, and when he knew I could play, he asked me to show him. So I did. But then the brothers said I shouldn't be risking my hands doing manual labor and Mallory, I mean Mr. Kirk, got mad and said I was hired to do ranch work...."

"I see where this is going," Darby replied quietly. "It must have been difficult."

She nodded again and drew in a long breath. "I didn't mean to start trouble. It was so wonderful to have a piano to play on." She smiled. "I've loved music all my life. I can play classical guitar, too, and I used to carry a guitar with me wherever I went. But you can't pack a piano around, so I sort of got out of the habit of playing." She closed her eyes. "I can hear sonatas in my mind, when I go to bed. I never met a classical score that I didn't love. Especially Debussy..."

"Am I paying you for musical commentary now?" Mallory asked coldly from the doorway.

She started, and almost dropped the saddle. "Sorry, boss. Sorry." She rushed out the door with the saddle over her shoulder, almost tripped and fell down the steps in her rush.

Darby put out a hand and pulled Mallory around. His blue eyes were blazing. "Lay off," he said in a menacing tone. "The girl's had enough for one day."

Mallory shook off the hand and glared at his foreman. "Don't push me."

"Then don't push her," Darby said. "Look at her, for God's sake!"

He didn't want to, but he did. She was fumbling with the saddle. Her hands were shaking. Tears were rolling down her cheeks. Mallory felt it through his heart, like a knife. He grimaced.

"If I was her, I'd quit right now," Darby said shortly. "And when she comes back tonight, that's what I'm going to advise her to do. I know a couple of ranchers who need help...."

"You'll keep your mouth shut, or you'll be the one leaving," Mallory told him angrily. "Don't interfere."

"Then you stop treating her like the black plague" came the short reply. "Honest to God, what's wrong with you? I've never seen you treat a kid like that!"

"She's no kid," Mallory said angrily. "She's a woman." He knew it far better than Darby.

"Well, maybe so," he conceded. "Still, she's twice the woman that blond headache you take around with you is," he told the boss. "You're letting her warp your idea of Morie. She's making you suspicious. Now you're picking holes in everything Morie does. All because you and your brothers were taken in by Vanessa Wilkes. It's your pride, hurting and making you suspect everybody. Even poor old Harry. He never stole that drill. Your girlfriend was in the bunkhouse just before she told you she'd seen him take it. She framed him, and you let her."

"That's enough," Mallory said. He looked dangerous. "He was guilty."

"He wasn't, but he knew he'd never convince you as long as Gelly was around. Now she's trying to do the same to Morie, to make you run her off." He straightened. "I've seen good people and I've seen bad people. I warned you about Vanessa and you wouldn't listen. Now I'm telling you, Morie isn't like that. She's pure gold. If you aren't careful, you'll ruin her life. Maybe your own, too."

"She's not what she seems," Mallory said.

"Who is?" Darby smiled gently. "But she's not devious. She's running from something. I don't know what. But she had no idea how to do ranch work, I'll tell you that."

"What!"

"She was desperate for a job," Darby said. "So I taught her how to do the chores, how to dip cattle, how to help brand, how to stack hay and ride fence and pull calves. You have to admit, she's turned into one of the best hires we've ever had. Works all hours, never complains about anything." His eyes narrowed and the smile thinned. "And you think someone like that could be dishonest? Wouldn't she be complaining at every turn and trying to get out of hard work?"

"I don't know," Mallory confessed. "Vanessa

made me question my judgment. I'm not certain about anyone anymore."

"If you want to distrust somebody, you take a hard look at that Bruner woman," Darby said. "Something's not right there. I'd bet money on it."

"She's just a friend," Mallory muttered.

"She doesn't think that. She wants you. And she'll find a way to get rid of Morie, you mark my words. She's not going to let her stay here."

"It's my ranch. I hire and fire."

"Think so? We'll see. Meanwhile, how about easing up on Morie?" he added. "God knows what that child's been through in her life to make her end up here, doing a job she was never intended to do. Hurts me to see that deep scratch on her face. Flawless complexion. She could have been a model."

Mallory frowned. He hadn't considered her complexion or her background. He'd only been concerned that she might be a con artist. He'd have to take a better look at her. On the one hand, he was suspicious. On the other, he trusted Darby's judgment when he couldn't trust his own.

He patted the old man on the shoulder. "Never could take back talk from anybody but you, you old pirate."

Darby grinned. "You'll always get the truth from me. Even if you don't want to hear it."

Mallory sighed. He was looking after Morie.

She'd gone galloping off, still crying. He felt like a villain. "Think I'll take a ride."

Darby smiled. "Good idea. You do that."

MORIE STOPPED AT THE CREEK and got off the horse. She bathed her face in the clean water and used her only handkerchief to mop up her tears. Ridiculous, letting that awful man make her cry. She should have kicked him and told him what he could do with his job. That's what her father would have done. He'd never have gone off crying. She tried to picture that and it made her smile.

She heard a horse coming up and turned, expecting Darby. But it was the boss. He looked oddly contrite, watching her with one arm crossed over the pommel, his dark eyes keen on her tearstained face.

"Maybe I could have chosen my words better," he said stiffly.

She shrugged and looked away. "I work here. You're the boss."

"Yes, but..." He drew in an angry breath. "Why didn't you fight back? Why did you run?"

She glared at him. "I've caused enough trouble for one day," she said flatly. She drew in a long breath. "Listen, I should quit...."

"No!"

He was out of the saddle in a heartbeat and standing over her the next. He took her by the shoulders. In the silence of the woods, she could hear her own heart beating as he looked into her eyes and didn't look away for so long that her heart ran wild. She had to part her full lips to breathe. Her heartbeat was strangling her.

He saw that helpless reaction and it touched him. She couldn't have faked her attraction to him. It was far too visible.

His hands relaxed and became caressing. They ran up and down her arms in the long-sleeved cotton T-shirt. "You puzzle me," he said, his voice deep and slow, like velvet. "I don't like it."

Her hands pressed against the soft cotton of his shirt. Underneath it she felt cushy, thick hair and hard muscle. She smelled the woodsy cologne and the masculine soap that clung to his skin. He made her tingle all over, just by standing close to her. She looked up at his wide, sensuous mouth and remembered how it felt to kiss him. She wanted him to kiss her. She wanted it, so much!

"Damn it," he ground out, because he knew. He could sense her hunger, even before her rapt gaze on his lips proved it to him.

Before she could question the sudden curse, his mouth went down on hers. He kissed her hungrily. His arms lifted her into the instantly hard contours of his powerful body and pulled her into him. His hand went to the base of her spine, insistent as he demonstrated the force of his desire for her.

She tried to protest, but her own body betrayed her. She moaned and pressed close against him, her mouth twisting under his, provoking, pleading, begging for more.

She felt him move, felt the ground suddenly under her back and the weight and warmth of his body melting down into hers. She felt his long leg parting both of hers as his hips moved down between them.

"Dear...God!" he bit off reverently as he felt the pleasure wash over him.

His hands were under her shirt, under her bra. He felt the softness of her small, firm breasts with their hard tips first against his fingers, and then, as he pushed the shirt up out of his way, under his mouth.

He suckled her, hard, feeling her arch under him and cry out. He thought he was hurting her in his ardor and started to lift his head, but her hands pulled, pleaded, dragged his mouth back down.

She tasted like honey. He was drowning in need. He pressed against her in a slow, sensuous rhythm that grew more insistent by the minute. His hand lifted her hips, pulled them against the hardness of him.

He worked feverishly at the buttons of his shirt and opened it so that he could feel her breasts under the crush of his bare chest. His mouth invaded hers. He was desperate to have her. He couldn't bear to stop, not now!

Neither could she. It was the most passionate interlude of her young life. She wasn't able to protest. She wanted to know him, as a man, as a lover. She wanted to feel him deep inside her, feel him taking her, possessing her. She wanted…a child…!

She hadn't realized she'd spoken aloud until he suddenly dragged himself away from her, rolled over in an agonized state of denial and groaned as if all the devils in purgatory were pummeling him.

She lay shocked, gasping, as she realized how far they'd gone. She jackknifed, quickly righting her clothing, shivering with denied pleasure. She got to her feet, shaking, and looked away while she fought to get her breath. She was horrified at her own lack of control. It had been so close!

She swallowed, hard, and then swallowed again. She couldn't force herself to look at him, although she heard him get to his feet, heard his own rasping breath as he worked to regain the control he'd lost.

After a minute, she heard a rough curse break from his throat as he looked at her stiff back.

"So that's your game, is it?" he asked coldly. "You'd like a child, would you? I don't suppose you're taking any sort of preventative. You seduce the boss, there's a child and you're set for life. That how it works?"

She turned, shocked. She stared at him with stark embarrassment and averted her eyes. She was flushed and sick at heart. "I...wasn't thinking at all."

"Obviously you were," he said coldly. He smiled. It wasn't a nice smile. "Good try. But I'm no novice with your sex, and I'm no easy mark."

"It wasn't like that." She faltered, flushing even more.

He gave her a long and very insulting look. "Sure." He picked up his hat from where he'd tossed it, dusted it off, slanted it over his eyes and went to find his horse, which had wandered off to eat green grass. He mounted and turned the horse. He stared at her, but she didn't look at him, or answer him. She went to get back on her own mount and rode away without another word.

She was going to have to leave. She knew it certainly. Mallory had made his opinion of her quite clear. What was unclear was why he'd suddenly started kissing her like that. She hadn't asked for it. Or had she? Her obvious attraction to him was going to be disastrous. He was already suspicious of her, thanks to his girlfriend. She'd blurted out that embarrassing comment and now he was surely going to think she was some gold digger.

Her subconscious must be working overtime,

she decided, because she had no conscious thought of starting a family. But to have a child, with a man like Mallory, who was so masculine and attractive...

And bullheaded and suspicious-minded and unkind, she added hotly to herself. Of course she wanted a child from a man like that!

Actually, in her young life, she'd never known passion or such hunger; she'd never thought of marrying and having children. She'd thought herself in love with the persistent accountant until she found out his true motives for courting her. But now she knew there had been nothing at all to that relationship. And he'd pressed her to sleep with him. He'd even said they had no need for birth control, because he wanted children with her. Somehow, she'd had the sense to deny him.

Mallory was thinking the exact same thing about her that she'd thought about her would-be lover. The accountant, she still couldn't bring herself to say his name even silently, had wanted to trap her into marriage. Mallory thought Morie was up to the same underhanded game. It was humiliating.

She should have had more control of herself. It was just that he was heaven to kiss. And kissing had so quickly not been enough to satisfy either of them. If she hadn't opened her mouth to say something so shocking, if he hadn't pulled back in time...

She flushed, remembering how sweet it had been. She couldn't allow that to happen again. Not that she'd be around long enough. She'd started trouble with the brothers, innocently, setting one against the other. Her presence here was causing problems. She should leave. Now. Today.

Yes. She should. She got back on her horse and started to turn him toward the ranch. But at the last minute, she couldn't force herself to do it. Just a little longer, she promised herself. Just a few more days to look at Mallory from a distance and talk to him and dream of him. What would it hurt?

She started back to the fence line.

SEVERAL DAYS PASSED with no other incidents. Mallory, however, said hardly two words to Morie. He relayed instructions through Darby, who seemed uncomfortable for some reason.

Cane found Morie at the line cabin, where she was spending the day watching for calves to drop. He got off his horse with some little effort and walked up on the porch. Morie was drinking coffee from her thermos and eating a cold, buttered biscuit.

"Hi," she greeted cheerily. "Want to share lunch?" She held out the half-eaten biscuit.

He shook his head. "No, thanks. I just had a

thick roast-beef sandwich with homemade French fries."

She groaned and looked at the biscuit. "I knew I wasn't living right."

He smiled. He pushed his wide-brimmed hat back on his head and his dark eyes narrowed. "What's going on between you and Mal?" he asked unexpectedly.

She fumbled and spilled coffee on her jeans. Well, they were dirty anyway. "What...what do you mean?" She faltered, and ruined her poise by flushing.

He pursed his lips. "I see."

"No, you don't," she shot back. "You don't see. There's nothing. Nothing at all!"

"Why, because he's the boss and you're the hired help?" he asked, leaning back against a post. "We aren't royalty."

"You might as well be," she said flatly. "He thinks I'm after his money."

His eyebrows arched. "He does?"

She lowered her eyes to the splash of coffee on her knee. She sipped more coffee. "I'm not," she said with quiet pride, "but it's what he thinks." She looked up. "I'm fairly certain his girlfriend is helping him to think it. She really hates my guts."

"I noticed."

She looked up at him solemnly. "You watch

her," she said with sudden passion. "She's pretending to be something she's not."

His eyebrows arched. "And you know this, how…?"

"For one thing, she's wearing last year's colors. For another, the shoes she favors are far out of style. Her jewelry is just as dated, and the purse she carries is couture, but it's not a new one."

His eyebrows arched more. "Excuse me?"

She shifted restlessly and averted her eyes. "I have a friend who models," she lied. It was her mother, who was her closest friend. "I know what's in style and what's not, something Ms. Bruner seems unaware of. I suppose she thinks men don't follow fashion and wouldn't know," She met his gaze. "She's trying to pose as a socialite, but something's not right about her. Want some advice? Get a private detective to do just a surface check of her background. I'm betting you'd find something interesting."

"Why don't you tell Mal?" he asked.

She laughed coldly. "Oh, sure, he'd listen to me. He already thinks I'm a gold-digging opportunist."

He sighed. "You're not what you're pretending to be, either, are you?"

She smiled wryly. "No," she confessed. "But I'm an honest person. I'm not hiding from the law or contemplating breaking it. Actually, I have a cousin who's a Texas Ranger. I've known him and looked up to him since I was able to walk. He'd disown me if I did anything criminal. So would my parents."

"Why are you working here?"

"You'd be surprised," she assured him.

"I might be, at that." He hesitated. "Want me to go ride fence with you? I've got some free time. That killer is still on the loose." He sobered. "I wouldn't want anything to happen to you."

She was pleasantly surprised at his protective attitude. "Thanks," she said and meant it. "But I'm fine. I've got the cell phone the boss was kind enough to provide, and I've got a gun that Darby loaned me. I'll be fine."

He regarded her quizzically. "Okay, then. I'll leave you to it. A cold biscuit. You call that lunch?"

She sighed. "It's a lovely biscuit. Mavie made them for me."

"She's a super cook."

"Yes, she is. Thanks again," she added as he mounted his horse and started to ride off.

"You're welcome."

He tipped his hat and rode away. Morie finished her biscuit and coffee and went back to work.

CHAPTER SEVEN

MORIE WAS CONFUSED about her feelings for Mallory and her growing concern about Gelly Bruner's interference and antagonism. The woman really hated her, and she was going to find a way to make trouble. Not that Morie was willing to run from a fight. If worse came to worst, she could always tell them the truth about herself. Except that Mallory, who hated lies, would think her a hopeless liar and probably never speak to her again.

She finished her cold biscuit and cooling coffee and sighed. Just as she started to get up, she heard a twig snap. There was another sound of movement, rhythmic. Any hunter knew that to walk normally was a dead giveaway to prey he was stalking. Animals never moved rhythmically. They'd hear the odd rhythm and know it was a human even before they caught his scent.

Morie looked toward her saddled horse, where her pistol was. She did have her cell phone in her pocket, though. She stood up and pulled it out, fumbling as she tried to turn it on. Of all the times not to have it activated…!

"Don't do that" came a curt, masculine command from behind her.

She whirled, frightened and shocked, to see a tall, sandy-haired man with a hunting rifle standing just a few yards away. She trembled and dropped the phone. Her wide brown eyes were appalled as she looked at the rifle and hoped that she'd lived a good enough life that she wouldn't go somewhere horrible when she died.

She didn't speak. It would be useless. Either he'd kill her or he wouldn't. But the bore of that rifle barrel looked ten inches wide as she stared down it. She lifted her hands and waited.

But surprisingly, he didn't shoot. He lowered the gun. "Where did Tank go?" he asked suddenly.

"T…tank?"

"Tank Kirk," he said curtly. His blue eyes were dark and glittery.

"That wasn't Tank. It was Cane." She faltered. "He just came to offer to ride the fence line with me, because there's an escaped murderer on the loose."

"Murderer," he scoffed. "It was an accident. The idiot fell into a brick wall and his even more idiotic girlfriend lied and said I did it deliberately. Getting even, because I knew what she was and I wanted no part of her."

She lowered her hands slowly. Her heart was slamming against her ribs. "You're Joe Bascomb." She faltered.

"Yes, unfortunately." He sighed. He stared at her. "Have you got anything to eat out here? I'm so sick of rabbit and squirrel—bad time of year to eat either. They're not really in season. But a man gets hungry."

"I have a biscuit left. No coffee, I'm sorry, but I have a bottle of water." She offered both.

He put down the rifle and ate the biscuit with odd delight, closing his eyes on the taste. "Mavie must have made these." He sighed. "Nobody cooks like she does." He finished it off in a heartbeat and washed it down with half the bottle of water.

Morie watched him with open curiosity. He didn't act like a murderer.

He noted her gaze and laughed shortly. "I wasn't going to end up in a maximum-security prison while my lawyer spins out appeal after appeal. I hate cages. God, I hate cages! To think I could ever end up like this because of some spiteful, vicious woman…!"

"If you'd had a good defense attorney, he could have taken her apart on the witness stand," she returned.

"My attorney is from legal aid, and they come in all sizes. This one's meek and mild and thinks that women have been victimized too much in courts, so she wouldn't say anything to hurt my accuser's feelings."

"You should have asked the judge to appoint someone else."

"I did. They couldn't get anyone else to volunteer." He sighed heavily and ran a restless big hand through his hair. "She did say she'd appeal. I think she finally realized that I was innocent, after I'd been convicted. She said she was sorry." He glared at Morie. "Sorry! I'm going to get the needle, and she's sorry!"

"So am I," she said gently. "The justice system usually works. But people are the odd element in any trial. Mistakes get made."

"You'd know this, how?" he asked, but with a smile.

"My uncle is a state supreme court judge," she replied. "In Texas."

His eyebrows arched. "Impressive."

She smiled. "Yes, it is. He used to work for legal aid and donate time, when he was younger. He still believes everyone is entitled to proper representation."

"I wish he sat on the bench in Wyoming," Bascomb replied sadly.

"You should turn yourself back in," she advised. "This is only going to make things worse for you."

"They couldn't get much worse," he replied. "I

lost my wife last year. She died of a heart attack. She was only twenty-nine years old. Who dies of a heart attack at twenty-nine?" he exclaimed.

"There was a football player at my high school who dropped dead on the playing field at age seventeen of an unknown heart problem," Morie replied. "He was a sweet boy. We all mourned him. People get all sorts of disorders at young ages. You don't think of little children having arthritis, either, do you? But some grammar-school kids have rheumatoid arthritis that limits them in all sorts of ways. Kids also have diseases like diabetes. We don't only get things wrong with us when we're old."

"I guess so. It's not a perfect world, is it?" he added.

She shook her head.

He finished the bottle of water. "Thanks. I've been going by my mom's place for food, but they've got people watching it. I don't want her to suffer for what I've done. I've been hunting for food."

"What about water?" she asked gently. "It's dangerous to drink water from springs…."

He pulled a packet of tablets out of his vest pocket and showed her. "It makes any water potable," he said. "I was in the military. Tank and I served together in Iraq. That seems like a hundred years ago." He grimaced. "He testified for me.

It was a real brave thing to do, when everybody thought I was guilty. The local boy's family is known and loved, and that made it a lot harder for me to get an unbiased jury. In fact—" he sighed "—one of the jurors was actually an illegitimate blood relation. My attorney didn't catch that on voir dire, either."

She caught her breath. "That's a disqualification. Grounds for a retrial."

"You think so?" he asked, curious.

"I do. You should speak to your attorney."

He laughed shortly. "She's not my attorney anymore. I read in a discarded newspaper that she said she couldn't represent someone who proved himself guilty by running away. So now I've got no defense and nobody to advise me."

She moved a step closer. "I'm advising you. Turn yourself in before it's too late."

He shook his head. "Can't do that. I can't survive locked up in a cage. I've had months of it. I'd rather die than go back, and that's the truth."

She could sympathize. She didn't like closed places, either. "It will go harder on you that you didn't wait for an appeal."

"I don't care," he said heavily. "My wife is dead…the life I had is all gone. I've got no reason to go on anyway. If they shoot me down in the woods, well, it won't be so bad. God forgives people.

Even bad people. I don't think He'll send me to purgatory."

"You can't give up," she said, driven to comfort him. "God puts us here for a reason. We may never know why. It may be to inspire one person, or give another a reason to keep them from suicide, or be in the right place to give aid to save someone's life who may one day save the world. Who knows? But I believe we have a purpose. All of us."

"And what do you think mine is?" he asked with amusement. She was so fervent in her beliefs.

"I don't know," she replied. "But you have a part to play. I'm sure of that. Don't give up. Don't ever give up."

"There was this movie *Galaxy Quest* with Tim Allen and Alan Rickman, kind of a *Star Trek* spoof," he recalled. "Their running line was 'Never give up, never surrender!'"

"I saw that one. It was terrific," she replied, smiling.

He shrugged. "I guess it wasn't such a bad credo, at that." He shouldered the gun. "Don't tell anybody I was here," he said.

She bit her lower lip. It sounded like a threat.

He gave her a long-suffering look. "You might get in trouble for giving me food and water," he added.

She relaxed. "Oh. Thanks."

"I'm a wanted man," he replied quietly. "I'm not giving up, no matter what. They'll have to take me down. Prison is a horrible place for an outdoorsman." He looked around at the towering trees and the blue, blue sky. "This is my cathedral," he said solemnly. "There's no place closer to God than the forest." He drew in the scent of it with closed eyes. "I should never have let her talk me into going to her apartment," he said. "She was screaming. She said her boyfriend was banging on the door threatening to kill her and I was the only person she knew that she could trust to deal with him. I must have been out of my mind," he added remorsefully. "She was fending him off when I got there, but he muttered something about her attacking him first. She set us both up. I don't think she meant for him to die, or me to go to prison... It was just a misguided plea for attention. But she caused it. Now she's the injured party and I'm being sued for wrongful death by his family." He gave her a long look.

She winced. "I'm sorry."

"Hell, so am I," he said heavily. "Don't know what I ever did to deserve this."

"It's a trial," she replied. "All of us have them. It's part of the process of life. You'll get through it," she added firmly.

"Think so? If I were a gambler, I'd take that bet and get rich on it." He looked at her clothing and laughed. "Well, maybe not. You don't look any better off than I was, no offense."

"None taken," she replied.

"I have to go. Thanks for the help. But if I'm caught, I'll swear you never did a thing to help me," he added.

"And I'll swear that I did," she said proudly. "I'm not afraid of due process. My uncle is a judge. He'd find someone good to represent me."

His blue eyes smiled at her. "Lucky you. Thanks, kid."

She laughed. "You're welcome. I wish I could help you."

His face softened. "You're a nice person. My wife was like that. She'd have helped anybody, in the law or out of it. I miss her so much."

"It's just a little separation," she said. "We all go, eventually. It's a matter of time."

He cocked his head. "She'd have said that, too." He looked around. "You be careful out here, all alone. It's dangerous sometimes. There are other people who shun society. Some of them are homeless people with various mental disturbances. They could hurt you."

"I know. I've got a phone."

"Keep it on," he advised drily.

"Yes, well if I'd had it on, the police would already be here, wouldn't they?" she said pointedly.

He chuckled. "I guess so." He gave her a last look. "Be safe."

"You, too."

He turned and walked back into the woods. She noted that when he was almost out of sight, the rhythm of his footsteps changed and became halting and unsteady. Like an animal's gait. She realized then that he'd walked in a human pattern to alert her to his presence, so that he wouldn't frighten her too much by appearing suddenly. She felt sorry for him. She wondered if she could get in touch with Uncle Danny and find him some help. Even if he was guilty as sin, he needed a lawyer. Uncle Danny would know someone. She was certain of it.

THAT NIGHT, SHE CALLED HIM. She knew his habits quite well, and one of them was to work very late at his office on nights when circuit court was in session. Sure enough, he answered the phone himself. He was surprised but pleased to hear from her.

"Having fun at your job?" he asked, amused that she'd defied King to work as a cowgirl on a ranch.

"Lots," she replied. "But I miss you."

"I miss you, too, sweetie," he replied. "Not prying, but is there some reason besides love that you're calling me at night? Got a problem?"

"Sort of," she said. "There's this escaped convict who was framed..."

"Oh, spare me," he said heavily. "Honey, you have no idea how many innocent people are serving life terms in federal prison. They were framed, the cops were dishonest, somebody was getting even with them..."

"But it's not like that." She faltered. "Tank Kirk was a character witness for him. The man fought in Iraq. His wife died. This other woman chased him and couldn't get him, so she set him up by crying for help when her boyfriend was beating her up. The guy came to her rescue, struggled with the man, who hit his head and died. The woman then swore that the convict did it deliberately. It's her word against his, and he only had a public defender."

"Careful, darlin', I was a public defender," he chided. "It's a noble calling."

"Yes, well this public defender was on the woman's side and wouldn't press the case. There's something else. There was a blood relative of the victim on the jury and it wasn't caught in voir dire."

"Now that's another matter, a very serious one," Danny replied. "His attorney should press for a retrial on that basis, if she can prove it."

"He isn't represented," she replied. "His attorney quit when he escaped and ran from the law."

"Oh, boy."

"I know. I shouldn't get involved. But he seems a decent man. You'd have to know the Kirk brothers to understand why I think he's innocent. Tank isn't easily fooled about people."

"Ah. But he's fooled about you, isn't he?"

She had to concede that point. "Touché."

"Tell you what. I know some people in the judiciary in Wyoming. I'll make a few phone calls. What's the man's name?"

"Joe Bascomb."

"Okay. But you stay out of it. Believe me, you don't want to be charged as an accessory, in aiding an escaped convict," he added.

"Yes, I know. I won't. Thanks."

"Hey, how could I turn down my favorite girl?" he teased. "See you soon. Take care."

"You, too."

She closed up the little phone with a sigh. It wasn't any of her business. But the man had seemed so personable. He could have killed her, attacked her, if he'd wanted to. There had been nobody to help her. But he'd been polite and courteous and kind. It spoke volumes about the sort of person he was. She had to help if she could. And you never knew, she considered. There was a pattern to life. He'd become entwined in hers. There had to be a reason, somewhere. She might find it out one day.

THE NEXT MORNING, Mallory was looking at her with more suspicion than ever. She walked over to him, trying not to notice how very attractive he was. She wished she could have met him in her real persona, as she was, so that things would have been on an equal footing from the beginning. As it was, he'd know someday that she'd lied to him about her status. Or perhaps he wouldn't. She could go home, go back to the old life, marry the nice clean-cut young millionaire her father was pressing her to marry and settle down. She could forget the rough rancher who lived in Wyoming and thought she was shady and untrustworthy. If only he could know how much those accusations hurt her.

She looked up at him with wide dark eyes. "Something wrong, boss?"

"You know that we keep a record of all outgoing phone calls here?" he asked solemnly.

Her heart jumped. She'd called Texas. In fact, she'd called her uncle's office.

"Do you?" she asked, trying to sound innocent.

"I'd like to know why you were phoning a superior court judge in Texas," he said simply. He shoved his hands into his pockets and gave her a cold smile. "In fact, the same superior court judge who flew up here for our party. Did you discuss something more than canapés when you met him outside and Gelly caught you? Is he your lover? Or do you have a lawsuit in mind and you're looking for advice? I do recall that you threatened to sue Gelly."

Her heart raced while she searched for excuses that wouldn't sound any more alarm bells. She didn't want to give away Tank's friend. If Mallory knew she'd seen the man in the woods, he might call the sheriff. She didn't want to cause the poor man any more trouble than she already had.

"I forgot to add something to the recipe I gave him," she blurted out.

He blinked and stared at her. "Excuse me?"

"The canapé recipe," she continued. "I forgot to tell him how long his housekeeper should cook them. He said they were having some big to-do on his family's ranch next month and he wanted the recipe for that."

"So you called him in the middle of the night to tell him?" he asked, incredulous.

She grimaced. "It was when I remembered it," she replied, and shrugged. "I forget stuff."

"Not his phone number, apparently," he mused.

"It was listed on the internet," she muttered, prevaricating because it was for a good cause. "I used a search engine. I knew his name and what he did for a living. The rest was easy."

He let out a long breath. He always seemed to be suspicious of her, and he hated himself for it. She seemed to be an honest, hardworking, kind young woman. But he didn't trust his instincts. He'd been taken in one time too many by a woman who wasn't what she seemed. This one knew her way around the law, despite her protests, and she could pose a real threat to the ranch if she was trying to set him up.

On the other hand, his heart started doing cartwheels every time he looked at her, and that was getting worse by the day. He wanted her. He was having a hard time hiding it, especially from his brothers, who noticed everything.

Gelly was furious that he even talked about Morie, which he did often, involuntarily. He'd mentioned her help in the kitchen, which Mavie had been overjoyed to have. Gelly wouldn't dirty her fingers in a kitchen, and she was already jealous. Too jealous. He'd let the woman get too familiar with him, just by not pushing her away when he still could. Now she was talking about marriage and interceding with him for a friend who wanted to buy some scrubland on the northernmost end of the ranch.

"It's just worthless land," she coaxed. "You can't run cattle on it. This poor man just lost everything he had. He just wants a few acres to live on. Maybe grow a little garden."

"If it's land you can't run cattle on, you sure as hell can't farm it, Gelly," he'd replied. "Besides, it's a family ranch and that would be a family decision. You need to have the man come and talk to us."

She didn't dare do that. The brothers would realize in a heartbeat that he was a businessman, not a down-on-his-luck rancher.

"Oh, he's out of town," she said, thinking quickly.

"Doing what?"

She thought. "Visiting his sick brother."

He shrugged. "No problem. Have him come see us when he gets back. Now, are you hell-bent on going to this movie?" he added, indicating it on the screen of his computer. "I don't like comedies."

"It's funny," she assured him. "At least, that's what I was told. You need a night out. You spend too much time working around here. You should hire a manager. You know, I just met a man who would do nicely. He's college educated and…"

"I run the ranch," he said coldly, looking up at her.

She hesitated. "Well, I was just mentioning it. About the movie," she added, and quickly changed the subject. He was too quick for her. She'd have to be more careful.

Mallory was remembering the conversation while he was staring pointedly at Morie. She flushed under the scrutiny. He could see her heart beating wildly against her shirt. Her breasts were

pointed suddenly, too, and he felt his own body re-
acting to her arousal. He wanted to back her into
the wall and kiss her forever.

He pulled himself up short. He had to get her
out of here before he did something stupid. "All
right," he said. "You can go back to work."

"Thanks." She didn't look at him again. She
could barely walk for the trembly feeling that went
over her. He'd looked at her with pure hunger. She
knew he wanted her, but he didn't trust her. He
was remembering her involuntary outburst in the
woods. If only she'd kept her mouth shut! He'd
never trust her again and she had only herself to
blame. But she could win his trust. She knew she
could. She just had to try.

HE TOLD GELLY, WITHOUT meaning to, about Morie's
phone call to the Texas judge.

"Well, that's not surprising," she commented
on the way to the movie.

"Why not?" he shot at her.

"They were all hugged up together when I went
out to tell her to get back to work and stop disturbing your guests," she replied, lying through her
teeth. She smiled secretively when she saw his expression. "He was very rude to me. He didn't like
it that I interrupted them."

"She said she was giving him a canapé recipe,"
he scoffed.

She laughed out loud. "Oh, come on!" She glanced at him with lowered eyelids. "And you actually believed her?"

He didn't like feeling foolish. "I suppose so. At first."

"I'm sure there's something going on there," she replied easily. "They obviously knew each other all along. And he's a judge." She glanced at him again. "What if she's trying to set you up for a lawsuit and he's helping her? Some judges are dishonest, you know."

That was what he'd thought himself. He didn't want to agree with her.

"She looks to me the sort who'd look for an easy way," she added. "She's so poor, she'd probably do anything to get out of debt, to have nice clothes that were currently in fashion, to be seen at the best places, to travel first-class around the world." She was daydreaming, not about her rival's wishes, but her own. Her face set in hard lines. "She's probably sick of having to do things she hates just to get ahead in life, to have the things she deserves and can't get any other way."

He gave her an astonished look.

She noted it, and cleared her throat. "I mean, that sort of woman obviously is hoping to make some rich man fall for her, and she'll do whatever it takes. You're rich. Of course she wants you. It's obvious."

"It is?"

"She stares at you all the time," she muttered. "Like a kid looking at the counter in an ice-cream shop."

"She does?" His heart jumped. He had to force himself not to react. "I hadn't noticed," he added in a droll tone.

"It's disgusting the way she falls all over herself to please you. Let me tell you, she's not like that around me," she said grimly. "She's all claws and teeth. She hates me. The way she talks to me...you should say something to her about it," she added firmly. "It's not right, to have a hired person speak that way to someone of my class."

Of her class. Her father was a retired textile worker, he'd found that out quite accidentally in conversation with a neighbor. Her late mother had been a bank clerk, an honorable profession but not something that gave her carte blanche to high society. Gelly had aspirations. She wanted money. He felt hunted, all of a sudden. She'd been sweet and clinging and flattering at first. Now she was becoming aggressive and demanding, pushing him toward her friends who wanted cheap land and jobs and other things. It was vaguely annoying.

"You're getting a little pushy lately yourself, Gelly," he remarked curtly.

She caught her breath. "Am I? How so?"

"You sure do know plenty of people I can help," he noted coolly.

She bit her lip. "Oh, that. I was asked about jobs here, that's all. I don't even know the man who wanted the managerial position—he's a friend of a friend. And the man who wants the land is a good friend of my father's. My father worked in a textile corporation, you know. He was quite well-known in certain circles."

He was a cloth cutter, but Mallory wasn't saying it. He'd keep his own counsel. There was something about Gelly that started to ring alarm bells in his brain. He just smiled and asked her where she'd like to eat after the movie let out.

BUT LATER HE SPOKE TO TANK.

"What do you really think of Gelly?" he asked when they were sipping coffee alone at the kitchen table. They rarely had it late at night, but they were helping with calving and it was a long and tedious job that never seemed to end when it was bedtime.

Tank's dark eyes narrowed. "I don't think about her, if I can help it. Why?"

"She's got a friend who wants us to sell him some scrubland we own, that tract on the northern boundary that we can't run cattle on. She says it's just worthless land. He's down on his luck and wants us to sell it to him cheap."

Tank pursed his lips. "Wasn't that the same land

that the oil company had its eye on for fracking and we refused to lease it to them?"

Mallory raised his head. His eyes narrowed. "The very same."

"I wonder if her friend has any ties to the oil and gas industry."

"I wonder," Mallory repeated, and he didn't smile.

"You were asking someone about phone records," Tank added. "May I ask why?"

He shifted restlessly and sipped coffee. "Morie called that superior-court-judge friend of Cane's in Texas late at night."

Tank's eyes lifted. "Danny Brannt?"

Mallory looked murderous. "Brannt?"

"Yes. His brother is Kingston Brannt. He has an empire down in Texas. Runs Santa Gertrudis cattle that make ours look like mongrels by comparison."

"Morie's last name is Brannt," Mallory replied thoughtfully.

"Yes, but there's no relation. I asked Danny. He said it's one of the most common names in his part of Texas." He added with a smile, "Like Smith in other places. Coincidence. Nothing more."

"Really?"

"Look at Morie, for God's sake," Tank replied. "She's sweet, but she's poor as Job's turkey, can't you see? She didn't even have a decent cell phone until we got one for her."

Mallory felt a chill. "She's courting a judge," he said. "I think she may be looking for a way to sue us."

"You tar and feather her every chance you get, don't you?" Tank replied. "I wonder why."

"Gelly thinks she's up to something."

"Yes? Well, I think Gelly's up to something, and to your detriment." He finished his coffee. "Better watch your step."

"Maybe so," he conceded after a minute. He finished his own coffee. "Guess we'd better grab a little sleep while we can," he added.

Tank nodded his agreement. "Good advice."

CHAPTER EIGHT

THE NEXT DAY, Morie found an excuse to talk to Tank after they moved cattle from one pasture to another.

"I need to tell you something. I don't quite know how," she said when they were resting for a minute with thermoses full of coffee while the cattle grazed in their new fenced area.

He pushed his hat back and wiped his sweaty brow with his forearm. "Go ahead."

She glanced around to make sure nobody was near enough to hear. "Joe Bascomb was at the line cabin," she said.

"What? Good Lord, girl…!"

"He didn't hurt me. He didn't even really threaten me," she said. "He was hungry, so I gave him a biscuit and some water. He's in awful shape."

He winced. "He was my friend. I don't believe he could deliberately kill anybody."

"Neither do I. He said that his attorney gave him up when he escaped." She hesitated. "He said there was a relative of the dead man on the jury that convicted him. That should be grounds for a retrial, shouldn't it?"

He glanced at her curiously. "That's why you called the judge in Texas, isn't it?"

She laughed ruefully. "Yes," she admitted.

"What did he say?"

"That it should be grounds for a retrial. But Joe needs to turn himself in, and he needs a new attorney."

"I'd pay for one myself if I could find anybody locally who'd agree to defend him. The dead man's family is much loved here," he added. "Nobody thinks the victim was a valuable member of society, but his family is powerful. Not many local attorneys want the stigma of defending his killer."

"The judge might know somebody who'd do it pro bono," she added.

"What did you do to talk him into that?" he exclaimed.

"I appealed to his sense of justice. He's a very nice man. He came into the kitchen to compliment the cook on the food. Whoever thinks to do that at a party?" she added, having been to dozens where the food was taken for granted.

"He must be a nice man," he agreed with a smile. "I'll see what I can do." He sobered. "But don't you talk to Joe again, regardless of the circumstances. You get on your horse and leave. It's dangerous, abetting an escaped criminal. I think he's innocent, but the court judged him guilty."

"And you'd ride away and refuse help, would you?" she asked placidly.

"Well, no, I wouldn't. But I'm in a different situation than you are." His eyes narrowed. "You work for us. So you do as we say. Got that?"

"Yes, sir," she said with a sigh.

"I'm not trying to be mean. I just want to keep you out of trouble, if I can. You'd better stay clear of Gelly, too," he added. "She's really got it in for you."

"I'm not afraid of her."

"You should be," he replied. "Because Mallory believes the things she tells him. I don't know why. He doesn't even particularly like her. She just flatters his ego. He's never had much luck with women wanting him for himself, and he's easily swayed because of it. He thinks he's ugly."

"Ugly? Mallory?" she exclaimed. "Good heavens, he's not ugly!"

He pursed his lips. "He's not?"

She flushed and cleared her throat. "Well, I'd better get back to work. But I wanted you to know about Joe. I hope somebody can help him."

"Me, too."

She got on her horse and rode off, leaving Tank more puzzled than ever about her.

MALLORY WAS PREOCCUPIED. Gelly gave him a long, searching look while they ate salads at the local restaurant.

"You're worried about something, aren't you?" she asked, smiling.

He shrugged. "My brothers are falling over themselves to help our newest hire," he muttered.

"That woman," Gelly scoffed. She put down her fork. "Mal, she's a con artist if I ever saw one! Why don't you fire her?"

He finished his salad. "I'd be lynched," he mused. "Everybody's crazy about her. Even old Mavie, who hates most people." It made him feel an odd sense of pride that the people who worked for him valued Morie. He didn't know why.

Gelly's blue eyes glittered. "She's going to cause big trouble if you let her stay. You already told me what happened with your brothers when she started playing that piano. How did she learn, do you think? Maybe she played piano in a bar," she suggested with just the right note of suspicion. "What do you really know about her? You should check her out. You really should. I'll bet she has a really terrible background."

"I wonder," he said. It was their policy to check out new hires, and he had. But the detective had run into a stone wall about her family background. She seemed to be without any family in Wyoming. But his investigation had noted that she'd worked for two other ranches and had glowing recommendations from the owners. He couldn't have known that Morie had provided those references deliberately and made sure the people involved were coached in what information to give out. She'd hoped the detective would do only a surface scan and not use her social-security number to derive damaging information. But, then, the privacy laws would prevent most of that incursion without proof of criminal intent. And she'd never broken the law. She didn't even have a parking or speeding ticket to her name.

"I think she's trying to trick you into having a relationship with her," Gelly suggested. "I've seen the way she looks at you. She wants you." She leaned forward earnestly. "She would love to be pregnant. You'd have to support her and the child or she'd go to the authorities. Maybe even the television stations! What a pathetic picture she could paint, about being victimized by her boss!"

He took that with a grain of salt. But what Gelly said made sense, especially in light of his last, urgent moment with her, the hired help. He felt shamed by his lack of control, and he was still suspicious about Morie's whispered desire for a child.

Gelly saw his indecision. She would have to act. The woman was getting to Mal, and she was going to lose him if she didn't get her off the place. She had plans, big plans, for Mal and this ranch.

All she needed was a little more time. She had a friend who wanted to make a huge development on land Mal owned. She was being cut in for a small fortune. All she had to do was ease Mal into a nice relationship and then convince him to give up those few worthless acres to her for a pittance. After all, it was scrubland; he didn't even run cattle on it. Her friend had connections to the gas industry and he wanted the land for fracking, to drill through shale deposits to force oil to the surface. He'd checked out geological surveys, and that land was rich in oil and gas deposits, worth a fortune, in fact!

It was a controversial technique that had, on occasion, polluted local water tables to the extent that water could be set on fire with a match, because of the gas that infiltrated the water. But that wasn't Gelly's concern; she only wanted the kickback she was promised. It would be formidable. Then she could buy anything she wanted, instead of wearing things from a consignment shop. Fortunately for her, the brothers knew nothing about fashion and didn't realize that she was only pretending the sophistication they saw. She had other plans, even bigger ones, once she cajoled Mal into marrying her. That would take more time. But Morie was a threat and she had to be removed.

It would be easy enough. Mal already distrusted the new hire, and Morie was as dim as a low-battery flashlight. All Gelly had to do was play up to one of the young cowboys who liked her and watched her whenever she was around. A few sweet words, a few kisses, and he'd do whatever she asked. She'd already gained his confidence, pretended affection and concern for him, brought him presents. Little presents, cheap ones, like a ring with his initials on it. But they did the trick. She could use him to help her.

Mal hated a thief more than anything. She smiled. It would be easy.

MORIE WAS HELPING DARBY doctor a sick bull. The bull didn't want help and made his resistance obvious by trying to kick both of them.

"Come on, now, old fellow," Darby said gently as he turned the bull around. "That sore place is infected, and it's not going to get better without help. The vet said to put this on twice a day and we're doing it, whether you like it or not!"

"He really doesn't like that salve." Morie chuckled. "Oof!" she exclaimed when he shifted and knocked her down into the hay.

"You okay?" Darby asked, worried.

"Sure, just winded."

"Hey, Bates, come over here and help us!" he called to a young cowboy who'd just entered the barn.

"Sure thing," he called. "Just let me put away

this horse. Ms. Bruner went riding and I showed her some of the good paths." He flushed, remembering how sweet that ride had been. "She's a real nice lady."

Darby and Morie gaped at him. He didn't notice. He was still floating. Gelly had kissed him and whispered that she would do anything he liked if he would just do one little thing for her. All he had to do was place a priceless jeweled egg she'd taken from the Kirks' living room in Morie's rucksack. Such a small favor. She wasn't going to get the girl in trouble; it had been Cane's idea. It was a practical joke, nothing more…would he help? Of course he would!

He chatted to Morie as he helped them with the reluctant bull. Boy, was Miss Morie in for a surprise, he thought merrily. She was a good sport. He didn't know why Cane wanted to play a trick on her, but then, he didn't understand rich people and their senses of humor in the first place.

"Thanks, Bates," Darby told him when they were finished. "You're a good man."

"No problem," he replied. "I love ranch work, even the dirty bits."

"Me, too," Morie agreed, laughing. "It's nice to be out in the open and not to work a nine-to-five job shut up in an office somewhere."

"That's why I like it here so much." Bates nodded. "Good land, fine cattle, nice people."

"Lots of nice people," Morie agreed, and smiled at Darby.

He returned her smile. "Okay, back to work. We'd better leave before Old Stomper here finds a way to corner us and kick us. Had that happen before. He sure hates being touched."

"Old Stomper?" Morie questioned when Bates had gone back to the horses.

"He likes to step on cowboys," he explained. "Broke a man's foot during roundup." He shook his head. "He's one bad customer. But he's the best breeding bull we've got, so he gets pampered."

"That's Kirk's Ransom 428, isn't he?" she wondered aloud.

His eyes almost popped. "Yes, how did you know?"

"I, uh, look at sales papers." She faltered. "I recognized him from his conformation."

Darby was speechless.

"I've been around cattlemen all my life," she said after a minute. "Certainly long enough to know a prize bull when I see one. I just didn't recognize him while I was trying to keep from being shoved to death," she added ruefully.

He gave a short laugh and gave up his suspicions. "Sure. I can understand that."

"I guess I'd better get back out to the line cabin…"

"Miss Brannt!"

She and Darby turned at the cold and belligerent address.

"Yes, sir, boss?" she asked.

His eyes were as cold as his face was hard. "Come to the bunkhouse, please." He turned and walked out.

"The bunkhouse?" she wondered aloud. She went out with Darby and noticed that Bates was smothering a grin.

Darby went with her. He knew the boss's moods. That look was dangerous. He'd seen it before, when the cook, Vanessa, had been fired. He had a bad feeling and he looked at Morie with concern.

They walked into the bunkhouse. Mallory was there, with Ms. Bruner and Cane and Tank. None of them were smiling.

"Open your rucksack, please," Mallory asked curtly.

She lifted both eyebrows. "Sure. But why?" she asked as she retrieved it from her room and handed it to the boss.

"Open it, please," he repeated.

She shrugged, put it down on the table near the door and opened it. She pulled out clothing, books and…

Her expression was genuinely shocked. That was a replica of one of the famous Romanov Easter eggs that had originally been made for the czar of Russia and his wife. It was made of pure gold, which was going for over a thousand dollars a gram at current market prices, and studded with diamonds and sapphires, rubies and emeralds. It was worth a king's ransom. She held it in her hand and gaped at it. She'd last seen it in the Kirks' living room in a locked case. How…?

She turned and looked at them. Ms. Bruner wasn't smiling, but there was a look on her face that made Morie want to put her out a window.

"This egg was left to us by our grandmother, who was given it as a Christmas gift from her husband decades ago," Mallory said with ice dripping from every syllable. "It's utterly priceless."

"At current gold prices, the gold alone would buy a Jaguar," she murmured, shocked.

"Interesting, that a poor working cowgirl would know that," Mallory replied.

She handed the egg to Mallory. Her eyes were full of abused pride. "You think that I would steal from you?" she asked quietly, and searched his face.

"The evidence pretty much speaks for itself," Mallory told her.

She looked from his angry face to Cane's shocked one and Tank's bland one. Darby lifted his chin.

"She's no thief," Darby said shortly. "I may not be the world's best judge of character, but I'd bet my retirement on this girl's honesty. Saw her run down a cowboy who dropped a five-dollar bill out of his wallet and didn't notice. Not the act of a thief," he added.

"This was missing out of the case." Mallory indicated the egg.

"How did she get the key?" Tank asked aloud.

"Mine is missing," Mallory said coldly. His eyes narrowed on Morie.

She just stared at him, with her heart breaking in her chest. She was damned without a trial. Everybody was looking at her with varying degrees of suspicion. She knew she'd been set up and she knew who did it—that Bruner woman, with some help, she would have bet, from that grinning cowboy in the barn who'd gone riding with her. Bates.

But it would do no good to condemn him on a stray thought. Nothing she said was going to convince Mallory that she'd been set up. She could see that in his face. It twisted her heart. If he'd cared for her at all, he'd never have believed her capable of this.

She stared at him with resignation. "I suppose you want to call the sheriff now," she said, and thought how she was going to explain this to her parents. Her father would be outraged. He'd come after Mallory with his team of family attorneys and it would be a major assault on the man's reputation and wealth. Her father was vindictive. Especially where his children were concerned. Mallory Kirk had no idea what a hornet's nest he was stirring up, nor did that Bruner woman, whose entire past would be laid out to public view when her dad got through.

"No," Mallory said, averting his eyes. "I won't do that. But you're resigning as of right now. I want you off my land in one hour. No more. And Darby will watch you pack, to make sure nothing else goes mysteriously missing."

Morie lifted her chin. Spanish royalty from three generations ago showed itself in her comportment and arrogance. "I have never stolen anything in my life," she said with quiet pride. "And you will regret this. I promise you."

"Threats!" Gelly scoffed. "The last resort of a thief caught red-handed!"

"You remember it," Morie told her evenly. "You're wearing last year's clothes, probably bought from a consignment shop, and trying to insinuate yourself into the boss's life," she said flatly, shocking everybody, especially Gelly. "You're a fraud, too, lady. I don't know what your game is, but sooner or later, you'll betray yourself."

Gelly moved closer to Mallory. There was something oddly dangerous in the other woman's delicate features. Something Gelly recognized, because she'd seen it before.

"How would you know anything about fashion?" Mallory asked coldly, indicating Morie's stained and torn jeans and old sweatshirt and disheveled condition.

"You might be surprised at what I know, and where I learned it," she told him. Her black eyes were snapping like fireworks under her long, black eyelashes. "One day you'll know the truth about me, too. And you'll regret to your dying day that you ever accused me of a crime."

"Criminals always say such things," Gelly chided.

Morie smiled coldly. "You'd know."

"How dare you!" Gelly stepped forward with her hand raised.

"Lawsuits will ensue if you hit me," Morie told her. "I promise."

Mallory caught the woman's arm and pulled her back. "Let's get this over without complications," he told her. He was feeling really sick at what he'd charged Morie with. He hadn't even let her speak.

"If you have a defense, let's hear it," he added, his eyes on hers.

Morie just laughed. "Sure. I've been set up and she—" she indicated Gelly "—knows it. But nobody is going to believe me. I'm just the new hire."

She put her things into the rucksack and gathered up her small television and iPod and coat. "This is all I brought with me. May I ask someone to drive me to the bus station in town, or would you like me to walk there?" she added icily.

Mallory felt even worse when he saw how little she had. Maybe she'd been desperate for money. But if she had, why not come to him and ask for help? His face hardened. He'd made that impossible, with his own antagonism.

"I'll drive you, honey," Cane said gently. "Let's go."

"I can drive her," Tank protested.

Neither of them believed her guilty, and it was obvious.

"Thanks," Morie told them sincerely. "I'll remember you both kindly, years from now."

Mallory was fuming. He hated being put in this position. And he really hated having his own brothers make him look like the villain.

"Darby, could you drive me to town, please?" she asked the older man. "If the boss doesn't mind."

"Drive her," Mallory said curtly. He glared at his brothers. "In case you didn't notice, she had Grandmother's jeweled egg in her rucksack!"

Both brothers looked at Gelly with veiled hostility.

She stepped closer to Mallory. "Why are you looking at me? I didn't steal anything!"

"Neither did I," Morie told her as Darby gathered up the heavy things and she shouldered her pack. She smiled at Gelly. It wasn't a nice smile. "When I get home, my father will want to know all about you," she added softly. "I'm sure he'll find interesting things."

Gelly panicked for just a minute. But she noted the other woman's pitiful clothing and lost her worry. "Oh, I'm sure." She laughed. "Does he even own a computer?"

You might be surprised, Morie thought, but she didn't speak. She looked up at Mallory as she passed him, with sadness and pain.

"You might have given me the benefit of the doubt," she said quietly.

"I did," he muttered.

She sighed. "You think I stole from you," she said in a soft, wounded tone.

"You did," he replied, digging in.

She shook her head. "One day, you'll find out the truth and you'll be sorry. But it will be too late," she added.

He felt cold chills down his spine. He wasn't in the wrong. Gelly had assured him that one of the hands knew something that he was afraid to tell. She'd learned about it accidentally while they were riding. The poor boy was almost in tears as he related how he'd seen Morie handling that beautiful egg he'd once seen in the display case inside the big ranch house. Of course, unbeknownst to him, Gelly had coaxed Bates into going to Mallory with his story and coached him on how to behave.

Mallory felt sick to his stomach. Morie was going to leave. He'd never see her again. It shouldn't bother him. He knew she was after him for his money; no woman had ever wanted him for any other reason. He knew he wasn't handsome. She was a gold digger. Why did it hurt so damned much to see that pain in her face, to hear it in her voice?

"If you're leaving, go," he said curtly. "Before I change my mind and have you prosecuted!"

"Oh, that would be very interesting," Morie replied with a twinge of her old audacity. "Very interesting, indeed. In fact, I'm quite tempted to dare you to do it," she added with a thoughtful look at Gelly, who was flushed and worried.

"No!" Gelly said, feeling suddenly unsure of herself at the other woman's confident smile. She was friends with the judge who knew Cane. She might dig up something that Gelly didn't want known. "No, it's too much. She's poor. Just let her go. One day, she'll get what's coming to her."

"More than likely, you will," Morie countered. She looked at the brothers. "I enjoyed my time here."

"I don't think you did it," Cane said flatly.

"Neither do I," Tank affirmed.

They both glared at Mallory.

"Well, she's got you blindsided," Mallory shot back. "What, you didn't notice the egg in her rucksack, huh? It got there by magic, I guess."

They started to argue, but she got between them. "I've caused enough trouble," she told them. "I guess I'll have to go back and take the consequences." She meant go back and let her father arrange that marriage to his best friend's son, who was a millionaire twice over and had a flourishing feedlot operation in North Texas. It would make for a great partnership.

"In trouble at home, are you?" Mallory asked curtly.

"Usually," she replied. "Thanks for the job," she added, and not with a great deal of sarcasm. "I learned a lot here." She turned to Darby. "Mostly from you," she said with a smile. "I'll miss you."

"I'll miss you, too," Darby said with a cold look at Mallory as he left.

She turned to continue out the door. She stopped, turned back to Mallory and glared up at him. "I won't miss you," she replied harshly. "I was totally wrong. I thought you were the last person on earth who would have convicted me on circumstantial evidence. But then, I can't expect a stranger to care about me. I had dreams..." Her eyes fell. "Foolish dreams. Anyway, take care, guys," she told the other two brothers and managed a smile for them. "See you someday, maybe."

They grimaced and turned back to glare at Mallory. But Morie was already in the ranch pickup with Darby at the wheel. Headed home to Texas.

"YOU MARK MY WORDS, that woman had something to do with it," Cane said angrily. "She set Morie up."

"I agree," Tank replied. "We should have stopped her from leaving. We should have made Mal listen."

"He won't. He was infatuated with Morie. He didn't like it. He wanted to believe she was a thief, so he had an excuse to fire her." He turned to his brother. "She almost dared him to prosecute her. Would a thief be willing to go to trial?"

"Not likely. I remember Joe Bascomb saying that he was anxious for his case to go to trial so he'd be cleared in the eyes of the community. Of course, we see how that played out!" His eyes narrowed as he looked toward the barn. "Interesting, how Bates just happened to notice Morie playing with that egg. She lives in a separate room, and the door's always closed, Darby said. So how did he see her?"

"And what the hell was he doing, riding around with Mal's girlfriend?" Cane added. "Something fishy there. Real fishy. It was Gelly who just happened to find the missing drill in our former employee's suitcase. And now, surprise, surprise, she just happened to hear a cowboy who noticed a thief playing with a rare objet d'art. How convenient."

Tank pursed his lips. "I really think we need to do some investigating of our own. I still have contacts in government, some of them covert operatives. It wouldn't take much work to look into Ms. Bruner's background, now would it?"

"Mal will never believe anything bad about her."

"Think so? Let's find out."

"I'm game. Go for it."

MORIE, UNAWARE OF the brothers' plotting, was on the bus to Jackson to get a commercial flight home. She hadn't let Darby see her buy the bus ticket to Jackson, because she was supposed to be going back to Texas. And in fact, she was, on her father's corporate jet. It would be waiting for her at the Jackson airport.

She didn't want to tell her parents what had happened for a number of reasons. First, it would be humiliating to have them know that their daughter had been accused of stealing. Second, her father would plow into the Kirks like an earthmover. He'd never stop until he'd utilized every legal resource at his command, and Gelly Bruner would be nailed to the wall, along with whoever had helped her set Morie up.

It had to be Bates, Morie decided. The stupid man was crazy about Gelly. God knew what she'd told him to make him help, but Morie couldn't get that odd smile out of her mind. How strange, for Bates to look at her with that smile and then, shortly afterward, for her to be fired for theft. He'd been with Gelly all morning. Gelly had also set up a former hand who was fired for stealing. It was all so useless.

Of course, nobody knew who Morie really was, or her real background. If they had, Gelly would have had her own head on the block. Morie was rich beyond the dreams of avarice. Gelly, however, would love to be rich. She just wanted to marry Mallory, so that she'd have whatever she wanted. Morie had been in the way. Gelly had been jealous of her from the start, and she had to know that Mallory was feeling something more than professional regard for his newest hire.

Those hungry kisses had knocked Morie off guard. She'd never expected that things would end like this. She choked back tears of anger and loss. Maybe it was just as well, she told herself. Mallory believed in her guilt. If he'd cared about her, nothing would have convinced him that she'd take something from him. That was absolute proof that anything he felt was just physical. He didn't care about Morie. He couldn't have cared, and treated her so coldly.

She dabbed at her eyes with her battered handkerchief. Her father was going to be livid when he found out where she'd been. But Shelby would stand up for her. It would be all right. She'd just have to get through the next few days and it would start getting better. She'd go on with her life, and Mallory would fade into the past, day by day, hour by hour. Maybe in a year she wouldn't even be able to remember what he looked like. Time was kind.

HER FATHER AND MOTHER were waiting at the ranch's airstrip. They were standing close together, as they always were, smiling at each other until Morie came down the steps of the small jet.

"Morie!" Shelby ran to her and embraced her, hugging her close. "Oh, it's so good to have you home again!"

"Been rolling in wheat straw?" her father asked, his black eyes that were so much like her own narrowed in suspicion.

She grinned and hugged him tight. "Yes, I have. Don't fuss, Daddy."

He hugged her, laughing. "Okay. Good to have you home, brat." He held her at arm's length. "Now.

Where the hell have you been for the past few weeks?"

She sighed. "Working on a ranch as a cowgirl," she confessed.

"Good God Almighty!" he raged. "Hell, I wouldn't even let you lift a hay bale here and you went to work on a...!"

"Please don't fuss," she interrupted. "I learned so much about ranching. I learned about calving and feed and fences, all the things you'd never teach me. I learned ranching from the ground up. And I had a good time doing it."

"Where did you work?" he persisted.

"In Wyoming, for people who had no idea who I was," she said. "And that's all I'm going to say about it. Ever."

"Was it a big ranch?" he asked.

She shrugged. "A family one."

"I see."

"Some brothers. They were nice. I even had my own room in the bunkhouse and all the cowboys looked out for me. It was just like here, only smaller," she added, to cover herself. "Much smaller."

"Did you tell them who you were when you left?" Shelby wondered.

"No. I just said I had to come home." She dropped her eyes.

Shelby, who knew her very well, was certain

that there was much more to this story that Morie didn't want to tell her parents.

"Well, we can talk about it later." Shelby said gently. She smiled at King. "Right now, let's get her home and cleaned up. Honestly, Morie, you do look ragged!"

Morie laughed. "It was fun, while it lasted."

"It's nice to have you home." Shelby sighed, hugging her again. "I'm surrounded by men when you aren't here. Nobody wants to discuss recipes or Paris sales and shopping."

King made a face. "I'll talk about the production sale late this month," he volunteered.

Shelby glowered at him. "I'm already tired of hearing about it. Who do you think is having to make all the arrangements, my darling? Not you! I'll bet you have no clue about caterers and musical entertainment and tables and chairs and awnings...."

"Gosh, is that the time?" King glanced at his big watch. "I have cattle to brand!"

Shelby made a face at him. "Then you can drop us off at the house on your way," she told him with a chuckle.

He smiled back. He shouldered the box and the rucksack that Morie had brought with her and headed for the big ranch SUV.

LATER, SHELBY CORNERED her daughter in the bedroom and closed the door.

"You can fool your dad," she said, "but you can't ever fool me. Now come clean," she told Morie and sat down beside her on the spotless comforter with its exquisite pastel floral design. "What really happened?"

Morie laid her head on Shelby's shoulder. "I fell in love."

"Really!"

"He was a beast. He had a girlfriend who was pretending to be something she's not. She had someone plant a jeweled egg in my rucksack and went to the boss and told him I stole it from him. So he fired me. I came home. End of story."

"He accused you of theft?" she exclaimed.

"Yes. He said he wouldn't call the sheriff, but he fired me."

Shelby's dark eyes flashed. "We'll sue him for defamation of character!"

"No, you won't," Morie said calmly. "It would be useless. That woman set me up. I can't prove it, but I know she did it. He believed her," she added with a pointed look at her mother. "No man who loved a woman would ever convict her on circumstantial evidence, no matter how damning it was."

Shelby drew in a long breath. In a minute, she nodded. "If that's the way you want it."

"Please don't tell Daddy."

Shelby grimaced. "I have to tell him something."

"Then embroider it a little, can't you?" She knew that her parents never had secrets from each other. She envied them their closeness. She felt now that she'd never have anyone to share secrets with.

"I'll soft-pedal it," Shelby promised. "But I don't like it. You're no thief."

"We know it. We don't have to prove it to anyone."

"That's true enough. But I'd like to jerk a knot in your boss, and his girlfriend," Shelby added. She wasn't a fiery woman, but she did have a temper.

Morie hugged her. "Thanks."

"You're my daughter. I love you." She kissed her cheek. She frowned. "What in the world happened to your face?"

"Just a scratch. I was moving a tree branch and it shifted. It's only a surface one. It will heal nicely, you'll see. Now how about a nice piece of broiled fish with herbs and butter? Please?"

Shelby laughed. "All right. Just for you. A homecoming present. I'm glad you're back."

"Yes." Morie sighed as she looked around at familiar things. "So am I."

CHAPTER NINE

MORIE THREW HERSELF into helping Shelby with details for the big production sale. In between, she had to cope with her father's matchmaking. Daryl Coleman was tall and dark and quite good-looking. His family had huge feedlots in Northern Texas and Daryl himself was CEO of an oil company that was based in Oklahoma. He was savvy about technical innovations and a whiz with computers. He had everything a woman could have wanted. He just wasn't Mallory Kirk.

But he liked Morie and he was always around. After Mallory's suspicion and alternating hot-and-cold treatment, Daryl was a breath of fresh air. He had exquisite manners and he loved to dance. So did Morie. It was one of the things she loved most in life.

Daryl flew her to Dallas in the corporate jet that his family had shares in, and took her to an authentic Latin dance club.

"So you want to learn to tango," he told her with a grin. "This is the place to learn."

"I'm not keen on it," she mumbled, looking around. "It looks a whole lot easier in movies."

"None of the movies it's in are authentic," he assured her. He took her right hand in his left one and rested his free hand on her waist. "Tango is a battle between a man and a woman. It's quick and slow, insistent and sensuous. Most of it is footwork. Just follow my lead. You're an excellent dancer. This should be easy for you."

"Easy!" she scoffed after she'd stumbled into him three times and almost upset a waiter with a tray of drinks headed for the restaurant at the other end of the club. No alcohol was allowed near the dance floor itself.

He chuckled. "You're rusty, kid," he teased. "You've been spending too much time around cattle and not enough around attractive, dashing men like me."

She looked up at his good looks and twinkling dark eyes and burst out laughing. "And so modest!"

"I'm modest. After all, I have so much to be modest about," he assured her.

She leaned against him with a breathless laugh. "Daryl, you're a wonder."

He hugged her close. "Sure I am. You really need to marry me," he added with a smile. "Your father says so every time he sees me."

She grimaced. "I like you a lot, but my dad is

looking at mergers, not relationships. It's a flat economy and he's diversifying his investments. Like your folks," she added drily.

He shrugged. "I haven't met anybody I really want to marry," he said honestly. "You're pretty and sweet, and you won't be marrying me for my money," he added in a cold tone.

She stopped dancing and looked up. "Somebody did want to marry you for it," she guessed.

He nodded. "She was sweet and pretty, too. I went nuts over her. Then, just before I was getting ready to propose, I saw her at a party sneaking into a bedroom with the host. They came back out a few minutes later, disheveled and laughing, and when I asked, she said sure she slept with him. He'd given her a diamond dinner ring and she wanted to pay him back for it." His face hardened. "She said everybody did it, why was I so uptight? It was just sex."

Morie searched his black eyes quietly. "That's the attitude most people have today. Everything is okay now. Multiple lovers are the rule. Funny, isn't it, that fifty years ago men and women alike were held to a higher standard of morality and families stayed together. Isn't the divorce rate something like fifty percent?"

"Probably higher." He sighed. "I'm so old-fashioned that I don't fit in anywhere."

"So am I, sweet man," she replied, and pressed

close to him, closing her eyes. "Maybe I should marry you, Daryl. We're alike in a lot of ways. I really do like you."

He hugged her close. "I like you, too, honey. I guess there are worse reasons to base a marriage on."

She kept her eyes closed as they danced and tried not to think about how it had felt when Mallory held her close and kissed her in that incredibly sexy way and made her head spin. Maybe it would be safer to marry a man she only liked. Passionate love surely made life more complicated.

He kissed her hair. "What kind of ring would you like?" he asked matter-of-factly.

She drew in a long breath. "I don't know. Maybe a ruby. I like rubies."

"Coincidentally, my family has investments in a jewelry chain," he teased. "So you can have whatever stone you fancy, and we'll have a designer make it into your dream wedding set."

Her dream wedding set would have included Mallory as the groom, but she couldn't say that. She was falling into her father's net headfirst, letting him rule her life. She'd tried rebellion, however, and it had ended badly. Very badly. It might be time to listen to her father's advice and do something sensible. After all, Daryl was highly eligible and quite good-looking, and they'd known each other for a long time. It wouldn't be a passionate relationship. But it would be a lasting one, she was certain.

Now all she had to do was stop thinking about Mallory Kirk. That wasn't going to be easy.

MALLORY WAS HAVING PROBLEMS of his own. His brothers refused to be in the same room with Gelly, and when she came to the ranch, they made their disapproval known by walking away the minute her small used car pulled up at the front porch.

"Do you have to make it so obvious that you don't like her?" Mallory raged to Cane.

Cane gave him a cold look. "She framed Morie."

"Damn it, she did not! Gelly just happened to be riding with Bates when he mentioned what he'd seen."

"Like she just happened to know about the stolen drill in our former employee's suitcase," Cane retorted. "Anybody who makes Gelly mad gets fired."

Mallory averted his dark eyes. "Coincidence."

Cane stuck his hand in his pocket and went to the picture window to look out over the acres of green pasture just starting to stick up through the latest snow. "And I won't agree to let her friend buy that so-called scrubland, in case you were going to ask."

"Neither will I," Tank added curtly as he joined them.

Mallory didn't reply. He'd had Gelly harping on it for days. He was almost ready to sell it just to get her off his back. When she wasn't being obnoxious, she was sweeter than she'd ever been. She caressed him and kissed him and told him how handsome he was, and how happy she was that he'd been saved from that money-grubbing girl he'd had to fire.

For a man whose lack of conventional good looks was imposing, it was an ego trip of the finest kind. It blinded him to her other faults. He wouldn't concede that he was vulnerable because he was guilt-ridden over firing Morie on flimsy circumstantial evidence.

"Did that key to the display case ever show up?" Cane asked suddenly and with narrowed eyes.

Mallory joined him at the picture window, his hands jammed deep into his jean pockets. "Yeah," he replied. "Found it in my coat pocket. I guess I forgot and put it there instead of back in the drawer where we keep it."

"Odd," Tank commented.

And Gelly knew about the key and where it was kept, because she'd admired that egg once and Mallory had pulled out the key to open the case and let her hold it. He didn't mention that.

They moved to the display case and studied the egg.

"You know," Mallory said suddenly, frowning, "it looks funny."

"I was just noticing that," Cane replied curtly. "Open it."

Mallory brought the key out of the drawer and opened the glass doors of the ornate, wood-scrolled cabinet. He picked up the egg and frowned. "These settings look slipshod. And here—" he indicated the jewels "—they don't look... Good God, it's a fake!"

Cane's jaw tautened. "A cheap fake."

Mallory was seething. "Morie," he said flatly. "She had the real one in her rucksack."

"She handed it back to you," Tank replied angrily. "You put it back in the case. I saw you do it. Morie was gone by then!"

Mallory didn't want to admit that. It suited him to think Morie was a thief. He'd sent her packing, wounded her pride, treated her like a criminal, all on the word of a cowboy he hardly knew and a woman who harried him night and day to employ her friends and sell land to them.

His lean face was harassed. "Yes," he had to concede, his eyes stormy. "She was gone by then."

And all the joy in his life had gone with her. He was left with the emptiness in his heart and the certainty of long years ahead with Gelly to assuage the ache Morie had left behind. She couldn't do it. He liked Gelly, but she didn't stir him, not even with her most passionate kisses, except in the most basic way. Intellectually, she was a no-show. Her conversational skills revolved around popular television shows and movies and the latest fashions.

"It's time to call in private detectives," Cane said flatly. "In fact, Morie advised that some time ago, when I talked to her at the line cabin."

Mallory glared at him. "What were you doing out there?"

His brother smiled coldly. "Looking for Morie after you'd upset her."

"She was a hire. She stuck her nose into everything around here," he muttered.

"Yes, like making canapés for a party and helping cook—and she didn't even ask for extra pay or complain that she didn't get it," Tank reminded him.

Mallory felt guilty. "I meant to compensate her for that. Of course, she was running around after that judge friend of yours," he added icily, turning to Cane.

"Danny Brannt is a gourmet chef," Cane replied. "He and his wife have a housekeeper who was trained in Paris as a cook, and they're always looking for new and exciting finger foods for parties. In fact, they're famous for it. I understand that his housekeeper is helping to cater that big to-do at the Brannt Ranch next month. We were invited, I believe."

"Yes," Mallory murmured absently. "King Brannt has some seed bulls that are the talk of the industry. I have in mind to buy one from him for our breeding program." He didn't add that the mention of that last name stung. Not that Morie had any connection to that famous Brannt; she was just a poor working cowgirl.

"Can we afford one?" Cane asked amusedly. "We're only just showing profit from the past two painful years of investments and stock adjustments."

"We can afford one," Mallory replied quietly. He glanced at his brother. "You and Tank are responsible for those successes as much as I am," he added. "I know it's been rough. I appreciate what you've done."

"Hell, I appreciate what you've done," Cane said. "You've got the business head. Tank may be the marketing specialist, and I do like showing off our bulls at cattle shows with a little help from our cowboys who travel with me, but you're the one with the genius to know where to put the money so that it will grow. That's no mean feat in a flat economy."

"I had help. Our stockbroker is the genius. I just followed his suggestions." He looked worried.

"Who could have taken that egg?" he wondered aloud. "And when did it go missing?"

"I don't know. Sometime between the time that Morie left and you found the key. The question is, who had the key and the opportunity to get into the cabinet?"

"Couldn't have been a break-in," Mallory said, thinking out loud. "Not with our security system in place."

"And I'd bet my stock portfolio on Mavie's honesty," Tank added.

Mallory nodded. "So would I. Her former boss isn't the sort to suffer a thief any more than we are. She was with him for twenty years until he had to give up his ranch and retire, leaving her unemployed. She's been a welcome addition to our staff."

Cane pursed his sensual lips. "Bates, maybe?" He was thinking out loud. "He was the one who claimed to see Morie playing with the egg. Interesting, because Darby says she kept her door closed anytime she was in the bunkhouse, and she kept it locked."

"Suspicious," Mallory said flatly.

"A woman in a bunkhouse full of men would lock her door," Cane shot back. "Especially one like Morie. Darby told me that she lived off campus when she was in college, because she refused to live in a coed dorm even if the whole world thought it was all right."

His eyebrows arched. "She could have been lying."

"Why do you think she lied in the first place?" Cane demanded. "Because Gelly said she did?"

"Let's not bring Gelly into this," Mallory said defensively. "I'm very fond of her." He pushed his hands deeper into his pockets. "She's having all sorts of financial problems because her father made bad investments." He shrugged. "Maybe I should marry her...."

"I'm leaving the day she comes in the door," Cane said harshly. "And Tank will go with me."

"In a heartbeat," Tank agreed. "We'll take our share of the ranch profits with us," he added in a cold tone. "You and Gelly try staying afloat financially with only a third of the land and cattle!"

"You wouldn't do that," Mallory returned, wounded.

"I'd do it in a heartbeat," Tank assured him with flashing brown eyes.

"So would I," Cane agreed. "I'm not living with Gelly."

"What has she ever done to make you two so hostile?" Mallory exclaimed, exasperated.

Cane looked at Tank. "Blind as a bat."

"And stubborn as a mule," Tank agreed. "Can't tell pyrite from gold."

"Morie stole the egg," Mallory roared. "She took it and hid it in her rucksack and was going to sell it!"

"Sure." Cane took the fake egg in his hand and showed it to Tank. "And she replaced it with this one after we put it back in the cabinet," he added with a droll look at his brother. "Of course, she was on her way home in a bus at the time. I guess it's magic."

Tank nodded. "And funny thing, the key reappeared in Mal's coat pocket."

"How convenient."

"Gelly couldn't have taken the egg," Mallory said doggedly, answering a charge they hadn't made verbally. "She hasn't ever been alone in here!"

"We had a conference call from the state cattlemen's association committee on grazing," Cane reminded him. "All three of us went into the office to take it. Mavie was in the kitchen cooking dinner and Gelly was in here alone. As soon as we came back, she said she had an urgent matter to attend to in town."

Mallory felt sick. "It couldn't be her," he protested, but it was a weak protest.

"If you believe her innocent, let's prove it," Cane said. "I know the best private detective in the business, Dane Lassiter from Houston. Let me have him do some investigating for us. If Gelly has nothing to hide, it will clear her."

"And if not," Tank put in, "it's better to know now, especially if you're bullheaded enough to try and marry her."

"She loves me," Mallory bit off. "She says she can't live without me." He averted his eyes. "She thinks I'm handsome."

"Nobody thinks you're handsome who isn't lying," Cane told him flatly. "Look in a mirror! But looks have nothing to do with character, and you've got plenty of that. Women don't care about looks. They care about actions."

Mallory glared at him.

"He's right." Tank clapped him on the back. "We love you. We won't lie to you. But you might ask yourself why Gelly is. And why she keeps trying to get jobs for her friends and land for some stranger that she barely knows."

Mallory was weakening. He'd been stubborn because he was guilt-ridden about the way he'd treated Morie. His brothers were right. Morie couldn't have taken the egg. She left the ranch just minutes after it was found in her rucksack, and Mallory was certain that he'd held the real egg in his hands in the bunkhouse. He'd put it back in the display case himself, after Morie was gone. So the real one had to have been replaced after Morie's departure...replaced with this cheap copy that would only have fooled someone from a distance. None of them had thought to look at it closely. There had been no reason to.

"Let me call Dane," Cane coaxed. "If you're right about Gelly, I'll apologize."

"So will I," Tank agreed.

Mallory drew in a long breath. "Okay," he said after a minute. His expression was grim. "Call him."

THE ESTATE WAS BRILLIANT with color and decoration, especially the huge stone patio where tables were going to be set up the following week for King's gala production show. Ranchers were coming from all over the world to look at his prize cattle, which would be offered for sale at auction.

"Dad really does things on a big scale," Morie mused as she and her mother went over the final plans with a staff of professionals who would complete the finishing touches and employ caterers for the occasion. It was much too large an endeavor for any one person, although Shelby kept a tight rein on the operation and dictated what she wanted done.

"Yes, he does," Shelby said with a smile. "He's very proud of his purebred herd."

"So am I," Morie replied. "Now that I know how a ranch operates from the ground up, I have even more admiration for the care Dad takes of his cattle and his men."

"My daughter, the cowgirl," Shelly chuckled.

"I enjoyed it. Most of it," she replied and lowered her eyes.

Shelby turned back to the woman who was carrying out the party plans. "You were able to get Desperado to play for us, weren't you?"

Tenny Welsh laughed. "Yes, I was," she said, "although the group is semiretired now. They all have kids and touring isn't conducive to raising a family, they say. But they'll do it for you," she told Shelby. "Heather Everett is best friends with the lead singer. She convinced them."

"God bless her," Shelby said fervently. "She's such a sweetie."

"So is her daughter, Odalie," Tenny replied with a sigh. "Have you ever heard her sing? She has the voice of an angel!"

"Where did you hear her?" Morie asked, curious.

"She goes to our church and is a soloist in the choir," the other woman replied with a smile. "It's such a joy to hear her."

"She's had an offer from the Met, by the way," Shelby told Morie. "She's deliberating whether or not to go."

"It would be a shame to waste a talent like that,"

the caterer replied dreamily. "Oh, I'd love to have such a voice!"

Morie didn't reply. She was thinking of her brother, Cort, who had such a hopeless passion for the shy blonde, who apparently hated him. Nobody knew why. Well, perhaps Cort did, but he was very tight-lipped about his private life.

"So here's the final menu." Shelby interrupted her thoughts as she handed the printed list to the caterer. "And please make certain that we have a variety of canapés to suit every taste, and plenty of fruit."

"I always do," Tenny reminded her with a smile. This wasn't the first time she'd catered big social parties for the Brannts. "I know your tastes very well, Shelby."

Shelby laughed. "It will be a gala occasion. We have a famous soccer star, four A-list actors and actresses, the CEO of a giant computer/software corporation, two government agents, a few assorted mercenaries and the former vice president."

"Vice president?" Morie asked, surprised.

"He's a friend of your father's," she replied. "Of course, so are the mercenaries," she added amusedly. "He likes black sheep."

"Well, they are interesting people," Tenny added. Her face changed. "Especially that man,

Grange, who works for the Pendletons. The stories I've heard about him!"

"Yes, he was a former major in the Green Berets," Shelby confided. "And there was a rumor that he actually led a group of mercs down into Mexico to rescue Gracie Pendleton when she was kidnapped by that deposed South American dictator, Emilio Machado."

"I've heard about him," Morie said. She frowned. "Wasn't something said about a connection between Machado and our Rick Marquez, who works as a homicide detective with San Antonio P.D.?" she added.

"Yes," Tenny replied in a soft tone. "Some document has surfaced that connects him with Marquez's mother."

"Barbara, who owns the café in Jacobsville," Morie commented. "She has wonderful food. I've eaten there when I visited a girlfriend...."

"No," Tenny interrupted gently. "Not his foster mother. His real mother."

Both women looked at her without speaking.

"Now isn't that interesting," Shelby said.

"And don't you dare repeat it," Tenny replied. "I heard it from someone I know and trust and I'm not supposed to tell. But you can keep a secret." She smiled as she met Shelby's eyes. "As I well know."

"Yes." Shelby didn't comment further, leaving her daughter to wonder about the strange remark.

DARYL CAME OVER TO TALK to King about a new seed bull that his father wanted to add to the breeding program, but he stopped by long enough to speak with Morie privately.

"You said you wanted rubies," he reminded her.

She flushed, because she hadn't really taken the engagement thing seriously. He had, apparently. "Daryl..."

"If you don't like the design, we can change it," he assured her. He opened the jeweler's box. "I had it made up like this, because I know how much you love roses."

She caught her breath when she saw the rings. They were the most unique and beautiful settings she'd ever seen in her life. They looked like living blood in their exquisite eighteen-karat-gold settings. The engagement ring was a rose, its petals outlined in gold and set in glittering pigeon's blood rubies, the largest of which made the center. The engagement ring was studded with rubies and made to interlock with the wedding band.

"Here." Daryl pulled them out of the box and took her hand. He hesitated with a grin. "Want to try them on? No sales pressure. They come with a demented fiancé, but you can dump him anytime you like if you find someone more deserving."

She looked into his black eyes with real pleasure. He'd taken her to movies and taught her to
tango, he'd ridden with her over the acres and
acres of her father's huge ranch. He'd been a friend
and even a confidant. She'd told him, although not
her parents, the whole truth of her sojourn on the
Rancho Real and found him a sympathetic and
caring listener. He was also as quiet as a clam.
He'd never divulged her secrets to her parents.

She could do worse.

He laughed, because she'd said it out loud. "Yes,
you could," he assured her. "I even still have most
of my own teeth!"

"Most of them?" she asked with a curious
frown.

His black eyes twinkled. "Your brother knocked
one of them out when we were in college together.
I can't even remember what we fought over. But he
said that since he couldn't beat me in a fair fight,
we'd be better off as friends, and we have been,
all these years."

"Yes, well, my brother has an attitude problem
from time to time," she conceded. He was hot-
tempered, the way Shelby had said their father
once was, and he tended to be impulsive to a fault.
But he was a good person. Like Daryl.

She shrugged. "Might as well try them on,
since you went to so much trouble having them designed for me," she teased and held out her hand.

They were a perfect fit. They complemented her beautiful hands with their faint olive tan, and the settings glittered in the light with a thousand reflections. The cut was exquisite.

"I love them," she confessed.

He smiled. "Good! So. When are we getting married?"

She stared at him in panic. Mallory was still out there somewhere, even if he hated her and considered her a thief. She should hate him, but she couldn't. She loved him. The thing was, if he'd had second thoughts about her, he'd have been in touch by now. He'd have phoned, written, something, anything. But there had been only silence from him. He still thought she was a thief. It tormented her.

"He won't change his mind, Morena," he said gently, using her real name. "Men like that are never wrong, in their own opinion. You're clinging to dreams. It's better, always better, to deal in reality."

"You're right, of course," she said in a subdued tone. "It's just…"

He bent and kissed her forehead. "An engagement isn't a marriage. Just say yes. We'll announce it at the production sale and make your father and my father very happy so they'll shut up trying to pressure us into getting married." He lifted his head. "And if things do somehow work out for you and your suspicious rancher, I'll take back the rings and go shopping elsewhere," he offered firmly. "You have nothing to lose, really."

She drew in a soft breath. He made sense. She didn't really agree, but she was certain that the future would be dark enough if she went through it alone. In some ways Daryl was perfect for her, and her father would be ecstatic. It might be enough to stop him from digging into her recent past and steamrolling over the Kirks in revenge if he found out why Mallory had fired her. That alone was reason enough to say yes. Daryl was right about one other thing—an engagement wasn't a marriage. She could break it anytime she liked, with no hard feelings.

She touched the rings. "Pity to waste them."

"Just what I was thinking," he agreed.

Her dark eyes twinkled. "Okay. We can be engaged. But it's like a trial engagement," she added firmly. "Just that."

He touched her nose with the tip of his forefinger. "Just that. I promise."

Her father was over the moon when they gave him the news. "Thank God you finally saw sense," he told her. He shook Daryl's hand. "Welcome to the family. You can be married very soon."

"We're not rushing it," Daryl said, when he

noted her discomfort. "We're going to take our time and get to know each other."

King's dark eyes narrowed. "Is that necessary? Why?"

"Now, Dad," Morie said gently. "Don't push."

"It's because of that damned Wyoming rancher who fired you, isn't it?" her father demanded suddenly. "The lowlife son of Satan is going to find himself on the wrong side of a defamation-of-character lawsuit just as soon as I find out who framed you! And his isn't the only head that's going to roll when I do!"

CHAPTER TEN

MORIE FELT HER HEART turn over at the anger and threat in her father's deep voice. "How did you…?" she exclaimed, horrified that he was going to try to ruin the Kirks. They were in a precarious financial situation. He could do it.

"I didn't buy that story that you came home voluntarily. I know you," he returned curtly. "You were devastated by whatever happened. I had a friend in Houston do some digging. My, my, what I found out," he added softly, although his eyes were glittering.

She went closer to him. "Words," she said quietly. "It was all just words. I was set up…you know that. Mallory Kirk has a jealous girlfriend. She thought I was getting too close to him so she found a way to get me fired."

"You should have made him prosecute you," King returned hotly. "I'd have had that blonde wannabe tied up in knots on the witness stand."

Witness stand. Jury. Her eyes narrowed. "You talked to Uncle Danny. He sold me out!"

He looked uncomfortable. "Danny didn't say anything. He just made some odd comments and I got suspicious about why you suddenly left a job you told him you loved."

"So you hired a private detective," she said with resignation. "Listen, Dad, it doesn't matter. I'm going to marry Daryl. Nobody knows me in Wyoming. Who cares what gossip goes around about why I left the ranch up there?"

"I care," he said flatly. "You're my child. You were accused of a crime. And now there's another crime that they may try to blame you for."

"Excuse me?" she asked, and her stomach flipped.

"A priceless jeweled egg was stolen from the house, and replaced with a cheap copy that went unnoticed until a few days ago," King said icily. "If they thought you stole it in the first place, they may come after you and have you prosecuted now that it's gone missing for real."

She felt sick. "I saw Mallory Kirk going back toward the house with it, just after he told me to leave."

"Yes, well, somebody took it soon afterward."

"I'd already left Wyoming," she protested.

"They could say you took it with you," he returned. "They could say you let Kirk find it in your rucksack because you had the real one hidden. It was an unsettling confrontation. He could say that he didn't notice it was a copy because of the emotional upset."

She sat down on the arm of the sofa, her expression tense and worried.

"I'm not about to let my daughter be labeled a thief," he said icily. "Your name is going to be cleared, and I don't care who else gets hurt. People who steal should be caught, Morena. You should have made them call the law and prosecute you."

"That's what Joe Bascomb did," she said bitterly. "And he was convicted of a murder, when he was innocent."

"Was he?" King asked, with narrowed yes. "Danny thinks there may be more to that story than you're aware of. He's the one who called in private detectives in the first place, to check out your friend Bascomb because you asked him for help, to get the man an attorney. In the process, they learned about the theft of the jeweled egg."

She felt even more terrible. Surely it couldn't get any worse. Could it?

She took a long breath. "Okay, you're right. But can it wait until after the production sale?" she asked gently. "Let's not spoil it with a lot of legal challenges. Mom's worked so hard."

King grimaced. He knew how hard Shelby had worked. She was the heart of the outfit, in many ways. "All right," he agreed after a minute. "That's only a few days away. But afterward," he added with ice in his tones, "we're going to set things straight in Wyoming."

She nodded. She wasn't looking forward to it. Mallory Kirk was in for a huge surprise, and not one he was going to enjoy. Her father would have him for breakfast. She studied her parent while he talked to Daryl. Under other circumstances, he might have liked Mallory. They were very similar in many ways. And hadn't her father been suspicious of Shelby and thought her an opportunist during their stormy relationship? He really didn't have much room to talk. Not that she was going to say that out loud.

UNCLE DANNY AND HIS VIVACIOUS wife, Edie, came with their sons, and their housekeeper/cook, Safie, to stay during the production sale. Morie and Daryl took the kids riding and to movies to keep them occupied while the adults got everything organized for the sale.

The house was huge, and additions had been constructed while the kids were in school so that they had entertainment areas for their friends. There was an immense ballroom, an indoor swimming pool, a tennis court out back, the stables and a barn for King's prize bulls. It was a lavish estate. Six Jaguars, two sedans, two convertibles and two antique sports cars graced the garage.

Cort and Morie owned the convertibles, although
it had taken a long time to convince King that they
were as safe as most other cars.

THE SATURDAY MORNING that kicked off the production sale came with a suddenness that Morie
hadn't anticipated. The small airport just south of
the ranch was kept busy as corporate jets landed,
refueled and took off again after depositing their
passengers.

Morie was fascinated by the guest list. She
watched famous people stroll around the prem-
ises with starstruck awe.

"Stop that," Daryl teased, holding her hand.
"You've seen them before."

"Yes, on television," she assured him. "Dad's
never gone whole hog like this for a production
sale!"

"He's making a statement," Daryl said in an odd
tone.

She frowned. "Excuse me?"

He sighed. "Never mind." He grinned. "Race
you to the sale barn!"

"I can't," she objected. "I have to help in the
kitchen, making canapés. Even with all of us helping, including Aunt Edie and Safie and the caterers, it's a pinch getting it done in time for the party
tonight. While all the visiting cattlemen are drooling over Dad's seed bulls, the women are grinding

their teeth trying to provide enough food. And that doesn't include the barbecue that's going on in the tents for lunch," she added, indicating the row of tents and the smokers that were going full tilt to provide barbecue. "At least the cowboys are handling that for us! Thank goodness we got old Rafe to come out of retirement long enough to make those famous Dutch-oven biscuits he's famous for. Not to mention his beef barbecue."

"It will be worth it if your dad sells enough bulls," Daryl observed.

She thought of something. "Daryl, you have oil holdings. Do you do fracking?"

He glared at her. "No. We do offshore drilling, and we have a few rigs set up in Oklahoma, but we're very careful where we drill and we have safeguards in place. We have a wonderful record for safety."

"I didn't mean to offend," she said quickly. "But I wondered if you knew any companies that do fracking up in Wyoming."

"I know one that's trying to," he said. "A man named Cardman owns it. He's been sued in two states for lax safety procedures—if it isn't done properly, it contaminates the local water table. See, you inject water, and chemicals, at high pressure into the ground to fracture the shale rock and release oil and gas. It's not popular at the moment.

There was even a documentary made about the dangers. That's one reason we don't invest in it."

"Cardman," she mused.

"He's a shady character," he affirmed. "He's known for buying up scrubland from unsuspecting landowners and then putting up operations on it. Several people have sued him. He just moves to another state and keeps going."

"Shame."

"Really."

SHE MENTIONED IT to her mother when they were loading the last silver tray with hors d'oeuvres that evening, just before the guests congregated in the ballroom.

"Fracking," her mother mused. "What a nasty sort of operation it sounds."

"I know we need oil. Nobody wants to live in grass huts and walk fifty miles to a city," Morie stated. "But there are safe ways to extract oil, and then there's this high-speed injection fracturing. That woman I told you about kept trying to get Mallory to sell her friend some scrubland on his property. She didn't say why, but now I'm curious."

"You should mention it to your uncle Danny. He knows the Kirks."

"I might do that."

Shelby touched her daughter's cheek. The

scratch had healed, and the skin was soft and velvety and blemishless, just like her own. "Sweetheart, are you really going to marry Daryl?"

"Dad wants me to."

"What do you want to do, Morena?"

Her dark eyes were sad. "I want to marry for love," she replied. "But when it isn't returned, maybe it's best to settle for someone honest and kind that you really like. Daryl is a wonderful person."

"He truly is. But if you don't love him, and he doesn't love you, the two of you are cheating each other." Her face was solemn. "I married for love. I've never regretted it. Not once."

"You were lucky," Morie said with a smile.

"Eventually." Shelby chuckled. "Oh, if you'd known your father as he used to be!" She rolled her eyes. "It was like domesticating a wolf!"

"It was?" Morie laughed.

"Worse! A grizzly bear." She pursed her perfect lips. "Your Mallory Kirk sounds just like your father. They'd butt heads at first, but then they'd be friends."

"Chance would be a fine thing." Morie sighed.

"I don't know. Life is funny," Shelby replied. "You never know what surprises are in store for you."

FIFTEEN MINUTES LATER, Morie had reason to remember that odd statement. Mallory Kirk walked in the door with Gelly Bruner.

Morie, standing beside Daryl, watched them come in with cold eyes. Her heart was cutting circles in her chest, but she was trying to act normally. In her exquisite white couture gown, with its thin strip of gold trim, and her long hair in an elegant upswept hairdo, dripping diamonds, she was the epitome of the wealthy debutante. Gelly was dressed in last year's fashion, again, a black dress that was passable but nothing to stir comment. Mallory, in evening dress, was impressive even if he didn't have movie-star looks. His tall, fit body was made for evening clothes. He looked elegant, if somber.

Morie saw her father moving toward Mallory with a sinking feeling in her stomach.

"You must be Kingston Brannt," Mallory said, extending a hand. "I'm Mallory Kirk. My brothers and I have a ranch in Wyoming. I came to get one of those seed bulls I've read so much about in cattle journals."

King didn't extend his own hand. He looked at the other man with black eyes that could have cut diamond. "I know who you are."

Mallory seemed puzzled. "This is my friend, Gelly Bruner."

"Mr. Brannt, I've heard so much about you," she purred.

King didn't even look at her.

"I've never seen so many famous people," Gelly was gushing. "You must know all the rich people on earth!"

"They're friends, Miss Bruner," King said curtly. "I don't choose them for their bank balances."

"Of course not," she said quickly.

"Hello, there," Danny Brant said to Mallory, and he did shake hands. "How are your brothers?"

"Working, as usual. Good to see you again."

"Same here." He glanced at his brother, who was still seething. "We're always happy to have fellow cattlemen visit."

"I can't get over the decorations," Gelly enthused. "I'd love to know where you found so many antique roses!"

"Oh, that would be my niece. She's crazy about them," Danny said easily. "Her fiancé had a set of rings made for her with the design. There she is! Come over here, honey."

He was setting the cat among the pigeons and grinning. King was irritated that his brother had stolen his thunder, because he'd had something else in mind for the introduction.

Morie clung to Daryl's big hand as she joined them.

"This is my niece, Morena," Danny introduced. "And her fiancé, Daryl Coleman. He's CEO of an oil corporation."

Morena lifted her head proudly. She was aware of Gelly's suddenly white face, and Mallory's utter stillness as he registered who she was.

"Yes, my daughter worked for you for several weeks, I believe," King said in a voice that promised retribution. "And was allowed to quit rather than be prosecuted for theft. It might interest you to know that I've retained a private detective to investigate those charges. And I assure you," he growled, "countercharges will be forthcoming. Nobody accuses my daughter of being a damned thief!"

Mallory gaped at her. This elegant young woman, dressed in couture, living in luxury, engaged to be married, was the same ragged little cowgirl who'd turned his life upside down and left under a cloud of suspicion.

"Well...well, what a surprise," Gelly managed with a nervous laugh.

"Isn't it?" Morie asked. "By the way, Ms. Bruner, that friend of yours who wanted to buy the scrubland on the ranch, his name wouldn't be Cardman, by any chance, would it? Because Daryl has had some very interesting things to say about his past, and the lawsuits he's facing in several states for unsafe drilling practices."

"It was Cardman," Mallory replied, and stared at Gelly blankly. He'd had one too many surprises for one night.

"You should sell him the land," Morie advised with a pleasant smile. "Then when you want to see fireworks, all you'll have to do is set a match to your water."

He glared at her. "You lied," he said in a rasping tone.

"Well, thieves do lie, don't they?" she shot back.

He looked uncomfortable.

"My daughter is no thief," King told Mallory with glittering eyes. "She has no need to steal. I understand a priceless jeweled egg is missing from your ranch. Since my daughter seems to be involved in the case, I've hired Dane Lassiter out of Houston to investigate the theft for me."

"Cane hired him to investigate it for us," Mallory said stiffly. "And I don't think Morie took it," he added without meeting her eyes. "It was stolen after she left the ranch."

"How kind of you to move me off the suspect list," she said. "A few weeks late, of course." She was looking at Gelly, who was pale and unsteady on her feet. "Perhaps in the future, you'll be more careful about whom you set up for a burglary charge, Ms. Bruner. This one seems to have backfired on you."

"I didn't set anybody up," Gelly muttered. She pressed close to Mallory. "Could we leave? I won't be harassed like this!"

"You didn't mind harassing me, as I recall," Morie replied. "Or that poor cowboy who was fired for a missing drill that conveniently turned up in his suitcase."

"We need to go!" Gelly said. She was sounding hysterical.

"If you have any part in the charges against my daughter, Miss Bruner," King continued, staring straight at Gelly, "I will have my attorneys nail you to a wall. That's a promise. If you have one skeleton in your closet, I promise you'll see it on the evening news!"

Gelly let go of Mallory's arm and literally ran for the front door.

"As for you," King told Mallory Kirk, "in the history of this ranch, I have never had anyone escorted off the property. But if you and your 'friend' aren't gone within the hour, I swear to God I'll have the local sheriff escort you personally to the airport!"

Mallory sighed heavily. He looked at Morie, so beautiful in her gown, with her face taut and her eyes hard. She clung to that damned handsome kid, her fiancé, and looked as if it would make her happy never to see Mallory Kirk again as long as she lived. And he was dying for her. He'd missed her, wanted her, blamed himself for her condition. He'd imagined her ragged and poor, in a shelter somewhere because she couldn't find another job. And here she turned up in a mansion, surrounded by wealth, pampered by her father, the richest cattleman in Texas!

He'd been taken in by Gelly, lock, stock and barrel. Morie hated him. Her father hated him. He'd never live this down. He'd been stupid and judgmental, and he was getting just what he deserved. Morie had wanted to love him. He'd slapped her down. Now she was engaged to some other man, set to marry and start a family. Mallory would go back to Wyoming alone to reflect on his idiocy and face the future all by himself.

He stuck his big hands in his slacks pockets. "Well, if I had hemlock, I guess I'd drink it about now," he mused.

Danny muffled a laugh. Nobody else was amused. King looked murderous. Morie was impassive, on the surface at least.

In the middle of the confrontation, Shelby arrived. She lifted her eyebrows at the tableau. "My goodness, are we hosting a murder?" she mused.

Mallory looked at her with sudden recognition. "I know your face," he said gently.

She smiled. "I was a professional model when I married King," she said, sliding her hand through King's arm.

"Your mother was Maria Kane, the actress," Mallory continued. She nodded.

"I've been watching her old movies on late-night television," he commented. He glanced at Morie. "Now I know why you looked so familiar to us."

"She favors my mother," Shelby replied. "Mr...?"

"Kirk. Mallory Kirk."

The smile immediately left Shelby's elfin face. Her dark eyes began to glitter.

Mallory sighed. "No need for further introductions." He nodded and glanced down at Morie. "For the record, nobody thought you took the damned egg. You had no opportunity. As for the charge I made, I apologize. I've been blind, deaf, dumb and stupid, as my brothers have reminded me every hour on the hour since you left. I guess it took a kick in the head to convince me." He shrugged. "I don't need a road map to see which direction I need to look for a thief." His face set in hard lines. "I'm genuinely sorry," he told the Brannts. "She was one of the hardest-working hires I've ever had. Never complained. Never fussed. Never asked for concessions or special treatment and took risks that I'd never have let her take if I'd known about them."

Morie didn't speak. She was too sick at heart. It was too late. Much too late.

"What risks?" King asked coldly.

"For one, a confrontation with an escaped convicted killer who's a friend of my brother Tank,"
he replied.

"He isn't guilty," Morie said defensively. "I'm
sure of it."

"And I'm sure that he is," Mallory replied.
"Tank's fond of him and he won't listen to reason."
He glanced wryly at King, who was still smolder-
ing. "Family character trait, I'm afraid. But the
fact is, Joe Bascomb has an atrocious temper and
he once beat a mule almost to death. Any man
who'll treat livestock like that will treat a man like
that."

"Nobody treats animals that way here," King
said.

"Or on my place," Mallory agreed.

"You should let him stay," Danny told King.

King smiled. It wasn't a nice smile. "He won't
like it here."

Mallory glanced at Morie's stiff little face and
he felt a cold, hollow place inside him. "You might
have just told me who you were in the first place."

"I wanted to learn ranch work and he—" she
nodded toward her father "—wouldn't let me near
it."

"You were raised to be a lady," King said curtly.
"Not a cowhand."

"You had no business lifting heavy limbs off
fences!" Mallory agreed hotly.

"Don't yell at my daughter," King said angrily.

"Your daughter was an idiot," Mallory shot back. "She could have ruined her health. I thought she was what she claimed to be, a poor girl down on her luck who needed a job desperately!"

"I did need a job," Morie said defensively. "I got sick and tired of men wanting me for what my father had instead of what I was!"

Mallory glared at Daryl.

Daryl grinned at him. "Wrong number," he said defensively. "My folks are on the Fortune 500 list, and I have my own very successful businesses. I don't need to marry money."

"He had the same problem," Morie replied. "That's why we're marrying each other."

"Not true," Daryl replied.

She gaped at him. "Not true?"

"She's marrying me because I can do the tango," Daryl said easily, and smiled down at her.

She shifted restlessly. "Well, yes. Most men can't dance." She looked pointedly at her father.

"Your mother didn't marry me for my dancing skills," King pointed out.

"Good thing," Shelby agreed, and she seemed to unbend just a little. She looked past Mallory. "I believe your friend is motioning to you."

He turned. Gelly was making frantic motions toward the door.

"She's just afraid that she'll be arrested before you can get her to an airplane," Morie said with a pleasant smile. The smile faded. "And that might be the truth."

Mallory felt like an insect under a magnifying glass. He knew he wasn't going to change minds or win hearts here, not in this atmosphere. He'd have to go back home and do what he could to undo the damage. Morie was going to marry that handsome yahoo, was she? Not if he could help it.

"Don't you marry him," he told her firmly, nodding toward Daryl.

"Well, you can't tango," she said sourly.

"How do you know?" he replied.

"He isn't staying long enough to demonstrate any dancing skills," King said impatiently.

"I'm going." Mallory turned away. But he hesitated. "We all make mistakes. It's why they put erasers on pencils."

"Some of us make bigger mistakes than others," Morie replied. "I'll concede that I shouldn't have applied for work without telling you the truth. But you should have given me the benefit of the doubt," she added coldly.

"Under the circumstances, that didn't seem possible."

"Not with your girlfriend planting evidence right and left," Morie replied curtly.

"Not my girlfriend," Mallory said quietly. "Not anymore." He looked right into Morie's eyes as he said it, and her whole body tingled.

"I'm getting married," Morie informed him with a tight smile. "So don't look at me to replace her."

"Fat chance," Mallory said with a glance at a glowering Kingston Brannt. "I'll be damned if I'll marry into any family he belongs to."

"That goes double for my daughter!" King snapped.

Mallory looked at Shelby and shook his head. "You must be one gutsy lady."

"Because I married him?" Shelby managed a smile. "He's not so bad, once you get to know him."

"Which you won't," King muttered. "Aren't you leaving?"

"I guess I am," Mallory agreed. He glanced at Morie again with faint pride and obvious regret. "You wouldn't like to hear my side of it?"

"Sure," she replied. "Just like you wanted to hear my side of it."

He glanced from one family member to another, turned and walked slowly away. Gelly grabbed his arm at the front door and started talking before they even got halfway out it. But Mallory wasn't listening.

"WELL, I CAN SEE WHY YOU HAD to leave Wyoming," Shelby said after the guests had gone home and they were sitting on Morie's bed.

"He's a pain," Morie agreed. "But did you see the look on Gelly's face when she realized who I was?" she mused. "It did my heart good."

"She's probably realized how much trouble she's going to be in, as well," Shelby replied. She studied her daughter's face. "You really love that man, don't you?"

Morie closed up like a sensitive plant at sundown. "I thought I did," she replied. "But if he could take someone else's word for my character, he doesn't know me. He doesn't want to know me. He's happy living as a bachelor with his brothers."

"I wonder."

"I lived in dreams," Morie said, fingering the expensive comforter. "I thought he was getting to know me and enjoying it, as I was. I thought he wanted me. All the time, he was just playing."

"Why would he do that?" Shelby wondered aloud. "He doesn't seem a frivolous man."

Morie blinked. "He isn't."

"Perhaps he's been hunted for his wealth, too."

"He's still being hunted for it, or didn't you notice Gelly?" Morie laughed.

"A woman with an eye to the main chance, and quite cold-blooded, if you ask me," Shelby agreed.

"Even his brothers suspected she was setting me up, but Mallory wouldn't listen. He's bull-headed to a fault!"

"Just like your father, dear."

"I guess so."

"You shouldn't marry Daryl when you're still in love with another man," Shelby said abruptly. "It's not fair to either of them."

Morie didn't answer. She was remembering the shock on Mallory's face when he saw her in the beautiful gown, holding Daryl's hand. It had been sweet vengeance. But it was a long step from that to forgiveness.

"How could I ever trust him again?" Morie wondered aloud. "Who's to say that he wouldn't do the same thing twice?"

Shelby kissed her cheek. "Love requires trust. Now I'm going to bed. We'll talk some more tomorrow, okay? I'm very tired."

"I know you are. Everything went perfectly. Well, except for Mallory walking in and spoiling the evening."

"He held his own against your father, you know," Shelby murmured drily. "That's not easy. Most other men are terrified of him. Mallory wasn't."

Morie had noticed that. It made her proud. But she wasn't going to say it.

"Sleep well," she told her mother, and hugged her tight.

Shelby kissed her dark hair. "You, too, my darling. Good night."

CHAPTER ELEVEN

"YOU CAN'T BELIEVE THEM!" Gelly exclaimed, almost hysterically. "She's rich, so she can accuse me of things and I can't defend myself!"

He glanced at Gelly in the seat of the corporate jet beside him. "Weren't you just on the other end of that argument?"

She glowered at him. "She stole the egg. I know she did. You saw it in her bag!"

"I did, didn't I?" He was still kicking himself mentally for believing Morie guilty in the first place.

"I did not plant it there. I swear!"

"They've hired a private detective. So have my brothers. The same detective—how's that for a coincidence?" he murmured.

She shifted in her seat. This was getting too close for comfort. She couldn't endure a thorough background check. "I'll sue for invasion of privacy!"

"Gelly, the detective is investigating the theft of

a priceless jeweled egg," he reminded her. "How does that involve your privacy?"

She cleared her throat. "I'm sorry." She forced a smile. "I wasn't thinking clearly. I'm very upset. Her father is obnoxious!"

"He loves her. He's very protective. I'd be that way about my own kids."

She snuggled up to him. "Wouldn't you like to have a family? I would. We could get married right away."

"We could. But we aren't going to."

"But you like me, don't you?"

He looked down into eyes like cash registers, as cold as ice, and realized that he'd never seen Gelly as she really was until now. It had taken a near tragedy to open his eyes to her real nature.

"You really want to be rich, don't you?"

She gaped at him. "Who doesn't?"

"There are things more important than money."

She laughed coldly. "Of course there are, if you've got it."

"I want to hear more about that friend of yours, Cardman," he said suddenly.

She looked around restlessly. "He's just someone I know. He's down on his luck."

"Would it be because of the lawsuits?"

She cleared her throat. "I think I'll try to have a little nap," she said with a practiced smile. "I've had a very upsetting evening. You don't mind?"

"I don't mind."

She curled up in her seat and pillowed her head on her arm. Mallory got up and went to sit in the front seat, where he had access to a laptop. He opened it and started doing some digging of his own.

WHEN HE GOT HOME, his brothers were both in the living room, having coffee and watching the news before bedtime.

They stared at him curiously. "You're back early," Tank said. "I thought the plan was to fly back in tomorrow."

"There was an unexpected surprise."

They both raised eyebrows.

Mallory stuck both hands in the pockets of his dress slacks and glared at them. "Kingston Brannt has a daughter."

"Oh?" Cane mused with a wicked smile.

"Does he, now?" Tank added. "And you noticed her?"

"It was hard not to," Mallory snapped. "She worked for us for several weeks."

There were shocked faces all around.

"Morie?" Cane asked. "She's the daughter of that Brannt?"

"Told you the name wasn't a coincidence, didn't I?" Tank mused. "She had quality and breeding."

"What the hell was she doing working for wages?" Cane wanted to know.

"She got tired of men wanting to marry her for her money," Mallory said tersely.

"I can understand that," Tank agreed.

"So she found a man who was loaded and now she's engaged to him," Mallory continued in a dull tone. "He's a pretty boy. His father's in the Fortune 500. No gold digging there. And her father likes *him*."

It was the emphasis on the last word that caught their attention.

"King doesn't like you, I'm assuming," Cane mused.

"Fat chance. I accused his daughter of theft and fired her," Mallory said heavily. He took off his jacket, loosened his tie and dropped down into his recliner. "I must have been blind, to think she'd steal from us."

"You had Gelly helping you think it," Cane said sourly.

"Gelly was half-hysterical when we left," Mallory confided. "Morie's father hired a private detective." He glanced at Cane. "The same one you hired, Dane Lassiter. When he mentioned that, Gelly almost fainted. And there's something else. That friend of hers, Cardman, who wanted to buy our scrubland, he's in the oil business. He does the fracturing process with injection wells to extract oil. He's being sued in several states for sloppy work that resulted in groundwater contamination."

"I seem to recall that you were in favor of selling him that land," Tank commented to Mallory.

"Go ahead, rub it in. I've been a complete idiot," Mallory grumbled. "No need to feel shy about commenting."

"Anybody can be fooled by a woman," Cane said sourly.

"Except me," Tank said with a grin.

Nobody said anything. It wasn't true. He used to have a fail-safe radar when it came to women. In fact, he'd been the first to suspect that Gelly wasn't what she seemed to be. But his own track record was blemished since his last failed romance.

"What about Morie?" Cane asked.

"What about her?" Mallory returned belligerently.

"Don't try to fool us...we're your family," Tank replied. "It was obvious that you felt something for her, even if you were fighting it tooth and nail."

Mallory's dark eyes grew narrow. "Maybe I did. But I'm not marrying into any family that belongs to King Brannt!"

"Ooooh," Tank murmured drily. "Venomous."

"Absolutely," Cane agreed.

"He's bullheaded, uncompromising, acid-tongued, confrontational, bad-tempered and he has the parlor manners of a rabid moose!"

"So you liked him, then," Cane replied, nodding and smiling.

"I've never seen a rabid moose," Tank commented.

"I'll fly you to Texas. You can see for yourself," Mallory muttered.

"To give the man credit, it would be offensive to have his only daughter charged with theft. And from what I've heard, nobody has a temper the equal of King Brannt's."

"I gather that you didn't get to meet Cort at the party?" Cane mused.

Mallory frowned. "Who's Cort?"

"Her older brother. If you think King's got a temper, you ain't seen nothing yet," Cane drawled. "A cattleman made a nasty remark about his conservation practices that he didn't like and he put the man through an antique screen in a restaurant. Police came, arrests were made. Cort just laughed. The cattleman was selling supposedly purebred cattle with bloodlines that were, shall we say, not of the purest. Cort exposed him at the hearing. The charges were dropped, very quickly, and the cattleman did a disappearing act. I hear they're still looking for him."

"Any cattleman worth his salt can spot a good bull by conformation alone," Tank scoffed.

"Yes, well, the cattleman was selling his stock to a newcomer from back east who'd just bought a ranch and was buying bulls for his new herd," he replied. "He was furious when he found out what he'd lost."

"God help us," Tank exclaimed. "So the perp skipped and left his pigeon holding the bag. Tragic."

"Perp? You still talk like a lawman," Cane remarked.

Tank shrugged. It was painful to remember how he'd been shot up during the border incident. But it was getting easier to live with.

"Sorry," Cane said gently. "I wasn't trying to bring back bad memories. I forget sometimes."

Tank smiled. "Me, too. No problem."

Mallory was listening, but not commenting. He was seeing Morie in her beautiful gown, her black hair upswept, her creamy shoulders on view. He was seeing that handsome yahoo holding her waist and feeling the anger rise in him at the sight. She'd been his, if he'd wanted her. He'd kissed her, held her, touched her. She was innocent. Was she still? Or had she gone rushing into that playboy's bed, full of grief and anguish at Mallory's rejection and distrust?

"Damned pretty boy," Mallory muttered to himself.

"Excuse me?" Cane replied.

"Morie's fiancé," he said coldly.

"I'm sure that she only likes him because he's handsome," Tank said with a wry glance at his brother.

"You can talk," Mallory said irritably. "Both of you got the looks in the family. I favor our grandfather, God help me. He looked like his face caught fire and somebody put it out with an ax."

They both practically rolled on the floor laughing.

"Well, we're still stuck with lawsuits drifting in," Mallory said heavily. "Brannt's going to sue us for defamation of character."

"He won't," Cane replied easily. "Morie won't let him. She's got a heart."

"A big one," Tank agreed. "She's as innocent as Joe Bascomb."

Cane was silent. Mallory stared at him pointedly. "You're loyal to your friends. It's one of your finest traits. But Joe beat his father's mule senseless and almost killed it. Have you forgotten that?"

"Joe said it was his dad," Tank replied tautly.

"There were witnesses, Tank," Mallory said gently. "His mother was taken to the emergency room around the same time with a fractured arm. The talk was that she tried to stop Joe from beating the mule and he hit her with the tire iron."

"She said she fell," Tank replied doggedly.

"You don't want to hear these things, but you

already know that Joe got out of the army on a mental," Cane reminded him. "He attacked two men in his barracks for making fun of him because he couldn't spell. Put one of them in the hospital."

"That might all be true, but he could still be innocent of deliberately causing the death of the man who was beating Laura Teasley."

"I know," Cane said. "But there's a pattern of violent behavior going back a long way. It came out at the trial. Besides that, Laura testified that Joe already had a grudge against the victim for a blacksmithing job he did and wasn't paid for."

"We were talking about the Brannts," Tank said, changing the subject abruptly. "And we still have the problem of who took that egg."

"The only people who had access to this room were Mavie—and we know she didn't do it—and us. And Gelly," Cane added quietly.

"That's not quite true, is it, Tank?" Mallory asked suddenly, and with a pointed stare.

Tank glared at him. "Joe was only in here once, just before he was arrested," he said.

"Tank, he came on the place without even being noticed when he approached Morie at the line cabin," Mallory reminded him. "He's a woodsman. He can get into and out of anything. He's a locksmith, in addition to being a blacksmith. He can open locks."

"Isn't it enough that he's being accused of a murder he didn't commit? Do we have to start accusing him of theft, as well?" Tank exclaimed, exasperated. He got up. "I'm going to bed. Arguing gets us nowhere."

"Me, too," Cane agreed. He got to his feet. "Dane Lassiter has one of his best detectives up here poking around. He'll dig up something. I'm sure of it."

"Most of it will probably concern Gelly, I'm afraid," Tank said with a worried look at Mallory. "I hope you aren't more involved with her than you seem to be."

"I'm not," Mallory said heavily. "She was just somebody to take around places."

"You'd better hope she doesn't come up with a better accusation than the ones she made against Morie and our former cowhand," Cane told him.

"Like what?" Mallory asked, stunned.

"Maybe she'll turn up pregnant," Cane said.

Mallory's dark eyes twinkled. "Not by me," he said. "I'm not that careless."

"She could lie."

"Bloodwork would exonerate me," Mallory said easily. "I was never intimate with her in the first place."

"Good thing," Tank said.

"Yes," Cane agreed.

Mallory didn't mention that there had been a

close call once, just once, after Morie left and he was depressed enough to need comforting. But he hadn't crossed the line with Gelly. So even if she made the charge, he'd be able to refute it. He did worry, though, that she might try to trap him. She wanted money and now she was desperate. He wondered if she might have taken that priceless egg. She did have the opportunity and the motive. It would have to wait for the private detective to iron it out, he supposed.

He went up to bed, his mind still full of Morie's real identity and the picture that he'd carry forever in his heart, of her in that white gown, looking as elegant as a princess and quite at home among the wealthiest cattlemen in the world.

A FEW DAYS LATER, A TALL, dark man with long black hair and pale gray eyes, wearing a suit, knocked at the front door.

Mavie let him in and called Mallory, who was the only brother in the house at the moment.

"Ty Harding." The man introduced himself and shook hands with Mallory. "I work for Dane Lassiter, out of Houston."

"Come in," Mallory invited. "Mavie, coffee?"

"Coming right up," she said, casting a last, smiling glance at the handsome newcomer. Not only was he handsome, he had the physique of a movie star, tall and muscular without being overtly so.

Harding sat down across from Mallory. "I've finished the investigation."

"Then you know who took the egg?" Mallory asked at once.

He nodded grimly. "It was sold to a fence in Denver through a third party for ten thousand dollars."

Mallory gaped at him. "It's worth ten times that!"

"Yes, we know. The fence has been arrested and the egg was confiscated from its new owner. He's pretty upset. He paid a quarter of a million for it. Luckily, the fence hadn't had time to distribute more than a third of the money."

Mallory was relieved. "That piece of art was our grandmother's," he explained. "It really is priceless, but it has a sentimental value, as well. Who stole it?"

Harding hesitated. Mavie came in with steaming cups of black coffee in mugs on a silver tray. There was pound cake, too. She put it down, grinning at the newcomer. She didn't smile much. Mallory was amused at her friendliness to the visitor. "Hope you like cake," she said. "It was made fresh yesterday."

"I love it. Thank you."

"Cream? Sugar?" she offered.

Harding shook his head and chuckled, showing perfect white teeth. "I got used to drinking it black years ago. It's hard to find condiments in some of the places I've worked."

"Thank you, Mavie," Mallory said pointedly.

She glanced at him, cleared her throat, excused herself and left.

"Nice lady," Harding commented as he sipped coffee. He closed his eyes. "Colombian," he decided. "My favorite."

Mallory's eyes widened. "You can tell the origin of the blend?"

"It's a hobby." His eyes twinkled with secret amusement.

Mallory didn't comment. "Now. Who took the egg?"

Harding had another sip of coffee and put the cup down. "A threesome, I'm afraid."

"What threesome?" Mallory's mind was working overtime as he searched for suspects.

"A local woman, Gelly Bruner, took the egg. She had a key to your cabinet, which was made for her by an escaped convict, Joe Bascomb, who needed money to avoid being captured. There was a third man involved, peripherally, a man named Bates. It seems he helped Ms. Bruner by planting evidence."

Mallory's face was thunderous. "Bates works

for me! He said he saw Morie Brannt holding the egg in the bunkhouse."

"I believe he also helped plant evidence on another cowboy who worked here, a man named Harry Rogers, who's retained counsel and plans to sue for false arrest."

"Great," Mallory said. "I guess we'll keep our lawyers busy."

"Rogers does have a case, but it's the sheriff who arrested him that he's suing, and also Ms. Bruner. He isn't suing you. He said you were set up, just as he was."

Mallory was touched. "In that case he can have his job back with a raise, if he wants it, and I'll pay for his attorney."

"You'd have to talk to him about that. Your cowboy Bob Bates has been arrested, however, and charged with aiding and abetting theft."

"I'm just astonished," Mallory said heavily. "I did suspect Gelly, but I had no idea Bates was that involved."

"He had feelings for her and he's very young," Harding replied. "He's sick at heart about what he did. She told him it was a prank. He didn't find out different until Ms. Brannt was fired, and then he was afraid to come forward."

"It doesn't excuse theft," Mallory said. "Not at all."

"He's a first offender," Harding said. "I'm

almost certain that he'll get probation. Ms. Bruner is, however, in a different situation. She has a record."

"For what?" Mallory asked, stunned.

"Theft. This isn't her first walk around the justice system. She's never been convicted, but she's been charged twice in the theft of priceless antiques from private homes. I'm afraid she's not going to have an easy time. Her signature was on the receipt for proceeds from the sale of the stolen egg, and Bates is turning state's evidence against her in return for first-offender status. He can put her in the house with a duplicate key at the time of the theft. It seems that Bascomb also made her a copy of your house key."

"Oh, good God," Mallory exclaimed.

"So it might be a good idea for you to check your other valuables and see if any are missing or have been replaced with copies," the detective suggested.

"I'll do that today," Mallory agreed. "That's a lot of good detective work for such a short time."

Harding shrugged. "I love my job. I used to be a cop, but I got tired of the hours, so I quit Houston P.D. and went to work for Dane Lassiter." He grinned. "He's some boss, let me tell you."

"So I've heard."

"There's a rumor going around that Joe Bascomb didn't get his cut of the money and he's out for revenge," Harding added. "If I were you, I'd put on extra patrols out here and watch where I went. He's really desperate now. They've brought in other law-enforcement personnel to go into the woods after him, including some trackers and some K-9 units."

"I'll make sure we're all armed," Mallory told him. "And thanks."

Harding smiled. "My pleasure."

MALLORY TOLD HIS BROTHERS what Harding had related, and they went around the house looking for other missing objects. To their shock, they found at least two priceless ceramic vases missing and one irreplaceable solid gold miniature goblet, not to mention an entire silver service that was kept apart from the others in a special cabinet. It was almost never unlocked and the brothers paid it little attention, because it was in an out-of-the-way place in the house.

Mallory called the sheriff's department and an officer took down the descriptions of the missing items and their value. He promised to have their investigator get in touch with the appropriate authorities in Denver and search for them. Mallory didn't expect them to be found. But there was always a chance, even if it was a small one.

Gelly had called him collect from the detention center, crying and begging for help. "I'm innocent," she wailed. "I'm being set up! It's a lie!"

"Gelly, you had duplicate keys that Bascomb made for you," he added. "The prosecutor has an eyewitness who saw you sell the jeweled egg to a dealer in Las Vegas. What do you expect me to do?"

"You have to help me!" she exclaimed. "I'll tell them I'm pregnant! I'll call the newspapers!"

"Go ahead," he said easily.

"I mean it!"

"So do I," he replied. "You'd have to prove it. We both know it's impossible."

"Well, I know that. But I can lie," she shot back. "I know how to lie and make people believe me!"

"You sure do," he agreed coldly. "You got Morie fired with your lies. Not to mention Harry Rogers, who worked for us and was fired for stealing a drill that he didn't even take."

"That silly girl," Gelly muttered. "I made up all sorts of stories about her, and you believed every one of them!"

"Yes. I did," he replied grimly.

"Maybe I can't have you, but you'll never have her, now!" she exclaimed. "I can't imagine that she'd really want you. You're as ugly as an old boot!"

His pride ached at the charge. "Maybe," he replied coldly. "But I'm rich."

"Humph!"

"Goodbye, Gelly."

He hung up and removed the cartridge that had the conversation on it. Even though he hadn't informed her that she was being recorded, this would serve as evidence that he wasn't responsible for any pregnancy she might claim in the future. He dropped it in the drawer of the telephone table, replaced it with a new one and then blocked the number she'd called from—the detention center— so that she couldn't reach him again. Her words stung. He knew he had nothing in the looks department. He turned and went out to work. But his mind wasn't at all on what he was doing. Which was a shame.

MORIE WAS WALKING AROUND the barn with her father and brother. She hadn't said two words all morning.

Cort was tall like their father, with jet-black hair and eyes. He was drop-dead gorgeous, Morie thought, even if he was her brother. Now he glanced at her with narrowed eyes. "Don't be thinking about that damned Wyoming coyote," he said hotly. "He's not worth a single thought."

"Amen," King Brannt muttered.

"Neither of you know a thing about him," Morie replied without looking up. "He has good qualities. He was taken in by Gelly Bruner."

"His brothers weren't," King replied.

"Love blinds men," Morie said with more pain than she realized. "Mallory is in love with Gelly."

Both men looked down at her.

King, undemonstrative to a fault, nevertheless put his arm around his daughter and hugged her close. "Daryl will make you a good husband," he told her firmly.

She smiled. "I know."

"If she doesn't love him, he won't," Cort cut in bluntly.

King glared at his son. "You're supposed to be on my side."

"I am on your side. But she's my sister and I love her," the younger man added. "It's not a good idea to jump into a new relationship when you haven't resolved the old one."

"I never had a relationship with that awful cattleman," Morie muttered.

King let her go and searched her face. "Are you sure?"

"I'm sure," she said firmly.

King raised an eyebrow. "He was looking at you the way I look at a juicy steak when your mother's been feeding me chicken for a week."

Morie's heart jumped. "He was?"

King shrugged. "He stood up to me, too."

"I thought you didn't like him." Morie faltered.

"I heard from the private detective," he continued. "It seems Ms. Bruner is in jail awaiting trial on theft by taking, along with one of the Kirks' cowboys. That escaped criminal they're looking for is on the list, too, but they still can't find him."

"It was on the news this morning," Cort said. "They've sent in tracking dogs."

"I feel sorry for Tank," Morie said. "Joe Bascomb was his friend."

"Tank?" Cort asked, blinking.

"He killed one overseas and his men gave him the nickname," Morie volunteered.

Cort sighed. "I guess it's better than Tub."

Tub was what they called one of their cowboys, who was thin as a rail and the best wrangler they'd ever had. Nobody knew how he'd come by the nickname.

"They said that Bascomb had told a family member that he had a score to settle before he was caught, and that they wouldn't take him alive."

Morie felt cold chills run down her arms. It was an odd sort of apprehension, as if she knew something terrible was about to happen and that she had no way of stopping it.

"I feel odd," she murmured.

"Odd, how?" her father asked.

Before she could answer, Shelby came into the barn, looking like a fashion plate even in jeans and a T-shirt. She was frowning.

"What's wrong, honey?" King asked, sensitive

to her moods. He caught her by her arms, gently, smiling down at her. "Can I help?"

She shook her head and looked at Morie with sorrow. "It's about that cattleman you worked for, Mallory Kirk."

Morie's heart stopped, skipped and ran away. "What about him?"

"That escaped criminal kidnapped him on his own ranch. He says he's going to kill him… Morie!"

Morie didn't hear her. She'd fainted dead away.

CHAPTER TWELVE

IF IT DISTURBED HER FAMILY that Morie fainted at the news that Mallory had been kidnapped, her next move horrified them. She announced plans to fly up to Wyoming.

"What in the world do you think you can do that the law can't?" King demanded hotly.

"I can talk to Joe Bascomb," she said flatly.

"Nobody can talk to him—he's desperate." Her brother tried to reason with her. "He might kidnap you and kill you, too."

"He won't," she said, certain of it. "I talked to him. I shared my lunch with him. He'll listen to me."

Shelby hadn't said anything yet. She was watching, listening, worrying.

"Mom, remember when old man Hughes got drunk?" she asked gently. "Remember who they'd call to come get him out of bars or fights? It was me. He'd always do what I asked, no matter how mad or mean he was."

"Yes, I remember," Shelby said. "You have a way with people."

"Joe Bascomb isn't going to listen to any man," she said quietly. "But he might listen to a woman."

King was grinding his teeth. "I won't let you risk it."

She went close to him. "Yes, you will, Dad," she said gently. "Because it's what you'd do, in my place, and you know it." Her eyes darkened. "I love Mallory Kirk. He may be gullible, and he may be a terror of a man, but I can't let him die and not try to save him."

King drew in a long breath. "I guess you can't."

She pulled off her engagement ring and put it in his hand. "Please give that back to Daryl and tell him I did find somebody better, but only because it's a man I love. He'll understand."

"He will," King agreed. "I'll have them fuel the jet."

"Thanks."

He kissed her forehead. "Don't get killed." He wasn't teasing.

"I won't. I promise." She hugged him and her brother and then her mother.

"I could go with you," Cort volunteered.

"They don't need any more troublemakers than they've already got up there," King mused, shaking his head at his son. "You're too much like me. You'd just put everybody's back up."

Cort shrugged, but he didn't dispute the assessment. He tugged at Morie's long black hair. "Be safe."

She nodded. "I will be. I promise."

SHE PHONED TANK FROM the airport. He and Cane both came to get her. But when she explained what she wanted to do, they were adamantly against it.

"He'd listen to me if he'd listen to anybody," Tank argued. He was gaunt, like Cane. It had been a rough couple of days since Mallory went riding fence out near the old line cabin and didn't return. Joe Bascomb had phoned a few hours later and told them that he had Mallory and he was going to kill him for messing up his financial coup. Tank had pleaded with his friend, but Joe said he had nothing to lose and he wasn't talking to them again. He hung up.

"Mal may already be dead," Tank said heavily. "We have no way of knowing."

"I don't think he is," she said, without explaining why she thought that. She knew inside herself, knew certainly, that Mallory was still alive. She knew it.

"You don't even know how to find Joe, if we were to agree to let you try," Cane argued.

"I do know," she said. "I'll go to the line cabin and wait for him. He'll come. He watches it."

They frowned.

"That's where he took Mal from," Cane recalled. "We saw signs of a struggle."

"Why the cabin?" Tank wondered.

She gave them a droll look. "It's provisioned, isn't it? There's even a bed. And nobody stays out there except when there's a need. Where do you think he's been living all this time, in a cave?"

"You might have voiced that suspicion earlier," Tank muttered.

"I was having a little problem with credibility around here at the time," she said drily.

They looked upset.

"I know you two believed I was innocent," she said. "Thanks."

Cane studied her curiously. "Mallory said you sparkled like a jewel at your family ranch. Kingston Brannt's daughter, riding fence lines." He shook his head. "We could hardly believe it."

"Dad wouldn't let me near the cattle," she said, beaming inside at their description of what Mallory had said about her. "Neither would my brother. And I was being forcefully courted for my father's money. I needed a break."

"Mallory's been kicking himself ever since he got home," Tank told her. "He thinks he's too ugly to appeal to a woman for himself, so all they want is his money."

"He's not ugly. Stupid, yes," she muttered. "Idiotic. Distrustful. Bad-tempered...!"

"We know all that," Cane acknowledged. "But we love him."

She glanced at them sadly. "Yes. So do I. It's why I came. And I won't be discouraged from doing this. I'm right."

"If Joe doesn't kill Mal," Tank said quietly, "and it works out that he lets him go, he'll kill us for letting you take the risk."

"We can deal with that when it happens. Right now, I need to change clothes, borrow a horse and ride out to the line cabin."

"It's pouring down rain," Cane said.

"No problem. I packed a raincoat!"

She'd also packed five thousand dollars in large bills, with which she was going to appeal to Joe to release Mallory. It was a calculated risk. He might grab her and the money, and kill her with Mallory. But she was willing to take the chance that he wouldn't. He was a basic sort of person. He needed money and he was angry that he'd been double-crossed. But he still needed money and he might bargain for it. The sheriff was closing in. He'd need to get out quickly. He wouldn't know that Morie had already spoken to the sheriff, who was another friend of Uncle Danny's, and outlined her plan. He would have two government agents in the woods overlooking the line cabin, woodsmen as good or better than Joe Bascomb. She couldn't tell the brothers that, in case they let something slip. So she kept her counsel.

Darby was upset when she had him saddle the horse for her.

"You can't do this," he protested as she loaded a small pouch, along with a bag of biscuits and a thermos of coffee that Mavie, protesting, too, had made for her to take along. "You can't let her do it!" he raged at the two brothers standing grimly nearby.

"Yes, they can, Darby," Morie told him gently. "I won't let Joe kill Mallory. No matter what I have to do to save him."

"It's not right."

She smiled. "Yes, it is. You just send up a prayer or two for me, okay?"

"Dozens," he promised grimly. "I wish I'd known who you were at the start. I'd never have let you go riding fence in the first place."

"If you hadn't, I wouldn't have gotten to know Joe Bascomb and I wouldn't have a prayer of convincing him to release Mallory. Things work the way they're supposed to. There's a plan, and a purpose, to everything," she said, shocking herself because she remembered saying that to Joe.

She mounted up gracefully and turned the gelding. Rain was peppering down over her slicker and wide-brimmed hat. It was getting dark, too, but she wouldn't let that deter her. She had a flashlight in her pack. "Try not to worry. I'll call you as soon as I know anything." She had a cell phone in the pocket of her slicker. She patted it.

"If we don't hear from you in an hour, we're coming in," Tank said quietly.

She nodded. "Fair enough."

She turned the horse again and galloped off toward the line cabin. All she had was hope. But hope was the very last thing anyone ever lost.

MORIE PULLED UP AT THE line cabin and dismounted. She took the biscuits and thermos and money out of her saddlebag, along with her flashlight.

She noticed movement at the curtain. She'd guessed right. Joe was in that cabin. She wondered if he had Mallory there, and prayed that he did. If he'd already killed Mallory, her life would be worth nothing.

She went up the steps and opened the door. She looked down the barrel of a loaded shotgun.

"What are you doing here?" Joe Bascomb demanded hotly.

She felt sick at her stomach, and she was scared to death. But she didn't dare show it. She only smiled. "Brought you something."

He blinked. The gun wavered. "Brought me something?"

She nodded.

He hesitated. She glanced around the single

room. Mallory wasn't there. Her heart sank. What if he was already dead?

The shotgun barrel lowered. "What did you bring?" he asked.

"Is Mallory Kirk alive?" she asked.

He drew in a long, worried breath. He stared at her.

"Is he alive?" she asked again, more unsteadily.

He put on the safety and laid the shotgun across the long, rough wooden table. "Yes," he said after an eternity of seconds.

She let out the breath she'd been holding. "Where is he?"

"Tied up against a tree, some distance from here," he said curtly. "Where he won't be found. He's roughed up—he fought me when I tried to take him from here. But he ain't dead. Yet," he added menacingly. "Why are you here? How did you know where to find me?"

"I didn't," she replied. "I was hoping you might come back here. It's where we met, remember?"

He blinked. "Yeah."

She put the leather pouch and the bags on the table. She opened the bag and produced two freshly buttered biscuits with strawberry preserves on them, along with a thermos of hot coffee. She presented them to him.

"Mavie's biscuits." His voice almost broke. He took one and bit into it and groaned with pleasure. He sipped coffee with the same expression. "Living in the wild, you miss some things so bad!" he exclaimed. He looked at her and winced. "Dangerous, you coming out here! Why did they let you?"

"They couldn't stop me," she said simply. She looked him in the eye. "I love Mallory Kirk."

That made him uncomfortable. He averted his eyes. "He ain't nothing to look at."

"It's what's inside him that makes him the man he is," she replied. "He's honest and hardworking and he never lies."

He laughed coldly. "That Bruner woman said she loved me," he said coldly. "I met her after my wife died. She wanted me to make her some keys. She said that man I killed owed her a ton of money and it was in his house in a box. She told him lies about his girlfriend to make him hit her. She knew the woman would call me for help, because I was close by."

"Good heavens," Morie exclaimed.

"So I got her out of the room and tried to make him tell me about the money in the box, but he fought me and I had to kill him. Gelly said it was all right…she had a way to make even more money," he said in a faraway tone. "She told me about the jeweled egg, but I already knew because Tank had showed it to me once. I didn't realize how much it was worth. So she took Mallory's keys and asked me to make her duplicates, to get into the Kirks' house and that curio cabinet. She put them back and Mallory thought he'd misplaced them. I had to sneak into the smith's shop at night and risk capture to do it for her. She said she'd get that egg and sell it and then we'd have money to run away. She got a cowboy to help her. Then she goes and sells the stuff to a fence and gets arrested, and I don't get a dime, because Mallory Kirk called in a private detective and he blew the lid off the case!"

"My father called the detective," she said matter-of-factly. "I was blamed for the theft of the egg in the first place."

"You were?" he exclaimed.

She nodded. "By Gelly. And Bates, the cowboy who planted it in my bag."

"I hate that," he said slowly. "I never meant to hurt you. You been kind to me. Most people don't care."

"I'm sorry for you, I really am," she told him. "But killing Mallory won't solve any problems. It will just guarantee you the death penalty."

He laughed again, a cold, chilling sound, and his eyes were opaque. "I won't go back. I killed that man deliberately," he said, his eyes suddenly as cold as his voice. "He wouldn't tell me where the money was. I was going to have money to take Gelly places and buy her nice things. She said she loved me more than anybody in the world. Nobody loved me since my wife died...."

Her heart stilled in her chest. She'd never known that Joe was involved with the woman. She would have bet that the Kirks didn't know, either.

"Did you know that she had a record?" she asked. "She was arrested twice and charged with theft, but she managed to get out of going to trial. She won't be that lucky this time."

"She said she had another way to get money, since this one fell through," he muttered. "She was going to claim that Mallory got her pregnant." He shook his head, while Morie stood frozen in place. "But after I kidnapped him, he told me he taped the conversation she had with him when she said it would be a lie but she could make people believe her. Can you believe she'd be that stupid?!"

Morie relaxed. She'd worried for a second that it could be true. It was such a relief! But she still had to save Mallory....

"I brought you something else," she said, and indicated the leather pouch.

He frowned. He put down the thermos cup and opened the pouch. He caught his breath. "This is a fortune!"

"Not really. It's just five thousand. It's part of my inheritance. My father owns a big cattle ranch in Texas. His mother left me the money."

She moved closer. "It will help you get away, won't it? So will you let Mallory go?"

His eyes narrowed suspiciously. "The bills are marked, huh?"

She threw up her hands. "How do you mark bills?" she exclaimed, exasperated. "I came straight from the bank to the airport, and I told nobody what I was going to do with the money. I didn't even tell my folks that I took it out of my account!"

He relaxed then. He took the money in his hands and looked at it with pure fascination. He'd done so many things, tried so hard, to get enough to get out of this county alive. Now he had the means. All he had to do was leave, now....

"Were you followed?" he asked her at once.

She shook her head. "I made them promise."

He was thinking, planning, plotting. The money would buy him a cheap car, and clothes and food. He could run to Montana, where he had other friends who would hide him. He could get away.

He turned back to her and picked up the shotgun. For an instant, her heart shivered as she wondered if he'd kill her now that she'd given him the cash.

"I won't hurt you," he said in an awkward way. "I just want to get away. I can't go back to jail. I can't be locked up." He stared at the money. "I hit my mother with a tire iron," he recalled in a faraway, shocked tone. "I never meant to hurt her. I never meant to hurt anybody. I get these rages. I go blind mad and I can't control it. I can't help myself." He closed his eyes. "Maybe I'd be better off dead, you know? I wouldn't hurt anybody else. Poor old Mallory…he was kind to me once, gave me a helping hand because Tank asked him to, after we got out of military service. Tank was my friend. I lied to him. I told him I was framed." He sighed. "I wasn't framed. I meant to kill the man. I've done terrible things. Things I never wanted to do." He looked at her. "But I can't let them take me alive, you understand? I can't be locked up."

She grimaced. "If you gave yourself up, maybe they could get a psychologist who could help you…."

"I killed a man," he reminded her. "And kidnapped another one. That means feds will come in. They'll track me all the way to hell. I can get away for a while. But in the end, the feds will hunt me down. I knew one, once. He was like a bulldog. Wouldn't eat, wouldn't sleep, just hunted until he found the man he was looking for. A lot of them are like that." He took the other biscuit and the thermos of coffee. "Thanks," he said. "For the food and coffee. For the money." He hesitated. "For listening. Nobody ever really listened to me except my wife. I beat her…." He groaned. "God knows why she didn't leave me. I never deserved her. She got cancer. They said she knew she had it and she wouldn't get treatment. I knew why. She loved me but she couldn't go on living with me, and she couldn't leave me. Damn me! I don't deserve to live!"

"That's not for you to say," she told him. "Life is a gift."

He swallowed, hard. He looked at her with eyes that were already dead. "My mama knew there was something wrong with me when I was little. She said so. But she had too much pride to tell anybody. Thought it was like saying there was something wrong with her. I could never learn nothing, you know? I quit school because they made fun of me. I saw words backward."

She went closer, totally unafraid. "I'm sorry. I'm so sorry."

He ground his teeth together. "I'm sorry I got you involved in this. Wasn't your problem. Mallory's a half mile down the trail," he said after a minute, "off to the right, in some bushes. He'll be hard to find, because I didn't want him found."

"I'll find him," she said with certainty.

He started to the door, hesitated, looked back at her. "Damn, he's a lucky man!" he said through his teeth. He closed the door and melted into the night.

MORIE DIDN'T WASTE a minute. She rushed out, mounted the horse and turned him down the narrow trail that she knew from weeks of riding fence. Mallory was out there somewhere, getting soaked in this cold rain. God knew how long he'd been tied up. He would certainly need some sort of medical attention. It was almost freezing, unseasonably cold. She felt her heartbeat shaking her as she worried about not being able to find him. She could call for help, but if Joe was still around and watching, he might think she'd sold him out and he might try to kill Mallory and her in revenge. She didn't dare take the risk.

She rode down the path for what she judged was a half mile, and she dismounted, tied her horse to a tree and started beating through the underbrush. But she found nothing. What if Joe had lied? What if he'd really killed Mallory, and she was going to stumble over his body instead of the living, breathing man? She felt terror rise in her throat like bile.

Maybe she'd misjudged the distance. Maybe it was farther away!

She mounted again and rode a little ways. Somewhere there was a sound, an odd sound, like a crack of thunder. But it was just drizzle. There was no storm. She shrugged it off. She was upset and hearing things. She dismounted and started searching off the path again. It was slow going. She could hardly see her hand in front of her face, and the flashlight was acting funny. She searched again and again, but she found nothing. There were trees, all around, but none with a man tied to it.

"Damn," she muttered, frantic to find Mallory. What if Bascomb had lied? What if he'd killed Mallory and dumped his body someplace else? If a man could kill, couldn't he lie, too?

She swallowed, hard, and fought tears. She had to think positively. Joe wasn't lying. Mallory was alive. He was somewhere around here. And she was going to find him! She had to find him. She had no life left without him.

She rode a few more yards, dismounted and searched off the path again. But, again, she found nothing. She repeated the exercise, over and over again, fearful that she might get careless and miss him. She could get help when it turned light, but that might be too late...!

She went down the path to a turn in the road, dismounted and walked through the underbrush. The glow of the flashlight began to give off a dull yellow light. She'd forgotten to change the batteries! She shook it and hit it, hoping the impact might prop it up for a few more precious minutes, but it didn't. Even as she watched, the light began to fade.

"Oh, damn!" she wailed to herself. "And I haven't got any spare batteries. Of all the stupid things to do!"

There was a sound. She stopped. She listened. Rain was getting louder on the leaves, but there was some muffled sound. Her heart soared.

"MALLORY!" SHE CALLED. Damn Joe, she wasn't going to let Mal die because she was afraid to raise her voice.

The muffled sound came again, louder, to her right.

She broke through the bushes wildly, blindly, not caring if they tore her skin, if they ruined her clothing, if they broke bones. She trampled over dead limbs, through patchy weeds, toward a thicket where tall pine trees were growing.

"Mallory!" she called again.

"Here." His voice was muffled and bone-tired and heavy.

She pushed away some brush that had been piled up around a tree. And there was Mallory. Bareheaded, pale, tied to the tree with his arms behind him, sitting. He was soaking wet. His face was bruised. He looked worn to the bone. But when he saw Morie, his eyes were so brilliant with feeling that she caught her breath.

She managed to untie the bandanna that Joe had used to gag him with.

He coughed. "Got anything to drink?" he asked huskily. "Haven't had water for a day and a half...."

"No," she groaned. "I'm so sorry!" She thought

with anguish of the thermos of coffee she'd given Joe Bascomb.

"I'll get you loose," she choked out. She got around the tree and tried to untie the bonds, but the nylon rope was wet and it wouldn't budge.

"Pocketknife. Left pocket."

She dug in his pocket for it, her face close to his as she worked.

His dry mouth brushed across her cheek. "Beautiful, brave girl," he whispered. "So...proud of you."

Tears ran down her cheeks with the rain. She bent and put her mouth against his, hard. "I love you," she whispered. "I don't care about the past."

He managed a smile. "I love you, too, baby."

Her heart soared. "You do?" she exclaimed. "Oh, Mal!" She bent and kissed him again with helpless longing.

"I'm not complaining. But think you might cut me loose anytime soon?" he murmured. "My hands have gone to sleep."

"Oh, dear!"

She ran around the tree, opened the knife and went to work on the bonds. His hands were white. The circulation ran back into them when he was free and he groaned at the pain.

"Can you stand up?" she asked, concerned.

He tried and slumped back down. "Sorry," he murmured. "Legs gone to sleep, too."

He was obviously suffering from exposure and God knows what other sort of injuries that Joe had inflicted on him.

"I'll get help," she said at once, and pulled out her cell phone.

Lights flashed around her as men came forward. "Miss Brannt?" someone called.

She gasped. "Yes!"

A tall, dark-haired man came into view. He was wearing jeans and a buckskin jacket. He had long black hair in a ponytail and a grim expression. "I'm Ty Harding. I work for Dane Lassiter."

"Hiya, Harding," Mallory managed. "Good to see you on the job."

"I can outtrack any of these feds," he teased the other two men, "so I volunteered to help search for you. Hey, Jameson, can you bring a Jeep up here?"

"Sure. Be right back."

There were running footsteps.

Harding knelt beside him. "I don't think you're going to be able to ride a horse back," he guessed.

"Probably not," Mallory agreed hoarsely. "Have you got any water?"

"I have," one of the feds said, and tossed a bottle to Harding, who handed it, opened, to Mallory. It was painful to Morie to watch how thirstily he drank it, choked and drank again.

"God, that's so sweet!" Mallory exclaimed when he'd drained the bottle. "I've been tied here for almost two days. Thought I'd die, sure. Then an angel came walking up and saved me," he added, smiling at Morie. "My own personal guardian angel."

"I gave Joe Bascomb a pouch with cash," she told Harding. "I spoke to the sheriff about it before I came up here, so he knows. I can't tell you which direction Joe took. It was raining...."

Harding's expression in the light of his flashlight was grim. "There's no need to concern yourself with that now."

"Have you caught him?" she exclaimed. "Already?"

"No," he said quietly. "We found him. Sitting up against a tree about half a mile away. Stone dead."

She caught her breath. Cold chills ran up and down her arms. That odd, high-pitched crack of thunder she thought she'd heard. A gunshot? "Dead?" She faltered.

He nodded. "Self-inflicted gunshot wound. He left a note." He pulled it out of his pocket. "He addressed it to you, Miss Brannt."

With trembling hands, she opened the dirty piece of paper. It was stained with blood. Joe's blood. It was only a few lines of scribbled writing.

I killed a man and kidnapped another on account of a no-good woman who just wanted

money. I'd never get out of jail. Thank you
for being kind, when nobody else ever was.
Your man is lucky. Be happy. Your friend,
Joe.

She burst into tears.

Mallory pulled her close and held her, despite the
pain in his arms from being in such a restrained
position. "It's all right. It's all over."

"Poor man," she choked out.

"He chose his life, Miss Brannt," Harding told
her quietly.

"But he didn't," she said through tears. "He had
a learning disability and all sorts of psychologi-
cal problems. But he didn't get help because his
mother thought they'd say there was something
wrong with her, too."

"Good Lord," Mallory said heavily. "If only
we'd known."

"We all have a purpose," Morie said again.

"Yes, we do," Harding said, surprisingly. "People
weave themselves into the fabric of our lives for
reasons we sometimes never understand. But there
is a purpose to everything. Even Bascomb's suicide."

"At least his mother didn't live to see him come
to this end," Mallory said. He tilted up Morie's wet
face. "And speaking of family, we'd better start
making telephone calls. My brothers must be out

of their minds, to say nothing of your mother and brother and your vicious, rabid father...."

"He isn't vicious. You'll learn to love him," she assured him.

"Think so?" Harding mused, pursing his lips. "I've met your father. And I have serious doubts about that."

She chuckled. "You don't know him. I do."

"My loss, I'm sure," Harding conceded. He looked up as the Jeep arrived. "Let's get you to the hospital, Mr. Kirk. You'll need to be checked out."

"Hospital? I'm not going to any damned hospital!" he burst out as they helped him into the Jeep.

"Yes, you are," Morie told him firmly. "Now sit back and shut up. We're saving you."

He gave her a blank stare. And then he chuckled. "Okay, boss," he drawled. "Whatever you say."

"You just remember that, and we'll get along famously." She batted her long lashes at him and grinned.

CHAPTER THIRTEEN

TANK AND CANE MET THEM at the emergency room. They hugged their pale, worn brother and choked up at the thought of how close he'd come to death.

"You let her come out after me alone," Mallory accused them.

"You can thrash us when you're better. Honest, we'll break you a pine limb," Cane promised.

Tank grinned. "But look what she did. She saved you."

Morie beamed. "Yes, I did," she agreed. "Despite the best efforts of my brother and mother and father and your brothers and Darby."

"We're all relieved," Cane said, smiling at her. "But she did what none of us could have done. Bascomb would have shot us on sight...."

There was a commotion in the hall followed by angry footsteps and a loud voice.

"Dad!" Morie exclaimed, because she recognized that voice.

King Brannt stormed into the examination room with flashing black eyes, trailed by a hospital clerk and a resident.

"Oh, Dad!" Morie ran and hugged him close. "I'm okay. It's all right!"

"Where is he?" They could hear Shelby's voice in the hall.

"Just follow the trail of bodies," Cort answered with a laugh.

"Mom! Cort! What are you doing here?" she exclaimed, hugging them, too.

"We were ten minutes behind you," King said, "but we couldn't get anybody to tell us anything, and they—" he pointed at Cane and Tank "—wouldn't answer their damned phones. I had to yell at a detective and a sheriff to find out anything!"

"You shouldn't yell at people. It's undignified," Shelby said gently.

He glared at her. "It's justified when you're scared to death that your daughter's been killed!"

The resident and the hospital clerk belatedly understood King's rampage. They smiled and left. The resident was back in a minute, however, to check out Mallory.

"Exposure, dehydration, some evidence of bruising on the ribs and a dislocated shoulder, but the tests don't reveal any broken bones or internal injuries," he told them. "You were very lucky, Mr. Kirk. Far luckier than your assailant. They've just taken him to the local hospital for an autopsy."

"What?" King exclaimed.

"Killed himself," the resident explained. He looked at Morie and shook his head. "If my wife had done what you did tonight, I'd have eaten her alive verbally before I hugged her to death. Does foolhardy behavior run in your family?"

"Yes, it does!" Shelby volunteered, pointing toward her husband and her son.

"Well, Mr. Kirk will be all right," the resident said with a smile. "He just needs rest and something for pain and a little patching up. We'll take care of that right now."

"Patching up," Mallory muttered. "It's just some cuts. I get worse than this doing ranch work every day."

"Me, too," King agreed, approaching him with his hands in his pockets. "Got kicked by a bull two days ago and had to have stitches."

"I got stepped on by one last week," Mallory said. "Damned things do it deliberately."

King stared at him. "You'd better be good to her."

"I will," Mallory replied quietly.

"You bet he will," Tank seconded. "Or we'll make him divorce her and I'll marry her and be good to her."

"She can marry me if she decides to get rid of him." Cane jerked his thumb toward Mallory. "I still have most of my own teeth and I can do the tango," he claimed with a straight face, because he'd heard from Mallory about Morie's fascination with the dance.

"I'm learning," Mallory protested. "It takes time. I need somebody to teach me."

Morie pursed her lips. "I think I'm up to that."

Mallory's dark eyes twinkled. "I think I'll learn even faster if you teach me. And there are a few things I can teach you, too."

"There are?" she asked, with mock fascination.

"Yes. Like how not to go riding off into the dark looking for escaped convicts!" he burst out. "What if he'd killed you?"

"Then I guess you'd have to find somebody else to teach you how to tango," she said simply.

Mallory let out an exasperated sigh.

"See?" King asked him. "Now you know how it's going to be. I've put up with it since she was old enough to stamp her foot at me and say no. It's your turn now."

Morie just laughed.

SHE DIDN'T GO HOME with her family. She moved into the big house at the Kirk ranch, into her own room, and Mallory bought her a beautiful set of rings, but emeralds instead of rubies. He wasn't duplicating the Fortune 500 heir's offering, he assured her. They were engaged although he'd never actually asked her to marry him. Shelby was helping with invitations. The ceremony would be held at the ranch in Texas.

The night before they flew back, Mallory held her in his lap in the recliner in the living room, after his brothers had discreetly gone to bed. He kissed her hungrily.

"I'm starving," he groaned as his hands found their way under her flimsy blouse and molded the soft skin. "I've never been so hungry in all my life."

She smiled under the warm press of his mouth. "Me, either."

"But we're going to wait anyway."

She laughed. "Yes."

He lifted his head. He was breathing hard. "Remind me again why we're going to do that, when nobody else does?"

"Just because the whole world's doing it, doesn't make it right in the view of people of faith," she replied simply. "I want a wedding night. A real one. Not an after-the-fact one that just comes after the wedding ceremony. I want oceans of lace in the gown I choose, the excitement of the ceremony and the reception, and the anticipation of how wonderful it's going to be during the night ahead. There's only one first time. Mine is going to be exactly the way I want it. Period."

He sighed. "Principles are very cumbersome sometimes."

She leaned forward and nibbled his lower lip. "You'll be happy you waited."

"Are you sure about that?" he mused.

She nodded. "Positively."

"All right. I'll have a cold shower and a colder beer and go to bed."

"Good man."

He made a face. "Not willingly."

"You're a good man," she disagreed. "And I'll be very proud to be your wife."

He smiled. "My beautiful Morena," he whispered. "Married to the ugliest tough man in Wyoming."

"Liar," she chided. "You're the most gorgeous man alive to me."

His eyebrows arched. "Me?"

"You. It isn't the way you look that makes you gorgeous. It's the man you are."

He flushed.

She grinned. She kissed him again and got to her feet. "We leave first thing in the morning. Mavie and Darby have to come, too, you know."

"They know, too. They're packed already."

She was somber for a moment. "I'm really sorry about Gelly. They say she'll probably do twenty years if they convict her."

"I'm sorry I blamed you," he replied, hugging her close. He sighed. "I had a close call there. She really had me with blinders on."

"You woke up in time, though. That's what counts."

"I suppose it does."

THE WEDDING WAS THE BIGGEST event Branntville could remember since Shelby Kane married King Brannt. The guest list was incredible. It included famous movie stars and television newsmen, sports stars, politicians and even European royalty.

Daryl was on the guest list. He had come by earlier to congratulate them, and to tell Morena he was happy for her. He hadn't been offended that Morena sent the rings back instead of returning them herself, especially when he knew what she'd risked to save Mallory's life. He was just happy that she was safe.

However, he added ruefully, now that he was no longer engaged, his enthusiastic parents were once again offering him as an entrée to any eligible young woman. He was resigned, he told her, to being hunted. But who knew, they might find him someone really nice. Like his friend Morena. Mallory stood by, not very patiently, while they spoke. But Daryl shook hands with him and after a few minutes, they were all smiling.

As they settled into the wedding ceremony, Morena, in a designer gown that one of Shelby's former colleagues had made up for her, was radiant and so much in love that she seemed to glow.

Her black hair, festooned with pale white pearl flowers, was loose around her shoulders under a veil of illusion with pearl highlights that covered her face. Her gown was traditional, with puff sleeves and a keyhole neckline, a long train...and it was accented with imported Belgian lace. Her jewelry was some of the finer pieces from her mother's collection along with a borrowed jeweled hair clasp from her shy maid of honor, Odalie Everett, who walked down the aisle tall and proud on the arm of Cane Kirk to stand with Mallory, pointedly ignoring Cort Brannt along the way.

The organ sounded the "Wedding March" as Morena walked slowly down the aisle of the ranch chapel to Mallory Kirk, who was standing at the altar with both his brothers as best man. She carried a bouquet of white and yellow roses tied with yellow ribbon. She looked at Mallory and almost tripped at the expression in his dark, loving eyes. *What a long way we've come,* she thought.

She looked up at him and the rest of the ceremony went by so quickly that she almost missed it. She let him put the ring on her finger, said the appropriate words and peered up at her new husband as he lifted the fingertip veil from her face and saw her for the first time as a wife. It was an old, beautiful tradition that both had looked forward to, in a time when tradition was routinely trampled and ridiculed by the world at large.

"My beautiful wife," he whispered, and smiled as he bent to kiss her with tender reverence.

She kissed him back, sighing as if she had the world in her arms. And she did.

The reception was fun. They fed each other cake, posed for pictures for the press and the photographer who was documenting the wedding, and danced to the live orchestra playing contemporary tunes.

"What a long way we've come," Mallory murmured into her ear as he waltzed her around the room.

"Funny, I was thinking that when we were standing at the altar," she exclaimed.

"Reading each other's minds already," he teased.

She nodded. Her eyes searched his. The electricity between them arced like a live current. She caught her breath at the intensity of feeling there.

"Not yet," she whispered.

He nodded, but his eyes never left hers. "Not yet."

TWO LONG HOURS LATER, they climbed into the limousine that was taking them to San Antonio, where they were spending their wedding night. The next day, they were off to the Caribbean, to a private island owned by a friend who was loaning them his estate for a week. It would be a dream honeymoon. Nothing to do but learn about each other and lie in the sun. Morena was looking forward to it.

They checked in to the suite Mallory had reserved. The bellboy was tipped. The door was locked. The phone was unplugged. Mallory took Morena by the waist and looked into her eyes for so long that she gasped with the feeling that passed between them.

He reached out with a long forefinger and traced a path around a nipple which quickly became erect. She gasped.

"I've dreamed about this for weeks," he whispered.

She nodded, breathless. "So have I."

He bent and nuzzled his nose against hers. The pressure of his finger increased, teasing and withdrawing. "You made me wait," he whispered with patient amusement. "Now I'm going to make you wait."

His mouth opened on hers. He kissed her slowly, with a mastery she was only just beginning to recognize. His big hands were deft and sure as he peeled her out of the exquisite dress and the slip and bra underneath. He kissed his way down her trembling body to her panty line as he eased the last flimsy scraps of clothing from her. His mouth opened on her flat belly and she cried out as his hands moved lower.

He let her go long enough to turn down the

bedcovers. He lifted her, kissed her tenderly and laid her on the cool sheets. His eyes made a meal of her nudity as his hands went to his coat. He removed it, and then the tie. He dropped them onto a chair and smiled as his hands worked buttons on his shirt to disclose a broad, muscular chest covered with thick, curling black hair.

She thought about how that was going to feel against her bare breasts and she moved, helpless, on the sheets, shivering a little at the intensity of his gaze.

He chuckled softly. "Anticipation is fun," he murmured.

"Says you," she teased, breathless.

He removed his shoes and socks, his belt, his trousers. Then, slowly, the black boxer shorts he fancied.

She stared at him with red cheeks. She'd seen photographs. Most women had, at some point, even if it was only by looking over a classmate's shoulder at a magazine. But she hadn't dreamed that men looked so, so...

As she looked, he began to swell from the pleasure of her rapt gaze, and she did gasp.

He eased down beside her on the bed. "As you might have guessed," he whispered in a voice gone husky with desire, "I'm a little better endowed than most men. But I won't hurt you. I promise."

"I'm not afraid."

"Bosh." His mouth smoothed over her firm, pretty little breasts. "Of course you are. It's the first time."

"Of course I am," she agreed huskily. "You don't mind...?"

He lifted his head and looked at her with open shock. "What?"

"I read this article," she said. "Some men said they wouldn't touch a virgin because they didn't want to have to worry about complications..."

"They did?" His hand slid down her belly and he smiled as she tried to withdraw when he touched her. "Easy," he whispered. "This is part of it. Don't be embarrassed. It's natural, what you're feeling."

She didn't know what she was feeling. Shock, at first, at being touched in a place where she only touched herself when she was bathing. And then, more shock, because when his hand moved, there was so much pleasure that she cried out and clutched at his arms.

"Unexpected, was it?" he teased gently. "Oh, it gets better."

His mouth opened on her soft breasts while he touched her, tasting and exploring in a veritable feast of the senses that lifted her in a helpless arch toward the source of all that delight.

"This may be a little uncomfortable," he whispered at her mouth as his hand moved again.

She flinched at first. But when she realized what he was doing, she didn't fight. She lay back, biting her lower lip, until he finished.

When he lifted his hand, there was a trace of blood. He reached beside the bed for a box of tissues and wiped it off, looking into her eyes the whole time.

"It wasn't bad," she whispered.

He nodded. "It will hurt less, now, when I go inside you," he whispered, moving down against her. He nudged her legs apart matter-of-factly, looking down. "I'll go slow."

"Okay."

She lifted her arms to him and welcomed the warm, slow crush of his chest against her breasts. She gasped as she felt him at the secret place, the dark place that had never known contact such as this. Her nails bit into his hard arms as he nudged at her gently.

He reassured her. "Nothing to be nervous about," he said softly. "Nothing at all."

His hand moved in between their bodies and touched her. This time she didn't flinch. She lifted up to it and shivered as pleasure throbbed into her like molten fire. She moaned and closed her eyes, so that she could savor it.

The pressure grew little by little, tracing and teasing, and then firm, and insistent, and maddening.

"Please!" she cried.

"Yes."

His hand moved and his body replaced it. He moved into her deliberately, confidently, resting on his forearm as he positioned her for even greater pleasure and guided her movements.

She sobbed. The tension was growing, building. She couldn't think. She could barely breathe. She focused on his face, coming closer, moving away, on the rhythm that brushed her against the mattress with every slow, deep thrust of his hips. She shivered as the pleasure kept building and building and building, breath by aching breath, until the whole world reduced itself to the sound of their bodies sliding against each other, the faint scraping sound of the sheets as they moved over them, the building rasp of their breathing.

"Mallory," she sobbed, arching, shuddering.

"Now, baby," he whispered, and the rhythm increased and his body became demanding, as control slipped away. "Now, now, now!"

She cried out, clutching him as she moved, too, desperate to twist up and meet that hard thrust, make it deeper, make it harder, make it, make it, make it...blaze up...like a furnace!

Her teeth bit into him as she climaxed, her body convulsing in a tense arch as she drowned in pleasure she'd never dreamed could exist. She was barely aware of his own rough movement, the hoarse cries of pleasure at her ears as he went over the edge with her. They clung together in ecstasy, as passion spent itself over a space of heated, mad seconds.

And even then, they couldn't stop moving. She ground her hips up against his, pleading for more.

"Oh, don't stop," she pleaded.

"I can't," he whispered in a hoarse chuckle. "Sweet. So damned sweet. I thought I was going to die of it!"

"Me, too!"

He lifted his head as he moved down against her, watching her pleasure grow all over again. Her response delighted him, made him feel ten feet tall. She showed no sign of wanting to stop at all.

"Go ahead, gloat," she whispered unsteadily.

"I love you," he whispered back, and kissed her hungrily. "My brave, beautiful, unbelievably sexy wife. I'd die for you."

She hugged him close. "I'd die for you."

His mouth crushed down over hers. "I'm spent, baby," he whispered against her lips. "But I can last a little longer. I'll pleasure you as long as I can, okay?"

She wasn't hearing him, or understanding him. She was in the grip of a fever so hot she thought she would burn to death. But finally, finally, she shuddered one last time and the tension snapped. She collapsed under him with a trembling sigh.

He rolled over beside her and gathered her close. "Satisfied?"

"Yes. I don't understand," she whispered into his throat.

"Women take longer than men do," he explained. "But a man spends himself and it takes time for him to be able to go again. Women last a lot longer in passion."

"Oh."

He lifted his head and searched her eyes. "You were right."

"I was? About what?"

He kissed her eyelids. "About waiting." He looked at her solemnly. "Right now, I'm sorry that I ever had a woman in my life before I met you."

She touched his mouth gently. "I'm not sure I'm sorry," she whispered drily.

He lifted both eyebrows.

"You are very, very good in bed," she mused. "From a beginner's standpoint, I mean. I was afraid," she confessed. "I'd heard some horror stories from other women about wedding nights. Especially about men losing control and hurting them badly."

"Oh, I couldn't hurt you," he replied softly and kissed her again. "I love you too much. It had to be good for you, or it wouldn't have been good for me at all."

She smiled lazily and moved against him, but suddenly she winced.

He lifted an eyebrow. "Sore?"

She flushed.

He laughed indulgently. "It's a side effect of headlong passion and abstinence. Not to worry, a couple of days' rest and we'll be back to normal. Meanwhile," he added with a chuckle, "we might consider ordering food and watching something on pay-per-view. What do you say?"

She sat up, gingerly, and nodded. "That might be a good idea."

He stood up, stretched and then grinned at her admiring gaze, picked her up and carried her into the bathroom. "But first we can have a nice relaxing shower and play doctor!"

She burst out laughing. Not only was marriage a passion feast, it also seemed to be the most fun she'd ever had.

A WEEK LATER, THEY WERE doing the tango in an exclusive club in Jamaica, right on the beach.

"I told you I'd learn quickly with the right teacher," Mallory teased, kissing her ear as they moved around the room.

"Yes, and you did."

"So did you," he whispered outrageously.

She peered up at him mischievously. "I bought this book today."

"You did? A book?" He leaned down. "What sort of book?"

"It's a detailed book about how to, well, how to do stuff. With your husband."

"I don't have a husband," he groaned. "What about me?"

"It's a book for a woman about how to do stuff with her husband," she informed him. "It's very detailed."

"Does it have pictures?" he asked with wide eyes.

She glared at him. "It doesn't need pictures."

"Then, can you demonstrate it for me?" he added, and his dark eyes were twinkling.

She laughed out loud. "Oh, I think I can do that."

"Now?" he asked, stopping in the middle of the dance floor.

"Here?" she asked, horrified.

"How dare you?" he huffed. "I'm a decent, up-right man, I am."

"You can't be upright while I demonstrate this book," she pointed out. She pursed her lips. "You have to be in a reclining position."

"This is getting better by the minute. Shall we go?"

He held out his arm. She put hers through it with a chuckle. "By all means. It might take some time," she added as they left the room. "I'm not sure I've got it down pat just yet."

"I promise not to complain, no matter how long it takes," he assured her with laughing dark eyes.

It did take a very long time. But he kept his promise. He didn't complain. Not even once.

* * * * *

DIAMOND IN THE ROUGH

For my friend Nancy C., who came all the way from Indiana just to meet me. Thanks for the beautiful cowboy quilt, Nancy—I'll never forget you!

And thanks to all of you on my bulletin board at my website, including Nancy and Amy, who spent hours of their precious free time making me a compendium of all the families in Jacobsville, Texas! Now, guys, maybe I can make fewer mistakes when I write about them! Love you all.

CHAPTER ONE

THE little town, Hollister, wasn't much bigger than Medicine Ridge, Montana, where John Callister and his brother Gil had a huge ranch. But they'd decided that it wasn't wise to confine their whole livelihood to one area. They needed to branch out a little, maybe try something different. On the main ranch, they ran a purebred bull and breeding operation with state-of-the-art science. John and Gil had decided to try something new here in Hollister, Montana; a ranch which would deal specifically in young purebred sale bulls, using the latest technology to breed for specific traits like low calving weight, lean conformation, and high weight gain ratio, among others. In addition, they were going to try new growth programs that combined specific organic grasses with mixed protein and grains to improve their production.

In the depressed economy, tailor-made beef cattle would cater to the discerning organic beef consumer. Gil and John didn't run beef cattle, but their champion bulls were bred to appeal to ranchers who did. It was a highly competitive field, especially with production costs going sky-high. Cattlemen could no longer depend on random breeding programs left up to nature. These days, progeny resulted from tailored genetics. It was a high-tech sort of agriculture. Gil and John had pioneered some of the newer computer-based programs that yielded high on profits coupled with less wasteful producer strategies.

For example, Gil had heard about a program that used methane gas from cattle waste to produce energy to run ranch equipment. The initial expense for the hardware had been high, but it was already producing results. Much of the electricity used to light the barns and power the ranch equipment was due to the new technology. Any surplus energy could be sold back to the electric company. The brothers had also installed solar panels to heat water in the main house and run hydraulic equipment in the breeding barn and the stockyard. One of the larger agricultural magazines had featured an article about their latest innovations. Gil's photo, and that of his daughters and his new wife had graced the pages of the trade publication. John had been at a cattle show and missed the photo shoot. He didn't mind. He'd never been one to court publicity. Nor was Gil. But they wouldn't miss a chance to advertise their genetically superior cattle.

John usually traveled to show the cattle. But he was getting tired of spending his life on the road. Now that Gil had married Kasie, the brothers' former secretary, and the small girls from Gil's first marriage, Bess and Jenny, were in school, John was feeling lonelier than ever, and more restless. Not that he'd had a yen for Kasie, but Gil's remarriage made him aware of the passing of time. He wasn't getting any younger; he was in his thirties. The traveling was beginning to wear on him. Although he dated infrequently, he'd never found a woman he wanted to keep. He was also feeling like a fifth wheel at the family ranch.

So he'd volunteered to come up to Hollister to rebuild this small, dilapidated cattle ranch that he and Gil had purchased and see if an injection of capital and new blood stock and high-tech innovation could bring it from bankruptcy to a higher status in the world of purebred cattle.

The house, which John had only seen from aerial photos, was a wreck. No maintenance had been done on it for years by its elderly owner. He'd had to let most of his full-time cowboys go when the market fell, and he wasn't able to keep up with the demands of the job with the part-timers he retained. Fences got broken, cattle escaped, the well went dry, the barn burned down and, finally, the owner decided to cut his losses. He'd offered the ranch for sale, as-is, and the Callister brothers had bought it from him. The old man had gone back East to live with a daughter.

Now John had a firsthand look at the monumental task facing him. He'd have to hire new cowboys, build a barn as well as a stable, spend a few thousand making the house livable, sink a well, restring the fences, buy equipment, set up the methane-based power production plant... He groaned at the thought of it. The ranch in Medicine Ridge was state-of-the-art. This was medieval, by comparison. It was going to take longer than a month or two. This was a job that would take many months. And all that work had to be done before any cattle could be brought onto the place. What had seemed like a pleasant hobby in the beginning now looked like it would become a career.

There were two horses in a corral with a lean-to for protection from the weather, all that remained of the old man's Appaloosas. The remuda, or string of working ranch horses, had been sold off long ago. The remaining part-time cowboys told John that they'd brought their own mounts with them to work, while there was still a herd of cattle on the place. But the old man had sold off all his stock and let the part-timers go before he sold the ranch. Lucky, John thought, that he'd been able to track them down and offer them full-time jobs again. They were eager for the work. The men all lived within a radius of a few miles. If John had to wait on replacing the ranch's horses, the men could bring their own to work temporarily while John restocked the place.

He planned to rebuild and restock quickly. Something would have to be done about a barn. A place for newborn calves and sick cattle was his first priority. That, and the house. He was sleeping on the floor in a sleeping bag, heating water on a camp stove for shaving and bathing in the creek. Thank God, he thought, that it was spring and not winter. Food was purchased in the town's only café, where he had two meals a day. He ate sandwiches for lunch, purchased from a cooler in the convenience store/gas station at the edge of town. It was rough living for a man who was used to five-star hotels and the best food money could buy. But it was his choice, he reminded himself.

He drove into town in a mid-level priced pickup truck. No use advertising that he was wealthy. Prices would skyrocket, since he wasn't on friendly terms with anyone here. He'd only met the cowboys. The people in town didn't even know his name yet.

The obvious place to start, he reasoned, was the feed store. It sold ranch supplies including tack. The owner might know where he could find a reputable builder.

He pulled up at the front door and strode in. The place was dusty and not well-kept. There seemed to be only one employee, a slight girl with short, wavy dark hair and a pert figure, wearing a knit pullover with worn jeans and boots.

She was sorting bridles but she looked up when he approached. Like many old-time cowboys, he was sporting boots with spurs that jingled when he walked. He was also wearing an old Colt .45 in a holster slung low on his hip under the open denim shirt he was wearing with jeans and a black T-shirt. It was wild country, this part of Montana, and he wasn't going out on the range without some way of protecting himself from potential predators.

The girl stared at him in an odd, fixed way. He didn't realize that he had the looks that would have been expected in a motion picture star. His blond hair, under the wide-brimmed cowboy hat, had a sheen like gold, and his handsome face was very attractive. He had the tall, elegant body of a rider, lean and fit and muscular without exaggerated lines.

"What the hell are you doing?" came a gruff, angry voice from the back. "I told you to go bring in those new sacks of feed before the rain ruins them, not play with the tack! Get your lazy butt moving, girl!"

The girl flushed, looking frightened. "Yes, sir," she said at once, and jumped up to do what he'd told her to.

John didn't like the way the man spoke to her. She was very young, probably still in her teens. No man should speak that way to a child.

He approached the man with a deadpan expression, only his blue eyes sparkling with temper.

The man, overweight and half-bald, older than John, turned as he approached. "Something I can do for you?" he asked in a bored tone, as if he didn't care whether he got the business or not.

"You the owner?" John asked him.

The man glared. "The manager. Tarleton. Bill Tarleton."

John tilted his hat back. "I need to find someone who can build a barn."

The manager's eyebrows arched. His eyes slid over John's worn jeans and boots and inexpensive clothing. He laughed. His expression was an insult. "You own a ranch around here?" he asked in disbelief.

John fought back his temper. "My boss does," he said, in an impulsive moment. "He's hiring. He just bought the Bradbury place out on Chambers Road."

"That old place?" Tarleton made a face. "Hell, it's a wreck! Bradbury just sat on his butt and let the place go to hell. Nobody understood why. He had some good cattle years ago, cattlemen came from as far away as Oklahoma and Kansas to buy his stock."

"He got old," John said.

"I guess. A barn, you say." He pursed his lips. "Well, Jackson Hewett has a construction business. He builds houses. Fancy houses, some of them. I reckon he could build a barn. He lives just outside town, over by the old train station. He's in the local telephone directory."

"I'm obliged," John said.

"Your boss…he'll be needing feed and tack, I guess?" Tarleton added.

John nodded.

"If I don't have it on hand, I can order it."

"I'll keep that in mind. I need something right now, though—a good tool kit."

"Sassy!" he yelled. "The man wants a tool kit! Bring one of the boxes from that new line we started stocking!"

"Yes, sir!" There was the sound of scrambling boots.

"She ain't much help," the manager grumbled. "Misses work sometimes. Got a mother with cancer and a little sister, six, that the mother adopted. I guess she'll end up alone, just her and the kid."

"Does the mother get government help?" John asked, curious.

"Not much," Tarleton scoffed. "They say she never did much except sit with sick folk, even before she got the cancer. Sassy's bringing in the only money they got. The old man took off years ago with another woman. Just left. At least they got a house. Ain't much of one, but it's a roof over their heads. The mother got it in the divorce settlement."

John felt a pang when he noticed the girl tugging a heavy toolbox. She looked as if she was barely able to lift a bridle.

"Here, I'll take that," John said, trying to sound nonchalant. He took it from her hands and set it on the counter, popping it open. His eyebrows lifted as he examined the tools. "Nice."

"Expensive, too, but it's worth it," Tarleton told him.

"Boss wants to set up an account in his own name, but I'll pay cash for this," John said, pulling out his wallet. "He gave me pocket money for essentials."

Tarleton's eyes got bigger as John started peeling

off twenty-dollar bills. "Okay. What name do I put on the account?"

"Callister," John told him without batting an eyelash. "Gil Callister."

"Hey, I've heard of him," Tartleton said at once, giving John a bad moment. "He's got a huge ranch down in Medicine Ridge."

"That's the one," John said. "Ever seen him?"

"Who, me?" The older man laughed. "I don't run in those circles, no, sir. We're just country folk here, not millionaires."

John felt a little less worried. It would be to his advantage if the locals didn't know who he really was. Not yet, anyway. Since he was having to give up cattle shows for the foreseeable future, there wasn't much chance that his face would be gracing any trade papers. It might be nice, he pondered, to be accepted as an ordinary man for once. His wealth seemed to draw opportunists, especially feminine ones. He could enjoy playing the part of a cowboy for a change.

"No problem with opening an account here, then, if we put some money down first as a credit?" John asked.

"No problem at all." Tarleton grinned. "I'll start that account right now. You tell Mr. Callister anything he needs, I can get for him!"

"I'll tell him."

"And your name...?" the manager asked.

"John," he replied. "John Taggert."

Taggert was his middle name. His maternal grandfather, a pioneer in South Dakota, had that name.

"Taggert." The manager shook his head. "Never heard that one."

John smiled. "It's not famous."

The girl was still standing beside the counter. John handed her the bills to pay for the toolbox. She worked the cash register and counted out his change.

"Thanks," John said, smiling at her.

She smiled back at him, shyly. Her green eyes were warm and soft. "You're welcome."

"Get back to work," Tarleton told her.

"Yes, sir." She turned and went back to the bags on the loading platform.

John frowned. "Isn't she too slight to be hefting bags that size?"

"It goes with the job," Tarleton said defensively. "I had a strong teenage boy working for me, but his parents moved to Billings and he had to go along. She was all I could get. She swore she could do the job. So I'm letting her."

"I guess she's stronger than she looks," John remarked, but he didn't like it.

Tarleton nodded absently. He was putting Gil Callister's name in his ledger.

"I'll be back," John told him as he picked up the toolbox.

Tarleton nodded again.

John glanced at the girl, who was straining over a heavy bag, and walked out of the store with a scowl on his face.

He paused. He didn't know why. He glanced back into the store and saw the manager standing on the loading platform, watching the girl lift the feed sacks. It wasn't the look a manager should be giving an employee. John's eyes narrowed. He was going to do something about that.

* * *

One of the older cowboys, Chad Dean by name, was waiting for him at the house when he brought in the toolbox.

"Say, that's a nice one," he told the other man. "Your boss must be stinking rich."

"He is," John mused. "Pays good, too."

The cowboy chuckled. "That would be nice, getting a paycheck that I could feed my kids on. I couldn't move my family to another town without giving up land that belonged to my grandfather, so I toughed it out. It's been rough, what with food prices and gas going through the roof."

"You'll get your regular check plus travel expenses," John told him. "We'll pay for the gas if we have to send you anywhere to pick up things."

"That's damned considerate."

"If you work hard, your wages will go up."

"We'll all work hard," Dean promised solemnly. "We're just happy to have jobs."

John pursed his lips. "Do you know a girl named Sassy? Works for Tarleton in the feed store?"

"Yeah," Dean replied tersely. "He's married, and he makes passes at Sassy. She needs that job. Her mama's dying. There's a six-year-old kid lives with them, too, and Sassy has to take care of her. I don't know how in hell she manages on what she gets paid. All that, and having to put up with Tarleton's harassment, too. My wife told her she should call the law and report him. She won't. She says she can't afford to lose the position. Town's so small, she'd never get hired again. Tarleton would make sure of it, just for spite, if she quit."

John nodded. His eyes narrowed thoughtfully. "I expect things will get easier for her," he predicted.

"Do you? Wish I did. She's a sweet kid. Always doing things for other people." He smiled. "My son had his appendix out. It was Sassy who saw what it was, long before we did. He was in the feed store when he got sick. She called the doctor. He looked over my Mark and agreed it was appendicitis. Doc drove the boy over to Billings to the hospital. Sassy went to see him. God knows how she got there. Her old beat-up vehicle would never make it as far as Billings. Hitched a ride with Carl Parks, I expect. He's in his seventies, but he watches out for Sassy and her mother. Good old fellow."

John nodded. "Sounds like it." He hesitated. "How old is the girl?"

"Eighteen or nineteen, I guess. Just out of high school."

"I figured that." John was disappointed. He didn't understand why. "Okay, here's what we're going to do about those fences temporarily..."

In the next two days, John did some amateur detective work. He phoned a private detective who worked for the Callisters on business deals and put him on the Tarleton man. It didn't take him long to report back.

The feed store manager had been allowed to resign from a job in Billings for unknown reasons, but the detective found one other employee who said it was sexual harassment of an employee. He wasn't charged with anything. He'd moved here, to Hollister, with his family when the owner of the feed store, a man named Jake McGuire, advertised in a trade paper for someone to manage it for him. Apparently Tarleton had been the only applicant and McGuire was desperate. Tarleton got the job.

"This McGuire," John asked over his cell phone, "how old is he?"

"In his thirties," came the reply. "Everyone I spoke to about him said that he's a decent sort."

"In other words, he doesn't have a clue that Tarleton's hassling the girl."

"That would be my guess."

John's eyes twinkled. "Do you suppose McGuire would like to sell that business?"

There was a chuckle. "He's losing money hand over fist on that place. Two of the people I spoke to said he'd almost give it away to get rid of it."

"Thanks," John said. "That answers my question. Can you get me McGuire's telephone number?"

"Already did. Here it is."

John wrote it down. The next morning, he put in a call to McGuire Enterprises in Billings.

"I'm looking to buy a business in a town called Hollister," John said after he'd introduced himself. "Someone said you might know the owner of the local feed store."

"The feed store?" McGuire replied. "You want to buy it?" He sounded astonished.

"I might," John said. "If the price is right."

There was a pause. "Okay, here's the deal. That business was started by my father over forty years ago. I inherited it when he died. I don't really want to sell it."

"It's going bankrupt," John replied.

There was another pause. "Yeah, I know," came the disgusted reply. "I had to put in a new manager there, and he didn't come cheap. I had to move him and his wife from Billings down here." He sighed. "I'm between a rock and a hard place. I own several businesses, and I don't have the time to manage them myself. That particular one has sentimental value. The manager just went to work. There's a chance he can pull it out of the red."

"There's a better chance that he's going to get you involved in a major lawsuit."

"What? What for?"

"For one thing, he was let go from his last job for sexual harassment, or that's what we turned up on a background check. He's up to his old tricks in Hollister, this time with a young girl just out of high school that he hired to work for him."

"Good Lord! He came with excellent references!"

"He might have them," John said. "But it wouldn't surprise me if that wasn't the first time he lost a job for the same reason. He was giving the girl the eye when I was in there. There's local gossip that the girl may sue if your manager doesn't lay off her. There goes your bottom line," he added dryly.

"Well, that's what you get when you're desperate for personnel," McGuire said wearily. "I couldn't find anybody else who'd take the job. I can't fire him without proper cause, and I just paid to move him there! What a hell of a mess!"

"You don't want to sell the business. Okay. How about leasing it to us? We'll fire Tarleton on the grounds that we're leasing the business, put in a manager of our

own, and you'll make money. We'll have you in the
black in two months."

"And just who is 'we'?" McGuire wanted to know.

"My brother and I. We're ranchers."

"But why would you want to lease a feed store in the
middle of nowhere?"

"Because we just bought the Bradbury place. We're
going to rebuild the house, add a stable and a barn, and
we're going to raise purebred young bulls on the place.
The feed store is going to do a lot of business when we
start adding personnel to the outfit."

"Old man Bradbury and my father were best friends,"
McGuire reminisced. "He was a fine rancher, a nice
gentleman. His health failed and the business failed with
him. It's nice to know it will be a working ranch again."

"It's good land. We'll make it pay."

"What did you say your name was?"

"Callister," John told him. "My brother and I have a
sizable spread over in Medicine Ridge."

"Those Callisters? My God, your holdings are
worth millions!"

"At least." John chuckled.

There was a soft whistle. "Well, if you're going to
keep me in orders, I suppose I'd be willing to lease the
place to you."

"And the manager?"

"I just moved him there," McGuire groaned again.

"We'll pay to move him back to Billings and give
him two weeks severance pay," John said. "I will not
agree to let him stay on," he added firmly.

"He may sue."

"Let him," John replied tersely. "If he tries it, I'll

make it my life's work to see that any skeleton in his past is brought into the light of day. You can tell him that."

"I'll tell him."

"If you'll give me your attorney's name and number, I'll have our legal department contact him," John said. "I think we'll get along."

There was a deep chuckle. "So do I."

"There's one other matter."

"Yes?"

John hesitated. "I'm going to be working on the place myself, but I don't want anyone local to know who I am. I'll be known as the ranch foreman—Taggert by name. Got that?"

There was a chuckle. "Keeping it low-key, I see. Sure. I won't blow your cover."

"Especially to Tarleton and his employee," John emphasized.

"No problem. I'll tell him your boss phoned me."

"I'm much obliged."

"Before we settle this deal, do you have someone in mind who can take over the business in two weeks if I put Tarleton on notice?"

"Indeed I do," John replied. "He's a retired corporate executive who's bored stiff with retirement. Mind like a steel trap. He could make money in the desert."

"Sounds like just the man for the job."

"I'll have him up here in two weeks."

"That's a deal, then."

"We'll talk again when the paperwork goes through."

"Yes."

John hung up. He felt better about the girl. Not that he expected Tarleton to quit the job without a fight. He hoped the threat of uncovering any past sins would work the magic. The thought of Sassy being bothered by that would-be Casanova was disturbing.

He phoned the architect and asked him to come over to the ranch the following day to discuss drawing up plans for a stable and a barn. He hired an electrician to rewire the house and do the work in the new construction. He employed six new cowboys and an engineer. He set up payroll for everyone he'd hired through the corporation's main offices in Medicine Ridge, and went about getting fences repaired and wells drilled. He also phoned Gil and had him send down a team of engineers to start construction on solar panels to help provide electricity for the operation.

Once those plans were underway, he made a trip into Hollister to see how things were going at the feed store. His detective had managed to dig up three other harassment charges against Tarleton from places he'd lived before he moved to Montana in the first place. There were no convictions, sadly. But the charges might be enough. Armed with that information, he wasn't uncomfortable having words with the man, if it was necessary.

And it seemed that it would be. The minute he walked in the door, he knew there was going to be trouble. Tarleton was talking to a customer, but he gave John a glare that spoke volumes. He finished his business with the customer and waited until he left. Then he walked up to John belligerently.

"What the hell did your employer tell my boss?" he demanded furiously. "He said he was leasing the store, but only on the condition that I didn't go with the deal!"

"Not my problem," John said, and his pale eyes glittered. "It was my boss's decision."

"Well, he's got no reason to fire me!" Tarleton said, his round face flushing. "I'll sue the hell out of him, and your damned boss, too!"

John stepped closer to the man and leaned down, emphasizing his advantage in height. "You're welcome. My boss will go to the local district attorney in Billings and turn over the court documents from your last sexual harassment charge."

Tarleton's face went from red to white in seconds. He froze in place. "He'll...what?" he asked weakly.

John's chiseled lips pulled up into a cold smile. "And I'll encourage your hired girl over there—" he indicated her with a jerk of his head "—to come clean about the way you've treated her as well. I think she could be persuaded to bring charges."

Tarleton's arrogance vanished. He looked hunted.

"Take my advice," John said quietly. "Get out while you still have time. My boss won't hesitate a second. He has two daughters of his own." His eyes narrowed menacingly. "One of our ranch hands back home tried to wrestle a temporary maid down in the hay out in our barn. He's serving three to five for sexual assault." John smiled. "We have a firm of attorneys on retainer."

"We?" Tarleton stammered.

"I'm a managerial employee of the ranch. The ranch is a corporation," John replied smoothly.

Tarleton's teeth clenched. "So I guess I'm fired."

"I guess you volunteered to resign," John corrected. "That gets you moved back to Billings at the ranch's expense, and gives you severance pay. It also spares you lawsuits and other…difficulties."

The older man weighed his options. John could see his mind working. Tarleton gave John an arrogant look. "What the hell," he said coldly. "I didn't want to live in this damned fly trap anyway!"

He turned on his heel and walked away. The girl, Sassy, was watching the byplay with open curiosity. John raised an eyebrow. She flushed and went back to work at once.

CHAPTER TWO

CASSANDRA PEALE told herself that the intense conversation the new foreman of the Bradbury place was having with her boss didn't concern her. The foreman had made that clear with a lifted eyebrow and a haughty look. But there had been an obvious argument and both men had glanced at her while they were having it. She was worried. She couldn't afford to lose her job. Not when her mother, dying of lung cancer, and her mother's ward, Selene, who was only six, depended on what she brought home so desperately.

She gnawed on a fingernail. They were mostly all chewed off. Her mother was sixty-three, Cassandra, who everyone called Sassy, having been born very late in life. They'd had a ranch until her father had become infatuated with a young waitress at the local cafeteria. He'd left his family and run away with the woman, taking most of their savings with him. Without money to pay bills, Sassy's mother had been forced to sell the cattle and most of the land and let the cowboys go. One of them, little Selene's father, had gotten drunk out of desperation and ran his truck off into the river. They'd found him the next morning, dead, leaving Selene completely alone in the world.

My life, Sassy thought, *is a soap opera*. It even has a villain. She glanced covertly at Mr. Tarleton. All he needed was a black mustache and a gun. He'd made her working life hell. He knew she couldn't afford to quit. He was always bumping into her "accidentally," trying to handle her. She was sickened by his advances. She'd never even had a boyfriend. The school she'd gone to, in this tiny town, had been a one-room schoolhouse with all ages included and one teacher. There had only been two boys her own age and three girls including Sassy. The other girls were pretty. So Sassy had never been asked out at all. Once, when she was in her senior year of high school, a teacher's visiting nephew had been kind to her, but her mother had been violently opposed to letting her go on a date with a man she didn't know well. It hadn't mattered. Sassy had never felt those things her romance novels spoke of in such enticing and heart-pattering terms. She'd never even been kissed in a grown-up way. Her only sexual experience—if you could call it that— was being physically harassed by that repulsive would-be Romeo standing behind the counter.

She finished dusting the shelves and wished fate would present her with a nice, handsome boss who was single and found her fascinating. She'd have gladly settled for the Bradbury place's new ramrod. But he didn't look as if he found anything about her that attracted him. In fact, he was ignoring her. Story of my life, she thought as she put aside the dust cloth. It was just as well. She had two dependents and no spare time. Where would she fit a man into her desperate life?

"Missed a spot."

She whirled. She flushed as she looked way up into dancing blue eyes. "W...what?"

John chuckled. The women in his world were sophisticated and full of easy wisdom. This little violet was as unaffected by the modern world as the store she worked in. He was entranced by her.

"I said you missed a spot." He leaned closer. "It was a joke."

"Oh." She laughed shyly, glancing at the shelf. "I might have missed several, I guess. I can't reach high and there's no ladder."

He smiled. "There's always a soapbox."

"No, no," she returned with a smile. "If I get on one of those, I have to give a political speech."

He groaned. "Don't say those words," he said. "If I have to hear one more comment about the presidential race, I'm having my ears plugged."

"It does get a little irritating, doesn't it?" she asked. "We don't watch the news as much since the television got hit by lightning. The color's gone whacky. I have to think it's a happy benefit of a sad accident."

His eyebrows arched. "Why don't you get a new one?"

She glowered at him. "Because the hardware store doesn't have a fifty-cent one," she said.

It took a minute for that to sink in. John, who thought nothing of laying down his gold card for the newest plasma wide screened TV, hadn't realized that even a small set was beyond the means of many lower-income people.

He grimaced. "Sorry," he said. "I guess I've gotten too used to just picking up anything I like in stores."

"They don't arrest you for that?" she asked with a straight face, but her twinkling eyes gave her away.

He laughed. "Not so far. I meant," he added, thinking fast, "that my boss pays me a princely salary for my organizational skills."

"He must, if you can afford a new TV," she sighed. "I don't suppose he needs a professional duster?"

"We could ask him."

She shook her head. "I'd rather work here, in a job I do know." She glanced with apprehension at her boss, who was glaring toward the two of them. "I'd better get back to work before he fires me."

"He can't."

She blinked. "He can't what?"

"Fire you," he said quietly. "He's being replaced in two weeks by a new manager."

Her heart stopped. She felt sick. "Oh, dear."

"You won't convince me that you'll miss him," John said curtly.

She bit a fingernail that was already almost gone. "It's not that. A new manager might not want me to work here anymore..."

"He will."

She frowned. "How can you know that?"

He pursed his lips. "Because the new manager works for my boss, and my boss said not to change employees."

Her face started to relax. "Really?"

"Really."

She glanced again at Tarleton and felt uncomfortable at the furious glare he gave her. "Oh, dear, did somebody say something to your boss about him...about him being forward with me?" she asked worriedly.

"They might have," he said noncommittally.

"He'll get even," she said under her breath. "He's that sort. He told a lie on a customer who was rude to him, about the man's wife. She almost lost her job over it."

John felt his blood rise. "All you have to do is get through the next two weeks," he told her. "If you have a problem with him, any problem, you can call me. I don't care when or what time." He started to pull out his wallet and give her his business card, until he realized that she thought he was pretending to be hired help, not the big boss. "Have you got a pen and paper?" he asked instead.

"In fact, I do," she replied. She moved behind the counter, tore a piece of brown paper off a roll, and picked up a marking pencil. She handed them to him.

He wrote down the number and handed it back to her. "Don't be afraid of him," he added curtly. "He's in enough trouble without making more for himself with you."

"What sort of trouble is he in?" she wanted to know.

"I can't tell you. It's confidential. Let's just say that he'd better keep his nose clean. Now. I need a few more things." He brought out a list and handed it to her. She smiled and went off to fill the order for him.

He took the opportunity to have a last word with Tarleton.

"I hear you have a penchant for getting even with people who cross you," John said. His eyes narrowed and began to glitter. "For the record, if you touch that girl, or if you even try to cause problems for her of any sort, you'll have to deal with me. I don't threaten people with lawsuits. I get even." The way he said it, added to his even, unblinking glare, had backed down braver men than this middle-aged molester.

Tarleton tried to put on a brave front, but the man's demeanor was unsettling. Taggert was younger than Tarleton and powerfully muscled for all his slimness. He didn't look like a man who ever walked away from a fight.

"I wouldn't touch her in a blind fit," the older man said haughtily. "I just want to work out my notice and get the hell back to Billings, where people are more civilized."

"Good idea," John replied. "Follow it."

He turned on his heel and went back to Sassy.

She looked even more nervous now. "What did you say to him?" she asked uneasily, because Tarleton looked at her as if he'd like her served up on a spit.

"Nothing of any consequence," he said easily, and he gave her a tender smile. "Got my order ready?"

"Most of it," she said, obviously trying to get her mind back to business. "But we don't carry any of this grass seed you want. It would be special order." She leaned forward. "The hardware store can get it for you at a lower price, but I think we will be faster."

He grinned. "The price won't matter to my boss," he assured her. "But speed will. He's experimenting with all sorts of forage grasses. He's looking for better ways to increase weight without resorting to artificial means. He thinks the older grasses have more nutritional benefit than the hybrids being sowed today."

"He's likely right," she replied. "Organic methods are gaining in popularity. You wouldn't believe how many organic gardeners we have locally."

"That reminds me. I need some insecticidal soap for the beans we're planting."

She hesitated.

He cocked his head. His eyes twinkled. "You want to tell me something, but you're not sure that you should."

She laughed. "I guess so. One of our organic gardeners gave up on it for beans. She says it works nicely for tomatoes and cucumbers, but you need something with a little more kick for beans and corn. She learned that the hard way." She grimaced. "So did I. I lost my first corn planting to corn borers and my beans to bean beetles. I was determined not to go the harsh pesticide route."

"Okay. Sell me something harsh, then," he chuckled.

She blushed faintly before she pulled a sack of powerful but environmentally safe insecticide off the shelf and put it on the counter.

Tarleton was watching the byplay with cold, angry eyes. So she liked that interfering cowboy, did she? It made him furious. He was certain that the new foreman of the Bradbury ranch had talked to someone about him and passed the information on to McGuire, who owned this feed store. The cowboy was arrogant for a man who worked for wages, even for a big outfit like the Callisters's. He was losing his job for the second time in six months and it would look bad on his record. His wife was already sick of the moving. She might leave him. It was a bad day for him when John Taggert walked into his store. He hoped the man fell in a well and drowned, he really did.

His small eyes lingered on Sassy's trim figure. She really made him hot. She wasn't the sort to put up much of a fight, and that man Taggert couldn't watch her day and night. Tarleton smiled coldly to himself. If he was losing his job anyway, he didn't have much to lose. Might as well get something out of the experience. Something sweet.

* * *

Sassy went home worn-out at the end of the week. Tarleton had found more work than ever before for her to do, mostly involving physical labor. He was rearranging all the shelves with the heaviest items like chicken mash and hog feed and horse feed and dog food in twenty-five and fifty-pound bags. Sassy could press fifty pounds, but she was slight and not overly muscular. It was uncomfortable. She wished she could complain to someone, but if she did, it would only make things worse. Tarleton was getting even because he'd been fired. He watched her even more than he had before, and it was in a way that made her very uncomfortable.

Her mother was lying on the sofa watching television when Sassy got home. Little Selene was playing with some cut-outs. Her soft gray eyes lit up and she jumped up and ran to Sassy, to be picked up and kissed.

"How's my girl?" Sassy asked, kissing the soft little cheek.

"I been playing with Dora the Explorer, Sassy!" the little blond girl told her. "Pippa gave them to me at school!"

Pippa was the daughter of a teacher and her husband, a sweet child who always shared her playthings with Selene. It wasn't a local secret that Sassy could barely afford to dress the child out of the local thrift shop, much less buy her toys.

"That was sweet of her," Sassy said with genuine delight.

"She says I can keep these ones," the child added.

Sassy put her down. "Show them to me."

Her mother smiled wearily up at her. "Pippa's mother is a darling."

Sassy bent and kissed her mother's brow. "So is mine."

Mrs. Peale patted her cheek. "Bad day?" she added.

Sassy only smiled. She didn't trouble her parent with her daily woes. The older woman had enough worries of her own. The cancer was temporarily in remission, but the doctor had warned that it wouldn't last. Despite all the hype about new treatments and cures, cancer was a formidable adversary. Especially when the victim was Mrs. Peale's age.

"I've had worse," Sassy told her. "What about pancakes and bacon for supper?" she asked.

"Sassy, we had pancakes last night," Selene complained as she showed her cut-outs to the woman.

"I know, baby," Sassy said, bending to kiss her gently. "We have what we can afford. It isn't much."

Selene grimaced. "I'm sorry. I like pancakes," she added apologetically.

"I wish we could have something better," Sassy said. "If there was a better-paying job going, you can bet I'd be applying for it."

Mrs. Peale looked sad. "I'd hoped we could send you to college. At least to a vocational school. Instead we've caused you to land in a dead-end job."

Sassy struck a pose. "I'll have you know I'm expecting a prince any day," she informed them. "He'll come riding up on a white horse with an enormous bouquet of orchids, brandishing a wedding ring."

"If ever a girl deserved one," Mrs. Peale said softly, "it's you, my baby."

Sassy grinned. "When I find him, we'll get you one of those super hospital beds with a dozen controls so you can sit up properly when you want to. And we'll get Selene the prettiest dresses and shoes in the world. And then, we'll buy a new television set, one that doesn't have green people," she added, wincing at the color on the old console TV.

Pipe dreams. But dreams were all she had. She looked at her companions, her family, and decided that she'd much rather have them than a lot of money. But a little money, she sighed mentally, certainly would help their situation. Prince Charming existed, sadly, only in fairy tales.

The architect had his plans ready for the big barn. John approved them and told the man to get to work. Within a few days, building materials started arriving, carried in by enormous trucks: lumber, steel, sand, concrete blocks, bricks, and mortar and other construction equipment. The project was worth several million dollars, and it created a stir locally, because it meant jobs for many people who were having to commute to Billings to get work. They piled onto the old Bradbury place to fill out job applications.

John grinned at the enthusiasm of the new workers. He'd started the job with misgivings, wondering if it was sane to expect to find dozens of laborers in such a small, economically depressed area. But he'd been pleasantly surprised. He had new men from surrounding counties lining up for available jobs, experienced workers at that. He began to be optimistic.

He was doing a lot of business with the local feed store, but his presence was required on site while the construction was in the early stages. He'd learned the hard way that it wasn't wise to leave someone in charge without making sure they understood what was required during every step.

He felt a little guilty that he hadn't been back to check that Sassy hadn't had problems with Tarleton, who only had two days left before he was being replaced. The new manager, Buck Mannheim, was already in town, renting a room from a local widow while he familiarized himself with the business. Tarleton, he told John, wasn't making it easy for him to do that. The man was resentful, surly, and he was making Sassy do some incredibly hard and unnecessary tasks at the store. Buck would have put a stop to it, but he felt he had no real authority until Tartleton's two weeks were officially up. He didn't want them to get sued.

As if that weasel would dare sue them, John thought angrily. But he didn't feel right putting Buck in the line of fire. The older man had come up here as a favor to Gil to run the business, not to go toe-to-toe with a belligerent soon-to-be-ex-employee.

"I'll handle this," John told the older man. "I need to stop by the post office anyway and get some more stamps."

"I don't understand why any man would treat a child so brutally," Buck said. "She's such a nice girl."

"She's not a girl, Buck," John replied.

"She's just nineteen," Buck replied, smiling. "I have a granddaughter that age."

John felt uncomfortable. "She seems older."

"She's got some mileage on her. A lot of responsibility. She needs help. That child her mother adopted goes to school in pitiful clothes. I know that most of the money they have is spent for utilities." He shook his head. "Hell of a shame. Her mother's little check is all used up for medicine that she has to take to stay alive."

John felt guilty that he hadn't looked into that situation. He hadn't planned to get himself involved with his employees' problems, and Sassy wasn't technically even that, but it seemed there was nobody else in a position to help. He frowned. "You said Sassy's mother was divorced? Where's her husband? Couldn't he help? Even if Sassy's not young enough for child support, she's still his child. She shouldn't have to be the breadwinner."

"He ran off with a young woman. Just walked out the door and left. He's never so much as called or written in the years he's been gone, since the divorce," Buck said knowledgeably. "From what I hear, he was a good husband and father. He couldn't fight his infatuation for the waitress." He shrugged. "That's life."

"I hope the waitress hangs him out to dry," John muttered darkly. "Sassy should never have been landed with so much responsibility at her age."

"She handles it well, though," Buck said admiringly. "She's the nicest young woman I've met in a long time. She earns her paycheck."

"She shouldn't be having to press weights to do that," John replied. "I got too wrapped up in my barn to keep an eye on her. I'll make up for it today."

"Good for you. She could use a friend."

John walked in and noticed immediately how quiet it was. The front of the store was deserted. It was mid-morning and there were no customers. He scowled, wondering why Sassy wasn't at the counter.

He heard odd sounds coming from the tack room. He walked toward it until he heard a muffled scream. Then he ran.

The door was locked from the inside. John didn't need ESP to know why. He stood back, shot a hard kick with his heavy work boots right at the door handle, and the door almost splintered as it flew open.

Tarleton had backed Sassy into an aisle of cattle feed sacks. He had her in a tight embrace and he was trying his best to kiss her. His hands were on her body. She was fighting for her life, panting and struggling against the fat man's body.

"You sorry, son of a…!" John muttered as he caught the man by his collar and literally threw him off Sassy.

She was gasping for air. Her blouse was torn and her shoulders ached. The stupid man had probably meant to do a lot more than just kiss her, if he'd locked the door, but thanks to John he'd barely gotten to first base. She almost gagged at the memory of his fat, wet mouth on her lips. She dragged her hand over it.

"You okay?" John asked her curtly.

"Yes, thanks to you," she said heavily. She glared at the man behind him.

He turned back toward Tarleton, who was flushed at being caught red-handed. He backed away from the homicidal maniac who started toward him with an expression that could have stopped traffic.

"Don't you…touch me…!" Tarleton protested.

John caught him by the shirtfront, drew back his huge fist, and knocked the man backward out into the feed store. He went after him, blue eyes sparking like live electricity, his big fists clenched, his jaw set rigidly.

"What the…?" came a shocked exclamation from the front of the store.

A man in a business suit was standing there, eyebrows arching.

"Mr….McGuire!" Tarleton exclaimed as he sat up on the floor holding his jaw. "He attacked me! Call the police!"

John glanced at McGuire with blazing eyes. "There's a nineteen-year-old girl in the tack room with her shirt torn off. Do you need me to draw you a picture?" he demanded.

McGuire's gray eyes suddenly took on the same sheen as John's. He moved forward with an odd, gliding step and stopped just in front of Tarleton. He whipped out his cell phone and pressed in a number.

"Get over here," he said into the receiver. "Tarleton just assaulted Sassy! That's right. No, I won't let him leave!" He hung up. "You should have cut your losses and gone back to Billings," he told the white-faced man on the floor, nursing his jaw. "Now, you're going to jail."

"She teased me into doing it!" Tarleton cried. "It's her fault."

John glanced at McGuire. "And I'm a green elf." He turned on his heel and went back to the tack room to see about Sassy.

She was crying, leaning against an expensive saddle, trying to pull the ripped bits of her blouse closed. Her ratty little faded bra was visible where it was torn. It was embarrassing for her to have John see it.

John stripped off the cotton shirt he was wearing over his black undershirt. He eased her hands away from her tattered blouse and guided her arms into the shirt, still warm from his body. He buttoned it up to the very top. Then he framed her wet face in his big hands and lifted it to his eyes. He winced. Her pretty little mouth was bruised. Her hair was mussed. Her eyes were red and swollen.

"Me and my damned barn," he muttered. "I'm sorry."

"For...what?" she sobbed. "It's not your fault."

"It is. I should have expected something like this."

The bell on the door jangled and heavy footsteps echoed on wood. There was conversation, punctuated by Tarleton's protests.

A tall, lean man in a police uniform and a cowboy hat knocked at the tack door and walked in. John turned, letting him see Sassy's condition.

The newcomer's thin mouth set in hard lines and his black eyes flashed fire. "You all right, Sassy?" he asked in a deep, bass voice.

"Yes, sir, Chief Graves," she said brokenly. "He assaulted me!" she accused, glaring at Tarleton. "He came up behind me while I was putting up stock and grabbed me. He kissed me and tore my blouse..." Her voice broke. "He tried to...to...!" She couldn't choke the word out.

Graves looked as formidable as John. "He won't ever touch you again. I promise. I need you to come down to my office when you feel a little better and give me a statement. Will you do that?"

"Yes, sir."

He glanced at John. "You hit him?" he asked, jerking his head toward the man still sitting on the floor outside the room.

"Damned straight I did," John returned belligerently. His blue eyes were still flashing with bad temper.

Chief Graves glanced at Sassy and winced.

The police chief turned and went back out into the other room. He caught Tarleton by his arm, jerked him to his feet, and handcuffed him while he read him his rights.

"You let me go!" Tarleton shouted. "I'm going back to Billings in two days. She lied! I never touched her that way! I just kissed her! She teased me! She set me up! She lured me into the back! And I want that damned cowboy arrested for assault! He hit me!"

Nobody was paying him the least bit of attention. In fact, the police chief looked as if he'd like to hit Tarleton himself. The would-be Romeo shut up.

"I'm never hiring anybody else as long as I live," McGuire told the police chief. "Not after this."

"Sometimes snakes don't look like snakes," Graves told him. "We all make mistakes. Come along, Mr. Tarleton. We've got a nice new jail cell for you to live in while we get ready to put you on trial."

"She's lying!" Tarleton raged, red-faced.

Sassy came out with John just behind her. The ordeal she'd endured was so evident that the men in the room grimaced at just the sight of her. Tarleton stopped shouting. He looked sick.

"Do you mind if I say something to him, Chief Graves?" Sassy asked in a hoarse tone.

"Not at all," the lawman replied.

She walked right up to Tarleton, with her green eyes glittering with fury, drew back her hand, and slapped him across the mouth as hard as she could. Then she turned on her heel and walked right back to the counter, picked up a sack of seed corn that she'd left there when the assault began, and went back to work.

The three men glanced from her to Tarleton. Their faces wore identical expressions.

"I'll get a good lawyer!" Tarleton said belligerently.

"You'll need one," John promised him, in a tone so full of menace that the man backed up a step.

"I'll sue you for assault!" he said from a safe distance.

"The corporation's attorneys will enjoy the exercise," John told him coolly. "One of them graduated from Harvard and spent ten years as a prosecutor specializing in sexual assault cases."

Tarleton looked sick.

Graves took him outside. John turned to McGuire.

The man in the suit rammed his hands into his pockets and grimaced. "I'll never be able to make that up to her," he said heavily.

"You might tell her that you recommended raising her salary," John replied.

"It's the least I can do," he agreed. "That new employee of yours—Buck Mannheim. He's sharp. I learned things I didn't know just from spending a half hour talking to him. He'll be an asset."

John nodded. "He retired too soon. Sixty-five is no great age these days." He glanced toward the back, where Sassy was moving things around. "She needs to see a doctor."

"Did Tarleton...?" McGuire asked with real concern.

John shook his head. "But he would have. If I'd walked in just ten minutes later..." His face paled as he considered what would have happened. "Damn that man! And damn me! I should have realized he'd do something stupid to get even with her!"

"I should have realized, too," McGuire added. "Don't

beat yourself to death. There's enough guilt to share. Dr. Bates is next to the post office. He has a clinic. He'll see her. He's been her family physician since she was a child."

"I'll take her right over there."

Sassy looked up when John approached her. She looked terrible, but she wasn't crying anymore. "Is he going to fire me?" she asked John.

"What in hell for? Almost getting raped?" he exclaimed. "Of course not. In fact, he's mentioned getting you a raise. But right now, he wants you to go to the doctor and get checked out."

"I'm okay," she protested. "And I have a lot of work to do."

"It can wait."

"I don't want to see Dr. Bates," she said.

He shrugged. "We're both pretty determined about this. I don't really think you'd like the way I deal with mutiny."

She stuck her hands on her slender hips. "Oh, yeah? Let's see how you deal with it."

He smiled gently. Before she could say another word, he picked her up very carefully in his arms and walked out the front door with her.

CHAPTER THREE

"YOU can't do this!" Sassy raged as he walked across the street with her, to the amusement of an early morning shopper in front of the small grocery store there.

"You won't go voluntarily," he said philosophically. He looked down at her and smiled gently. "You're very pretty."

She stopped arguing. "W...what?"

"Pretty," he repeated. "You've got grit, too." He chuckled. "I wish you'd half-closed that hand you hit Tarleton with, though." The smile faded. "That piece of work should be thrown into the county detention center wearing a sign telling what he tried to do. They'd pick him up in a shoebox."

Her small hands clung to his neck. "I didn't see it coming," she said, still in shock. "He pushed me into the tack room and locked the door. Before I could save myself, he pushed me back into the feed sacks and started kissing me and trying to get inside my blouse. I never thought I'd get away. I was fighting for all I was worth..." She swallowed hard. "Men are so strong. Even pudgy men like him."

"*I* should have seen it coming," he said, staring ahead

with a set face. "A man like that doesn't go quietly. This could have been a worse tragedy than it already is."

"You saved me."

He looked down into her wide, green eyes. "Yes. I saved you."

She managed a wan smile. "Funny. I was just talking to Selene—my mother's little ward—about how Prince Charming would come and rescue me one day." She studied his handsome face. "You do look a little like a prince."

His eyebrow jerked. "I'm too tall. Princes are short and stubby, mostly."

"Not in movies."

"Ah, but that's not real life."

"I'll bet you don't know a single prince."

She'd have been amazed. He and his brother had rubbed elbows with crowned heads of Europe any number of times. But he couldn't admit that, of course.

"You could be right," he agreed easily.

He paused to open the door with one hand with Sassy propped on his knee. He walked into the doctor's waiting room with Sassy still in his arms and went up to the receptionist behind her glass panel. "We have something of an emergency," he said in a low tone. "She's been the victim of an assault."

"Sassy?" the receptionist, a girl Sassy had gone to school with, exclaimed. She took one look at the other girl's face and went running to open the door for John. "Bring her right in here. I'll get Dr. Bates!"

The doctor was a crusty old fellow, but he had a kind heart and it showed. He asked John to wait outside while he examined his patient. John stood in the hall, staring at anatomy charts that lined the painted concrete block wall. In no time the sliding door opened and he motioned John back into the cubicle.

"Except for some understandable emotional upset, and a few light bruises, she's not too hurt." The doctor glowered. "I would like to see her assailant spend a few months or, better yet, a few years, in jail, however."

"So would I," John told him, looking glittery and full of outrage. "In fact, I'm going to work on that."

The doctor nodded. "Good man." He turned to Sassy, who was quiet and pale now that her ordeal was over and reaction was starting to set in. "I'm going to inject you with a tranquilizer. I want you to go home and lie down for the rest of the day." He held up a hand when she protested. "Selene's in school and your mother will cope. It's not a choice, Sassy," he added as he leaned out of the cubicle and motioned to a nurse.

While he was giving the nurse orders, John stuck his hands in his jeans pockets and looked down at Sassy. She had grit and style, for a woman raised in the back of beyond. He admired her. She was pretty, too, although she didn't seem to realize it. The only real obstacle was her age. His face closed up as he faced the fact that she was years too young for him, even without their social separation. It was a pity. He'd been looking all his adult life for a woman he could like as well as desire. This sweet little firecracker was unique in his female acquaintances. He admired her.

His pale eyes narrowed on Sassy's petite form. She had a very sexy body. He loved those small, pert breasts under the cotton shirt. He thought how bruised they probably were from Tarleton's fingers and he wanted to hurt the man all over again. He knew she was untouched. Tarleton had stolen her first intimacy from her, soiled it, demeaned it. He wished he'd wiped the floor with the man before the police chief came.

Sassy saw his expression and felt uneasy. Did he think she was responsible for the attack? She winced. He didn't know her at all. Maybe he thought she had lead Tarleton on. Maybe he thought she'd deserved what happened to her.

She lowered her eyes in shame. The doctor came back in with a syringe, rolled up her sleeve, swiped her upper arm with alcohol on a cotton ball, and injected her. Sassy didn't even flinch. She rolled down her sleeve.

"Go home before that takes effect, or you'll be lying down in the road," the doctor chuckled. He glanced at John. "Can you...?"

"Of course," John said. He smiled at Sassy, allaying her fears about his attitude. "Come on, sprout. I'll drive you."

"There's new stock that has to be put up in the store," she began to protest.

"It will still be waiting for you in the morning. If Buck needs help, I'll send some of my men into town to help him."

"But it's not your responsibility..."

"My boss has leased the feed store," he reminded her. "That makes it my responsibility."

"All right, then." She turned her head and smiled at the doctor. "Thanks."

He smiled back. "Don't you let this take over your life," he lectured her. "If you have any problems, you come back. I know a psychologist who works for the school system. She also takes private patients. I'll send you to her."

"I'll be okay."

John nodded at the doctor and followed Sassy out the door.

On the way home, Sassy sat beside him in the cab of the big pickup truck, fascinated by all the high-tech gadgets. "This is really nice," she remarked, smoothing over the leather dash. "I've never seen so many buttons and switches in a truck before."

He smiled lazily, steering with his left hand while he toyed with a loaded key ring in one of the big cup holders. "We use computers for roundup and GPS to move cattle and men around."

"Do you have a phone in here?" she asked, looking for one.

He indicated the second cup holder, where his cell phone was sitting. "I've got Bluetooth wiring in here," he explained. "The phone works through the speaker system. It's hands free. I can shorthand the call by saying the first or last name of the person I want to call. The phone does the rest. I get the Internet on it, and my e-mail as well."

"Wow," she said softly. "It's like the *Starship Enterprise*, isn't it?"

He could have told her that his brand-new Jaguar XF was more in that line, with controls that rose out of the console when the push-button ignition was activated, backup cameras, heated seats and steering wheel, and a supercharged V8 engine. But he wasn't supposed to be able to afford that sort of luxury, so he kept his mouth shut.

"This must be a very expensive truck," she murmured.

He grinned. "Just mid-range. Our bosses don't skimp on tools," he told her. "That includes working equipment for assistant feed store managers as well."

She looked at him through green eyes that were becoming drowsy. "Are we getting a new assistant manager to go with Mr. Mannheim?" she asked.

"Sure. You," he added, glancing at her warmly. "That goes with a rise in salary, by the way."

Her breath caught. "Do you mean it?"

"Of course."

"Wow," she said softly, foreseeing better used appliances for the little house and some new clothes for Selene. "I can't believe it!"

"You will." He frowned. "Don't fall over in your seat."

She laughed breathily. "I think the shot's taking effect." She moved and grimaced, absently touching her small breasts. "A few bruises are coming out, too. He really was rough."

His face hardened. "I hate knowing he manhandled you," he said through his teeth. "I wish I'd come to the store sooner."

"You saved me, just the same," she replied. She smiled. "My hero."

He chuckled. "Not me, lady," he mused. "I'm just a working cowboy."

"There's nothing wrong with honest labor and hard work," she told him. "I could never wrap my mind around some rich, fancy man with a string of women following him around. I like cowboys just fine."

The words stung. He was living a lie, and he shouldn't have started out with her on the wrong foot.

She was an honest person. She'd never trust him again if she realized how he was fooling her. He should tell her who he really was. He glanced in her direction. She was asleep. Her head was resting against the glass, her chest softly pulsing as she breathed.

Well, there would be another time, he assured himself. She'd had enough shocks for one day.

He pulled up in her driveway, went around and lifted her out of the truck in his arms. He paused at the foot of the steps to look down at her sleeping face. He curled her close against his chest, loving her soft weight, loving the sweet face pressed against his shirt pocket. He carried her up the steps easily, knocked perfunctorily at the door, and opened it.

Her mother, Mrs. Peale, was sitting in a chair in her bathrobe, watching the news. She cried out when she saw her daughter.

"What happened to her?" she exclaimed, starting to rise.

"She's all right," he said at once. "The doctor sedated her. Can I put her down somewhere, and I'll explain."

"Yes. Her bedroom…is this way." She got to her feet, panting with the effort.

"Mrs. Peale, you just point the way and sit back down," he said gently. "You don't need to strain yourself."

Her kind face beamed in a smile. "You're a nice young man. It's the first door on the left. Her bedroom."

"I'll be right back."

He carried Sassy into the bare little room and pulled back the worn blue chenille coverlet that was on the twin bed where she slept. Everything was spotless, if old. He lifted Sassy's head onto the pillow, tugged off her boots, and drew the coverlet over her, patting it down at her waist.

She breathed regularly. His eyes went from her disheveled, wavy dark hair to the slight rise of her firm breasts under the shirt he'd loaned her, down her narrow waist and slender hips and long legs. She was attractive. But it was more than a physical attractiveness. She was like a warm fireplace on a cold day. He smiled at his own imagery, took one last look at her pretty, sleeping face, went out, and pulled the door gently closed behind him.

Mrs. Peale was watching for him, worried. "What happened to her," she asked at once.

He sat down on the sofa next to her chair. "Yes. She's had a rough day…"

"That Tarleton man!" Mrs. Peale exclaimed furiously. "It was him, wasn't it?"

His eyebrows arched at her unexpected perception. "Yes," he agreed slowly. "But how would you know…?"

"He's been creeping around her ever since McGuire hired him," she said in her soft, raspy voice. She paused to get her breath. Her green eyes, so much like Sassy's, were sparking with temper. "She came home crying one day because he touched her in a way he shouldn't have, and she couldn't stop him. He thought it was funny."

John's usually placid face was drawn with anger as he listened.

Mrs. Peale noticed that, and the caring way he'd brought her daughter home. "Forgive me for being blunt, but, who are you?" she asked gently.

He smiled. "Sorry. I'm John…Taggert," he added, almost caught off guard enough to tell the truth. "My boss bought the old Bradbury place, and I'm his foreman."

"That place." She seemed surprised. "You know, it's haunted."

His eyebrows arched. "Excuse me?"

"I'm sorry. I shouldn't have said that...!" she began quickly.

"No. Please. I'd like to know," he said, reassuring her. "I collect folk tales."

She laughed breathily. "I guess it could be called that. You see, it began a long time ago when Hart Bradbury married his second cousin, Miss Blanche Henley. Her father hated the Bradburys and opposed the marriage, but Blanche ran away with Hart and got married to him anyway. Her father swore vengeance. One day, not long afterward, Hart came home from a long day gathering in strays, and found Blanche apparently in the arms of another man. He threw her out of his house and made her go back home to her father."

"Don't tell me," John interrupted with a smile. "Her father set her up."

"That's exactly what he did, with one of his men. Blanche was inconsolable. She sat in her room and cried. She did no cooking and no housework and she stopped going anywhere. Her father was surprised, because he thought she'd take up her old responsibilities with no hesitation. When she didn't, he was stuck with no help in the house and a daughter who embarrassed him in front of his friends. He told her to go back to her husband if he'd have her.

"So she did. But Hart met her at the door and told her he'd never live with her again. She'd gone from him to another man, or so he thought. Blanche gave up. She walked right out the side porch onto that bridge beside the old barn, and threw herself off the top. Hart heard her scream and ran after her, but she hit her head on a boulder when she went down, and her body washed up on the shore. Hart knew then that she was innocent. He sent word to her father that she'd killed herself. Her father went rushing over to Hart's place. Hart was waiting for him, with a double-barreled shotgun. He gave the old man one barrel and saved the other for himself." She grimaced. "It was almost ninety years ago, but nobody's forgotten."

"But they call the ranch the Bradbury place, don't they?" John asked, puzzled.

Mrs. Peale smiled. "Hart had three brothers. One of them took over the property. That was the great-uncle of the Bradbury you bought the ranch from."

"Talk about tragedies that stick in the mind," John mused. "I'm glad I'm not superstitious."

"How is it that you ended up bringing my daughter home?" she wondered aloud.

"I walked into the tack room in time to save her from Tarleton," he replied simply. "She didn't want to go to the doctor, so I carried her across the street and into his office." He sighed. "I suppose gossips will feed on that story for a week."

Mrs. Peale laughed. She had to stop suddenly, because her weak lungs wouldn't permit much of it. "Sassy is very stubborn."

He nodded. "I noticed." He smiled. "But she's got grit."

"Will she be all right?" she asked, worried.

"The doctor said that, apart from some bruises, she will. Of course there's the trauma of the attack itself."

"We'll deal with that…if we have to," the old woman

said quietly. She bit her lower lip. "Do you know about me?" she asked suddenly.

"Yes, I do," he replied.

Her thin face was drawn. "Sassy has nobody. My husband ran off and left me with Sassy still in school. I took in Selene when her father died while he was working for us, just after Sassy's father left. We have no living family. When I'm gone," she added slowly, "she won't have anybody at all."

"She'll be all right," John assured her quietly. "We've promoted her to assistant manager of the feed store. It comes with a raise in salary. And if she ever needs help, she'll get it. I promise."

She turned her head like a bird watching him. "You have an honest face," she said after a minute. "Thank you, Mr. Taggert."

He smiled. "She's sweet."

"Sweet and unworldly," she said heavily. "This is a good place to raise children, but it doesn't give them much sense of modern society. She's a babe in the woods, in some ways."

"She'll be fine," he assured her. "Sassy may be naïve, but she has an excellent self-image and she's a strong woman. If you could have seen her swinging on Tarleton," he added on a chuckle, with admiration in his pale eyes.

"She hit him?" she exclaimed.

"She did," he replied. "I wish they'd given her five minutes alone with him. It might have cured him of ever wanting to force himself on another woman. Not," he added darkly, "that he's going to have the opportunity for a very long time. The police chief has him in jail pending arraignment. He'll be brought up on assault charges and, I assure you, he won't be running around town again."

"Mr. McGuire should never have hired him," she muttered.

"I can assure you that he knows that."

She bit her lip. "What if he gets a good lawyer and they turn him loose?"

"In that case," John chuckled, "we'll search and find enough evidence on crimes in his past to hang him out to dry. Whatever happens, he won't be a threat to Sassy ever again."

Mrs. Peale beamed. "Thank you for bringing her home."

"Do you have a telephone here?" he asked suddenly.

She hesitated. "Yes, of course."

He wondered at the hesitation, but not just then. "If you need anything, anything at all, you can call me." He pulled a pencil and pad out of his pocket, one he'd bought in town to list supplies, and wrote the ranch number on it. He handed it to Mrs. Peale. "Somebody will be around all the time."

"That's very kind of you," she said quietly.

"We help each other out back home," he told her. "That's what neighbors are for."

"Where is back home, Mr. Taggert?" she asked curiously.

"The Callisters we work for live at Medicine Ridge," he told her.

"Those people!" She caught her breath. "My goodness, everybody knows who they are. In fact, we had a man who used to work for them here in town."

John held his breath. "You did?"

"Of course, he moved on about a year ago," she

added, and didn't see John relax. "He said they were the best bosses on earth and that he'd never have left if his wife hadn't insisted she had to be near her mother. Her mother was like me," she added sadly, "going downhill by the day. You can't blame a woman for feeling like that. I stayed with my own mother when she was dying." She looked up. "Are your parents still living?"

He smiled. "Yes, they are. I don't know them very well yet, but all of us are just beginning to get comfortable with each other."

"You were estranged?"

He nodded. "But not anymore. Can I do anything for you before I leave?"

"No, but thank you."

"I'll lock the door on my way out."

She smiled at him.

"I'll be out this way again," he said. "Tell Sassy she doesn't have to come in tomorrow unless she just wants to."

"She'll want to," Mrs. Peale said confidently. "In spite of that terrible man, she really likes her work."

"I like mine, too," John told her. He winked. "Good night."

"Good night, Mr. Taggert."

He drove back to the Bradbury place deep in thought. He wished he could make sure that Tarleton didn't get out of jail anytime soon. He was still worried. The man was vindictive. He'd assaulted Sassy for reporting his behavior. God knew what he'd do to her if he managed to get out of that jail. He'd have to talk to Chief Graves and see if there was some way to get his bond set sky-high.

* * *

The work at the ranch was coming along quickly. The framework for the barn was already up. Wiring and plumbing were in the early stages. A crew was starting to remodel the house. John had one bedroom as a priority. He was sick of using a sleeping bag on the floor.

He phoned Gil that night. "How are things going at home?" he asked.

Gil chuckled. "Bess brought a snake to the dinner table. You've never seen women run so fast!"

"I'll bet Kasie didn't run," he mused.

"Kasie ticked it under the chin and told Bess it was the prettiest garter snake she'd ever seen."

"Your new wife is a delight," John murmured.

"And you can stop right there," Gil muttered. "She's my wife. Don't you forget that."

John burst out laughing. "You can't possibly still be jealous of her now!"

"I can, too."

"I could bring her truckloads of flowers and hands full of diamonds, and she'd still pick you," John pointed out. "Love trumps material possessions. I'm just her brother-in-law now."

"Well, okay," Gil said after a minute. "How are the improvements coming along?"

"Slowly," John sighed. "I'm still using a sleeping bag on the hard floor. I've given them orders to finish my bedroom first. Meanwhile, I'm getting the barn put up. Oh, and I've leased us a feed store."

There was a pause. "Should I ask why?"

"The manager tried to assault a young woman who's working for the store. He's in jail."

"And you leased the store because…?"

John sighed. "The girl's mother is dying of lung cancer," he said heavily. "There's a young girl they took in when her father died...she's six. Sassy is the only one bringing in any money. I thought if she could be promoted to assistant manager, she might be able to pay her bills and buy a few new clothes for the little girl."

"Sassy, hmmm?"

John flushed at that knowing tone. "Listen, she's just a girl who works there."

"What does she look like?"

"She's slight. She has wavy, dark hair and green eyes and she's pretty when she smiles. When I pulled Tarleton off her, she walked up and slapped him as hard as she could. She's got grit."

"Tarleton would be the manager?"

"Yes," John said through his teeth. "The owner of the store, McGuire, hired him long distance and moved him here with his wife. Tarleton's lost at least one job for sexual harassment."

"Then why the hell did McGuire hire him?"

"He didn't know about the charges—there was never a conviction. He said he was desperate. Nobody wanted to work in this outback town."

"So who are we going to get to replace him?"

"Buck Mannheim."

"Good choice," Gil said. "Buck was dying of boredom after he retired. The store will be a challenge for him."

"He's a good manager. Sassy likes him already, and she knows every piece of merchandise on the place and the ordering system like the back of her hand. She keeps the place stocked."

"Is she all right?"

"A little bruised," John said. "I took her to the doctor and then drove her home. She slept all the way there."

"She didn't fuss about having the big boss carting her around?" Gil asked amusedly.

"Well, she doesn't know that I am the big boss," John returned.

"She what?"

John scowled. "Why does she have to know who I am?"

"You'll get in trouble if you start playing with the truth."

"I'm not playing with it. I'm just sidestepping it for a little while. I like having people take me at face value for a change. It's nice to be something more than a walking checkbook."

Gil cleared his throat. "Okay. It's your life. Let's just hope your decision doesn't come back to bite you down the line."

"It won't," John said confidently. "I mean, it isn't as if I'm planning anything permanent here. By the time I'm ready to come back to Medicine Ridge, it won't matter, anyway."

Gil changed the subject. But John wondered if there might not be some truth in what his big brother was saying. He hoped there wasn't. Surely it wasn't a bad thing to try to live a normal life for once. After all, he asked himself, how could it hurt?

CHAPTER FOUR

SASSY settled in as assistant manager of the feed store. Buck picked at her gently, teased her, and made her feel so much at home that it was like belonging to a family. During her second week back at work, she asked permission to bring Selene with her to work on the regular Saturday morning shift. Her mother had had a bad couple of days, she explained, and she wasn't well enough to watch Selene. Buck said it was all right.

But when John walked into the store and found a six-year-old child putting up stock, he wasn't pleased.

"This is a dangerous place for a kid," he told Sassy gently. "Even a bridle bit falling from the wall could injure her."

Sassy stopped and stared at him. "I hadn't thought about that."

"And there are the pesticides," he added. "Not that I think she'd put any in her mouth, but if she dropped one of those bags, it could fly up in her face." He frowned. "We had a little girl on the ranch back in Medicine Ridge who had to be transported to the emergency room when a bag of garden insecticide tore and she inhaled some of it."

"Oh, dear," Sassy said, worried.

"I don't mind her being here," John assured her. "But find her something to do at the counter. Don't let her wander around. Okay?"

She cocked her head at him. "You know a lot about kids."

He smiled. "I have nieces about Selene's age," he told her. "They can be a handful."

"You love them."

"Indeed I do," he replied, his eyes following Selene as she climbed up into a chair at the counter, wearing old but clean jeans and a T-shirt. "I've missed out on a family," he added quietly. "I never seemed to have time to slow down and think about permanent things."

"Why not?" she asked curiously.

His pale eyes searched hers quietly. "Pressure of work, I suppose," he said vaguely. "I wanted to make my mark in the world. Ambition and family life don't exactly mesh."

"Oh, I get it," she said, and smiled up at him. "You wanted to be something more than just a working cowboy."

His eyebrow jerked. "Something like that," he lied. The mark he meant was to have, with his brother, a purebred breeding herd that was known all over the world—a true benchmark of beef production that had its roots in Montana. The Callisters had attained that reputation, but John had sacrificed for it, spending his life on the move, going from one cattle show to another with the ranch's prize animals. The more awards their breeding bulls won, the more they could charge for their progeny.

"You're a foreman now," she said. "Could you get higher up than that?"

"Sure," he said, warming to the subject. He grinned. "We have several foremen, who handle everything from grain production to cattle production to AI," he added. "Above that, there's ranch management."

Her eyebrows drew together. "AI?" she queried. "What's that?"

If she'd been older and more sophisticated, he might have teased her with the answer. As it was, he took the question at face value. "It's artificial breeding," he said gently. "We hire a man who comes out with the product and inseminates our cows and heifers."

She looked uncomfortable. "Oh."

He smiled. "It's part of ranch protocol," he said, his tone soft. "The old-fashioned way is hit or miss. In these hard times, we have to have a more reliable way of insuring progeny."

She smiled back shyly. "Thanks for not explaining it in a crude way," she said. "We had a rancher come in here a month ago who wanted a diaper for his female dog, who was in heat." She flushed a little. "He thought it was funny when I got uncomfortable at the way he talked about it."

His thumb hooked into his belt as he studied her. The comment made him want to find the rancher and have a long talk with him. "That sort of thing isn't tolerated on our spread," he said shortly. "We even have dress requirements for men and women. There's no sexual harassment, even in language."

She looked fascinated. "Really?"

"Really." He searched her eyes. "Sassy, you don't have to put up with any man talking to you in a way that embarrasses you. If a customer uses crude language, you go get Buck. If you can't find him, you call me."

"I never thought…I mean, it seemed to go with the job," she stammered. "Mr. Tarleton was worse than some of the customers. He used to try to guess the size of my…of my…well—" she shrugged, averting her eyes "—you know."

"Sadly, I do," he replied tersely. "Listen, you have to start standing up for yourself more. I know you're young, but you don't have to take being talked down to by men. Not in this job."

She rubbed an elbow and looked up at him like a curious little cat. "I was going to quit," she recalled, and laughed a little nervously. "I'd already talked to Mama about it. I thought even if I had to drive to Billings and back every day, I'd do it." She grimaced. "That was just before gas hit over four dollars a gallon." She sighed. "You'd have to be a millionaire to make that drive daily, now."

"I know," he said with heartfelt emotion. He and Gil had started giving their personnel a gas ration allowance in addition to their wages. "Which reminds me," he added with a smile, "we're adding gas mileage to the checks now. You won't have to worry about going bankrupt at the pump."

"That's so nice of you!"

He pursed his lips. "Of course. I am nice. It's one of my more sterling qualities. I mean, along with being debonair, a great conversationalist, and good at poker." He watched her reaction, smiling wickedly when she didn't quite get it. "Did I mention that dogs love me, too?"

She did get it then, and laughed shyly. "You're joking."

"Trying to."

She grinned at him. It made her green eyes light up, her

face radiant. "You must have a lot of responsibility, considering how much work they're doing out at your ranch."

"Yes, I do," he admitted. "Most of it involves organization."

"That sounds very stressful," she replied, frowning. "I mean, a big ranch would have an awful lot of people to organize. I would think that you'd have almost no free time at all."

He didn't have much free time. But he couldn't tell her why. Actually the little bit of time he'd already spent here, even working, was something like a holiday, considering the load he carried when he was at home. He and Gil between them were overworked. They delegated responsibility where they could, but some decisions could only be made by the boss. "Well, it's still sort of a goal of mine," he hedged. "A man has to have a little ambition to be interesting." He studied her with pursed lips. "What sort of job goals do you have?"

She blinked, thinking. "I don't have any, really. I mean, I want to take care of Mama as long as I can. And I want to raise Selene and make sure she has a good education, and to save enough to help her go to college."

He frowned. Her goals were peripheral. They involved helping other people, not in advancing herself. He'd never considered the future welfare of anyone except himself—well, himself and Gil and the girls and, now, Kasie. But Sassy was very young to be so generous, even in her thoughts.

Young. She was nineteen. His frown deepened as he studied her youthful, faintly flushed little face. He found her very attractive. She had a big heart, a nice smile, a pretty figure, and she was smart, in a common-sense sort of way. But that age hit him right in the gut every time he considered her part in his life. He didn't dare become involved with her.

"What's wrong?" she asked perceptively.

He shifted from one big, booted foot to the other. "I just had a stray thought," he told her. He glanced at Selene. "You've got a lot of responsibilities for a woman your age," he added quietly.

She laughed softly. "Don't I know it!"

His eyes narrowed. "I guess it cramps your social life. With men, I mean," he added, hating himself because he was curious about the men in her life.

She laughed. "There are only a couple of men around town who don't have wives or girlfriends, and I turn them off. One of them came right out and said I had too much baggage, even for a date."

His eyebrows arched. "And what did you say to that?"

"That I loved my mother and Selene and any man who got interested in me would have to take them on as well. That didn't go over big," she added with twinkling eyes. "So I've decided that I'm going to be like the Lone Ranger."

He blinked. "Masked and mysterious?"

"No!" she chuckled. "I mean, just me. Well, just me and my so-called dependents." She glanced toward Selene, who was quietly matching up seed packages from a box that had just arrived. Her eyes softened. "She's very smart. I can never sort things the way she can. She's patient and quiet, she never makes a fuss. I think she might grow up to be a scientist. She already has that sort of introspective personality, and she's careful in what she does."

"She thinks before she acts," he translated.

"Exactly. I tend to go rushing in without thinking about the consequences," she added with a laugh. "Not Selene. She's more analytical."

"Being impulsive isn't necessarily a bad thing," he remarked.

"It can be," she said. "But I'm working on that. Maybe in a few years, I'll learn to look before I leap." She glanced up at him. "How are things going out at the Bradbury place?"

"We've got the barn well underway already," he said. "The framework's done. Now we're up to our ears in roofers and plumbers and electricians."

"We only have a couple of each of those here in town," she pointed out, "and they're generally booked a week or two ahead except for emergencies."

He smiled. "We had to import some construction people from Billings," he told her. "It's a big job. Simultaneously, they're trying to make improvements to the house and plan a stable. We've got fencing to replace, wells to bore, agricultural equipment to buy…it's a monumental job."

"Your boss," she said slowly, "must be filthy rich, if he can afford to do all that right now when we've got gas prices through the roof!"

"He is," he confided. "But the ranch will be self-sufficient when we're through. We're using solar panels and windmills for part of our power generation."

"We had a city lawyer buy land here about six years ago," she recalled. "He put in solar panels to heat his house and all sorts of fancy, energy-saving devices." She winced. "Poor guy."

"Poor guy?" he prompted when she didn't continue.

"He saw all these nature specials and thought grizzly bears were cute and cuddly," she said. "One came up into his backyard and he went out with a bag full of bread to feed to it."

"Oh, boy," he said slowly.

She nodded. "The bear ate all the bread and when he ran out, it started eating him. He did manage to get away finally by playing dead, but he lost the use of an arm and one eye." She shook her head. "He was a sad sight."

"Don't tell me," he said. "He was from back East."

She nodded. "Some big city. He'd never seen a real bear before, except in zoos and nature specials. He saw an old documentary on this guy who lived with bears and he thought anybody could make friends with them."

"Reminds me of a story I heard about a lady from D.C. who moved to Arizona. She saw a rattlesnake crawling across the road, so the story goes, and thought it was fascinating. She got out of her car and walked over to pet it."

"What happened to her?"

"An uncountable number of shots of antivenin," he said, "and two weeks in the hospital."

"Ouch."

"You know all those warning labels they have on food these days? They ought to put warning labels on animals." He held both hands up, as if holding a sign. "Warning: Most wild reptiles are not cute and cuddly and they will bite and can kill you. Or, Grizzly bears will eat bread, fruit, and some people."

She laughed at his expression. "I ran from a grizzly bear once and managed to get away."

"Fast, are you?"

"He was old and slow, and I was close to town. But I had great incentive," she agreed.

"I've never had to outrun anything," he recalled. "I did once pet a moose who came up to serenade one of our milk cows. He was friendly."

"Isn't that unusual?"

"It is. Most wild animals that will let you close enough to pet them are rabid. But this moose wasn't sick. He just had no fear of humans. I think maybe he was raised as a pet by people who were smart enough not to tell anybody."

"Because…?" she prompted.

"Well, it's against the law to make a pet of a wild animal in most places in the country," he explained. He smiled. "That moose loved corn."

"What happened to him?"

"He started charging other cattle to keep his favorite cow to himself, so we had to move him up farther into the mountains. He hasn't come back so far."

She grinned. "What if he does? Will you let him stay?"

He pursed his lips. "Sure! I plan to spray-paint him red, cut off his antlers, and tell people he's a French bull."

She burst out laughing at the absurd comment.

Selene came running up with a pad and pencil. "'Scuse me," she said politely to John. She turned to her sister. "There's a man on the telephone who wants you to order something for him."

Sassy chuckled. "I'll go right now and take it down. Selene, this is John Taggert. He's a ranch foreman."

Selene looked up at him and grinned. She was missing one front tooth, but she was cute. "When I grow up, I'm going to be a fighter pilot!"

His eyebrows arched. "You are?"

"Yup! This lady came by to see my mama. She's a nurse. Her daughter was a fighter pilot and now she flies big airplanes overseas!"

"Some role model," John remarked to Sassy, awed.

She laughed. "It's a brave new world."

"It is." He went down on one knee in front of Selene, so that her eyes could look into his. "And what sort of plane would you like to fly?" he teased, not taking her seriously.

She put a small hand on his broad shoulder. Her blue eyes were very wide and intent. "I like those F-22 Raptors," she said breathlessly. "Did you know they can actually stand still in the sky?"

He was fascinated. He wasn't sure he even knew what sort of military airplane that was. His breath exhaled. "No," he confessed. "I didn't."

"There was this program on TV about how they're built. And they were in a new movie about robots that come to our planet and pretend to be cars. I think Raptors are just beautiful," she said with a dreamy expression.

"I hope you get to fly one," he told her.

She smiled. "I got to grow up, first, though," she told him. She gasped. "Sassy!" she exclaimed. "That man's still on the phone!"

Sassy made a face. "I'm going, I'm going!"

"You coming back to see us again?" Selene asked John when he stood up.

He chuckled. "Thought I might."

"Okay!" She grinned and ran back to the counter, where Sassy was just picking up the phone.

John went to find Buck. It was a new world, indeed.

* * *

Tarleton was taken before the circuit judge for his arraignment and formally charged with the assault on Sassy. He pleaded not guilty. He had a city lawyer who gave the local district attorney a haughty glance and requested that his client, who was blameless, be let out on his own recognizance in lieu of bail. The prosecutor argued that Tarleton was a flight risk.

The judge, after reviewing the charges, did agree to set bail. But he set it at fifty thousand dollars, drawing furious protests from the attorney and his client. With no ability to raise such an amount, even using a bail bondsman, Tarleton would have to wait it out in the county detention facility. It wasn't a prospect he viewed with pleasure.

Sassy heard about it and felt guilty. Mr. Tarleton, for all his flaws, had a wife who was surely not guilty of anything more than bad judgment in her choice of a husband. It seemed unfair that she would have to suffer along with the defendant.

She said so, to John, when he turned up at the store the end of the next week.

"His poor wife," she sighed. "It's so unkind to make her go through it with him."

"Would you rather let him walk?" he asked quietly. "Set him free, so that he could do it to another young woman—perhaps with more tragic results?"

She flushed. "No. Of course not."

He reached out and touched her cheek with the tips of his fingers. "You have a big heart, Sassy," he said, his voice very deep and soft. "Plenty of other people don't, and they will use your own compassion against you."

She looked up curiously, tingling and breathless from just the faint contact of his fingers with her skin. "I guess some people are like that," she conceded. "But most people are kind and don't want to hurt others."

He laughed coldly. "Do you think so?"

His expression was saying things that she could read quite accurately. "Somebody hurt *you*," she guessed. Her eyes held his. They had an odd, blank look in them. "A woman. It was a long time ago. You never talk about it. But you hold it inside, deep inside, and use it to keep the world at a distance."

He scowled. "You don't know me," he said, defensive.

"I shouldn't," she agreed. Her green eyes seemed darker, more piercing. "But I do."

"Don't tell me," he murmured with faint sarcasm, "you can read minds."

She shook her head. "I can read wrinkles."

"Excuse me?"

"Your frown lines are deeper than your smile lines," she told him, not wanting to confess that her family had the "second sight," in case he thought she was peculiar. "It's a public smile. You leave it at the front door when you go home."

His eyes narrowed on her face. He didn't speak. She was incredibly perceptive for a woman her age.

She drew in a long breath. "Go ahead, say it. I need to mind my own business. I do try to, but it bothers me to see other people so unhappy."

"I am not unhappy," he said belligerently. "I'm very happy!"

"If you say so."

He glowered at her. "Just because a woman threw me over, I'm not damaged goods."

"How did she throw you over?"

He hadn't talked about it for years, not even to Gil. In one sense he resented this young woman, this stranger, prying into his life. In another, it made him want to talk about it, to stop the festering wound of it from growing even larger inside him.

"She got engaged to me while she was living with a man down in Colorado."

She didn't speak. She just watched him, like a curious little cat, waiting.

He grimaced. "I was so crazy about her that I never suspected a thing. She'd go away for weekends with her girlfriend and I'd watch movies and do book work at home while she was away. One weekend I had nothing to do, so I drove over to Red Lodge, where she'd said she was checked into a motel so that she could go fly-fishing with her girlfriend." He sighed. "Red Lodge isn't so big that you can't find people in it, and it does a big business in tourism. Turned out, her friend was male, filthy rich, and they had a room together. She had the most surprised look on her face when they came downstairs and found me sitting in the lobby."

"What did she say?" she asked.

"Nothing. Not one thing. She bit her lip and pretended that she didn't know the man. He was furious, and I felt like a fool. I went back home. She called and tried to talk to me, but I hung up on her. Some things don't take a lot of explaining."

He didn't add that he'd also hired a private detective, much too late, to find out what he could about the woman. It hadn't been the first time she'd kept a string of wealthy admirers, and she'd taken one man for a quarter of a million dollars before he found her out. She'd been after

John's money, all along; not himself. He wasn't as forth-coming as the millionaire she'd gone fly-fishing with, so she'd been working on the millionaire while she left John simmering on a back burner. As a result, she'd lost both men, which did serve her right. But the experience had made him bitter and suspicious of all women. He still thought they only wanted him for his money.

"The other guy, was he rich?" Sassy asked.

John's lips made a thin line. "Filthy rich."

She touched the front of his shirt with a shy, hesitant little hand. "I'm sorry about that," she told him. "But in a way, you're lucky that you aren't rich," she added.

"Why?"

"Well, you never have to worry if women like you for yourself or your wallet," she said innocently.

"There isn't much to like," he said absently, concentrating on the way she was touching him. She didn't even seem to be aware of it, but his body was rippling inside with the pleasure it gave him.

"You're kidding, right?" she asked. Her eyes laughed up into his. "You're very handsome. You stand up for people who can't take care of themselves. You like children. And dogs like you," she added mischievously, recalling one of his earlier quips. "Besides that, you must like animals, since you work around cattle."

While she was talking, the hand on his chest had been joined by her other one, and they were flat on the broad, hard muscles, idly caressing. His body was beginning to respond to her touch in a profound way. His blue eyes became glittery with suppressed desire.

He caught her hands abruptly and moved them. "Don't do that," he said curtly, without thinking how it was going to affect her. He was in danger of losing control of himself. He wanted to reach for her, slam her against him all the way up and down, and kiss that pretty mouth until he made it swell and moan under his lips.

She jerked back, appalled at her own boldness. "I'm sorry," she said at once, flushing. "I really am. I'm not used to men. I mean, I've never done that...excuse me!"

She turned and all but ran back down the aisle to the counter. When she got there, she jerked up the phone and called a customer to tell him his order was in. She'd already phoned him, and he hadn't answered, so she called again. It gave her something to do, so that John thought she was getting busy.

He muttered under his breath. Now he'd done it. He hadn't meant to make her feel brassy with that comment, but she was starting to get to him. He wanted her. She had warmth and compassion and an exciting little body, and she was getting under his skin. He needed a break.

He turned on his heel and walked out of the store. He should have gone back and apologized for being so abrupt, but he knew he'd never be able to explain himself without telling her the truth. He couldn't do that. She was years too young for him. He had to get out of town for a while.

He left Bradbury's former ranch foreman, Carl Baker, in charge of the place while he packed and went home to Medicine Ridge for the weekend.

It was a warm, happy homecoming. His big brother, Gil, met him at the door with a bear hug.

"Come on in," he said, chuckling. "We've missed you."

"Uncle John!"

Bess and Jenny, Gil's daughters by his first wife, came running down the hall to be picked up and cuddled and kissed.

"Oh, Uncle John, we missed you so much!" Bess, the eldest, cried, hugging him tightly around the neck.

"Yes, we did," Jenny seconded, kissing his bronzed cheek. "You can't stay away so long!"

"Did you bring us a present?" Bess asked.

He grinned. "Don't I always?" he laughed. "In the bag, next to my suitcase," he said, putting them down.

They ran to the bag, found the wrapped presents and literally tore the ribbons off to delve inside. There were two stuffed animals with bar codes that led children to Web sites where they could dress their pets and have adventures with them online in a safe environment.

"Web puppies!" Bess exclaimed, clutching a black Labrador.

Jenny had a Collie. She cuddled it close. "We seen these on TV!"

"Can we use the computer, Daddy?" Bess pleaded. "Please?"

"Use the computer?" Kasie, Gil's new wife, asked, grinning. "What are you babies up to, now?" she added, pausing to hug John before she pressed against Gil's side with warm affection.

"It's a Web puppy, Kasie!" Bess exclaimed, showing hers. "Uncle John bought them for us."

"I got a Collie, just like Lassie," Jenny beamed.

"We got to use the computer," Bess insisted.

Kasie chuckled. "I'll go start it up, then. Come on, babies. You staying for a while?" she asked John.

"For the weekend," John replied, smiling at the girls. "I needed a break."

"I guess you did," Gil replied. "You've taken on a big task up there. Sure you don't need more help? We could spare Green."

"I'm doing fine. Just a little complication."

Kasie led the girls off into Gil's office, where the computer lived. When they were out of earshot, Gil turned to John.

"What sort of complication?" he asked his younger brother.

John sighed. "There's a girl."

Gil's pale eyes sparkled. "It's about time."

John shook his head. "You don't understand. She's nineteen."

Gil only smiled. "Kasie was twenty-one. Barely. And I'm older than you are. Age doesn't have a lot to do with it."

John felt something of a load lift from his heart. "She's unworldly."

Gil chuckled. "Even better. Come have coffee and pie and tell me all about it!"

CHAPTER FIVE

SASSY put on a cheerful face for the rest of the day, pretending for all she was worth that having John Taggert push her away didn't bother her at all. It was devastating, though. She was shy with most men, but John had drawn her out of her shell and made her feel feminine and charming. Then she'd gone all googly over him and edged closer as if she couldn't wait to have him put his arms around her and kiss her. Even the memory of her behavior made her blush. She'd never been so forward with anyone.

Of course, she knew she wasn't pretty or desirable. He was a good deal older than she was, too, and probably liked beautiful and sophisticated women who knew their way around. He might not be a ranch boss, but he drove a nice truck and obviously made a good salary. In addition to all that, he was very handsome and charming. He'd be a woman magnet in any big city.

He'd saved her from Bill Tarleton, gotten her a raise and a promotion, and generally been kinder to her than she deserved. He probably had the shock of his life when she moved close to him as if she had the right, as if he belonged to her. The shame of it wore on her until she was pale and almost in tears when she left the shop that afternoon.

"Something bothering you, Sassy?" Buck Mannheim asked as they were closing up.

She glanced at him and forced a smile. "No, sir. Nothing at all. It's just been a long day."

"It's that Tarleton thing, isn't it?" he asked quietly. "You're upset that you'll have to testify."

She was glad to have an excuse for the way she looked. The assault did wear on her, but it was John Taggert's behavior, not her former boss's, that had her upset. "I guess it is a little worrying," she confessed.

He sighed. "Sassy, it's a sad fact of life that there are men like him in the world. But if you don't testify, he could get away with it. The reason you had trouble with him is that some other poor girl didn't want to have to face him in front of a jury. She let him walk. If he'd been convicted of sexual harassment, instead of just charged with it, he'd probably be in jail now. It might have stopped him from coming on to you."

She had to agree. "I suppose that's true. It's just… well, you know, Mr. Mannheim, some men think a woman leads them on if she just looks at them."

"I know. But that isn't the case here. John… Taggert—" he caught himself in the nick of time from letting John's real surname out "—will certainly testify to what he saw. He'll be there to back you up."

Which didn't make her feel any better, because John would probably think she worked at leading men on, considering how he'd had to push her away from him for being forward. She couldn't say that to Mr. Mannheim. It was too embarrassing.

"You just go on home, have a nice dinner, and stop worrying," he said with a smile. "Everything is going to be all right."

She let out a breath and smiled. "You remind me of my grandfather. He always used to tell me that things worked out, if we just sat back and gave them a chance. He was the most patient person I ever knew."

"I'm not patient." Buck chuckled. "But I do agree with your grandfather. Time heals."

"Don't I wish," she mused. "Good night, Mr. Mannheim. See you in the morning."

"I'll be here."

She got into the battered old truck her grandfather had willed her on his death, and drove home with black smoke pouring out behind her. The vehicle was an embarrassment, but it was all she had. Just putting gas in it and keeping the engine from blowing up was exorbitant. She was grateful for the gas allowance that she'd gotten with her promotion. It would help financially.

She parked at the side of the rickety old house and studied it for a minute before she walked up onto the porch. It needed so much repair. The roof leaked, there was a missing board on the porch, the steps were starting to sag, at least two windows were rotting out...the list went on and on. She recalled what John had said about the improvements that were being made on the Bradbury place, and it wasn't in nearly as bad a shape as this place. She despaired about what she was going to do when winter came. Last winter, she'd barely been able to afford to fill one third of the propane tank they used to heat the house. There were small space heaters in both bedrooms and a stove with a blower in the living room. They'd had to ration carefully, so they'd used a lot of quilts during the coldest months, and tried their best to save on fuel costs. It looked as though this year the fuel price would be twice as much.

She didn't dare think about the obstacles that lay ahead, especially her mother's worsening health. If the doctor prescribed more medicine, they'd be over their heads in no time. She already owed the local pharmacy half her next week's paycheck, because she'd had to supplement the cost of her mother's extra pills.

Well, she had to stop thinking about that, she decided. People were more important than money. It was just that she was the only person making any money. Now she was going to be involved in a court case, and it was just possible that John's boss might hear about it and not want such a scandalous person working in his store. Worse, John might tell him about how forward she'd been in the feed store today. She couldn't forget how angry he'd been when he walked out.

Just as she started up the steps, the sky opened up and it began to rain buckets. There was no time to lose. There were three big holes in the ceiling. One was right over the television set. She couldn't afford to replace the enormous console television, which was her mother's only source of pleasure. It was almost twenty years old, and the color wasn't good, but it had lasted them since Sassy was a baby.

"Hi!" she called on her way down the hall.

"It's raining, dear!" her mother called from the bedroom.

"I know! I'm on it!"

She made a dash for the little plastic tub under the sink, ran into the living room, and made it just in the nick of time to prevent drips from overwhelming the TV set. It was too big and heavy to move by herself. Her mother couldn't do any lifting at all, and Selene was too small. Sassy couldn't budge it, so the only alternative was to protect it. She put the tub on the flat top and breathed a sigh of relief.

"Don't forget the leak in the kitchen!" Mrs. Peale called again. Her voice was very hoarse and thin.

Sassy grimaced. She sounded as if she was getting a bad case of bronchitis, and she wondered how she'd ever get her mother willingly loaded into the truck if she had to take her to town to Dr. Bates. Maybe the dear old soul would make a house call, if he had to. He was a good man. He knew how stubborn Sassy's mother was, too.

She finished protecting the house with all sorts of buckets and pots. The drips on metal and plastic made a sort of soothing rhythm.

She peeked into her mother's bedroom. "Bad day?" she asked gently.

Her mother, pale and listless, nodded. "Hurts to cough."

Sassy felt even worse. "I'll call Dr. Bates…"

"No!" Her mother paused to cough again. "I've got antibiotic, Sassy, and I've used my breathing machine today already," she said gently. "I just need some cough syrup. It's on the kitchen counter." She managed a smile. "Try not to worry so much, darling," she coaxed. "Life just happens. We can't stop it."

Sassy bit her lower lip and nodded as tears threatened.

"Now, now." Mrs. Peale held out her thin arms. Sassy

ran to the bed and into them, careful not to press on her mother's frail chest. She cried and cried.

"I'm not going to die yet," Mrs. Peale promised. "I have to see Selene through high school first!"

It was a standing joke. Usually they both laughed, but Sassy had been through the mill for the past week. Her life was growing more complicated by the hour.

"We had a visitor today," her mother said. "Guess who it was?"

Sassy wiped at her eyes and sat up, smiling through the tears. "Who?"

"Remember Brad Danner's son Caleb, that you had a crush on when you were fifteen?" she teased.

Memory produced a vague portrait of a tall, lanky boy with black eyes and black hair who'd never seemed to notice her at all. "Yes."

"He came by to see you," Mrs. Peale told her. "He's been in the Army, serving overseas. He stopped by to visit and wanted to say hello to you." She grinned. "I told him to come to supper."

Sassy caught her breath. "Supper?" She sat very still. "But we've only got stew, and just barely enough for us," she began.

Mrs. Peale chuckled hoarsely. "He said we needed some take-out, so he's bringing a bucket of chicken with biscuits and honey and cottage fries all the way from Billings. We can heat it back up in the oven if it's cold when he gets here."

"Real chicken?" Sassy asked, her eyes betraying her hunger for protein. Mostly the Peales ate stews and casseroles, with very little meat because it was so expensive. "And biscuits with honey?"

"I guess I looked like I was starving," Mrs. Peale said wistfully. "I didn't have the heart to refuse. He was so persuasive." She smiled sheepishly.

"You wicked woman," Sassy teased. "What did you do?"

"Well, I was very hungry. He was talking about what he'd gotten himself and his aunt for supper last night, and I did mention that I'd forgotten what a chicken tasted like. He volunteered to come to dinner and bring it with him. What could I say?"

Sassy bent and hugged her mother warmly. "At least you'll get one good meal this week," she mused. "So will Selene." She sat up, frowning. "Where is Selene?"

"She's in her room, doing homework," Mrs. Peale replied. "She studies so hard. We have to find a way to let her go to college if she wants to."

"We'll work it out," Sassy promised. "Her grades will probably be so high that she'll get scholarships all over the place. She's a good student."

"Just like you were."

"I goofed off more than Selene does."

"You should put on a nice pair of jeans and a clean shirt," she told her daughter. "You can borrow some of my makeup. Caleb is a handsome young man, and he isn't going with anybody."

"You didn't ask?" Sassy burst out, horrified.

"I asked in a very polite way."

"Mother!"

"You should never turn down a prospective suitor," she chuckled. The smile faded. "I know you like Mr. Taggert, Sassy, but there's something about him…"

Her heart sank. Her mother was oddly accurate with

her "feelings." "You don't think he's a criminal or something?"

"Silly girl. Of course not. I just mean that he seems out of place here," Mrs. Peale continued. "He's intelligent and sophisticated, and he doesn't act like the cowboys who work around here, haven't you noticed? He's the sort of man who would look at home in elegant surroundings. He's immaculate and educated."

"He told me that he wanted to be a ranch manager one day," Sassy confided. "He probably works at building the right image, to impress people."

"That could be. But I think there's more to him than shows."

"You and your intuition," Sassy chided.

"You have it, too," the older woman reminded her. "It's that old Scotch-Irish second sight. My grandmother had it as well. She could see far ahead." She frowned. "She made a prediction that never made sense. It still doesn't."

"What sort?"

"She said I would be poor, but my daughter would live like royalty." She laughed. "I'm sorry, darling, but that doesn't seem likely."

"Everyone's entitled to a few misses," Sassy agreed.

"Anyway, go dress up. I told Caleb that we eat at six."

Sassy grinned at her. "I'll dress up, but it won't help. I'll still look like me, not some beauty queen."

"Looks fade. Character doesn't," her mother reminded her.

She sighed. "You don't find many young men in search of women with character."

"This may be the first. Hurry!"

* * *

Caleb was rugged-looking, tall and muscular and very polite. He smiled at Sassy and his dark eyes were intent on her face while he sat at the table with the two women and the little girl. He was serving in an Army unit in Afghanistan, where he was a corporal, he told them. He was a communications specialist, although he was good at fixing motors as well. The Army hadn't needed a mechanic when he enlisted, but they did need communications people, so he'd trained for that.

"Is it very bad over there, where you were?" Mrs. Peale asked, having struggled to the table with Caleb's help over Sassy's objections.

"Yes, it has been," Caleb said. "But we're making progress."

"Do you have to shoot people?" Selene asked.

"Selene!" Sassy exclaimed.

Caleb chuckled. "We try very hard not to," he told her. "But sometimes the warlords shoot at us. We're stationed high up in the mountains, where terrorists like to camp. We come under fire from time to time."

"It must be frightening," Sassy said.

"It is," Caleb said honestly. "But we do the jobs we're given, and try not to think about the danger." He glanced at Selene and smiled. "There are lots of kids around our camp. We get packages from home and they beg for candy and cookies from us. They don't get many sweets."

"Is there lots of little girls?" Selene asked.

"Now, we don't see many little girls," he told her. "Their customs are very different from ours. The girls mostly stay with their mothers. The boys tag along after their fathers."

"I'd like to tag along with my father," Selene said sadly. "But he went away."

"Away?"

Sassy mouthed "he died," and Caleb nodded quickly.

"Do have some more coffee, Caleb," Mrs. Peale offered.

"Thank you. It's very good."

Sassy had rationed out enough for a pot of the delicious beverage. It was expensive, and they rarely drank it. But Mrs. Peale said that Caleb loved coffee and he had, after all, contributed the meal. Sassy felt that a cup of good coffee wasn't that much of a sacrifice, under the circumstances.

After dinner, they gathered around the television to watch the news. Caleb looked at his watch and said he had to get back to Billings, because his aunt wanted to go to a late movie, and he'd promised to take her.

"But I'd like to come back again before I return to duty, if I may," he told them. "I had a good time tonight."

"So did we," Sassy said at once. "Please do."

"We'll make you a nice macaroni and cheese casserole next time, our treat," Mrs. Peale offered.

He hesitated. "Would you mind if I contributed the cheese for it?" he asked. "I'm partial to a particular brand."

They saw right through him, but they pretended not to. It had to be obvious that they were managing at a subsistence level.

"That would be very kind of you," Mrs. Peale said with genuine gratitude.

He smiled. "It would be my pleasure. Sassy, would you walk me out?"

"Sure!"

She jumped up and walked out to his truck with him. He turned to her before he climbed up into the cab.

"My aunt has a cousin who lives here. She says your mother is in very bad shape," he said.

She nodded. "Lung cancer."

He grimaced. "If there's anything I can do, anything at all," he began. "Your mother was so good to my cousin when she lost her husband in the blizzard a few years ago. None of us have forgotten."

"You're very kind. But we're managing." She grinned. "Thanks for the chicken, I'd forgotten what they tasted like," she added, mimicking her mother's words.

He laughed at her honesty. "You always did have a great sense of humor."

"It's easier to laugh than to cry," she told him.

"So they say. I'll come by tomorrow afternoon, if I may, and tell you when I'm free. My aunt has committed me to no end of social obligations."

"You could phone me," she said.

He grinned. "I'd rather drive over. Humor me. I'll escape tea with one of aunt's friends who has an eligible daughter."

She chuckled. "Avoiding matrimony, are you?"

"Apparently," he agreed. He pursed his lips. "Are you attached?"

She sighed. "No. Sorry." Her eyes widened. "Are you?"

He grimaced. "I'm trying not to be." He shrugged. "She's my best friend's girl."

She relaxed. He wasn't hunting for a woman. "I have one of those situations, too. Except that he doesn't have a girlfriend, that I know of."

"And he doesn't like you?"

"Apparently not."

"Well, if that doesn't take the cake. Two fellow sufferers, and we meet by accident."

"That's life."

"It is." He studied her warmly. "You know, I was so shy in high school that I never got up the nerve to ask you out. I wanted to. You were always so cheerful, always smiling. You made me feel good inside."

That was surprising. She remembered him as a standoffish young man who seemed never to notice her.

"I was shy, too," she confessed. "I just learned to bluff."

"The Army taught me how to do that," he said, smiling. "This man you're interested in—somebody local?"

She sighed. "Actually, he's sort of the foreman of a ranch. The men he works for bought the old Bradbury place…"

"That wreck?" he exclaimed. "Whatever for?"

"They're going to run purebred calves out there, once they build a new barn and stable and remodel the house and run new fences. It's going to be quite a job."

"A very expensive job. Who are his bosses?"

"The Callister brothers. They live in Medicine Ridge."

He nodded. "Yes. I've heard of them. Hard working men. One of their ranch hands was in my unit when I first shipped out. He said it was the best place he'd ever worked." He laughed. "He said the brothers got right out in the pasture at branding time and helped. They weren't the sort to sit in parlors and sip expensive alcohol."

"Imagine, to be that rich and still go out to work cattle," she said with a wistful smile.

"I can't imagine it," he told her. "But I'd love to be able to. I'm getting my college degree in the military. When I come out, I'm going to apprentice at a mechanic's shop in Billings and, hopefully, work my way up to partnership one day. I love fixing motors."

She gave him a wry look. "I wish you'd love fixing mine," she said. "It's pouring black smoke."

"How old is it?" he asked curiously.

"About twenty years…"

"Rings and valves," he said at once. "It's probably going to need rebuilding. At today's prices, you'd come out better to sell it for scrap and buy a new one."

"Pipe dreams," she laughed. "We live up to the last penny I bring home. I could never make a car payment."

"Have you thought about moving to Billings, where you could get a better job?"

"I'd have to take Mama and Selene with me," she said simply, "and we'd have to rent a place to live. At least we still have the house, such as it is."

He frowned. "You landed in a fine mess," he said sympathetically.

"I did, indeed. But I love my family," she added. "I'd rather have what I have than be a millionaire."

His dark eyes met her green ones evenly. "You're a nice girl, Sassy. I wish I'd known you better before I met my best friend's girl."

"I wish I'd known you better before John Taggert came to town," she sighed. "As it is, I'll be very happy to have you for a friend." She grinned. "We can cry on each others' shoulders. I'll even write to you when you go back overseas if you'll give me your address."

His face lit up. "I'd like that. It will help throw my

buddy off the trail. He caught me staring at his girl-friend's photo a little too long."

"I'll send you a picture of me," she volunteered. "You can tell him she reminded you of me."

His eyebrows lifted. "That won't be far-fetched. She's dark haired and has light eyes. You'd do that for me?"

"Of course I would," she said easily. "What are friends for?"

He smiled. "Maybe I can do you a good turn one day."

"Maybe you can."

He climbed into the truck. "Tell your family I said good-night. I'll drive over tomorrow."

She smiled up at him. "I'll look forward to it."

He threw up a hand and pulled out into the road. She watched him go, remembering that there were still a few pieces of chicken left. She'd have to rush inside and put them up quickly before Selene grew reckless and ate too much. If they stretched out that bucket of chicken, they could eat on it for most of the week. It was a godsend, considering their normal grocery budget. God bless Caleb, she thought warmly. He really did have a big heart.

John Callister had spent a pleasant weekend with his brother and Kasie and the girls. Mrs. Charters had made him his favorite foods, and even Miss Parsons, Gil's former governess who was now his bookkeeper, seemed to enjoy his visit. There was a new secretary since Gil had married Kasie. He was a male secretary, Arnold Sims, who seemed nice and was almost as efficient as Kasie had been. He was an older man, and he and Miss Parsons spent their days off together.

It was nice to get away from the constant headache

of construction and back to the bosom of his family. But he had to return to Hollister, and mend fences with Sassy. He should have found a kinder way to keep her at arm's length while he found his footing in their changing relationship. Her face had gone pale when he'd jerked back from her. She probably thought he found her offensive. He hated leaving her with that false impression, but his sudden desire for her had shocked and disturbed him. He hadn't been confident enough to go back and face her until he could hide his feelings.

There had to be some way to make it up to her. He'd think of a way when he got back to Hollister, he assured himself. He could explain it away without too much difficulty. Sassy had a kind heart. He knew she wouldn't hold grudges.

But when he walked into the store Monday afternoon, he got a shock. Sassy was leaning over the counter, smiling broadly at a very handsome young man in jeans and a chambray shirt. And if he wasn't mistaken, the young man was holding her hand.

He felt something inside him explode with pain and resentment. She'd put her hands on his chest and looked up at him with melting green eyes, and he'd wanted her to the point of madness. Now she was doing the same thing to another man, a younger man. Was she just a heartless flirt?

He walked up to the counter, noting idly that the younger man didn't seem to be disturbed by him, or even interested in him.

"Hi, Sassy," he said coolly. "Did you get in that special feed mix I asked you to order?"

"I'll check, Mr. Taggert," she said politely and with

a quiet smile. She walked into the back to check the invoice of the latest shipment that had just come that morning, very proud that she'd been able to disguise her quick breathing and shaky legs. John Taggert had a shattering effect on her emotions. But he didn't want her, and she'd better remember it. What a blessing that Caleb had come to the store today. Perhaps John would believe that she had other interests and wasn't chasing after him.

"Nice day," John said to the young man. "I'm John Taggert. I'll be ramrodding the old Bradbury ranch."

The boy smiled and extended a hand. "I'm Caleb Danner. Sassy and I went to school together."

John shook the hand. "Nice to meet you."

"Same here."

John looked around at the shelves with seeming nonchalance. "You work around here?" he asked carelessly.

"No. I'm in the Army Rangers," the boy replied, surprising his companion. "I'm stationed overseas, but I've been home on leave for a couple of weeks. I'm staying with my aunt in Billings."

John's pale eyes met the boy's dark ones. "That's a substantial drive from here."

"Yes, I know," Caleb replied easily. "But I promised Sassy a movie and I'm free tonight. I came to see if she'd go with me."

CHAPTER SIX

THE boy was an Army Ranger he said, and he was dating Sassy. John felt uncomfortable trying to pump the younger man for information. He wondered if Caleb was seriously interested in Sassy, but he had no right to ask.

She was poring over bills of lading. He watched her with muted curiosity and a little jealousy. It disturbed him that this younger man had popped up right out of the ground, so to speak, under his own nose.

It took her a minute to find the order and calm her nerves. But she managed to do both. She looked up as John approached the counter. He looked very sexy in those well-fitting jeans and the blue-checked Western-cut shirt he was wearing with his black boots and wide-brimmed hat. She shouldn't notice that, she told herself firmly. He wouldn't like having her interested in him; he'd already made that clear. She had to be businesslike.

"The feed was backordered," she said politely. "But it should be here by Friday, if that's all right. If it isn't," she added quickly when he began to look irritated, "I can ask Mr. Mannheim to phone them…"

"No need," he said abruptly. "We can wait. We aren't

moving livestock onto the place until we have the fences mended and the barn finished. I just want to have the feed on hand when they arrive."

"We'll have it by next week. No problem."

He nodded. He tried to avoid looking at her directly. She was wearing jeans with a neat little white peasant blouse that had embroidery on it, and she looked very pretty with her dark hair crisp and clean, and her green eyes shimmering with pleasure. Her face was flushed and she was obviously unsettled. The boy at the counter probably had something to do with that, he thought irritably. She seemed pretty wrapped up in him already.

"That's fine," he said abruptly. "I'll check back with you next week, or I'll have one of the boys come in."

"Yes, sir," she replied politely.

He nodded at Caleb and stalked out of the store without another glance at Sassy.

Caleb pursed his lips and noted Sassy's heightened color. "So that's him," he mused.

She drew in a steadying breath. "That's him."

"Talk about biting off more than you can chew," he murmured dryly.

"What do you mean?"

"Nothing," he returned, thinking privately that Taggert looked like a man who'd forgotten more about women than Sassy would ever learn about men. Taggert seemed sophisticated, for a cattleman, and was obviously used to giving orders. Sassy was too young for that fire-eater, too unsophisticated, too everything. Besides all that, the ranch foreman had spoken to her politely, but in a manner that was decidedly impersonal.

Caleb didn't want to upset Sassy by putting all that into words. Still, he felt sympathy for her. She was as likely to land that big fish as he was to find himself out on the town with his best friend's girl.

"How about that movie?" he asked quickly, changing the subject. "The local theater has three new ones showing…"

They went to Hollister's only in-town movie theater, a small building in town that did a pretty good business catering to families. There was a drive-in movie on the outskirts of town, in a cow-pasture, but Caleb wasn't keen on that, so they went into town.

The movie they chose was a cartoon movie about a robot, and it was hilarious. Sassy had worried about leaving her mother and Selene alone, but Mrs. Peale refused to let her sacrifice a night out. Sassy did leave her prepaid cell phone with her mother, though, in case of an emergency. Caleb had one of his own, so they could use it if they were in any difficulties.

Caleb drove her back home. He had a nice truck; it wasn't new, but it was well-maintained. He was sending home the payments to his aunt, who was making them for him.

"I only have a year to go," he told her. "Yesterday, I got a firm offer of a partnership in Billings at a cousin's car dealership. He has a shop that does mechanical work. I'd be in charge of that, and do bodywork as well. I went by to see him on a whim, and he offered me the job, just like that." His dark eyes twinkled. "It's what I've wanted to do my whole life."

"I hope you make it," she told him with genuine feeling.

He bent and kissed her cheek. "You're a nice girl, Sassy," he said softly. "I wish…"

"Me, too," she said, reading the thought in his face. "But life makes other plans, sometimes."

"Doesn't it?" he chuckled.

"When do you report back to duty?" she asked.

"Not for a week, but my aunt has every minute scheduled. She had plans for tonight, too, but I outfoxed her," he said, grinning.

"I enjoyed the movie. And the chicken," she told him.

"I enjoyed the macaroni and cheese we had tonight," he replied. He was somber for a minute. "If you ever need help, I hope you'll ask me. I'd do what I can for you."

She smiled up at him. "I know that. Thanks, Caleb. I'd make the same offer. But," she sighed, "I have no clue what I'd ever be able to help you with."

"I'll send you my address," he said, having already jotted hers down on a piece of paper. "You can send me that photo, to throw my buddy off the track."

She laughed. "Okay. I'll definitely do that."

"I'll phone you before I leave. Take care."

"You, too. So long."

He got into his truck and drove away.

Sassy walked slowly up the porch and into the house, her mind still on the funny movie.

She was halfway into the living room when she realized that one of the muffled voices she'd been hearing was male.

As she entered the room, John Taggert looked up from the sofa, where he was sitting with her mother. Her mother, she noted, was grinning like a Cheshire cat.

"Mr. Taggert came by to see how I was doing. Wasn't that sweet of him?" she asked her daughter.

"It really was," Sassy replied politely.

"Had a good time?" John asked her. He wasn't smiling.

"Yes," she said. "It was a cartoon movie."

"Just right for children," he replied, and there was something in his blue eyes that made her heart jump.

"We're all children at heart. I'm sure that's what you meant, wasn't it, Mr. Taggert?" Mrs. Peale asked sweetly.

He caught himself. "Of course," he replied, smiling at the older woman. "I enjoy them myself. We take the girls to movies all the time."

"Girls?" Mrs. Peale asked, frowning.

"My nieces," he explained. "They love cartoons. My brother and his wife take them mostly, but I fill in when I'm needed."

"You like children?"

He smiled. "I love them."

Mrs. Peale opened her mouth.

Sassy knew what was coming, so she jumped in. "Caleb's going to phone us before he goes back overseas," she told her mother.

"That's nice of him." Mrs. Peale beamed. "Such a kind young man."

"Kind." Sassy nodded.

"Would you like something to drink, Mr. Taggert?" Mrs. Peale asked politely. "Sassy could make some coffee…?"

John glanced at his watch. "I've got to go. Thanks anyway. I just wanted to make sure you were all right," he told Mrs. Peale, and he smiled at her. "Sassy's…boyfriend mentioned that he was taking her to a movie, and I thought about you out here all alone."

Sassy gave him a glare hot enough to scald. "I left Mama my cell phone in case anything happened," she said curtly.

"Yes, she did," Mrs. Peale added quickly. "She takes very good care of me. I insisted that she go with Caleb. Sassy hasn't had a night out in two or three years."

John shifted, as if that statement made him uneasy.

"She doesn't like to leave me at all," Mrs. Peale continued. "But it's not fair to her. So much responsibility, and at her age."

"I never mind it," Sassy interrupted. "I love you."

"I know that, sweetheart, but you should get to know nice young men," she added. "You'll marry one day and have children. You can't spend your whole life like this, with a sick old woman and a child..."

"Please," Sassy said, hurting. "I don't want to think about getting married for years yet."

Mrs. Peale's face mirrored her sorrow. "You should never have had to handle this all alone," she said regretfully. "If only your father had...well, that's not something we could help."

"I'll walk Mr. Taggert to the door," Sassy offered. She looked as if she'd like to drag him out it, before her mother could embarrass her even more.

"Am I leaving?" he asked Sassy.

"Apparently," she replied, standing aside and nodding toward the front door.

"In that case, I'll say good night." He smiled at Mrs. Peale. "I hope you know that you can call on me if you ever needed help. I'm not in the Army, but I do have skills that don't involve an intimate knowledge of guns—"

"This way, Mr. Taggert." Sassy interrupted emphatically, catching him firmly by the sleeve.

He grinned at Mrs. Peale, whose eyes were twinkling now. "Good night."

"Good night, Mr. Taggert. Thank you for stopping by."

"You're very welcome."

He followed Sassy out onto the front porch. She closed the door.

His eyebrows arched. "Why did you close the door?" he asked. His voice deepened with amusement. "Are you going to kiss me good night and you don't want your mother to see?"

She flushed. "I wouldn't kiss you for all the tea in China! There's no telling where you've been!"

"Actually," he said, twirling his wide-brimmed hat in his big hands, "I've been in Medicine Ridge, reporting to my bosses."

"That's nice. Do drive safely on your way back to your ranch."

He stopped twirling the hat and studied her stiff posture. He felt between a rock and a hard place.

"The Army Ranger seems like a good sort of boy," he remarked. "Responsible. Not very mature yet, but he'll grow up."

She wanted to bite him. "He's in the Army Rangers," she reminded him. "He's been in combat overseas."

His eyebrows lifted. "Is that a requirement for your dates, that they've learned to dodge bullets?"

"I never said I wanted a man who could dodge bullets!" she threw at him.

"It might be a handy skill for a man—dodging things, I mean, if you're the sort of woman who likes to throw pots and pans at men."

"I have never thrown a pot at a man," she said emphatically. "However, if you'd like to step into our kitchen, I could make an exception for you!"

He grinned. He could have bet that she didn't talk like that to the soldier boy. She had spirit and she didn't take guff from anyone, but it took a lot to get under her skin. It delighted him that he could make her mad.

"What sort of pot did you have in mind throwing at me?" he taunted.

"Something made of cast iron," she muttered. "Although I expect you'd dent it."

"My head is not that hard," he retorted.

He stepped in, close to her, and watched her reaction with detached amusement. He made her nervous. It showed.

He put his hat back on, and pushed it to the back of his head. One long arm went around Sassy's waist and drew her to him. A big, lean hand spread on her cheek, coaxing it back to his shoulder.

"You've got grit," he murmured deeply as his gaze fell to her soft mouth. "You don't back away from trouble, or responsibility. I like that."

"You…shouldn't hold me like this," she protested weakly.

"Why not? You're soft and sweet and I like the way you smell." His head began to bend. "I think I'll like the way you taste, too," he breathed.

He didn't need a program to know how innocent she was. He loved the way her hands gripped him, almost in fear, as his firm mouth smoothed over the parted, shocked warmth of her lips.

"Nothing heavy," he whispered as his mouth played with hers. "It's far too soon for that. Relax. Just relax, Sassy. It's like dancing, slow and sweet…"

His mouth covered hers gently, brushing her lips apart, teasing them to permit the slow invasion. Her hands relaxed their death-grip on his arms as the slow rhythm began to increase her heartbeat and make her breathing sound jerky and rough. He was very good at this, she thought dizzily. He knew exactly how to make her shiver with anticipation as he drew out the intimate torture of his mouth on her lips. He teased them, playing with her lower lip, nibbling and rubbing, until she went on tiptoe with a frustrated moan, seeking something far rougher and more passionate than this exquisite whisper of motion.

He nipped her lower lip. "You want more, don't you, honey?" he whispered roughly. "So do I. Hold tight."

Her hands slid up to his broad shoulders as his mouth began to burrow hungrily into hers. She let her lips open with a shiver, closing her eyes and reaching up to be swallowed whole by his arms.

It was so sweet that she moaned with the ardent passion he aroused in her. She'd never felt her body swell and shudder like this when a man held her. She'd never been kissed so thoroughly, so expertly. Her arms tightened convulsively around his neck as he riveted her to the length of his powerful body, as if he, too, had lost control of himself.

A minute later, he came to his senses. She was just nineteen. She worked for him, even though she didn't know it. They were worlds apart in every way. What the hell was he doing?

He pulled away from her abruptly, his blue eyes shimmering with emotion, his grasp a little bruising as he tried to get his breath back under control. His jealousy of the soldier had pushed him right into a situation he'd left town to avoid. Now, here he was, faced with the consequences.

She hung there, watching him with clouded, dreamy eyes in a face flushed with pleasure from the hungry exchange.

"That was a mistake," he said curtly, putting her firmly at arm's length and letting her go.

"Are you sure?" she asked, dazed.

"Yes, I'm sure," he said, his voice sharp with anger.

"Then why did you do it?" she asked reasonably.

He had to think about a suitable answer, and his brain wasn't working very well. He'd pushed her away at their last meeting and felt guilt. Now he'd compounded the error and he couldn't think of a good way to get out of it.

"God knows," he said heavily. "Maybe it's the full moon."

She gave him a wry look. "It's not a full moon. It's a crescent moon."

"A moon is a moon," he said doggedly.

"That's your story and you're sticking to it," she agreed.

He stared down at her with conflict eating him alive. "You're nineteen, Sassy," he said finally. "I'm thirty-one."

She blinked. "Is that supposed to mean something?"

"It means you're years too young for me. And not only in age."

She raised her eyebrows. "It isn't exactly easy to get

experience when you're living in a tiny town and supporting a family."

He ground his teeth. "That isn't the point…"

She held up a hand. "You had too much coffee
today and the caffeine caused you to leap on unsuspecting women."

He glowered. "I did not drink too much coffee."

"Then it must be either my exceptional beauty or my
overwhelming charm," she decided. She waited, arms
folded, for him to come up with an alternate theory.

He pulled his hat low over his eyes. "It's been a long,
dry spell."

"Well, if that isn't the nicest compliment I ever had,"
she muttered. "You were lonely and I was the only
eligible woman handy!"

"You were," he shot back.

"A likely story! There's Mrs. Harmon, who lives a
mile down the road."

"Mrs. Harmon?"

"Yes. Her husband has been dead fifteen years. She's
fifty, but she wears tight skirts and a lot of makeup and
in dim light, she isn't half bad."

He glowered even more. "I am not that desperate."

"You just said you were."

"I did not!"

"Making passes at nineteen-year-old girls," she
scoffed. "I never!"

He threw up his hands. "It wasn't a pass!"

She pursed her lips and gave him a sarcastic look.

He shrugged. "Maybe it was a small pass." He stuck
his hands in his pockets. "I have a conscience. You'd
wear on it."

So that was why he'd pushed her away in the store, before he left town. Her heart lifted. He didn't find her unattractive. He just thought she was too young.

"I'll be twenty next month," she told him.

It didn't help. "I'll be thirty-two in two months."

"Well, for a month we'll be almost the same age," she said pertly.

He laughed shortly. "Twelve years is a lot, at your age."

"In the great scheme of things, it isn't," she pointed out.

He didn't answer her.

"Thanks for stopping by to check on my mother," she said. "It was kind."

He lifted a shoulder. "I wanted to see if the soldier was hot for you."

"Excuse me?!"

"He didn't even kiss you good night," he said.

"That's because he's in love with his best friend's girl."

His expression brightened. "He is?"

"I'm somebody to talk about her with," she told him. "Which is why I don't get out much, unless a man wants to tell me about his love life and ask for advice." She studied him. "I don't guess you've got relationship problems?"

"In fact, I do. I'm trying not to have one with an inappropriate woman," he said, tongue-in-cheek.

That took a minute to register. She laughed. "Oh. I see."

He moved closer and toyed with a strand of her short hair. "I guess it wouldn't hurt to take you out once in a while. Nothing serious," he added firmly. "I am not in the market for a mistress."

"Good thing," she returned, "because I have no intention of becoming one."

He grinned. "Now, that's encouraging. I'm glad to know that you have enough willpower to keep us on the straight and narrow."

"I have my mother," she replied, "who would shoot you in the foot with a rusty gun if she even thought you were leading me into a life of sin. She's very religious. She raised me to be that way."

"In her condition," he said solemnly, "I'm not surprised that she's religious. She's a courageous soul."

"I love her a lot," she confessed. "I wish I could do more to help her."

"Loving her is probably what helps her the most," he said. He bent and brushed a soft kiss against her mouth. "I'll see you tomorrow."

She smiled. "Okay."

He started to walk down the steps, paused, and turned back to her. "You're sure it's not serious with the soldier?"

She smiled more broadly. "Very sure."

He cocked his hat at a jaunty angle and grinned at her. "Okay."

She watched him walk out to his vehicle, climb in, and drive away. She waved, but she noticed that he didn't look back. For some reason, that bothered her.

John spent a rough night remembering how sweet Sassy was to kiss. He'd been fighting the attraction for weeks now, and he was losing. She was too young for him. He knew it. But on the other hand, she was independent. She was strong. She was used to responsibility. She'd had years of being the head of her family, the bread-winner. She might be young, but she was more mature than most women her age.

He could see how much care she took for her mother and her mother's little ward. She never shirked her duties, and she worked hard for her paycheck.

The bottom line was that he was far too attracted to her to walk away. He was taking a chance. But he'd taken chances before in his life, with women who were much inferior to this little firecracker. It wouldn't hurt to go slow and see where the path led. After all, he could walk away whenever he liked, he told himself.

The big problem was going to be the distance between them socially. Sassy didn't know that he came from great wealth, that his parents were related to most of the royal houses of Europe, that he and his brother had built a world-famous ranch that bred equally famous breeding bulls. He was used to five-star hotels and restaurants, stretch limousines in every city he visited. He traveled first-class. He was worldly and sophisticated. Sassy was much more used to small town life. She wouldn't understand his world. Probably, she wouldn't be able to adjust to it.

But he was creating hurdles that didn't exist yet. It wasn't as if he was in love with her and aching to rush her to the altar, he told himself. He was going to take her out a few times. Maybe kiss her once in a while. It was nothing he couldn't handle. She'd just be companionship while he was getting this new ranching enterprise off the ground. When he had to leave, he'd tell her the truth.

It sounded simple. It was simple, he assured himself. She was just another girl, another casual relationship. He was going to enjoy it while it lasted.

He went to sleep, finally, having resolved all the problems in his mind.

The next day, he went back to the feed store with another list, this one of household goods that he was going to need. He was looking forward to seeing Sassy again. The memory of that kiss had prompted some unusually spicy dreams about her.

But when he got there, he found Buck Mannheim handling the counter and looking worried.

He waited while the older man finished a sale. The customer left and John approached the counter.

"Where's Sassy?" he asked.

Buck looked concerned. "She phoned me at home. Her mother had a bad turn. They had to send an ambulance for her and take her up to Billings to the nearest hospital. Sassy was crying…"

He was talking to thin air. John was already out the door.

He found Sassy and little Selene in the emergency waiting room, huddled together and upset.

He walked into the room and they both ran to him, to be scooped up and held close, comforted.

He felt odd. It was the first time he could remember being important to anyone outside his own family circle. He felt needed.

His arms contracted around them. "Tell me what happened," he asked at Sassy's ear.

She drew away a little, wiping at her eyes with the hem of her blouse. It was obvious that she hadn't slept. "She knocked over her water carafe, or I wouldn't even have known anything was wrong. I ran in to see what had happened and I found her gasping for breath. It was so bad that I just ran to the phone and called Dr. Bates. He sent for the ambulance and called the oncologist on staff here. They've been with her for two hours. Nobody's told me anything."

He eased them down into chairs. "Stay here," he said softly. "I'll find out what's going on."

She was doubtful that a cowboy, even a foreman, would be able to elicit more information than the patient's own family, but she smiled. "Thanks."

He turned and walked down the hall.

CHAPTER SEVEN

JOHN had money and power, and he knew how to use both. Within two minutes, he'd been ushered into the office of the hospital administrator. He explained who he was, why he was there, and asked for information. Even in Billings, the Callister empire was known. Five minutes later, he was speaking to the physician in charge of Sassy's mother's case. He accepted responsibility for the bill and asked if anything more could be done than was being done.

"Sadly, yes," the physician said curtly. "We're bound by the family's financial constraints. Mrs. Peale does have insurance, but she told us that they simply could not afford anything other than symptomatic relief for her. If she would consent, Mrs. Peale could have surgery to remove the cancerous lung and then radiation and chemotherapy to insure her recovery. In fact, she'd have a very good prognosis…"

"If money's all that's holding things up, I'll gladly be responsible for the bill. I don't care how much it is. So what are you waiting for?" John asked.

The physician smiled. "You'll speak to the financial officer?"

"Immediately," he replied.

"Then I'll speak to the patient."

"They don't know who I am," John told him. "That's the only condition, that you don't tell them. They think I'm the foreman of a ranch."

The older man frowned. "Is there a reason?"

"Originally, it was to insure that costs didn't escalate locally because the name was known," he said. "But by then, it was too late to change things. They're my friends," he added. "I don't want them to look at me differently."

"You think they would?"

"People see fame and money and power. They don't see people. Not at first."

The other man nodded. "I think I understand. I'll get the process underway. It's a very kind thing you're doing," he added. "Mrs. Peale would have died. Very soon, too."

"I know that. She's a good person."

"And very important to her little family, from what I've seen."

"Yes."

He clapped John on the shoulder. "We'll do everything possible."

"Thanks."

When he wrapped up things in the financial office, he strolled back down to the emergency room. Sassy was pacing the floor. Selene had curled up into a chair with her cheek pillowed on her arm. She was sound asleep.

Sassy met him, her eyes wide and fascinated. "What did you *do?*" she exclaimed. "They're going to operate on Mama! The doctor says they can save her life, that she can have radiation and chemotherapy, that there's a grant for poor people...she can live!"

Her voice broke into tears. John pulled her close and rocked her in his strong, warm arms, his mouth against her temple. "It's all right, honey," he said softly. "Don't cry."

"I'm just so happy," she choked at his chest. "So happy! I never knew there were such things as grants for this sort of thing, or I'd have done anything to find one! I thought...I thought we'd have to watch her die..."

"Never while there was a breath in my body," he whispered. His arms contracted. A wave of feeling rippled through him. He'd helped people in various ways all his life, but it was the first time he'd been able to make this sort of difference for someone he cared about. He'd grown fond of Mrs. Peale. But he'd thought that her case was hopeless. He thanked God that the emergency had forced Sassy to bring her mother here. What a wonderful near-tragedy. A link in a chain that would lead to a better life for all three of them.

She drew back, wiping her eyes again and laughing. "Sorry. I seem to spend my life crying. I'm just so grateful. What did you do?" she asked again.

He grinned. "I just asked wasn't there something they could figure out to do to help her. The doctor said he'd check, and he came up with the grant."

She shook her head. "It happened so fast. They've got some crackerjack surgeon who's teaching new techniques in cancer intervention here, and he's the one they're getting to operate on Mama. What's more, they're going to do it tomorrow. They already asked her, and she just almost jumped out of the bed she was so excited." She wiped away more tears. "We brought her up here to die," she explained. "And it was the most wonderful, scary experience we ever had. She's going to live, maybe long enough to see Selene graduate from college!"

He smiled down at her. "You know, I wouldn't be surprised at all if that's not the case. Feel better?"

She nodded. Her eyes adored him. "Thank you."

He chuckled. "Glad I could help." He glanced down at Selene, who was radiant. "Hear that? You'll have to go to college."

She grinned. "I want to be a doctor, now."

"There are scholarships that will help that dream come true, at the right time," he assured her.

Sassy pulled the young girl close. "We'll find lots," she promised.

"Thank you for helping save our mama," Selene told John solemnly. "We love her very much."

"She loves you very much," John replied. "That must be pretty nice, at your age."

He was saying something without saying it.

Sassy sent Selene to the vending machines for apple juice. While she was gone, Sassy turned to John. "What was your mother like when you were little?"

His face hardened. "I didn't have a mother when I was little," he replied curtly. "My brother and I were raised by our uncle."

She was shocked. "Were your parents still alive?"

"Yes. But they didn't want us."

"How horrible!"

He averted his eyes. "We had a rough upbringing. Until our uncle took us in, we were in—" he started to say boarding school, but that was a dead giveaway "—in a bad

situation at home," he amended. "Our uncle took us with
him and we grew up without a mother's influence."

"You still don't have anything to do with her? Or
your father?"

"We started seeing them again last year," he said
after a minute. "It's been hard. We built up resentments
and barriers. But we're all working on it. Years too late,"
he added on a cold laugh.

"I'm sorry," she told him. "Mama's been there for me
all my life. She's kissed my cuts and bruises, loved me,
fought battles for me... I don't know what I would have
done without her."

He drew in a long breath and looked down into
warm green eyes. "I would have loved having a
mother like her," he said honestly. "She's the most optimistic person I ever knew. In her condition, that
says a lot."

"I thought we'd be planning her funeral when we
came in here," Sassy said, still shell-shocked.

He touched her soft cheek gently. "I can understand that."

"How did you know where we were?" she asked
suddenly.

"I went into the feed store with a list and found
Buck holding down the fort," he said. "He said you
were up here."

"And you came right away," she said, amazed.

He put both big hands on her small waist and held
her in front of him. His blue eyes were solemn. "I never
planned to get mixed up with you," he told her honestly.
"Or your family. But I seem to be part of it."

She smiled. "Yes. You are a part of our family."

His hands contracted. "I just want to make the point that my interest isn't brotherly," he added.

The look in his eyes made her heartbeat accelerate. "Really?"

He smiled. "Really."

She felt as if she could fly. The expression on her face made him wish that they were in a more private place. He looked down to her full mouth and contemplated something shocking and potentially embarrassing.

Before he could act on what was certainly a crazy impulse, the doctor who'd admitted Mrs. Peale came walking up to them with a taller, darker man. He introduced himself and his companion.

"Miss Peale, this is Dr. Barton Crowley," he told Sassy. "He's going to operate on your mother first thing in the morning."

Sassy shook his hand warmly. "I'm so glad to meet you. We're just overwhelmed. We thought we'd brought Mama up here to die. It's a miracle! We never even knew there were grants for surgery!"

John shot a warning look at the doctor and the surgeon, who nodded curtly. The hospital administrator had already told them about the financial arrangements.

"We can always find a way to handle critical situations here," the doctor said with a smile. He nodded toward Dr. Crowley. "He's been teaching us new surgical techniques. It really was a miracle that he was here when you arrived. He works at Johns Hopkins, you see," he added.

Sassy didn't know what that meant.

John leaned down. "It's one of the more famous hospitals back East," he told her.

She laughed nervously. "Sorry," she told Dr. Crowley, who smiled. "I don't get out much."

"She works at our local feed store," John told them, beaming down at her. "She's the family's only support. She takes care of her mother and their six-year-old ward as well. She's quite a girl."

"Stop that," Sassy muttered shyly. "I'm not some paragon of virtue. I love my family."

His eyebrows arched and his eyes twinkled. "All of it?" he asked amusedly.

She flushed when she recalled naming him part of the family. She forced her attention back to the surgeon. "You really think you can help Mama? Our local doctor said the cancer was very advanced."

"It is, but preliminary tests indicate that it's confined to one lobe of her lung. If we can excise it, then follow up with chemotherapy and radiation, there's a good chance that we can at least prolong her life. We might save it altogether."

"Please do whatever you can," Sassy pleaded gently. "She means so much to us."

"She was very excited when I spoke with her," Dr. Crowley said with a smile. "She was concerned about her daughters, she told me, much more than with her own condition. A most unique lady."

"Yes, she is," Sassy agreed. "She's always putting other people's needs in front of her own. She raised me with hardly any help at all, and it was rough."

"From what I see, young woman," the surgeon replied, "she did a very good job."

"Thanks," she said, a little embarrassed.

"Well, we'll get her into surgery first thing. When we

see the extent of the cancerous tissue, we'll speak again. Try to get some rest."

"We will."

He and the doctor shook hands with John and walked back down the hall.

"I wish I'd packed a blanket or something," Sassy mused, eyeing the straight, lightly padded chairs in the distant waiting room. "I can sleep sitting up, but it gets cold in hospitals."

"Sitting up?" He didn't understand.

"Listen, you know how we're fixed," she said. "We can't afford a motel room. I always sleep in the waiting room when Mama's in the hospital." She nodded toward Selene, who was now asleep in the corner. "We both do it. Except Selene fits in these chairs a little better, because she's so small."

He was shocked. It was a firsthand look at how the rest of the world had to live. He hadn't realized that Sassy would have to stay at the hospital.

"Don't look like that," she said. "You make me uncomfortable. I don't mind being poor. I've got so many blessings that it's hard to count them."

"Blessings." He frowned, as if he wondered what they could possibly be.

"I have a mother who sacrificed to raise me, who loves me with her whole heart. I have a little sort-of sister who thinks I'm Joan of Arc. I have a roof over my head, food to eat, and, thanks to you, a really good job with no harassment tied to it. I even have a vehicle that gets me to and from work most of the time."

"I wouldn't call that vehicle a blessing," he observed.

"Neither would I, if I could afford that fancy truck

you drive," she chided, grinning. "The point is, I have things that a lot of other people don't. I'm happy," she added, curious about his expression.

She had nothing. Literally nothing. But she could count her blessings as if they made her richer than a princess. He had everything, but his life was empty. All the wealth and power he commanded hadn't made him happy. He was alone. He had Gil and his family, and his parents. But in a very personal sense, he was by himself.

"You're thinking that you don't really have a family of your own," Sassy guessed from his glum expression. "But you do. You have me, and Mama, and Selene. We're your family." She hesitated, because he looked hunted. She flushed. "I know we're not much to brag about…"

His arm shot out and pulled her to him. "Don't run yourself down. I've never counted my friends by their bank books. Character is far more important."

She relaxed. But only a little. He was very close, and her heart was racing.

"You suit me just the way you are," he said gently. He bent and kissed her, tenderly, before he let her go and walked toward Selene.

"What are you doing?" she exclaimed when he lifted the sleeping child in his arms and started toward the exit.

"I'm taking baby sister here to a modest guest room for the night. You can come, too."

She blinked. "John, I can't afford—"

"If I hear that one more time," he interrupted, "I'm going to say bad words. You don't want me to say bad words in front of the child. Do you?"

She was asleep and wouldn't hear them, but he

was making a point and being noble. She gave in, smiling. "Okay. But you have to dock my wages for it or I'll stay here and Selene can just hear you spout bad words."

He smiled over Selene's head on his chest. "Okay, honey."

The word brought a soft blush into Sassy's cheeks and he chuckled softly. He led the way out the door to his truck.

John's idea of a modest guest room was horrifying to Sassy when he stopped by the desk of Billings's best hotel to check in Sassy and Selene.

The child stirred sleepily in John's strong arms. She opened her eyes, yawning. "Mama?" she exclaimed, worried.

"She's fine," John assured her. "Go back to sleep, baby. Curl up in this chair until I get the formalities done, okay?" He placed her gently into a big, cushy armchair near the desk.

"Okay, John," Selene said, smiling as she closed her eyes and nodded off again.

"You'd better stay with her while I do this," John told Sassy, not wanting her to hear the clerk when he gave her his real name to pay for the room.

"Okay, John," she echoed her little sister, with a grin.

He winked at her and went back to the desk. The smile faded as he spoke to the male clerk.

"Their mother is in the hospital, about to have cancer surgery. They were going to sleep in the waiting room. I want a room for them, near mine, if it's possible."

The clerk, a kindly young man, smiled sympathetically. "There's one adjoining yours, Mr. Callister," he said politely. "It's a double. Would that do?"

"Yes."

The clerk made the arrangements, took John's credit card, processed the transaction, handed back the card, and then went to program the card-key for the new guests. He was back in no time, very efficient.

"I hope their mother does all right," he told John.

"So do I. But she's in very good hands."

He went back to Selene, lifted her gently, and motioned to Sassy, who was examining the glass coffee table beside the chairs.

She paused at a pillar as they walked into the elevator. "Gosh, this looks like real marble," she murmured, and then had to run to make it before the elevator doors closed. "John, this place looks expensive…"

"I'll make sure to tell Buck to dock your salary over several months, okay?" he asked gently, and he smiled.

She was apprehensive. It was going to be a big chunk of her income. But he'd already been so nice that she felt guilty for even making a fuss. "Sure, that's fine."

He led them down the hall and gave Sassy the card-key to insert in the lock. She stared at it.

"Why are you giving me a credit card?" she asked in all honesty.

He gaped at her. "It's the door key."

She cocked an eyebrow. "Right." She looked up at him as if she expected men with white nets to appear.

He laughed when he realized she hadn't a clue about modern technology. "Give it here."

He balanced Selene on one lifted knee, inserted the

card, jerked it back out so the green light on the lock blinked, and then opened the door.

Sassy's jaw dropped.

"It's a card-key," he repeated, leading the way in.

Sassy closed the door behind them, turning on the lights as she went. The room was a revelation. There was a huge new double bed—two of them, in fact. There were paintings on the wall. There was a round table with two chairs. There was a telephone. There was a huge glass window, curtained, that looked out over Billings. There was even a huge television.

"This is a palace," Sassy murmured, spellbound as she looked around. She peered into the bathroom and actually gasped. "There's a hair dryer right here in the room!" she exclaimed.

John had put Selene down gently on one of the double beds. He felt two inches high. Sassy's life had been spent in a small rural town in abject poverty. She knew nothing of high living. Even this hotel, nice but not the five-star accommodation he'd frequented in his travels both in this country and overseas, was opulent to her. Considering where, and how, she and her family lived, this must have seemed like kingly extravagance.

He walked back to the bathroom and leaned against the door facing while she explored tiny wrapped packets of soap and little bottles of shampoo and soap.

"Wow," she whispered.

She touched the thick white towels, so plush that she wanted to wrap up in one. She compared them to her thin, tatty, worn towels at home and was shocked at the contrast. She glanced at John shyly.

"Sorry," she said. "I'm not used to this sort of place."

"It's just a hotel, Sassy," he said softly. "If you've never stayed in one, I imagine it's surprising at first."

"How did you know?" she asked.

"Know what?"

"That I'd never stayed in a hotel?"

He cleared his throat. "Well, it shows. Sort of."

She flushed. "You mean, I'm acting like an idiot."

"I mean nothing of the sort." He shouldered away from the door facing, caught her by the waist, pulled her close, and bent to kiss the breath out of her.

She held on tight, relieved about her mother, but worried about the surgery, and grateful for John's intervention.

"You've made miracles for us," she said when he let her go.

He searched her shimmering green eyes. "You've made one for me," he replied, and he wasn't kidding.

"I have? How?"

His hands contracted on her small waist. "Let's just say, you've taught me about the value of small blessings. I tend to take things for granted, I guess." His eyes narrowed. "You appreciate the most basic things in life. You're so...optimistic, Sassy," he added. "You make me feel humble."

"Oh, that's rich," she chuckled. "A backwoods hick like me making a sophisticated gentleman like you feel humble."

"I'm not kidding," he replied. "You don't have a lot of material things. But you're happy without them." He shrugged. "I've got a lot more than you have, and I'm..." He searched for the word, frowning. "I'm... empty," he said finally, meeting her quiet eyes.

"But you're the kindest man I've ever known," she argued. "You do things for people without even thinking twice what problems you may cause yourself in the process. You're a good person."

Her wide-eyed fascination made him tingle inside. In recent years, women had wanted him because he was rich and powerful. Here was one who wanted him because he was kind. It was an eye-opener.

"You look strange," she remarked.

"I was thinking," he said.

"About what?"

"About how late it is, and how much you're going to need some sleep. We'll get an early start tomorrow," he told her.

The horror came back, full force. The joy drained out of her face, to be replaced with fear and uncertainty.

He drew her close and rocked her in his arms, bending his head over hers. "That surgeon is rather famous," he said conversationally. "He's one of the best oncologists in the country, and it's a blessing that he ended up here just when your mother needed him. You have to believe that she's going to be all right."

"I'm trying to," she said. "It's just hard. We've had so many trips to the hospital," she confessed, and sounded weary.

John had never had to go through this with his family. Well, there was Gil's first wife who died in a riding accident. That had been traumatic. But since then, John had never worried about losing a relative to disease. He had, he decided, been very lucky.

"I'll be right there with you," he promised her. "All the time."

She drew back and looked up at him with fascinated eyes. "You will? You mean it? Won't you get in trouble with your boss?"

"I won't," he said. "But it wouldn't matter if I did. I'm not leaving you. Not for anything."

She colored and smiled at him.

"After all," he teased, "I'm a member of the family."

She smiled even more.

"Kissing kin," he added, and bent to brush a whisper of a kiss over her soft mouth. He forced himself to step away from her. "Go to bed."

"Okay. Thanks, John. Thanks for everything."

He didn't answer her. He just winked.

The surgery took several hours. Sassy bit her fingernails off into the quick. Selene sat very close to her, holding her hand.

"I don't want Mama to die," she said.

Sassy pulled her close. "She won't die," she promised. "She's going to get better. I promise." She prayed it wasn't going to be a lie.

John had gone to check with the surgical desk. He came back grinning.

"Tell me!" Sassy exclaimed.

"They were able to get all the cancerous tissue," he said. "It was confined to a lobe of her lung, as he suspected. They're cautiously optimistic that your mother will recover and begin to lead a full life again."

"Oh, my goodness!" Sassy exclaimed, hugging Selene close. "She'll get better!"

Selene hugged her back. "I'm so happy!"

"So am I."

Sassy let her go, got up, and went to hug John close, laying her cheek against his broad, warm chest. He enveloped her in his arms. She felt right at home there.

"Thank you," she murmured.

"For what?"

She looked up at him. "For everything."

He smiled at her, his eyes crinkling.

"What happens now?" she asked.

"Your mother recovers enough to go home, then we bring her back up here for the treatments. Dr. Crowley said that would take a few weeks, but except for some nausea and weakness, she should manage it very well."

"You'll come with us?" she asked, amazed.

He glowered at her. "Of course I will," he said indignantly. "I'm part of the family. You said so."

She drew in a long, contented breath. She was tired and worried but she felt newborn. "You're the nicest man I've ever known," she said.

He cocked an eyebrow. "Nicer than the Army guy?"

She smiled. "Even nicer than Caleb."

He looked over her head and glowered even more. "Speak of the devil!"

A tall, dark-haired man in an Army uniform was striding down the hall toward them.

CHAPTER EIGHT

SASSY turned and, sure enough, Caleb was walking toward them in his Army uniform, complete with combat boots and beret. He looked very handsome.

"Caleb," Sassy said warmly, going to meet him. "How did you know we were here?"

He hugged her gently. "I have a cousin who works here. She remembered that I'd been down to see you in Hollister, and that your last name was Peale. How is your mother?"

"She just came out of surgery. Her prognosis is good. John found us a grant to pay for it all, isn't that incredible? I didn't know they had programs like that!"

Caleb knew they didn't. He looked at John and, despite the older man's foreboding expression, he smiled at him. He was quick enough to realize that John had intervened for Sassy's mother and didn't want anybody to know. "Yes, they do have grants, don't they? Nice of you to do that for them," he added, his dark eyes saying things to John that Sassy didn't see.

John relaxed a little. The boy might be competition, but his heart was in the right place. Sassy had said he was a friend, but Caleb here must care about her, to come right to the hospital when he knew about her mother. "They're a great bunch of people," he said simply.

"Yes, they are," Caleb agreed. He turned to smile down at Sassy while John fumed silently.

"Thank you for coming to see us," Sassy told the younger man.

"I wish I could stay," he told her, "but I'm on my way to the rimrocks right now. I'm due back at my assignment."

"The rimrocks?" Sassy asked, frowning.

"It's where the airport is," Caleb told her, grinning. "That's what we call it locally."

"I hope you have a safe flight back," she told him. "And a safe tour of duty."

"Now, that makes two of us," he agreed. "Don't forget to send me that photograph."

"I won't. So long, Caleb."

"So long." He bent and kissed her cheek, smiled ruefully at John, and walked back down the hall.

"What photograph?" John asked belligerently.

"It's not for him," she said, delighted that he looked jealous. "It's to throw his best friend off the track."

John was unconvinced. But just as he started to argue, the surgeon came into the waiting room, smiling wearily.

He shook hands with John and turned to Sassy. "Your mother is doing very well. She's in recovery right now, and then she'll go to the intensive care unit. Just for a couple of days," he added quickly when Sassy went pale and looked faint. "It's normal procedure. We want her watched day and night until she's stabilized."

"Can Selene and I see her?" Sassy asked. "And John?" she added, nodding to the man at her side.

The surgeon hesitated. "Have you ever seen anyone just out of surgery, young woman?" he asked gently.

"Well, there was Great-Uncle Jack, but I only got a glimpse of him...why?"

The surgeon looked apprehensive. "Post surgical patients are flour-white. They have tubes running out of them, they're connected to machines...it can be alarming if you aren't prepared for it."

"Mama's going to live, thanks to you," Sassy said, smiling. "She'll look beautiful. I don't mind the machines. They're helping her live. Right?"

The surgeon smiled back. Her optimism was contagious. "Right. I'll let you in to see her for five minutes, no longer," he said, "as soon as we move her into intensive care. It will be a little while," he added.

"We're not going anywhere," she replied easily.

He chuckled. "I'll send a nurse for you, when it's time."

"Thank you," Sassy said. "From the bottom of my heart."

The surgeon shifted. "It's what I do," he replied. "The most rewarding job in the world."

"I've never saved anybody's life, but I expect it would be a great job," she told him.

After he left, John gave her a wry look.

"I saved a man's life, once," he told her.

"You did? How?" she asked, waiting.

"I threw a baseball bat at him, and missed."

"Oh, you," she teased. She went close to him, wrapped her arms around him, and laid her head on his broad chest. "You're just wonderful."

His hand smoothed over her dark hair. Over her head, Selene was smiling at him with the same kind of happy, affectionate expression that he imagined was on Sassy's face. Despite the fear and apprehension of the ordeal, it was one of the best days of his life. He'd never felt so necessary.

Sassy was allowed into the intensive care unit just long enough to look at her mother and stand beside her. John was with her, the surgeon's whispered request getting him past the fiercely protective nurse in charge of the unit. Sassy was uneasy, despite her assurances, and she clung to John's hand as if she were afraid of falling without its warm support.

She stared at the still, white form in the hospital bed. Machines beeped. A breathing machine made odd noises as it pumped oxygen into Mrs. Peale's unconscious body. The shapeless, faded hospital gown was unfamiliar, like all the monitors and tubes that seemed to extrude from every inch of her mother's flesh. Mrs. Peale was white as a sheet. Her chest rose and fell very slowly. Her heartbeat was visible as the gown fluttered over her ample bosom.

"She's alive," John whispered. "She's going to get well and go home and be a different woman. You have to see the future, through the present."

Sassy looked up at him with tears in her eyes. "It's just...I love her so much."

He smiled tenderly and bent to kiss her forehead. "She loves you, too, honey. She's going to get well."

She drew in a shaky breath and got control of her emotions. She wiped at the tears. "Yes." She moved closer to the bed, bending over her mother. She remembered that when she was a little girl she'd had a debilitating virus that had almost dehydrated her. Mrs. Peale had perched on her bed, feeding her ice chips around the clock to keep fluids in her. She'd fetched wet cloths and whispered that she loved Sassy, that everything was going to be all right. That loving touch had chased the fear and misery and sickness right out of the room. Mrs. Peale seemed to glow with it.

"It's going to be all right, Mama," she whispered, kissing the pale, cool brow. "We love you very much. We're going home, very soon."

Mrs. Peale didn't answer her, but her hand on its confining board jumped, almost imperceptibly.

John squeezed Sassy's hand. "Did you see that?" he asked, smiling. "She heard you."

Sassy squeezed back. "Of course she did."

Three days later, Mrs. Peale was propped up in bed eating Jell-O. She was weak and sore and still in a lot of pain, but she was smiling gamely.

"Didn't I tell you?" John chided Sassy. "She's too tough to let a little thing like major surgery get her down."

Mrs. Peale smiled at him. "You've been so kind to us, John," she said. Her voice was still a little hoarse from the breathing tubes, but she sounded cheerful just the same. "Sassy told me all about the palace you're keeping her and Selene in."

"Some palace," he chuckled. "It's just a place to sleep." He stuck his hands into his jeans and his eyes twinkled. "But being kind goes with the job. I'm part of the family. She—" he pointed at Sassy "—said so."

"I did," Sassy confessed.

Mrs. Peale gave him a wry look. "But not too close a member…?"

"Definitely not," he agreed at once, chuckling. He looked at Sassy in a way that made her blush. Then he compounded the embarrassment by laughing.

In the weeks that followed, John divided his time between Mrs. Peale's treatments in Billings and the growing responsibility for the new ranch that was just beginning to shape up. The barn was up, shiny and attractive with bricked aisles and spotless stalls with metal gates. The corral had white fences interlaced with hidden electrical fencing that complemented the cosmetic look of the wood. The pastures had been sowed with old prairie grasses, with which John was experimenting. The price of corn had gone through the roof, with the biofuel revolution. Ranchers were scrambling for new means of sustaining their herds, so native grasses were being utilized, along with concentrated pelleted feeds and vitamin supplements. John had also hired a nearby farmer to plant grains for him and keep them during the growing season. His contractor was building a huge new concrete feed silo to house the grains when they were harvested at the end of summer. It was a monumental job, getting the place renovated. John had delegated as much authority as he could, but there were still management decisions that had to be made by him.

Meanwhile, Bill Tarleton's trial went on the docket and pretrial investigations were going on by both the county district attorney and the public defender's office for the judicial circuit where Hollister was located. Sassy was interviewed by both sides. The questions made her very nervous and uneasy. The public defender seemed to think she'd enticed Mr. Tarleton to approach her in a sexual manner. It hurt her feelings.

She told John about it when he stopped by after supper one Friday evening to check on Mrs. Peale. He hadn't been into the feed store the entire week because of obligations out at the ranch.

"He'll make me sound like some cheap tart in court," she moaned. "It will make my mother and Selene look bad, too."

"Telling the truth won't make anyone look bad, dear," Mrs. Peale protested. She was sitting up in the living room knitting. A knitted cap covered her head. Her hair had already started to fall out from the radiation therapy she was receiving, but she hadn't let it get her down. She'd made a dozen caps in different colors and styles and seemed to be enjoying the project.

"You should listen to your mother," John agreed, smiling. "You don't want him to get away with it, Sassy. It wasn't your fault."

"That lawyer made it sound like it was. The assistant district attorney who questioned me asked what sort of clothes I wore to work, and I told him jeans and T-shirts, and not any low-cut ones, either. He smiled and said that it shouldn't have mattered if I'd worn a bikini. He said Mr. Tarleton had no business making me uncomfortable in my workplace, regardless of my clothing."

"I like that assistant district attorney," John said. "He's a firecracker. One day he'll end up in the state attorney general's office. They say he's got a perfect record of convictions in the two years he's prosecuted cases for this judicial circuit."

"I hope he makes Mr. Tarleton as uncomfortable as that public defender made me," Sassy said with feeling. She rubbed her bare arms, as if it chilled her, thinking about the trial. "I don't know how I'll manage, sitting in front of a jury and telling what happened."

"You just remember that the people in that jury will most likely be people who've known you all your life," Mrs. Peale interrupted.

"That's the other thing," Sassy sighed. "The D.A.'s victim assistance person said the defending attorney is trying to get the trial moved to Billings, on account of Mr. Tarleton can't get a fair trial here."

John frowned. That did put another face on things. But he'd testify, as would Sassy. Hopefully Tarleton would get what he deserved. John knew for a fact that if he hadn't intervened, it would have been much more than a minor assault. Sassy knew it, too.

"It was a bad day for Hollister when that man came to town," Mrs. Peale said curtly. "Sassy came home every day upset and miserable."

"You should have called the owner and complained," John told Sassy.

She grimaced. "I didn't dare. He didn't know me that well. I was afraid he'd think I was telling tales on Mr. Tarleton because I wanted his job."

"It's been done," John had to admit. "But you're not like that, Sassy. He'd have investigated and found that out."

She sighed. "It's water under the bridge now," she replied sadly. "I know it's the right thing to do, taking him to court. But what if he gets off and comes after me, or Mama or Selene for revenge?" she added, worried.

"If he does," John said, and his blue eyes glittered

dangerously, "it will be the worst decision of his life. I promise you. As for getting off, if by some miracle he does, you'll file a civil suit against him for damages and I'll bankroll you."

"I knew you were a nice man from the first time I laid eyes on you," Mrs. Peale chuckled.

Sassy was smiling at him with her whole face. She felt warm and protected and secure. She blushed when he looked back, with such an intent, piercing expression that her heart turned over.

"Why does life have to be so complicated?" Sassy asked after a minute.

John shrugged. "Beats me, honey," he said, getting to his feet and obviously unaware of the endearment that brought another soft blush to Sassy's face. "But it does seem to get more that way by the day." He checked his watch and grimaced. "I have to get back to the ranch. I've got an important call coming through. But I'll stop by tomorrow. We might take in a movie, if you're game."

Sassy grinned. "I'd love to." She looked at her mother and hesitated.

"I have a phone," her mother pointed out. "And Selene's here."

"You went out with the Army guy and didn't make a fuss," John muttered.

Mrs. Peale beamed. That was jealousy. Sassy seemed to realize it, too, because her eyes lit up.

"I'm not making a fuss," Sassy assured him. "And I love going to the movies."

John relented a little and grinned self-consciously. "Okay. I'll be along about six. That Chinese restaurant that just opened has good food—suppose I bring some along and we'll have supper before we go?"

They hesitated to accept. He'd done so much for them already...

"It's Chinese food, not precious jewels," he said. "Would you like to go out and look at my truck again? I make a handsome salary and I don't drink, smoke, gamble or run around with predatory women!"

Now Mrs. Peale and Sassy both looked sheepish and grinned.

"Okay," Sassy said. "But when I get rich and famous one day for my stock-clerking abilities, I'm paying you back for all of it."

He laughed. "That's a deal."

The Chinese food was a huge assortment of dishes, many of which could be stored in the refrigerator and provide meals for the weekend for the women and the child. They knew what he'd done, but they didn't complain again. He was bighearted and he wanted to help them. It seemed petty to argue.

After they ate, he helped Sassy up into the cab of the big pickup truck, got in himself, and drove off down the road. It was still light outside, but the sun was setting in brilliant colors. It was like a symphony of reds and oranges and yellows, against the silhouetted mountains in the distance.

"It's so beautiful here," Sassy said, watching the sunset. "I'd never want to live anyplace else."

He glanced at her. He was homesick for Medicine Ridge from time to time, but he liked Hollister, too. It was a small, homey place with nice people and plenty of wide-open country. The elbow room was delightful. You could drive for miles and not meet another car or even see a house.

"Are we going to the theater in town?" she asked John.

He grinned like a boy. "We are not," he told her. "I found a drive-in theater just outside the city limits. The owner started it up about a month ago. He said he'd gone to them when he was young and thought it was time to bring them back. I don't know that he'll be able to stay open long, but I thought we'd check it out, anyway."

"Wow," she exclaimed. "I've read about them in novels."

"Me, too, but I've never been to one. Our uncle used to talk about them."

"Is it in a town?" she asked.

"No. It's in the middle of a cowpasture. Cattle graze nearby."

She laughed delightedly. "You're watching a movie with the windows open and a cow sticks its head into the car with you," she guessed.

"I wouldn't be surprised."

"I like cows," she sighed. "I wouldn't mind."

"He runs beef cattle. Steers."

She looked at him. "Steers?"

"It's a bull with missing equipment," he told her, tongue-in-cheek.

"Then what's a cow?"

"It's a cow, if it's had calves. If it hasn't, it's a heifer."

"You know a lot about cattle."

"I've worked around them all my life," he said comfortably. "I love animals. We're going to have horses out at the ranch, too. You can come riding and bring Selene, any time you want."

"You'd have to teach Selene," she said. "She's never been on a horse and you'd have to coach me. It's been a long time since I've been riding."

He glanced at her with warm eyes. "I'd love that."

She laughed. "Me, too."

The drive-in was in a cleared pasture about a quarter of a mile off the main highway. There was a marquee, which listed the movie playing, this time a science-fiction one about a space freighter and its courageous crew which was fighting a technological empire that ran the inner planets of the solar system where it operated. They drove through a tree-lined dirt road down to the cleared pasture. There was room for about twenty cars, and six were already occupying one of three slight inclines that faced a huge blank screen. Each space had a pole, which contained two speakers, one for cars on either side of it. At the ticket stand, which was a drive-through affair manned by a teenager who looked like the owner John had already met, most likely his son, John paid for their tickets.

He pulled the truck up into an unoccupied space and cut off the engine, looking around amusedly. "The only thing missing is a concession stand with drinks and pizza and a rest room," he mused. "Maybe he'll add that, later, if the drive-in catches on."

"It's nice out here, without all that," she mused, looking around.

"Yes, it is." He powered down both windows and brought the speaker in on his side of the truck. He turned up the volume just as the screen lit up with welcome messages and previews of coming attractions.

"This is great!" Sassy laughed.

"It is, isn't it?"

He tossed his hat into the small back seat of the double-cabbed truck, unfastened his seat belt, and stretched out. As an afterthought, he unfastened Sassy's belt and drew her into the space beside him, with his long arm behind her back and his cheek resting on her soft hair.

"Isn't that better?" he murmured, smiling.

One small hand went to press against his shirtfront as she curled closer with a sigh. "It's much better."

The first part of the movie was hilarious. But before it ended, they weren't watching anymore. John had looked down at Sassy's animated face in the flickering light from the movie screen and longing had grown in him like a hot tide. It had been a while since he'd felt Sassy's soft mouth under his lips and he was hungry for it. Since he'd known her, he hadn't had the slightest interest in other women. It was only Sassy.

He tugged on her hair so that she lifted her face to his. "Is this all you'll ever want, Sassy?" he asked gently. "Living in a small, rural town and working in a feed store? Will you miss knowing what it's like to go to college or work in a big city and meet sophisticated people?" he asked solemnly.

Her soft eyes searched his. "Why would I want to do that?" she asked with genuine interest.

"You're very young," he said grimly. "This is all you know."

"Mr. Barber, who runs the Ford dealership here, was born in Hollister and has never been outside the county in his whole life," she told him. "He's been married to Miss Jane since he was eighteen and she was sixteen. They have five sons."

He frowned. "Are you saying something?"

"I'm telling you that this is how people live here," she said simply. "We don't have extravagant tastes. We're country people. We're family. We get married. We have kids. We grow old watching our grandchildren grow up. Then we die. We're buried here. We have beautiful country where we can walk in the forest or ride through fields full of growing crops, or pass through pastures where cattle and horses graze. We have clear, unpolluted streams and blue skies. We sit on the porch after dark and listen to the crickets in the summer and watch lightning bugs flash green in the trees. If someone gets sick, neighbors come over to help. If someone dies, they bring food and comfort. Nobody in trouble is ever ignored. We have everything we need and want and love, right here in Hollister." She cocked her head. "What can a city offer us that would match that?"

He stared at her without speaking. He'd never heard it put exactly that way. He loved Medicine Ridge. But he'd been in college back East, and he'd traveled all over the world. He had choices. Sassy had never had the chance to make one. On the other hand, she sounded very mature as she recounted the reasons she was happy where she lived. There were people in John's acquaintance who'd never known who they were or where they belonged.

"What are you thinking?" she asked.

"That you're an old soul in a young body," he said.

She laughed. "My mother says that all the time."

"She's right. You have a profound grasp of life. So

you're happy living here. What if you had a scholarship and you could go to college and study anything you liked?"

"Who'd take care of Mama and Selene?" she asked softly.

"Most women would be more interested in a career than being tied down to family responsibilities in this day and age."

"I've noticed," she sighed. "They interviewed this career woman on the news one night," she continued. "She'd moved to three different cities in a year, looking for a job where she felt fulfilled. She was divorced and had an eight-year-old son. I wonder how he enjoyed being in three different schools in one year so that she could feel fulfilled?"

He frowned. "Kids adjust."

"Of course they do," she replied. "Mostly they adjust to having one parent, because so many people divorce, or they adjust to being suddenly part of somebody else's family. They adjust to parents who work all the time and are too tired to play or talk to them after school. They're encouraged to participate in all sorts of after-school activities as well, so they have baseball and football and soccer and band and theater and all those time-consuming responsibilities when they're not studying." She settled closer to John. "So exactly when do parents have time to get to know their kids? Everybody's so busy these days. I've read that some kids have to text-message their parents and make appointments to meet. And they wonder why kids are so screwed up."

He sighed. "I guess my brother and I were protected from a lot of that. Our uncle kept us close on the ranch. We played sports, but we were confined to one, and we had chores every day that had to be done. We didn't have cell phones or cars, and we mostly stayed at home until he thought we were old enough to drive. We always ate together and most nights we played board games or went outside with the telescopes to learn about the stars. He wasn't big on school activities, either. He said they were a corrupting influence, because we had city kids in our school with what he called outrageous ideas of morality."

She laughed. "That's what Mama called some of the kids at my school." She grimaced. "I guess I've been very sheltered. I do have a cell phone, but I don't know how to do text-messages."

"I'll teach you," he told her, smiling. "I do it a lot."

"I guess your phone does stuff besides just making calls."

"I have the Internet, movies, music, sports, and e-mail on mine," he told her.

"Wow. Mine just gets phone calls."

He laughed. She was so out of touch. But he loved her that way. The smile faded as he looked down into her soft, melting eyes. He dropped his gaze to her mouth, faintly pink, barely parted.

"I suppose the future doesn't come with guarantees," he said to himself. He bent slowly. "I've been sitting here for five minutes remembering how your soft lips felt under my mouth, Sassy," he whispered as his parted lips met hers. "I ache like a boy for you."

As he spoke, he drew her across the seat, across his lap, and kissed her with slow, building hunger. His big hand deftly moved buttons out of buttonholes and slid right inside her bra with a mastery that left her breathless and too excited to protest.

He caressed the hard tip with slow, teasing movements while he fed on her mouth, teasing it, too, with slow, brief contacts that eventually made her moan and arch up toward him.

Her skin felt hot. She ached to have him take off her blouse and everything under it and look at her. She wanted to feel his lips swallowing that hard-tipped softness. It was madness. She could hear her own heartbeat, feel the growing desire that built inside her untried body. She'd never wanted a man before. Now she wanted him with a reckless abandon that blasted every sane reason for protest right out of her melting body.

John lifted his head, frustrated, and glanced around him in the darkness. The scene on the screen was subdued and so was the lighting. Nobody could see them. He bent his head again and, unobtrusively, suddenly stripped Sassy's blouse and bra up to her chin. His blazing eyes found her breasts, adored them. He shivered with need.

She arched faintly, encouraging him. He bent to her breasts and slowly drew one of them right inside his mouth, pulling at it gently as his tongue explored the hardness and drew a harsh moan from her lips.

The sound galvanized him. His mouth became rough. The arm behind her was like steel. His free hand slid down her bare belly and right into the opening of her jeans. He was so aroused that he didn't even realize where they were.

At least, he didn't realize it until something wet and rubbery slid over his bent head through the passenger window.

It took him a minute to realize it wasn't, couldn't be,

Sassy's mouth. It was very wet. He forced his own head up and looked toward Sassy's window. A very large bovine head was inside the open window of the truck. It was licking him.

CHAPTER NINE

"S<small>ASSY</small>?" he asked, his voice hoarse with lingering passion.

She opened her eyes. "What?"

"Look out your window."

She turned her head and met the steer's eyes. "Aaaah!" she exclaimed.

He burst out laughing. He smoothed down her blouse and bra and sat up, his hand going gingerly to his hair. "Good Lord! I wondered why my hair felt so wet."

She fumbled her bra back on, embarrassed and amused at the same time. The little steer had moved back from the window, but it was still curious. It let out a loud "MOOOO." Muffled laughter came from a nearby car.

"Well, so much for my great idea that this was a good place to make out," John chuckled, straightening his shirt with a sigh. "I guess it wasn't a bad thing to get interrupted," he added, with a rueful smile at Sassy's red face. "Things were getting a little intense."

He didn't seem to be embarrassed at all, but Sassy had never gone so far with a man before and she felt fragile. She was uneasy that she hadn't denied him such intimate access to her body. And she couldn't forget where his other hand had been moving when the steer came along.

"Don't," John said softly when he read her expression. His fingers caught hers and linked into them. "It was perfectly natural."

"I guess you…do that all the time," she stammered.

He shrugged. "I used to. But since I met you, I haven't wanted to do it with anyone else."

If it was a line, it sounded sincere. She looked at him with growing hope. "Really?"

His fingers tightened on hers. "We've been through a lot of intense situations together in a little bit of time. Tarleton's assault. Your mother's close call. The cancer treatments." He looked into her eyes. "You said that I was like part of your family and that's how I feel, too. I'm at home when I'm with you." He looked down at their linked hands. "I want it to go on," he said hesitantly. "I want us to be together. I want you in my life from now on." He drew in a long breath. "I ache to have you."

She was uncomfortable with the way he said it, not understanding that he'd never tried to make a commitment to another woman in his life; not even when he was intimate with other women.

"You want to sleep with me," she said bluntly.

He smoothed his thumb over her cold fingers. "I want to do everything with you," he replied. "You're too young," he added quietly. "But, then, my brother just married a woman ten years his junior and they're ecstatically happy. It can work. I guess it depends on the woman, and we've already agreed that you're mature for your age."

"You aren't exactly over the hill, John," she replied,

still curious about what he was suggesting. "And you're very attractive." She gave him a gamine look. "Even small hoofed animals are drawn to you."

He glared at her.

"Don't look at me," she laughed. "It was you that the little steer was kissing."

He touched his wet hair and winced. "God knows where his mouth has been."

She laughed again. "Well, at least he has good taste."

"Thanks. I think." He pulled a red work rag from the console and dried his hair where the steer had licked it. He was watching Sassy. "You don't understand what I'm saying, do you?"

"Not really," she confessed.

"I suppose I'm making a hash of it," he muttered. "But I've never done this before."

"Asked someone to live with you, you mean," she said haltingly.

He met her eyes evenly. "Asked someone to marry me, Sassy."

She just stared. For a minute, she wasn't sure she wasn't dreaming. But his gaze was intent, intimate. He was waiting.

She let out the breath she'd been holding. She started to speak and then stopped, confused. "I…"

"If you've noticed any bad habits that disturb you, I'll try to change them," he mused, smiling, because she wasn't refusing.

"Oh, no, it's not that. I…I have a lot of baggage," she began nervously.

Then he remembered what she told him some time back, that her infrequent dates had said they didn't want to get involved with a woman who had so much responsibility for her family.

He grinned. "I love your baggage," he said. "Your mother and adopted sister are like part of my family already." He shrugged. "So I'll have more dependents." He gave her a wicked look. "Income tax time won't be so threatening."

She laughed out loud. He wasn't intimidated. He didn't mind. She threw her arms around him and kissed him so fervently that he forgot what they'd been talking about and just kissed her back until they had to come up for air.

"But I'll still work," she promised breathlessly, her eyes sparkling like fireworks. "I'm not going to sit down and make you support all three of us, I'll carry my part of the load!" She laughed, unaware of his sudden stillness, of the guilty look on his face. "It will be fun, making our way together. Hard times are what bring people close, you know, even more than the good times."

"Sassy, there are some things we're going to have to talk about," he said slowly.

"A lot of things," she agreed dreamily, laying her cheek against his broad, warm chest. "I never dreamed you might want to marry me. I'll try to be the best wife in the world. I'll cook and clean and work my fingers to the bone. I like horses and cattle. I'll help you with chores on the ranch, too."

She was cutting his heart open and she didn't know it. He'd lied to her. He hadn't thought of the consequences. He should have been honest with her from the beginning. But he realized then that she'd never have come near him if he'd walked into that feed store in his real persona. The young woman who worshipped the lowly cattle foreman would draw back and stand in awe of the wealthy cattle baron who could walk into a store and buy anything he fancied without even looking at a price tag. It was a sickening thought. She was going to feel betrayed, at best. At worst, she might think he was playing some game with her.

He smoothed his hand over her soft hair. "Well, it can wait another day," he murmured as he kissed her forehead. "There's plenty of time for serious discussions." He tilted her mouth up to his. "Tonight, we're just engaged and celebrating. Come here."

By the time they got back to her house, they were both disheveled and their mouths were swollen. Sassy had never been so happy in her life.

John had consoled himself that he still had time to tell Sassy the truth. He had no way of knowing that Bill Tarleton and his attorney had just gone before the district circuit judge in the courthouse in Billings for a hearing on a motion to dismiss all charges against him. The reason behind the motion, the attorney stated, was that the eyewitness who was to testify against Tarleton was romantically involved with the so-called victim and was, in fact, no common cowboy, but a wealthy cattleman from Medicine Ridge. The defense argued that this new information changed the nature of the accusation from a crime to an act of jealousy. It was a rich man victimizing a poor man because he was jealous of the man's attentions to his girlfriend.

The state attorney, who was also present at the hearing, argued that the new information made no difference to the primary charge, which was one of sexual assault and battery. A local doctor would testify to the young lady's physical condition after the assault. The public defender argued that he'd seen the doctor's report and it only mentioned reddish marks and bruising, on the young lady's arms, nothing more. That could not be construed as injury sustained in the course of a sexual assault, so only the alleged assault charge was even remotely applicable.

The judge took the case under advisement and promised a decision within the week. Meanwhile, the assistant district attorney handling the case in circuit court, showed up at Sassy's home the following Monday evening soon after Sassy had put Selene to bed to discuss the case. His name was James Addy.

"Mr. Tarleton is alleging that Mr. Callister inflated the charges out of jealousy because of the attention Mr. Tarleton was paying you," Addy said in a businesslike tone, opening his briefcase on the dining room table while Sassy sat gaping at him.

"Mr. Callister? Who is that?" she asked, confused. "John Taggert rescued me. Mr. Tarleton kissed me and was trying to force me down on the floor. I screamed for help and Mr. Taggert, who came into the store at that moment, came to my assistance. I don't know any Mr. Callister."

The attorney stared at her. "You don't know who John Callister is?" he asked, aghast. "He and his brother Gil own the Medicine Ridge Ranch. It's world famous as a breeding bull enterprise. Aside from that, they have massive land holdings not only in Montana, but in adjoining states, including real estate and mining interests. Their parents own the Sportsman Enterprises chain of magazines. The family is one of the wealthiest in the country."

"Yes," Sassy said, trying to wrap her mind around the strange monolog, "I've heard of them. But what do they have to do with John Taggert, except that they're his bosses?" she asked innocently.

The attorney finally got it. She didn't know who her suitor actually was. A glance around the room was enough to tell him her financial status. It was unlikely that a millionaire would be seriously interested in such a poor woman. Apparently Callister had been playing some game with her. He frowned. It was a cruel game.

"The man's full name is John Taggert Callister," he said in a gentler tone. "He's Gil Callister's younger brother."

Sassy's face lost color. She'd been dreaming of a shared life with John, of working to build something good together, along with her family. He was a millionaire. That sort of man moved in high society, had money to burn. He was up here overhauling a new ranch for the conglomerate. Sassy had been handy and she amused him, so he was playing with her. It hadn't been serious, not even when he asked her to marry him! She felt sick to her stomach. She didn't know what to do now. And how was she going to tell her mother and Selene the truth?

She folded her arms around her chest and sat like a stone, her green eyes staring at the attorney, pleading with him to tell her it was all a lie, a joke.

He couldn't. He grimaced. "I'm very sorry," he said genuinely. "I thought you knew the truth."

"Not until now," she said in a subdued tone. She closed her eyes. The pain was lancing, enveloping. Her life was falling apart around her.

He drew in a long breath, searching for the right words. "Miss Peale, I hate to have to ask you this. But was there an actual assault?"

She blinked. What had he asked? She met his eyes. "Mr. Tarleton kissed me and tried to handle me and I resisted him. He was angry. He got a hard grip on me and was trying to force me down on the floor when Mr. Taggert—" She stopped and swallowed, hard. "Mr. Callister, that is, came to help me. He pulled Mr. Tarleton off me. Then he called law enforcement."

The lawyer was looking worried. "You were taken to a doctor. What were his findings?"

"Well, I had some bruises and I was sore. He ripped my blouse. I guess there wasn't a lot of physical evidence. But it did scare me. I was upset and crying."

"Miss Peale, was there an actual *sexual* assault?"

She began to understand what he meant. "Oh! Well…no," she stammered. "He kissed me and he tried to fondle me, but he didn't try to take any of my other clothes off, if that's what you mean."

"That's what I mean." He sat back in his chair. "We can't prosecute for sexual assault and battery on the basis of an unwanted kiss. We can charge him with sexual assault for any sexual contact which is unwanted. However, the law provides that if he's convicted, the maximum sentence is six months in jail or a fine not to exceed $500. If in the course of sexual contact the perpetrator inflicts bodily injury, he can get from four years to life in prison. In this case, however, you would be required to show that injury resulted from the attempted kiss. Quite frankly," he added, "I don't think a jury, even under the circumstances, would consider unwanted touching and bruising to be worth giving a man a life sentence."

She sighed. "Yes. It does seem a bit drastic, even to me. Is it true that he doesn't have any prior convictions?" she asked curiously.

He shook his head. "We found out that he was arrested on a sexual harassment charge in another city, but he was cleared, so there was no conviction."

She was tired of the whole thing. Tired of remembering Tarleton's unwanted advances, tired of being tied to the memory as long as the court case dragged on. If she insisted on prosecuting him for an attack, she couldn't produce any real proof. His attorney would take her apart on the witness stand, and she'd be humiliated yet again.

But as bad as that thought was, it was worse to think about going into court and asking them to put a man, even Tarleton, in prison for the rest of his life because he'd tried to kiss her. The lawyer was right. Tarleton might have intended a sexual assault, but all he managed was a kiss and some bruising. That was uncomfortable, and disgusting, but hardly a major crime. Still, she hated letting him get off so lightly.

She almost protested. It had been a little more than bruising. The man had intended much more, and he'd done it to some other poor girl who'd been too shamed to force him to go to trial. Sassy had guts. She could do this.

But then she had a sudden, frightening thought. If John Taggert Callister was called to appear for the prosecution, she realized suddenly, it would become a media event. He was famous. His presence at the trial would draw the media. There would be news crews, cameras, reporters. There might even be national exposure. Her mother would suffer for it. So would Selene. For herself, she would have taken the chance. For her mother, still undergoing cancer treatments and unsuited to stress of any kind right now, she could not.

Her shoulders lifted. "Mr. Addy, the trial will come with a media blitz if Mr...Mr. Callister is called to testify for me, won't it? My mother and Selene could be talked about on those horrible entertainment news programs if it came out that I was poor and John was rich and there was an attempted sexual assault in the mix. Think how twisted they could make it sound. It would be the sort of sordid subject some people in the news media love to get their hands on these days. Just John's name would guarantee that people would be interested in what happened. They could make a circus out of it."

He hesitated. "That shouldn't be a consideration..."

"My mother has lung cancer," she replied starkly. "She's just been through major surgery and is now undergoing radiation and chemo for it. She can't take any more stress than she's already got. If there's even a chance that this trial could bring that sort of publicity, I can't take it. So what can I do?"

Mr. Addy considered the question. "I think we can plea bargain him to a charge of sexual assault with the lighter sentence. I know, it's not perfect," he told her. "He'd likely get the fine and some jail time, even if he gets probation. And it would at least go on the record as a conviction and any future transgression on his part would land him in very hot water. He has a public defender, but he seems anxious to avoid spending a long time in jail waiting for the trial. I think he'll agree to the lesser charge.

Especially considering who the witness is. When he has time to think about the consequences of trying to drag John Callister's good name through the mud, and consider what sort of attorneys the Callisters would produce for a trial, I believe he'll jump at the plea bargain."

She considered that, and then the trauma of a jury trial with all the media present. This way, at least Tarleton would now have a criminal record, and it might be enough to deter him from any future assaults on other women. "Okay," she said. "As long as he doesn't get away with it."

"Oh, he won't get away with it, Miss Peale," he said solemnly. "I promise you that." He pondered for a minute. "However, if you'd rather stand firm on the original charge, I'll prosecute him, despite the obstacles. Is this plea bargain what you really want?"

She sighed sadly. "Not really. I'd love to hang him out to dry. But I have to consider my mother. It's the only possible way to make him pay for what he tried to do without hurting my family. If it goes to a jury trial, even with the media all around, he might walk away a free man because of the publicity. You said they were already trying to twist it so that it looks like John was just jealous and making a fuss because he could, because he was rich and powerful. I know the Callisters can afford the best attorneys, but it wouldn't be right to put them in that situation, either. Mr. Callister has two little nieces…" She grimaced. "You know, the legal system isn't altogether fair sometimes."

He smiled. "I agree. But it's still the best system on earth," he replied.

"I hope I'm doing the right thing," she said on a sigh.

"If he gets out and hurts some other woman because I backed down, I'll never get over it."

He gave her a long look. "You aren't backing down, Miss Peale. You're compromising. It may look as if he's getting away with it. But he isn't."

She liked him. She smiled. "Okay, then."

He closed his briefcase and got to his feet. He held out his hand and shook hers. "He'll have a criminal record," he promised her. "If he ever tries to do it again, in Montana, I can promise you that he'll spend a lot of time looking at the world through vertical bars." He meant every word.

"Thanks, Mr. Addy."

"I'll let you know how things work out. Good evening."

Sassy watched him go with quiet, thoughtful eyes. She was compromising on the case, but on behalf of a good cause. She couldn't put her mother through the nightmare of a trial and the vicious publicity it would bring on them. Mrs. Peale had suffered enough.

She went back into the house. Mrs. Peale was coming out of the bedroom, wrapped in her chenille housecoat, pale and weak. "Could you get me some pineapple juice, sweetheart?" she asked, forcing a smile.

"Of course!" Sassy ran to get it. "Are you all right?" she asked worriedly.

"Just a little sick. That's nothing to worry about, it goes with the treatments. At least I'm through with them for a few weeks." She frowned. "What's wrong? And who was that man you were talking to?"

"Here, back to bed." Sassy went with her, helping her down on the bed and tucking her under the covers with her glass of cold juice. She sat down beside her. "That was the assistant district attorney—or one of them, anyway. A Mr. Addy. He came to talk to me about Mr. Tarleton. He wants to offer him a plea bargain so we don't end up in a messy court case."

Mrs. Peale frowned. "He's guilty of harassing you. He assaulted you. He should pay for it."

"He will. There's jail time and a fine for it," she replied, candy-coating her answer. "He'll have a criminal record. But I won't have to be grilled and humiliated by his attorney on the stand."

Mrs. Peale sipped her juice. She thought about what a trial would be like for Sassy. She'd seen such trials on her soap operas. She sighed. "All right, dear. If you're satisfied, I am, too." She smiled. "Have you heard from John? He was going to bring me some special chocolates when he came back."

Sassy hesitated. She couldn't tell her mother. Not yet. "I haven't heard from him," she said.

"You don't look well…"

"I'm just fine," Sassy said, grinning. "Now you go back to bed. I'm going to reconcile the bank statement and get Selene's clothes ready for school tomorrow."

"All right, dear." She settled back into the pillows. "You're too good to me, Sassy," she added. "Once I get back on my feet, I want you to go a lot of places with John. I'm going to be fine, thanks to him and those doctors in Billings. I can take care of myself and Selene, finally, and you can have a life of your own."

"You stop that," Sassy chided. "I love you. Nothing I do for you, or Selene, is a chore."

"Yes, but you've had a ready-made family up until now," Mrs. Peale said softly. "It's limited your social life."

"My social life is just dandy, thanks."

The older woman grinned. "I'll say! Wait until John gets back. He's got a surprise waiting for you."

"Has he, really?" Sassy wondered if it was the surprise the attorney had just shared with her. She was too sick to care, but she couldn't let on. Her mother was so happy. It would be cruel to dash all her hopes and reveal the truth about the young man Mrs. Peale idolized.

"He has! Don't you stay up too late. You're looking peaked, dear."

"I'm just tired. We've been putting up tons of stock in the feed store," she lied. She smiled. "Good night, Mama."

"Good night, dear. Sleep well."

As if, Sassy thought as she closed the door. She gave up on paperwork a few minutes later and went to bed. She cried herself to sleep.

John walked into the feed store a day later, back from an unwanted but urgent business trip to Colorado. He spotted Sassy at the counter and walked up to it with a beaming smile.

She looked up and saw him, and he knew it was all over by the expression on her face. She was apprehensive, uncomfortable. She fidgeted and could barely meet his intent gaze.

He didn't even bother with preliminary questions. His eyes narrowed angrily. "Who told you?" he asked tersely.

She drew in a breath. He looked scary like that. Now that she knew who he really was, knew the power and fame behind his name, she was intimidated. This man could write his own ticket. He could go anywhere, buy anything, do anything he liked. He was worlds away from Sassy, who lived in a house with a leaky roof. He was like a stranger. The smiling, easygoing cowboy she thought he was had become somebody totally different.

"It was the assistant district attorney," she said in a faint tone. "He came to see me. Mr. Tarleton was going to insinuate that you were jealous of him and forced me to file a complaint..."

He exploded. "I'll get attorneys in here who will put him away for the rest of his miserable life," he said tersely. He looked as if he could do that single-handed.

"No!" She swallowed. "No. Please. Think what it would do to Mama if a whole bunch of reporters came here to cover the story because of...because of who you are," she pleaded. "Stress makes everything so much worse for her."

He looked at her intently. "I hadn't thought about that," he said quietly. "I'm sorry."

"Mr. Addy says that Mr. Tarleton will probably agree to plead guilty or no contest to the sexual assault charge." She sighed. "There's a fine and jail time. He was willing to prosecute on the harder charge, but there would have to be proof that he did more than just kiss me and handle me..."

He frowned. He knew what she meant. A jury would be unlikely to convict for sexual assault and battery on an unwanted kiss and some groping, and how could they prove that Tarleton had intended much more? It made him angry. He wanted the man to go to prison. But Mrs. Peale would pay the price. In her delicate condition, it would probably kill her to have to watch Sassy go through the trial, even if she didn't get to court. John's name would guarantee news interest. Just the same, he was going to have a word with Mr. Addy. Sassy never had to know.

"How is your mother?" he asked.

"She's doing very well," she replied, her tone a little stilted. He did intimidate her now. "The treatments have left her a little anemic and weak, and there's some nausea, but they gave her medicine for that." She didn't add that it was bankrupting her to pay for it. She'd already had to pawn her grandfather's watch and pistol to manage a month's worth. She wasn't admitting that.

"I brought her some chocolates," he told her. He smiled gently. "She likes the Dutch ones."

She was staring at him with wide, curious eyes. "You'll spoil her," she replied.

He shrugged. "So? I'm rich. I can spoil people if I want to."

"Yes, I know, but…"

"If you were rich, and I wasn't," he replied solemnly, "would you hesitate to do anything you could for me, if I was in trouble?"

"Of course not," she assured him.

"Then why should it bother you if I spoil your mother a little? Especially, now, when she's had so much illness."

"It doesn't, really. It's just—" She stopped dead. The color went out of her face as she stared at him and suddenly realized how much he'd done for them.

"What's wrong?" he asked.

"There was no grant to pay for that surgery, and the treatments," she said in a choked tone. "You paid for it! You paid for it all!"

CHAPTER TEN

JOHN grimaced. "Sassy, there was no other way," he said, trying to reason with her. She looked anguished. "Your mother would have died. I checked your company insurance coverage when I had Buck put you on the payroll as assistant manager. It didn't have a major medical option. I told Buck to shop around for a better plan, but your mother's condition went critical before we could find one."

She knew her heart was going to beat her to death. She'd never be able to pay him back, not even the interest on the money he'd spent on her mother. She'd been poor all her life, but she'd never felt it like this. It had never hurt so much.

"You're part of my life now," he said softly. "You and your mother and Selene. Of course I was going to do all I could for you. For God's sake, don't try to reduce what we feel for each other to dollars and cents!"

"I can't pay you back," she groaned.

"Have I asked you to?" he returned.

"But…" she protested, ready for a long battle.

The door opened behind them and Theodore Graves, the police chief walked in. His lean face was set in hard lines. He nodded at John and approached Sassy.

He pushed his Stetson back over jet-black hair. "That assistant district attorney, Addy, said you agreed to let Tarleton plea bargain to a lesser charge," he said. "He won't discuss the case with me and I can't intimidate him the way I intimidate most people. So I'd like to know why."

She sighed. He made her feel guilty. "It's Mama," she told him. "He—" she indicated John "—is very well-known. If it goes to court, reporters will show up to find out why he's mixed up in a sexual assault case. Mama will get stressed out, the cancer will come back, and we'll bury her."

Graves grimaced. "I hadn't thought about that. About the stress, I mean." He frowned. "What do you mean, he's well-known?" he added, indicating John. "He's a ranch foreman."

"He's not," Sassy said with a long sigh. "He's John Callister."

Graves lifted a thick, dark eyebrow. "Of the Callister ranching empire over in Medicine Ridge?"

John lifted a shoulder. "Afraid so."

"Oh, boy."

"Listen, at least he'll have a police record," Sassy said stubbornly. "Think about it. Do you really want a media circus right here in Hollister? Mr. Tarleton would probably love it," she added miserably.

"He probably would," Graves had to agree. He stuck his hands into his slacks pockets. "Seventy-five years ago, we'd have turned him out into the woods and sent men with guns after him."

"Civilized men don't do things like that," Sassy reminded him. "Especially policemen."

Graves shrugged. "So sue me. I never claimed to be civilized. I'm a throwback." He drew in a long breath. "All right, as long as the polecat gets some serious time in the slammer, I can be generous and put up the rope I just bought."

Sassy wondered how the chief thought Tarleton would get a jail sentence when Mr. Addy had hinted that Tarleton would probably get probation.

"Good of you," John mused.

"Pity he didn't try to escape when we took him up to Billings for the motion hearing," Graves said thoughtfully. "I volunteered to go along with the deputy sheriff who transported him. I even wore my biggest caliber revolver, special, just in case." He pursed his lips and brightened. "Somebody might leave a door open, in the detention center…"

"Don't you dare," John said firmly. "You're not the only one who's disappointed. I was looking forward to the idea of having him spend the next fifteen years or so with one of the inmates who has the most cigarettes. But I'm not willing to see my future mother-in-law die over it."

"Mother-in-law?" Graves gave him a wry look from liquid black eyes in a lean, tanned face.

Sassy blushed. "Now, we have to talk about that," she protested.

"We already did," John said. "You promised to marry me."

"That was before I knew who you were," she shot back belligerently.

He grinned. "That's more like it," he mused. "The deference was wearing a little thin," he explained.

She flushed even more. She had been behaving like

a working girl with the boss, instead of an equal. She shifted. She was still uncomfortable thinking about his background and comparing it to her own.

"I like weddings," Graves commented.

John glanced at him. "You do?"

He nodded. "I haven't been to one in years, of course, and I don't own a good suit anymore." He shrugged. "I guess I could buy one, if I got invited to a wedding."

John burst out laughing. "You can come to ours. I'll make sure you get an invitation."

Graves smiled. "That's a deal." He glanced at Sassy, who still looked undecided. "If I lived in a house that looked like yours, and drove a piece of scrap metal like that vehicle you ride around in, I'd say yes when a financially secure man asked me to marry him."

Sassy almost burst trying not to laugh. "Has any financially secure man asked you to marry him lately, Chief?"

He glared at her. "I was making a point."

"Several of them," Sassy returned. "But I do appreciate your interest. I wouldn't mind sending Mr. Tarleton to prison myself, if the cost wasn't so high."

He pursed his lips and his black eyes twinkled. "Now that's a coincidence. I've thought about nothing else except sending Mr. Tarleton to prison for the past few weeks. In fact, it never hurts to recommend a prison to the district attorney," he said pleasantly. "I know one where even the chaplain has to carry a Taser."

"Mr. Addy already said he isn't likely to get jail time, since he's a first offender," Sassy said sadly.

"Now isn't that odd," the chief replied with a wicked grin. "I spent some quality time on the computer yesterday and I turned up a prior conviction for sexual assault over in Wyoming, where Mr. Tarleton was working two years ago. He got probation for that one. Which makes him a repeat offender." He looked almost angelic. "I just told Addy. He was almost dancing in the street."

Sassy gasped. "Really?"

He chuckled. "I thought you'd like hearing that. I figured that a man with his attitude had to have a conviction somewhere. He didn't have one in Montana, so I started looking in surrounding states. I checked the criminal records in Wyoming, got a hit, and called the district attorney in the court circuit where it was filed. What a story I got from him! So I took it straight to Addy this morning." He gave her a wry look. "But I did want to know why you let him plead down, and Addy wouldn't tell me."

"Now I feel better, about agreeing to the plea bargain," Sassy said. "His record will affect the sentence, won't it?"

"It will, indeed," Graves assured her. "In another interesting bit of irony, the judge hearing his case had to step down on account of a family emergency. The new judge in his case is famous for her stance on sexual assault cases." He leaned forward. "She's a woman."

Sassy's eyes lit up. "Poor Mr. Tarleton."

"Right." John chuckled. "Good of you to bring us the latest news."

Graves smiled at him. "I thought it would be a nice surprise." He glanced at Sassy. "I understand now why you made the decision you did. Your mom's a sweet lady. It's like a miracle that the surgery saved her."

"Yes," Sassy agreed. Her eyes met John's. "It is a miracle."

Graves pulled his wide-brimmed hat low over his eyes. "Don't forget that wedding invitation," he reminded John. "I'll even polish my good boots."

"I won't forget," John assured him.

"Thanks again," she told the chief.

He smiled at her. "I like happy endings."

When he was gone, John turned back to Sassy with a searching glance. "I'm coming to get you after supper," he informed her. "We've got a lot to talk about."

"John, I'm poor," she began.

He leaned across the counter and kissed her warmly. "I'll be poor, if I don't have you," he said softly. He pulled a velvet-covered box out of his pocket and put it in her hands. "Open that after I leave."

"What is it?" she asked dimly.

"Something for us to talk about, of course." He winked at her and smiled broadly. He walked out the door and closed it gently behind him.

Sassy opened the box. It was a gold wedding band with an embossed vine running around it. There was a beautiful diamond ring that was its companion. She stared at them until tears burned her eyes. A man bought a set of rings like this when he meant them to be heirlooms, handed down from generation to generation. She clutched it close to her heart. Despite the differences, she knew what she was going to say.

It took Mrs. Peale several minutes to understand what Sassy was telling her.

"No, dear," she insisted. "John *works* for Mr. Callister. That's what he told us."

"Yes, he did, but he didn't mention that Taggert was

his middle name, not his last name," Sassy replied patiently. "He and his brother, Gil, own one of the most famous ranches in the West. Their parents own that sports magazine Daddy always used to read before he left."

The older woman sat back with a rough sigh. "Then what was he doing coming around here?" she asked, and looked hurt.

"Well, that's the interesting part," Sassy replied, blushing. "It seems that he…well, he wants to…that is…" She jerked out the ring box, opened it, and put it in her mother's hands. "He brought that to me this morning."

Mrs. Peale eyed the rings with fascination. "How beautiful," she said softly. She touched the pattern on the wedding band. "He means these to be heirlooms, doesn't he? I had your grandmother's wedding band," she added sadly, "but I had to sell it when you were little and we didn't have the money for a doctor when you got sick." She looked up at her daughter with misty eyes. "He's really serious, isn't he?"

"Yes, I think he is," Sassy sighed. She sat down next to her mother. "I still can't believe it."

"That hospital bill," Mrs. Peale began slowly. "There was no grant, was there?"

Sassy shook her head. "John said that he couldn't stand by and let you die. He's fond of you."

"I'm fond of him, too," she replied. "And he wants to marry my daughter." Her eyes suddenly had a faraway look. "Isn't it funny? Remember what I told you my grandmother said to me, that I'd be poor but my daughter would live like royalty?" She laughed. "My goodness!"

"Maybe she really did know things." Sassy took the

rings from her mother's hand and stared at them. It did seem that dreams came true.

John came for her just at sunset. He took time to kiss Mrs. Peale and Selene and assure them that he wasn't taking Sassy out of the county when they married.

"I'm running this ranch myself," he assured her with a warm smile. "Sassy and I will live here. The house has plenty of room, so you two can move in with us."

Mrs. Peale looked worried. "John, it may not look like much, but I was born in this house. I've lived in it all my life, even after I married."

He bent and kissed her again. "Okay. If you want to stay here, we'll do some fixing up and get you a companion. You can choose her."

Her old eyes brightened. "You'd do that for me?" she exclaimed.

"Nothing is too good for my second mama," he assured her, and he wasn't joking. "Now Sassy and I are going out to talk about all the details. We'll be back later."

She kissed him back. "You're going to be the nicest son-in-law in the whole world."

"You'd better believe it," he replied.

John took her over to the new ranch, where the barn was up, the stable almost finished, and the house completely remodeled. He walked her through the kitchen and smiled at her enthusiasm.

"We can have a cook, if you'd rather," he told her.

She looked back at him, running her hand lovingly over a brand-new stove with all sorts of functions. "Oh,

I'd love to work in here myself." She hesitated. "John, about Mama and Selene…"

He moved away from the doorjamb he'd been leaning against and pulled her into his arms. His expression was very serious. "I know you're worried about her. But I was serious about the companion. It's just that she needs to be a nurse. We won't tell your mother that part of it just yet."

"She's not completely well yet. I know a nurse will look out for her, but…"

He smiled. "I like the way you care about people," he said softly. "I know she's not able to stay by herself and she won't admit it. But we're close enough that you can go over there every day and check on her."

She smiled. "Okay. I just worry."

"That's one of the things I most admire about you," he told her. "That big heart."

"You have to travel a lot, to show cattle, don't you?" she asked, recalling something she'd read in a magazine about the Callisters, before she knew who John was.

"I used to," he said. "We have a cattle foreman at the headquarters ranch in Medicine Ridge who's showing Gil's bulls now. I'll put on one here to do the same for us. I don't want to be away from home unless I have to, now."

She beamed. "I don't want you away from home, unless I can go with you."

He chuckled. "Two minds running in the same direction." He shifted his weight a little. "I didn't tell your mother, but I've already interviewed several women who might want the live-in position. I had their backgrounds checked as well," he added, chuckling. "When I knew I was going to marry you, I started thinking about how your mother would cope without you."

"You're just full of surprises," she said, breathless.

He grinned. "Yes, I am. The prospective housemates will start knocking on the door about ten Friday morning. You can tell her when we get home." He sobered. "She'll be happier in her own home, Sassy. Uprooting her will be as traumatic as the chemo was. You can visit her every day and twice on Sundays. I'll come along, too."

"I think you're right." She looked up at him. "She loves you."

"It's mutual," he replied. He smiled down at her, loving the softness in her green eyes. "We can add some more creature comforts for her, and fix what's wrong with the house."

"There's a lot wrong with it," she said worriedly.

"I'm rich, as you reminded me," he replied easily. "I can afford whatever she, and Selene, need. After all, they're family."

She hugged him warmly and laid her cheek against his chest. "Do you want to have kids?" she asked.

His eyebrows arched and his blue eyes twinkled. "Of course. Do you want to start them right now?" He looked around. "The kitchen table's just a bit short...ouch!"

She withdrew her fist from his stomach. "You know what I mean! Honestly, what am I going to do with you?"

"Want me to coach you?" he offered, and chuckled wickedly when she blushed.

"Look out that window and tell me what you see," she said.

He glanced around. There were people going in and out of the unfinished stable, working on the interior by portable lighting. There were a lot of people going in and out.

"I guarantee if you so much as kiss me, we'll be on every Internet social networking site in the world," she told him. "And not because of who you are."

He laughed out loud. "Okay. We'll wait." He glanced outside again and scowled. "But we are definitely not going to try to honeymoon here in this house!"

She didn't argue.

He tugged her along with him into a dark hallway and pulled her close. "They'll need night vision to see us here," he explained as he bent to kiss her with blatant urgency.

She kissed him back, feeling so explosively hot inside that she thought she might burst. She felt shivery when he kissed her like that, with his mouth and his whole body. His hands smoothed up under her blouse and over her breasts. He felt the hard tips and groaned, kissing her even harder.

She knew nothing about intimacy, but she wanted it suddenly, desperately. She lifted up to him, trying to get even closer. He backed her into the wall and lowered his body against hers, increasing the urgency of the kiss until she groaned out loud and shivered.

The frantic little sound got through his whirling mind. He pushed away from her and stepped back, dragging in deep breaths in an effort to regain the control he'd almost lost.

"You're stopping?" she asked breathlessly.

"Yes, I'm stopping," he replied. He took her hand and pulled her back into the lighted kitchen. There was a flush along his high cheekbones. "Until the wedding, no more time alone," he added huskily. His blue eyes met her green ones. "We're going to have it conventional, all the way. Okay?"

She smiled with her whole heart. "Okay!"

He laughed. "It's just as well," he sighed.

"Why?"

"We don't have a bed. Yet."

Her eyes twinkled. He was so much fun to be with, and when he kissed her, it was like fireworks. They were going to make a great marriage, she was sure of it. She stopped worrying about being poor. When they held each other, nothing mattered less than money.

But the next hurdle was the hardest. He announced a week later that his family was coming up to meet John's future bride. Sassy didn't sleep that night, worrying. What would they think, those fabulously wealthy people, when they saw where Sassy and her mother and Selene lived, how poor they were? Would they think she was only after John's wealth?

She was still worrying when they showed up at her front door late the next afternoon, with John. Sassy stood beside him in her best dress, as they walked up onto the front porch of the Peale homeplace. Her best dress wasn't saying much because it was off the rack and two years old. It was long, beige, and simply cut. Her shoes were older than the dress and scuffed.

But the tall blond man and the slender, dark-haired woman didn't seem to notice or care how she was dressed. The woman, who didn't look much older than Sassy, hugged her warmly.

"I'm Kasie," she introduced herself with a big smile. "He's Gil, my husband." Gil smiled and shook her hand warmly. "And these are our babies…" She motioned to two little blond girls, one holding the other by the hand. "That's Bess," she said, smiling at the taller of the two, "and that's Jenny. Say hello! This is Uncle John's fiancée!"

Bess came forward and looked up at Sassy with wide, soft eyes. "You going to marry Uncle John? He's very nice."

"Yes, he is," Sassy said, sliding her hand into John's. "I promise I'll take very good care of him," she added with a smile.

"Okay," Bess said with a shy returning smile.

"Come on in," Sassy told them. "I'm sorry, it isn't much to look at..." she added, embarrassed.

"Sassy, we were raised by an uncle who hated material things," Gil told her gently. "We grew up in a place just like this, a rough country house. We like to think it gave us strength of character."

"What he means is, don't apologize," John said in a loud whisper.

She laughed when Gil and Kasie agreed. Later she would learn that Kasie had grown up in even rougher conditions, in a war zone in Africa with missionary parents who were killed there.

Mrs. Peale greeted them with Selene by her side, a little intimidated.

"Stop looking like that," John chided, and hugged her warmly. "This is my future little mother-in-law," he added with a grin, introducing her to his family. "She's the sweetest woman I've ever known, except for Kasie."

"You didn't say I was sweet, too," Sassy said with a mock pout.

"You're not sweet. You're precious," he told her with a warm, affectionate grin.

"Okay, I'll go with that," she laughed. She turned to the others. "Come in and sit down. I could make coffee…?"

"Please, no," Gil groaned. "She pumped me full of it all the way here. We were up last night very late trying to put fences back up after a storm. Kasie had to drive most of the way." He held his stomach. "I don't think I ever want another cup."

"You go out with your men to fix fences?" Mrs. Peale asked, surprised.

"Of course," he said simply. "We always have."

Mrs. Peale relaxed. So did Sassy. These people were nothing like they'd expected. Even Selene warmed to them at once, as shy as she usually was with strangers. It was a wonderful visit.

"Well, what do you think of them?" John asked Sassy much later, as he was getting ready to leave for the ranch.

"They're wonderful," she replied, pressed close against him on the dark porch. "They aren't snobs. I like them already."

"It's as Gil said," he replied. "We were raised by a rough and tumble uncle. He taught us that money wasn't the most important thing in life." He tilted her mouth up and kissed it. "They liked you, too," he added. He smiled. "So, no more hurdles. Now all we have to do is get married."

"But I don't know how to plan a big wedding," she said worriedly.

He grinned. "Not to worry. I know someone who does!"

The wedding was arranged beautifully by a consultant hired by John, out of Colorado. She was young and pretty and sweet, and apparently she was very discreet.

Sassy was fascinated by some of the weddings she'd planned for people all over the country. One was that of Sassy's favorite country western singing star.

"You did that wedding?" Sassy exclaimed.

"I did. And nobody knew a thing about it until they were on their honeymoon," she added smugly. "That's why your future husband hired me. I'm the soul of discretion. Now, tell me what colors you like and we'll get to work!"

They ended up with a color scheme of pink and yellow and white. Sassy had planned a simple white gown, until Mary Garnett showed her a couture gown with the three pastels embroidered in silk into the bodice and echoed in the lace over the skirt, and in the veil. It was the most beautiful gown Sassy had ever seen in her life. "But you could buy a house for that!" Sassy exclaimed when she heard the price.

John, walking through the living room at the Peale house, paused in the doorway. "We're only getting married once," he reminded Sassy.

"But it's so expensive," she wailed.

He walked to the sofa and peered over her shoulder at the color photograph of the gown. His breath caught. "Buy it," he told Mary.

Sassy opened her mouth. He bent and kissed it shut. He walked out again.

Mary just grinned.

He had another surprise for her as well, tied up in a small box, as an early wedding present. He'd discovered that she'd had to pawn her grandfather's watch and pistol to pay bills and he'd gotten them out of hock. She cried like a baby. Which meant that he got to kiss the tears away. He was, she thought as she hugged him, the most thoughtful man in the whole world.

Sassy insisted on keeping her job, regardless of John's protests. She wanted to help more with the wedding, and felt guilty that she hadn't, but Mary had everything organized. Invitations were going out, flower arrangements were being made. A minister was engaged. A small orchestra was hired to play at the reception.

The wedding was being held at the family ranch in Medicine Ridge, to ensure privacy. Gil had already said that he was putting on more security for the event than the president of the United States had. Nobody was crashing this wedding. They'd even outfoxed aerial surveillance by putting the entire reception inside and having blinds on every window.

Nobody, he told John and Sassy, was getting in without an invitation and a photo ID.

"Is that really necessary?" Sassy asked John when they were alone.

"You don't know how well-known our parents are," he sighed. "They'll be coming, too, and our father can't keep his mouth shut. He's heard about you from Gil and Kasie, and he's bragging to anybody who'll listen about his newest daughter-in-law."

"Me?" She was stunned. "But I don't have any special skills and I'm not even beautiful."

John smiled down at her. "You have the biggest heart of any woman I've ever known," he said softly. "It isn't what you do or what you have that makes you special, Sassy. It's what you are."

She flushed. "What about your mother?"

He kissed her on the tip of her nose. "She's so happy

to have access to her grandchildren, that she never raises a fuss about anything. But she's happy to have some-body in the family who can knit."

"How did you know I can knit?"

"You think I hadn't noticed all the afghans and chair covers and doilies all over your house?"

"Mama could have made them."

"But she didn't. She said you can even knit sweaters. Our mother would love to learn how. She wants you to teach her."

She caught her breath. "But, it's easy! Of course, I'll show her. She doesn't mind—neither of them minds—that I'm poor? They don't think I'm marrying you for your money?"

He laughed until his eyes teared up. "Sassy," he said, catching his breath, "you didn't know I had money until after I proposed."

"Oh."

"They know that, too."

She sighed. "Okay, then."

He bent and kissed her. "Only a few more days to go," he murmured. "I can hardly wait."

"Me, too," she said. "It's exciting. But it's a lot of work."

"Mary's doing the work so you don't have to. Well, except for getting the right dresses for your mother and Selene."

"That's not work," she laughed. "They love to shop. I'm so glad Mama's getting over the chemo. She's better every day. I was worried that she'd be too weak to come to the wedding, but she says she wouldn't miss it for anything."

"We'll have a nurse practitioner at the wedding," he assured her. "Just in case. Don't worry."

"I'll do my best," she promised.

"That's my girl."

Finally there was a wedding! Sassy had chewed her nails to the quick worrying about things going wrong. John assured her that it would be smooth as silk, but she couldn't relax. If only she didn't trip over her own train and go headfirst into the minister, or do something else equally clumsy! All those important people were going to be there, and she had stage fright.

But once she was at the door of the big ballroom at the Callister mansion in Medicine Ridge where the wedding was taking place, she was less nervous. The sight of John, in his tuxedo, standing at the altar, calmed her. She waited for the music and then, clutching her bouquet firmly, her veil in place over her face, she walked calmly down the aisle. Her heart raced like crazy as John turned and smiled down at her when she reached him. He was the most handsome man she'd ever seen in her life. And he was going to marry her!

The minister smiled at both of them and began the service. It was routine until he asked if John had the rings. John started fishing in his pockets and couldn't find them. He grimaced, stunned.

"Uncle John! Did you forget?" Jenny muttered at his side, shoving a silken pillow up toward him. "I got the rings, Uncle John!"

The audience chuckled. Sassy hid a smile.

John fumbled the rings loose from the pillow and

bent and kissed his little niece on the forehead. "Thanks, squirt," he whispered.

She giggled and went to stand beside her sister, Bess, who was holding a basket full of fresh flower petals in shades of yellow, pink, and white.

The minister finished the ceremony and invited John to kiss his bride. John lifted the beautiful embroidered veil and pushed it back over Sassy's dark hair. His eyes searched hers. He framed her face in his big hands and bent and kissed her so tenderly that tears rolled down her cheeks, and he kissed every one away.

The music played again. Laughing, Sassy took the hand John held out and together they ran down the aisle and out the door. The reception was ready down the hall, in the big formal dining room that had been cleared of furniture for the occasion. As they ate cake and paused for photographs, to the strains of Debussy played by the orchestral ensemble, Sassy noticed movie stars, politicians, and at least two multimillionaires among the guests. She was rubbing elbows with people she'd only seen in magazines. It was fascinating.

"One more little hurdle, Mrs. Callister," John whispered to her, "and then we're going to Cancún for a week!"

"Sun and sand," she began breathlessly.

"And you and me. And a bed." He wiggled his eyebrows.

She laughed, pressing her face against him to hide her blushes.

"Well, it wasn't a bad wedding," came a familiar drawl from behind them.

Chief Graves was wearing a very nice suit, and nicely

polished dress boots, holding a piece of cake on a plate. "But I don't like chocolate cake," he pointed out. "And there's no coffee."

"There is so coffee," John chuckled, holding up a cup of it. "I don't go to weddings that don't furnish coffee."

"Where did you get that?" he asked.

John nodded toward the far corner, where a coffee urn was half-hidden behind a bouquet of flowers.

Graves grinned. "I hope you have a long and happy life together."

"Thanks, Chief," Sassy told him.

"Glad you could make it," John seconded.

"I brought you a present," he said unexpectedly. He reached into his pocket and drew out a small package. "Something useful."

"Thank you," Sassy said, touched, as she took it from his hand.

He gave John a worldly look, chuckled, and walked off to find coffee.

"What is it, I wonder?" Sassy mused, tearing the paper open.

"Well!" John exclaimed when he saw what was inside.

She peered over his arm and smiled warmly. It was a double set of compact discs of romantic music and classical love themes.

They glanced toward the coffee urn. Graves lifted his cup and toasted them. They laughed and waved.

CHAPTER ELEVEN

THEY stayed on the beach in a hotel shaped like one of the traditional Maya pyramids. Sassy lay in John's strong arms still shivering with her first taste of intimacy, her face flushed, her eyes brilliant as they looked up into his.

"It gets better," he whispered as his mouth moved lightly over her soft lips. "First times are usually difficult."

"Difficult?" She propped up on one elbow. "Are we remembering the same first time? Gosh, I thought I was going to die!"

His blue eyes twinkled. "Forgive me. I naturally assumed from all the moaning and whimpering that you were…stop that!" He laughed when she pinched him.

An enthusiastic bout of wrestling followed.

He kissed her into limp submission. "We really must do this again, so that I can get my perspective back," he suggested. "I'll pay attention this time."

She laughed and kissed his broad shoulder. "See that you do," she replied. She pushed him back into the pillows and followed him down.

"Now don't be rough with me, I'm fragile," he protested. "See here, take your hand off that…I'm not that sort of man!"

"Yes, you are," she chuckled, and put her mouth squarely against his. He was obediently silent for a long time afterward. Except for various involuntary sounds.

They held hands and walked down the beach at sunrise, watching seagulls soar above the incredible shades of blue that were the Gulf of Mexico.

"I never dreamed there were places like this," Sassy said dreamily. "The sand looks just like sugar."

"We'll have to take some postcards back with us. I can't believe I forgot to pack a digital camera," he sighed.

"We could buy one at the shop in the lobby," she suggested. "I have to have at least one picture of you in a bathing suit to put up in our house."

"Turnabout is fair play," he teased.

She laughed. "Okay."

"While we're at it, we'll buy presents for everybody."

"We should get something for Chief Graves."

"What would you suggest?"

"Something musical."

He pursed his lips. "We'll get him one of those wooden kazoos."

"No! Musical."

He drew her close. "Musical it is."

After the honeymoon, they stopped for the weekend at the Callister ranch in Medicine Ridge, where Sassy had time to sit down and get acquainted with John's sister-in-law, Kasie.

"I was so worried about fitting in here," Sassy confessed as they walked around the house, where the flowers were blooming in abundance around the huge swimming pool. "I mean, this is a whole world away from anything I know."

"I know exactly how you feel," Kasie said. "I was born in Africa, where my parents were missionaries," she recalled, going quiet. "They were killed right in front of us, me and my brother, Kantor. We went to live with our aunt in Arizona. Kantor grew up and married and had a little girl. He was doing a courier service by air in Africa when an attack came. He and his family were shot down in his plane and died." She sat down on one of the benches, her eyes far away. "I never expected to end up like this," she said, meeting the other girl's sympathetic gaze. "Gil didn't even like me at first," she added, laughing. "He made my life miserable when I first came to work here."

"He doesn't look like that sort of man," Sassy said. "He seems very nice."

"He can be. But he'd lost his first wife to a riding accident and he didn't ever want to get married again. He said I came up on his blind side. Of course, he thought I was much too young for him."

"Just like John," Sassy sighed. "He thought I was too young for him." She glanced at Kasie and grinned. "And I was sure that he was much too rich for me."

Kasie laughed. "I felt that way, too. But you know, it doesn't have much to do with money. It has to do with feelings and things you have in common." Her eyes had a dreamy, faraway look. "Sometimes Gil and I just sit and talk, for hours at a time. He's my best friend, as well as my husband."

"I feel that way with John," Sassy said. "He just fits in with my family, as if he's always known them."

"Mama Luke took to Gil right away, too." She noted the curious stare. "Oh, she's my mother's sister. She's a nun."

"Heavens!"

"My mother was pregnant with me and Kantor and a mercenary soldier saved her life," she explained. "His name was K.C. Kantor. My twin and I were both named for him."

"I've heard of him," Sassy said hesitantly, not liking to repeat what she'd heard about the reclusive, crusty millionaire.

"Most of what you've heard is probably true," Kasie laughed, seeing the words in her expression. "But I owe my life to him. He's a kind man. He would probably have married Mama Luke, if she hadn't felt called to a religious life."

"Is he married?"

Kasie frowned. "You know, I heard once that he did get married, to some awful woman, and divorced her right afterward. I don't know if it's true. You don't ask him those sort of questions," she added.

"I can understand why."

"Gil's parents like you," Kasie said out of the blue.

"They do?" Sassy was astonished. "But I hardly had time to say ten words to them at the wedding!"

"John said considerably more than ten words." Kasie grinned. "He was singing your praises long before he went back to marry you. Magdalena saw that beautiful shawl you'd packed and John told her you knitted it yourself. She wants to learn how."

"Yes, John said that, but I thought he was kidding!"

"She's not. She'll be in touch, I guarantee. She'll

turn up at your ranch one of these days with her knitting gear and you'll have to chase her out with a broom."

Sassy blushed. "I'd never do that. She's so beautiful."

"Yes. She and the boys didn't even speak before I married Gil. I convinced him to meet them on our honeymoon. He was shocked. You see, they were married very young and had children so early, long before they were ready for them. John and Gil's uncle took the boys to raise and sort of shut their parents out of their lives. It was a tragedy. They grew up thinking their parents didn't want them. It wasn't true. They just didn't know how to relate to their children, after all those years."

"I think parents and children need to be together those first few years," Sassy said.

"I agree wholeheartedly," Kasie said. She smiled. "Gil and I want children of our own, but we want the girls to feel secure with us first. There's no rush. We have years and years."

"The girls seem very happy."

Kasie nodded. "They're so much like my own children," she said softly. "I love them very much. I was heartbroken when Gil sent me home from Nassau and told me not to be here when they got home."

"What?"

Kasie laughed self-consciously. "We had a rocky romance. I'll have to tell you all about it one day. But for now, we'd better get back inside. Your husband will get all nervous and insecure if you're where he can't see you."

"He's a very nice husband."

"He's nice, period, like my Gil. We got lucky, for two penniless children, didn't we?" she asked.

Sassy linked her arm into Kasie's. "Yes, we did. But we'd both live in line cabins and sew clothes by hand if they asked us to."

"Isn't that the truth?" Kasie laughed.

"What were you two talking about for so long?" John asked that night, as Sassy lay close in his arms in bed.

"About what wonderful men we married," she said drowsily, reaching up to kiss him. "We did, too."

"Did Kasie tell you about her background?"

"She did. What an amazing story. And she said Gil didn't like her!"

"He didn't," he laughed. "He even fired her. But he realized his mistake in time. She was mysterious and he was determined not to risk his heart again."

"Sort of like you?" she murmured.

He laughed. "Sort of like me." He drew her closer and closed his eyes. "We go home tomorrow. Ready to take on a full-time husband, Mrs. Callister?"

"Ready and willing, Mr. Callister," she murmured, and smiled as she drifted off to sleep.

Several weeks later, Sassy had settled in at the ranch and was making enough knitted and crocheted accessories to make a home of the place. Mrs. Peale had a new companion, a practical nurse named Helen who was middle-aged, sweet, and could cook as well as clean house. She had no family, so Mrs. Peale and Selene filled an empty place in her life. Her charges were very happy with her. Sassy and John found time to visit regularly. They were like lovebirds, though. People rarely saw one without the other. Sassy mused that it was like they were joined at the hip. John grinned and kissed her for that. It was, indeed, he said happily.

One afternoon, John walked in the back door with Chief Graves, who was grinning from ear to ear.

"We have company," John told her, pausing to kiss her warmly and pull her close at his side. "He has news."

"I thought you'd like to know that Mr. Tarleton got five years," he said pleasantly. "They took him away last Friday. He's appealing, of course, but it won't help. He was recorded on DVD agreeing to the terms of the plea bargain. I told you that judge hated sexual assault cases."

Sassy nodded. "I'm sorry for him," she said. "I wish he'd learned his lesson the last time, in Wyoming. I guess when you do bad things for a long time, you just keep doing them."

"Repeat offenders repeat, sometimes," Graves replied solemnly. "But he's off the street, where he won't be hurting other young women." He pursed his lips. "I also wanted to thank you for the gift you brought back from Mexico. But I'm curious."

"About what?" she asked.

"How did you know I could play a flute?"

Her eyebrows arched. "You can?" she asked, surprised.

He chuckled. "Maybe she reads minds," he told John. "Better take good care of her. A woman with that rare gift is worth rubies."

"You're telling me," John replied, smiling down at his wife.

"I'll get back to town. Take care."

"You, too," Sassy said.

He sauntered out to his truck. John turned to Sassy with pursed lips. "So you can read minds, can you?" He leaned his forehead down against hers and linked his hands behind her. "Think you can tell me what I'm thinking right now?" he teased.

She reached up and whispered in his ear, grinning.

He laughed, picked her up, and stalked down the hall carrying her. She held on tight. Some men's minds, she thought wickedly, weren't all that difficult to read after all!

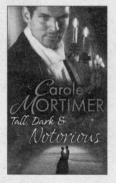

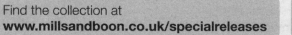

Sheikhs Collection

Rugged desert rulers, desire as hot as the burning sands...

On sale 5th July   On sale 2nd August   On sale 6th September

On sale 4th October   On sale 1st November   On sale 6th December

Collect all six books in this fabulous 3-in-1 collection
featuring powerful and wealthy Sheikh heroes!

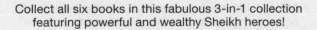

Find the collection at
www.millsandboon.co.uk/specialreleases

*Visit us
Online*

0713/MB423